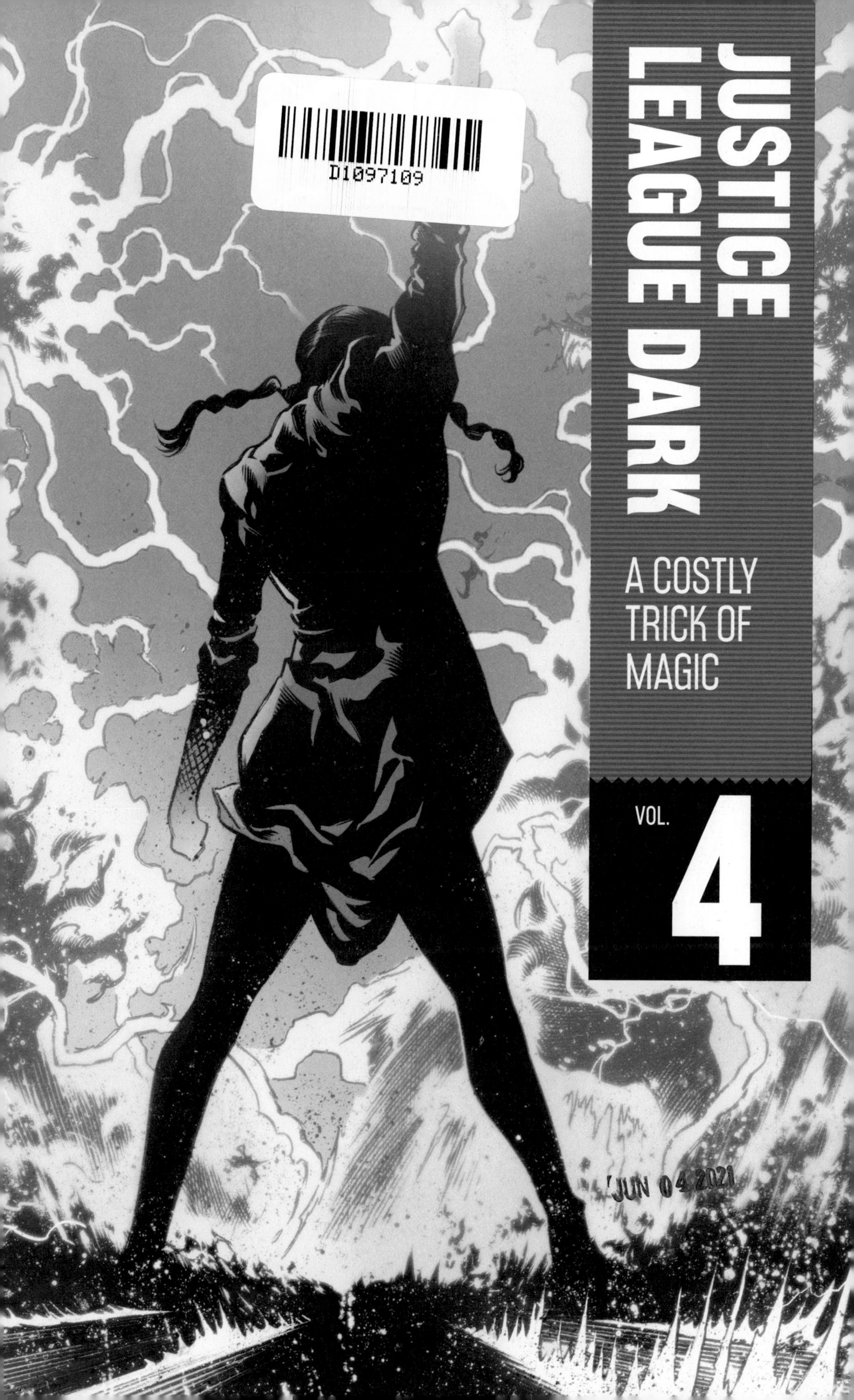

JUSTICE LEAGUE DARK

A COSTLY TRICK OF MAGIC

VOL. 4

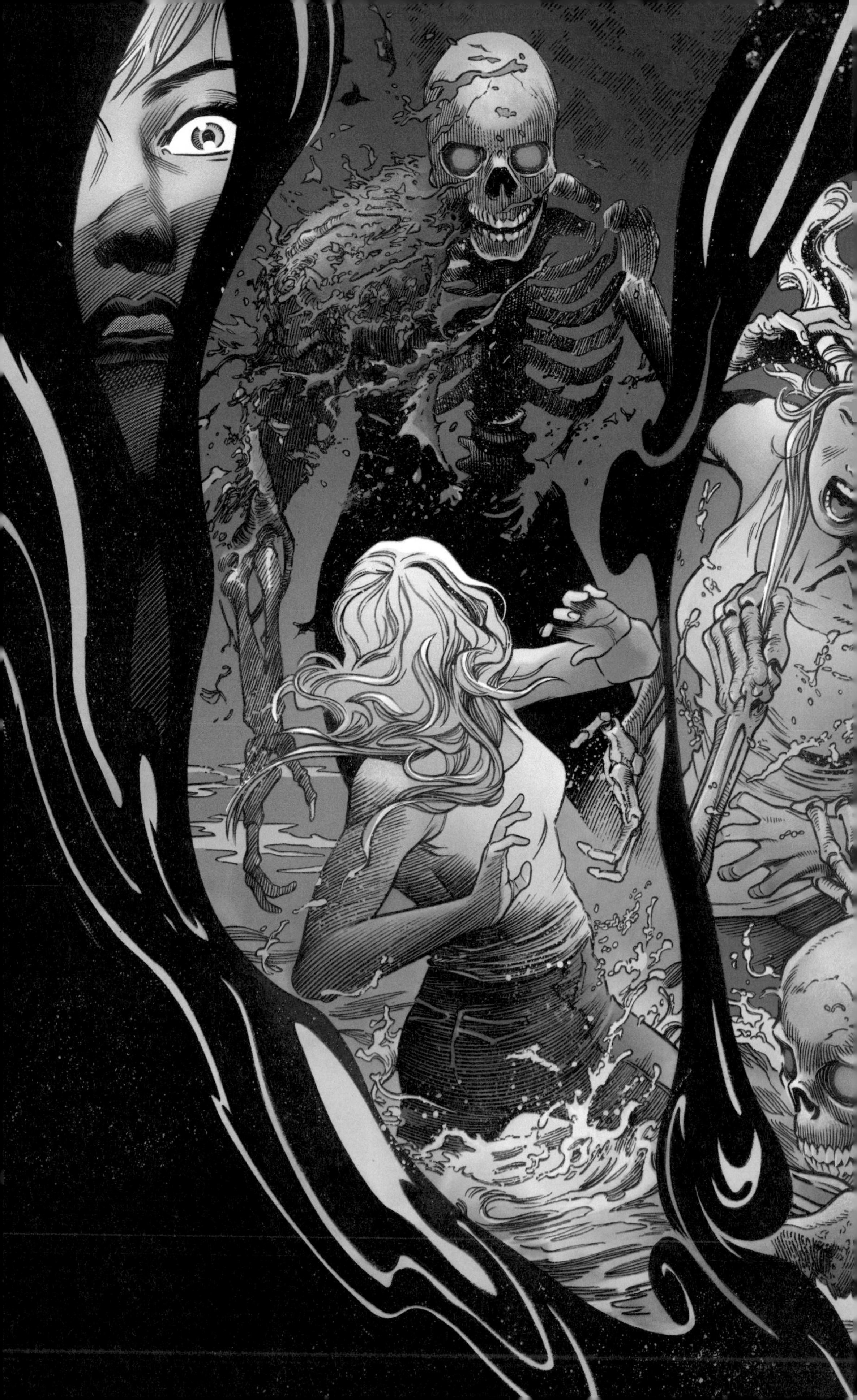

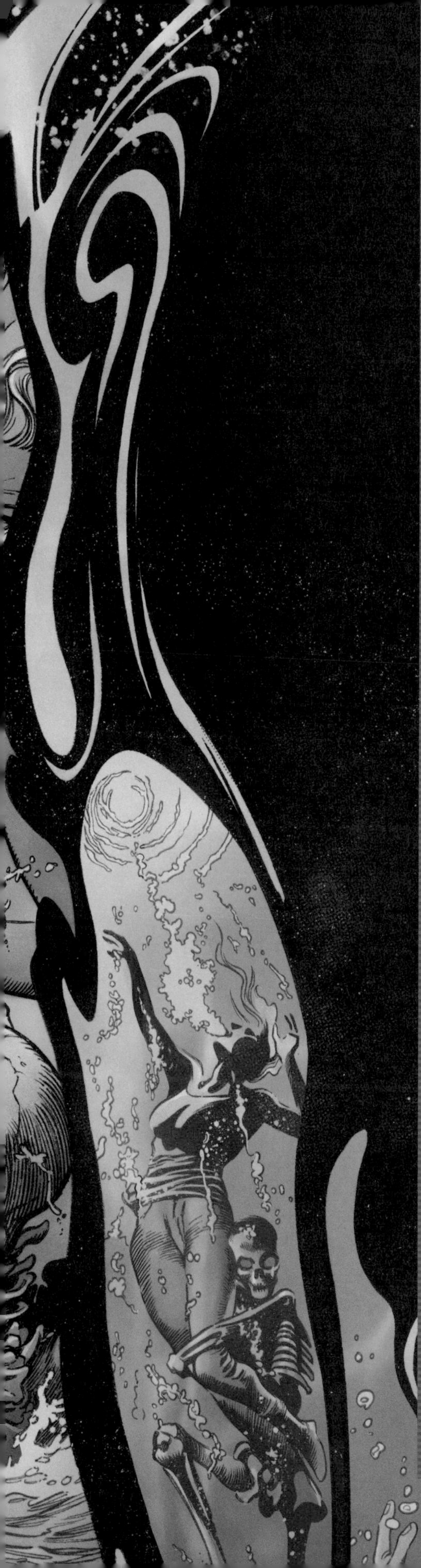

JUSTICE LEAGUE DARK

A COSTLY TRICK OF MAGIC

writers

RAM V
JAMES TYNION IV

artists

AMANCAY NAHUELPAN
KYLE HOTZ
ÁLVARO MARTÍNEZ BUENO
RAÚL FERNÁNDEZ

colorists

JUNE CHUNG
FCO PLASCENCIA

letterer

ROB LEIGH

collection cover artists

YANICK PAQUETTE and
NATHAN FAIRBAIRN

VOL. **4**

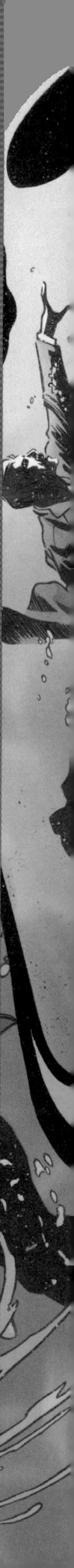

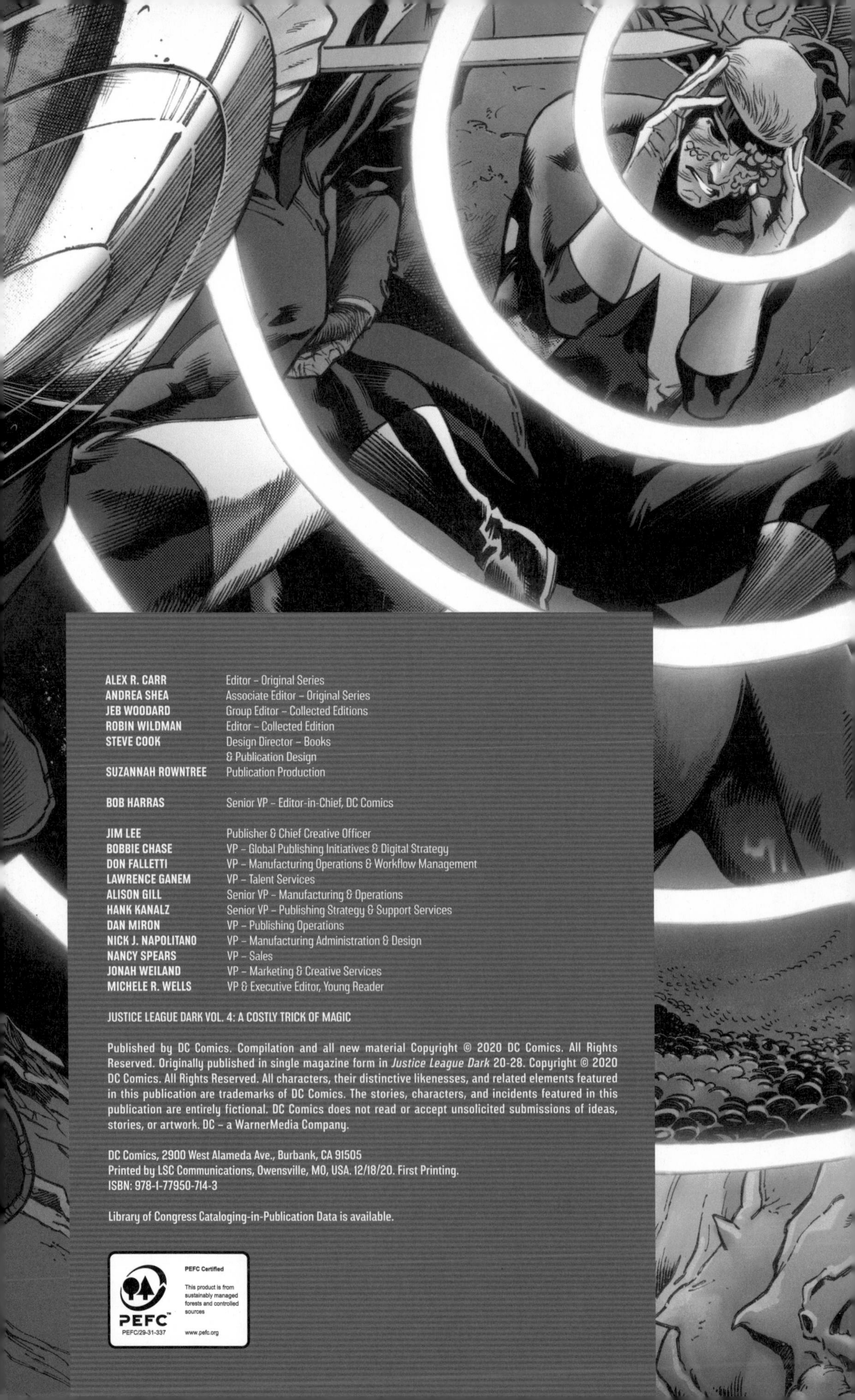

ALEX R. CARR Editor – Original Series
ANDREA SHEA Associate Editor – Original Series
JEB WOODARD Group Editor – Collected Editions
ROBIN WILDMAN Editor – Collected Edition
STEVE COOK Design Director – Books & Publication Design
SUZANNAH ROWNTREE Publication Production

BOB HARRAS Senior VP – Editor-in-Chief, DC Comics

JIM LEE Publisher & Chief Creative Officer
BOBBIE CHASE VP – Global Publishing Initiatives & Digital Strategy
DON FALLETTI VP – Manufacturing Operations & Workflow Management
LAWRENCE GANEM VP – Talent Services
ALISON GILL Senior VP – Manufacturing & Operations
HANK KANALZ Senior VP – Publishing Strategy & Support Services
DAN MIRON VP – Publishing Operations
NICK J. NAPOLITANO VP – Manufacturing Administration & Design
NANCY SPEARS VP – Sales
JONAH WEILAND VP – Marketing & Creative Services
MICHELE R. WELLS VP & Executive Editor, Young Reader

JUSTICE LEAGUE DARK VOL. 4: A COSTLY TRICK OF MAGIC

DC Comics, 2900 West Alameda Ave., Burbank, CA 91505
Printed by LSC Communications, Owensville, MO, USA. 12/18/20. First Printing.
ISBN: 978-1-77950-714-3

Library of Congress Cataloging-in-Publication Data is available.

PEFC Certified
This product is from sustainably managed forests and controlled sources
PEFC/29-31-337
www.pefc.org

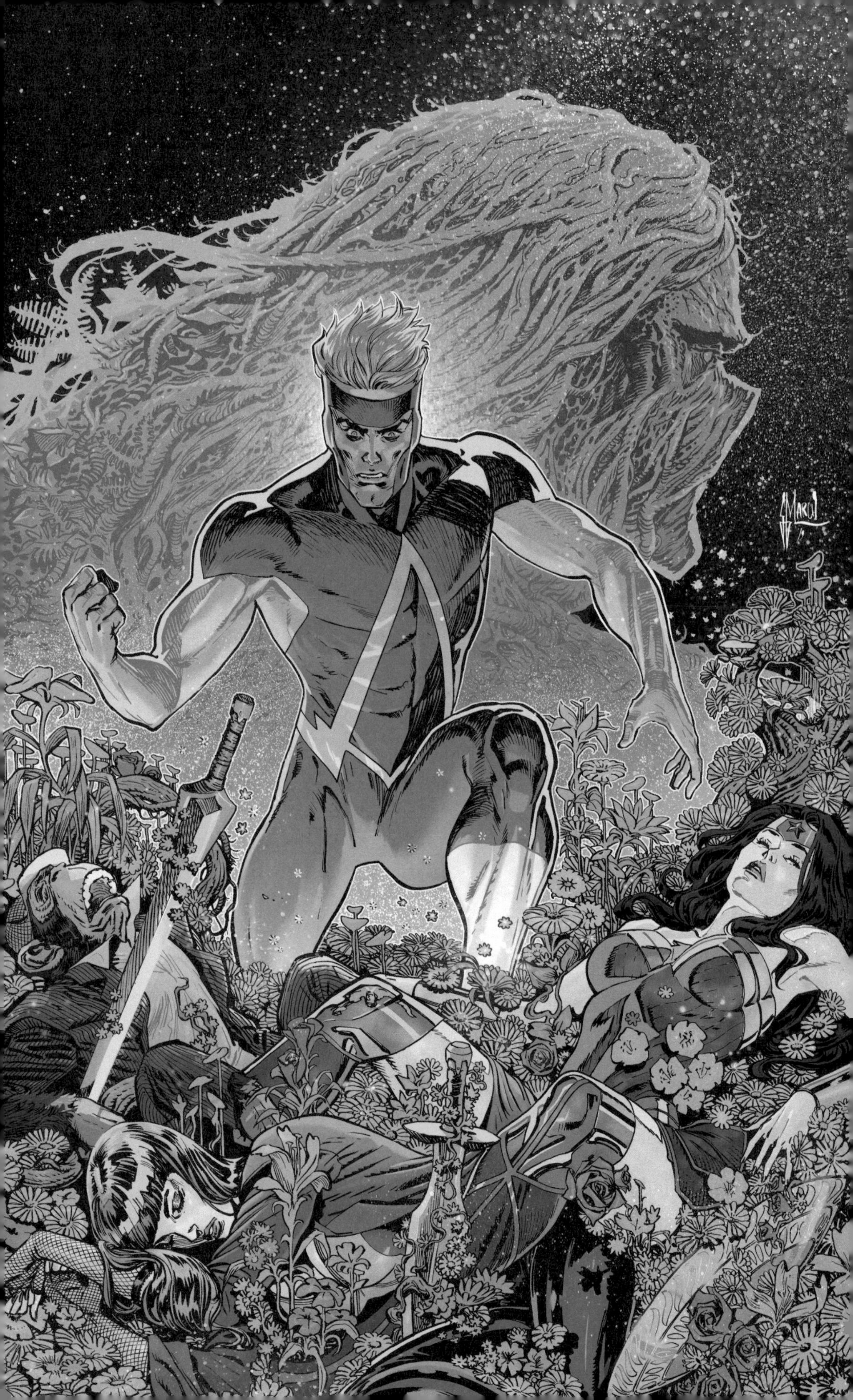

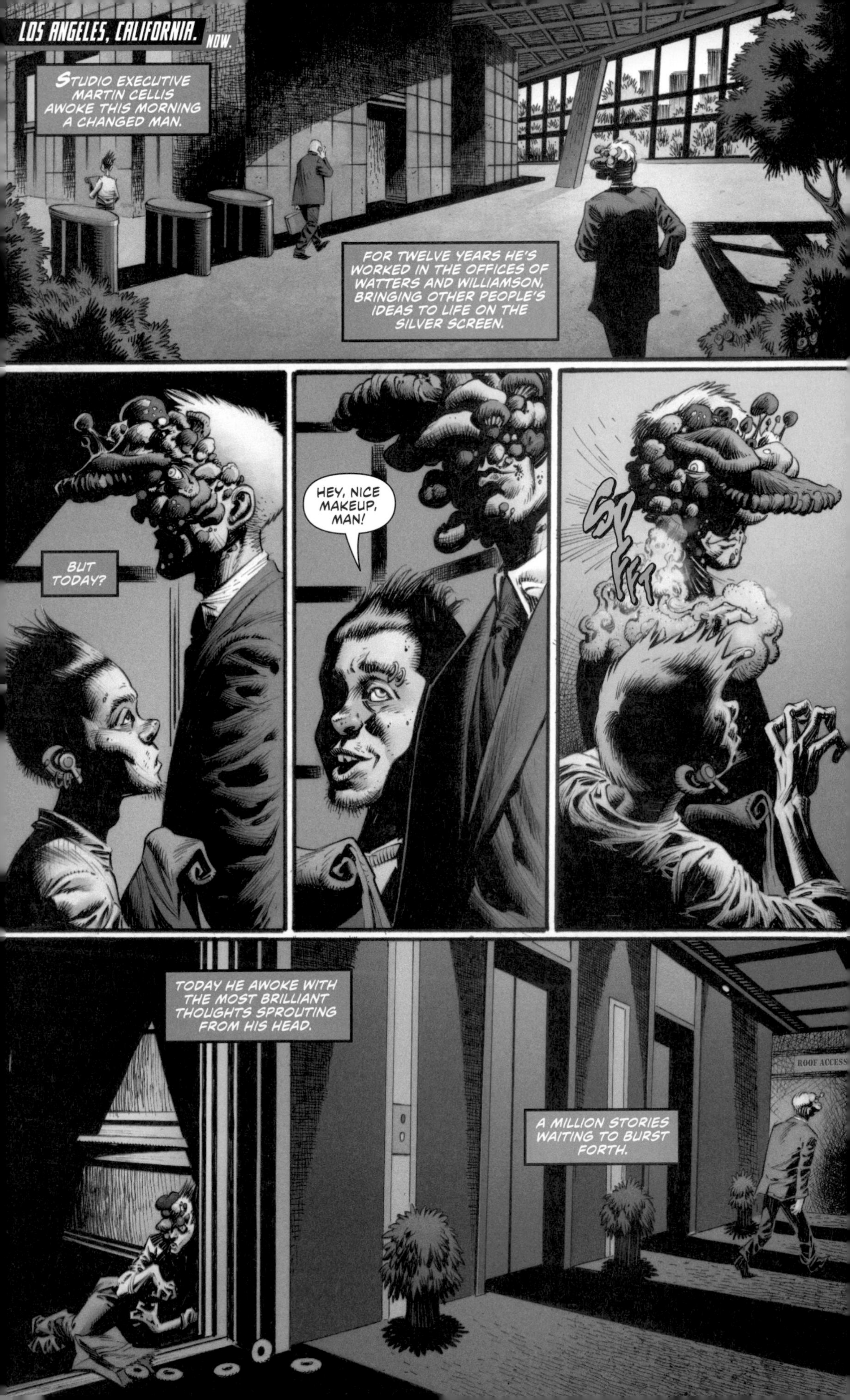
LOS ANGELES, CALIFORNIA. NOW.
STUDIO EXECUTIVE MARTIN CELLIS AWOKE THIS MORNING A CHANGED MAN.
FOR TWELVE YEARS HE'S WORKED IN THE OFFICES OF WATTERS AND WILLIAMSON, BRINGING OTHER PEOPLE'S IDEAS TO LIFE ON THE SILVER SCREEN.
BUT TODAY?
HEY, NICE MAKEUP, MAN!
SPLT
TODAY HE AWOKE WITH THE MOST BRILLIANT THOUGHTS SPROUTING FROM HIS HEAD.
A MILLION STORIES WAITING TO BURST FORTH.
ROOF ACCESS

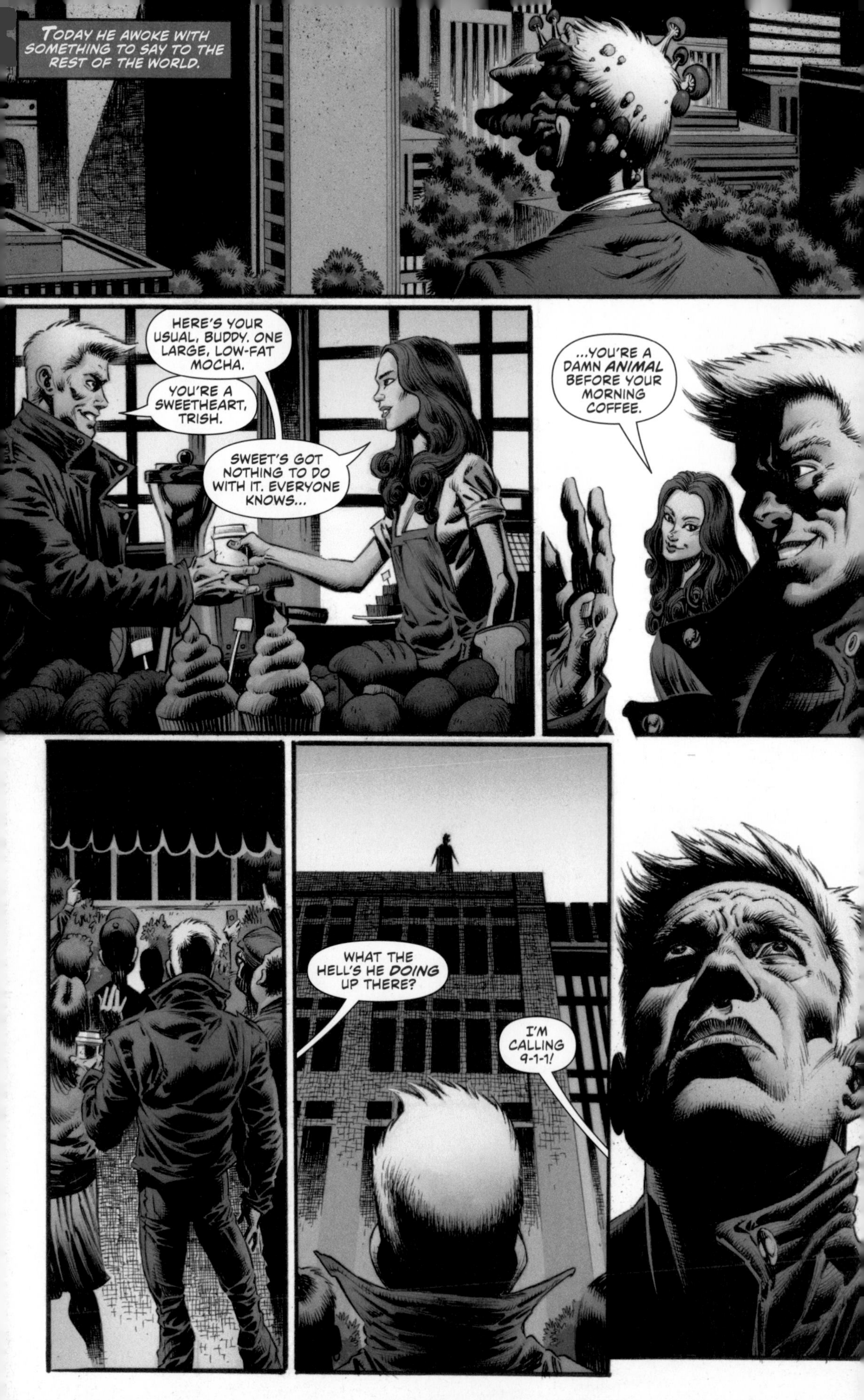
TODAY HE AWOKE WITH SOMETHING TO SAY TO THE REST OF THE WORLD.
HERE'S YOUR USUAL, BUDDY. ONE LARGE, LOW-FAT MOCHA.
YOU'RE A SWEETHEART, TRISH.
SWEET'S GOT NOTHING TO DO WITH IT. EVERYONE KNOWS...
...YOU'RE A DAMN ANIMAL BEFORE YOUR MORNING COFFEE.
WHAT THE HELL'S HE DOING UP THERE?
I'M CALLING 9-1-1!

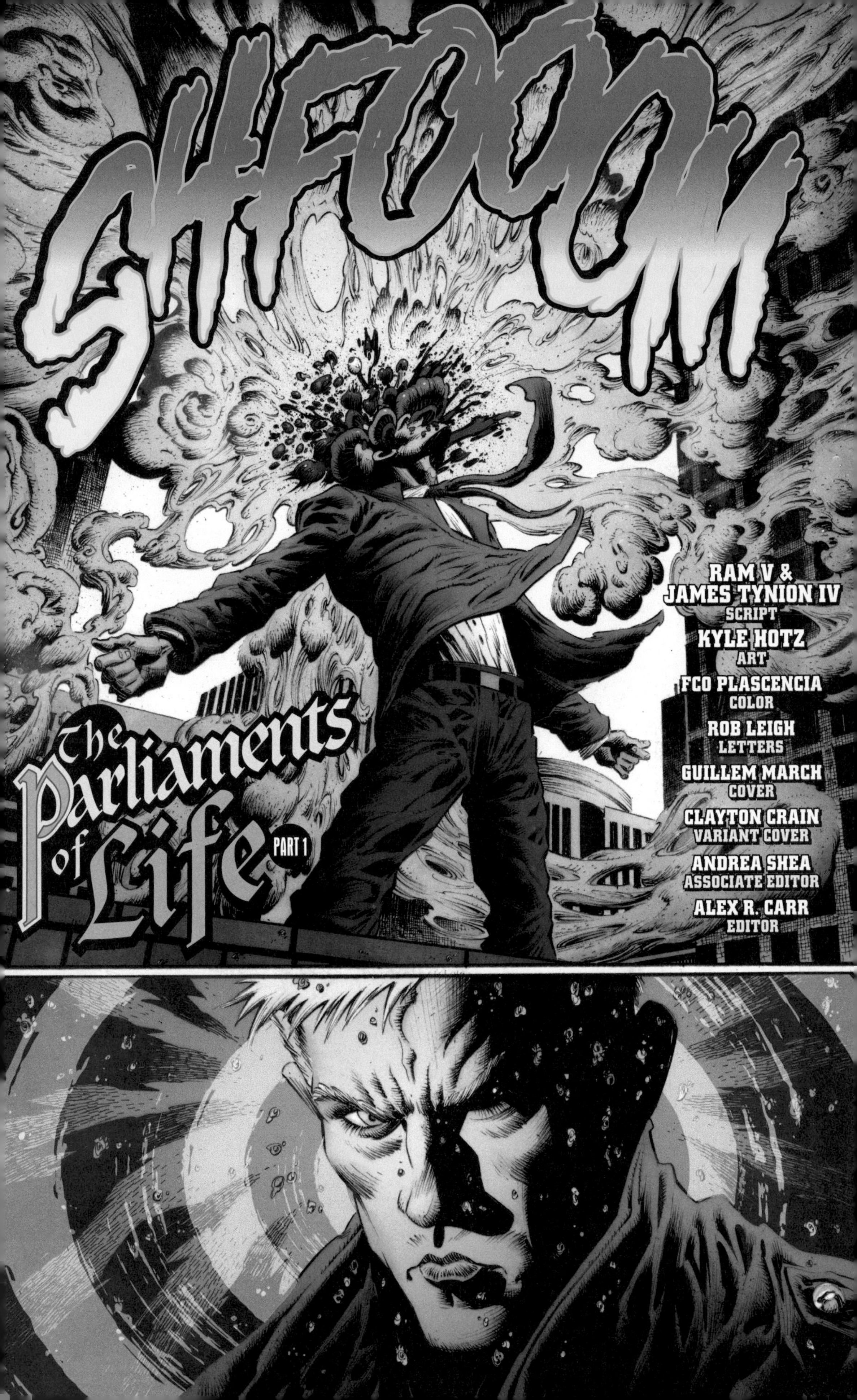
SHFOOM
The Parliaments of Life
PART 1
RAM V & JAMES TYNION IV
SCRIPT
KYLE HOTZ
ART
FCO PLASCENCIA
COLOR
ROB LEIGH
LETTERS
GUILLEM MARCH
COVER
CLAYTON CRAIN
VARIANT COVER
ANDREA SHEA
ASSOCIATE EDITOR
ALEX R. CARR
EDITOR

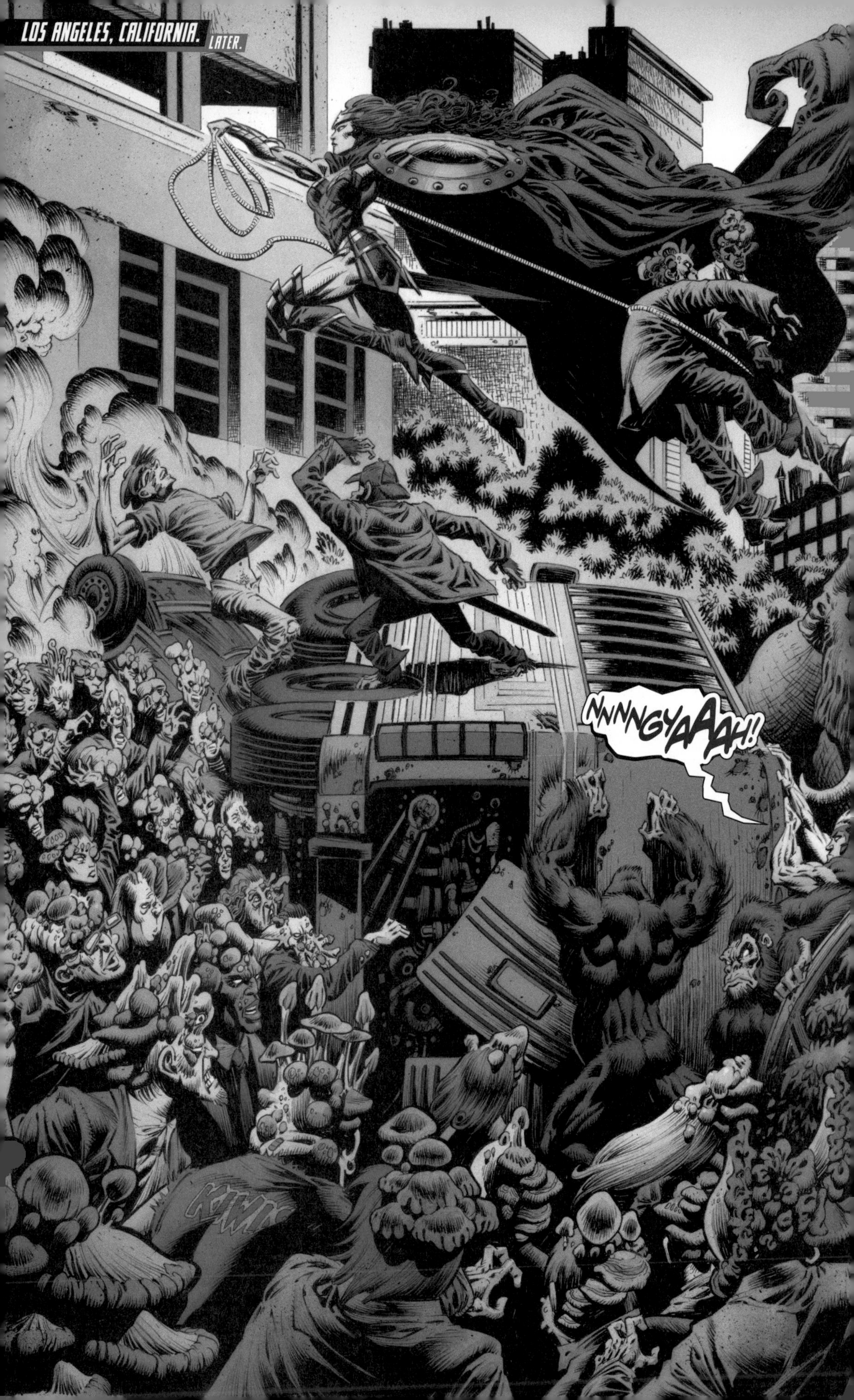
LOS ANGELES, CALIFORNIA.
LATER.
NNNNGYAAAH!

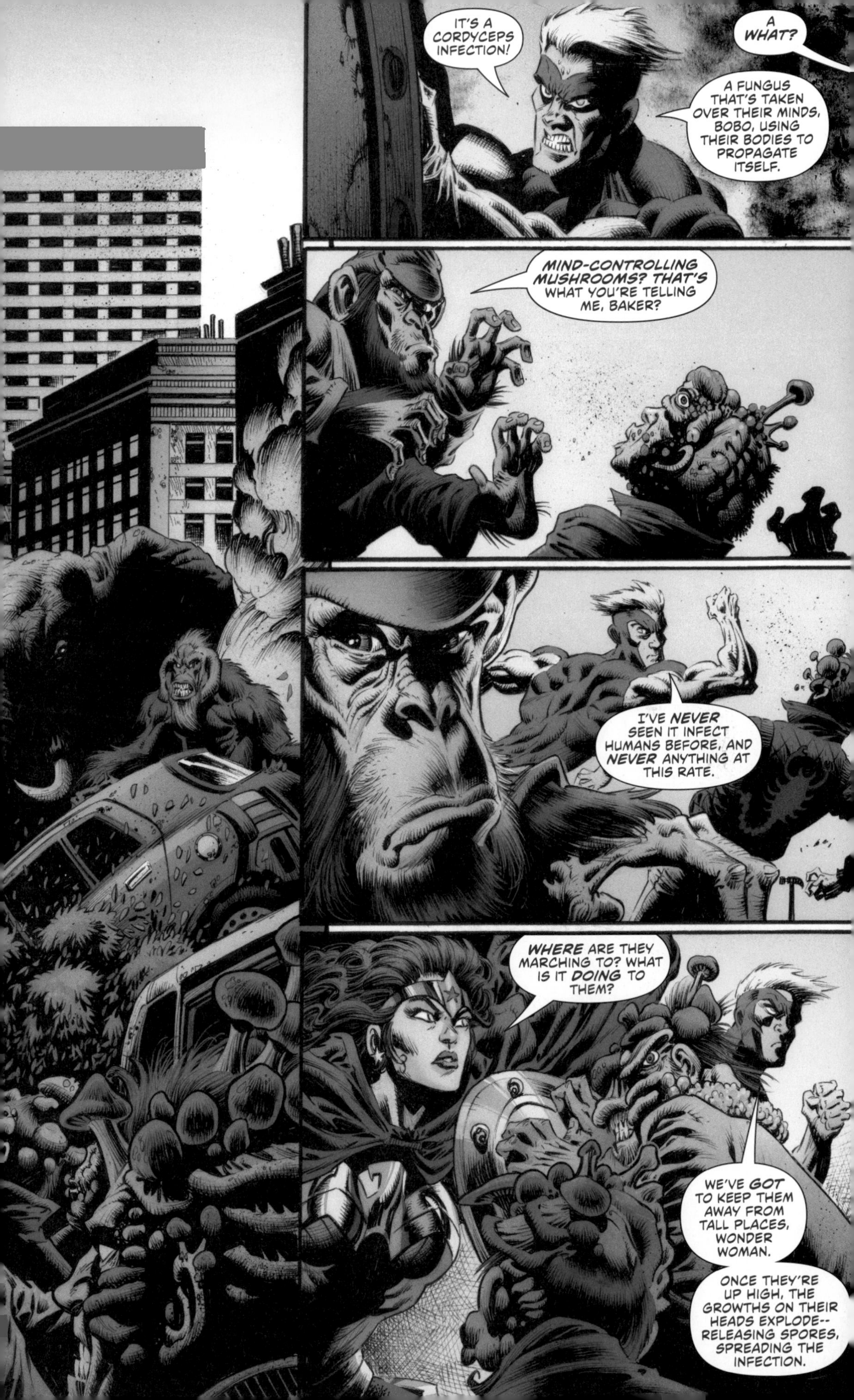
IT'S A CORDYCEPS INFECTION!
A WHAT?
A FUNGUS THAT'S TAKEN OVER THEIR MINDS, BOBO, USING THEIR BODIES TO PROPAGATE ITSELF.
MIND-CONTROLLING MUSHROOMS? THAT'S WHAT YOU'RE TELLING ME, BAKER?
I'VE NEVER SEEN IT INFECT HUMANS BEFORE, AND NEVER ANYTHING AT THIS RATE.
WHERE ARE THEY MARCHING TO? WHAT IS IT DOING TO THEM?
WE'VE GOT TO KEEP THEM AWAY FROM TALL PLACES, WONDER WOMAN.
ONCE THEY'RE UP HIGH, THE GROWTHS ON THEIR HEADS EXPLODE--RELEASING SPORES, SPREADING THE INFECTION.

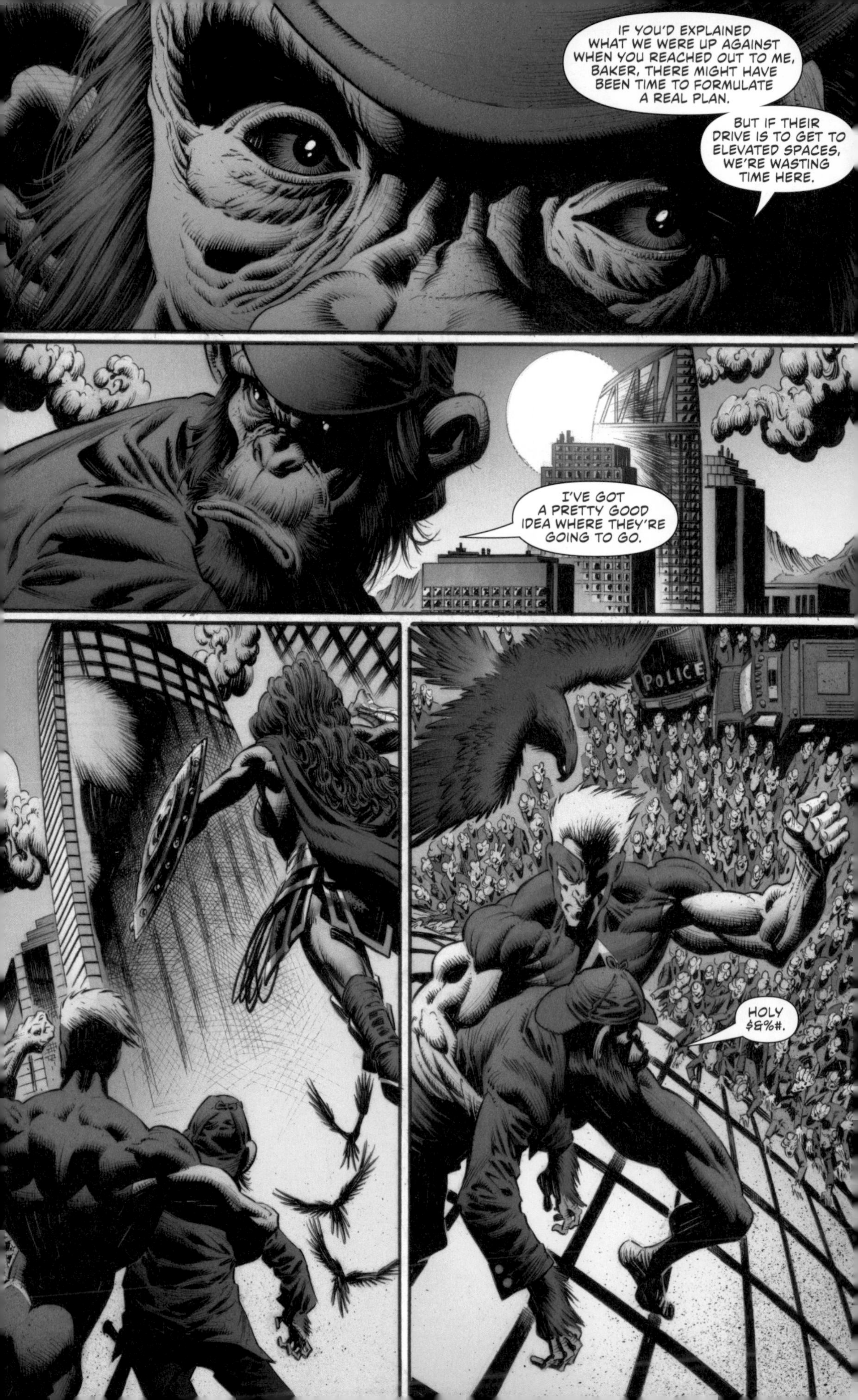
IF YOU'D EXPLAINED WHAT WE WERE UP AGAINST WHEN YOU REACHED OUT TO ME, BAKER, THERE MIGHT HAVE BEEN TIME TO FORMULATE A REAL PLAN.
BUT IF THEIR DRIVE IS TO GET TO ELEVATED SPACES, WE'RE WASTING TIME HERE.
I'VE GOT A PRETTY GOOD IDEA WHERE THEY'RE GOING TO GO.
POLICE
HOLY $&%#.

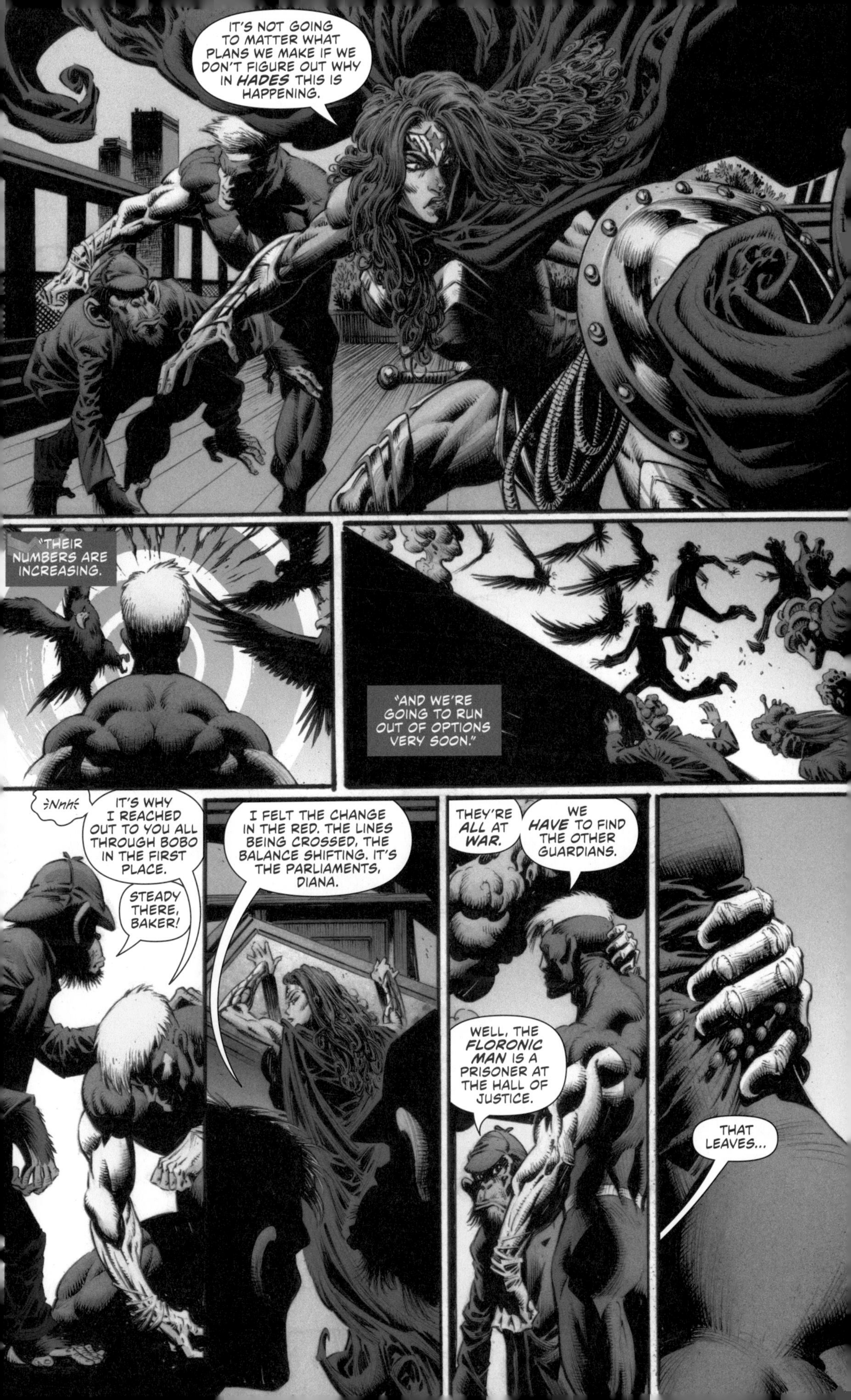

IT'S NOT GOING TO MATTER WHAT PLANS WE MAKE IF WE DON'T FIGURE OUT WHY IN *HADES* THIS IS HAPPENING.
"THEIR NUMBERS ARE INCREASING.
"AND WE'RE GOING TO RUN OUT OF OPTIONS VERY SOON."
Nnh
IT'S WHY I REACHED OUT TO YOU ALL THROUGH BOBO IN THE FIRST PLACE.
STEADY THERE, BAKER!
I FELT THE CHANGE IN THE RED. THE LINES BEING CROSSED, THE BALANCE SHIFTING. IT'S THE PARLIAMENTS, DIANA.
THEY'RE *ALL* AT *WAR*.
WE *HAVE* TO FIND THE OTHER GUARDIANS.
WELL, THE *FLORONIC MAN* IS A PRISONER AT THE HALL OF JUSTICE.
THAT LEAVES...

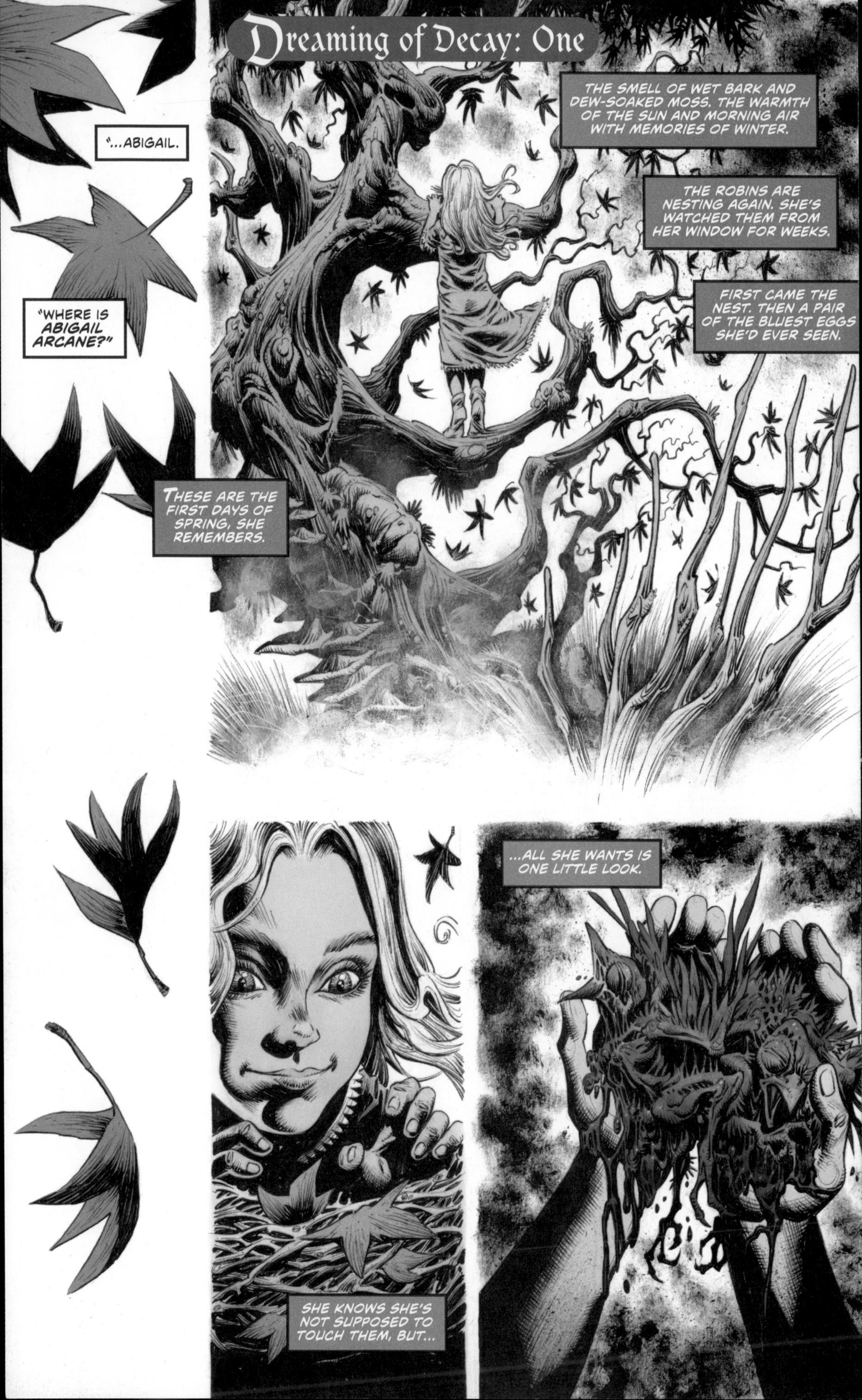
Dreaming of Decay: One
"...ABIGAIL.
"WHERE IS ABIGAIL ARCANE?"
THE SMELL OF WET BARK AND DEW-SOAKED MOSS. THE WARMTH OF THE SUN AND MORNING AIR WITH MEMORIES OF WINTER.
THE ROBINS ARE NESTING AGAIN. SHE'S WATCHED THEM FROM HER WINDOW FOR WEEKS.
FIRST CAME THE NEST. THEN A PAIR OF THE BLUEST EGGS SHE'D EVER SEEN.
THESE ARE THE FIRST DAYS OF SPRING, SHE REMEMBERS.
SHE KNOWS SHE'S NOT SUPPOSED TO TOUCH THEM, BUT...
...ALL SHE WANTS IS ONE LITTLE LOOK.

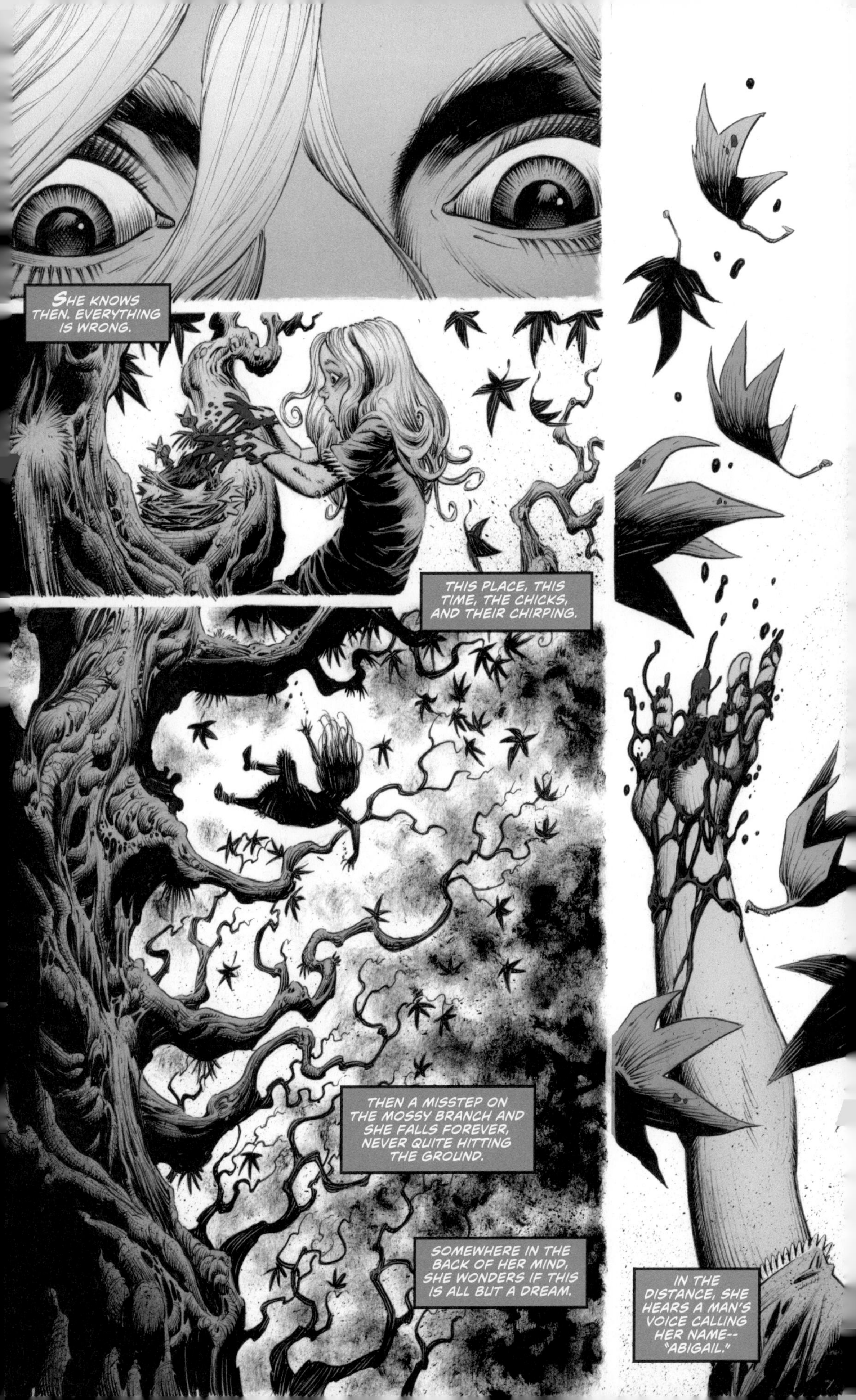
SHE KNOWS THEN. EVERYTHING IS WRONG.
THIS PLACE, THIS TIME, THE CHICKS, AND THEIR CHIRPING.
THEN A MISSTEP ON THE MOSSY BRANCH AND SHE FALLS FOREVER, NEVER QUITE HITTING THE GROUND.
SOMEWHERE IN THE BACK OF HER MIND, SHE WONDERS IF THIS IS ALL BUT A DREAM.
IN THE DISTANCE, SHE HEARS A MAN'S VOICE CALLING HER NAME-- "ABIGAIL."

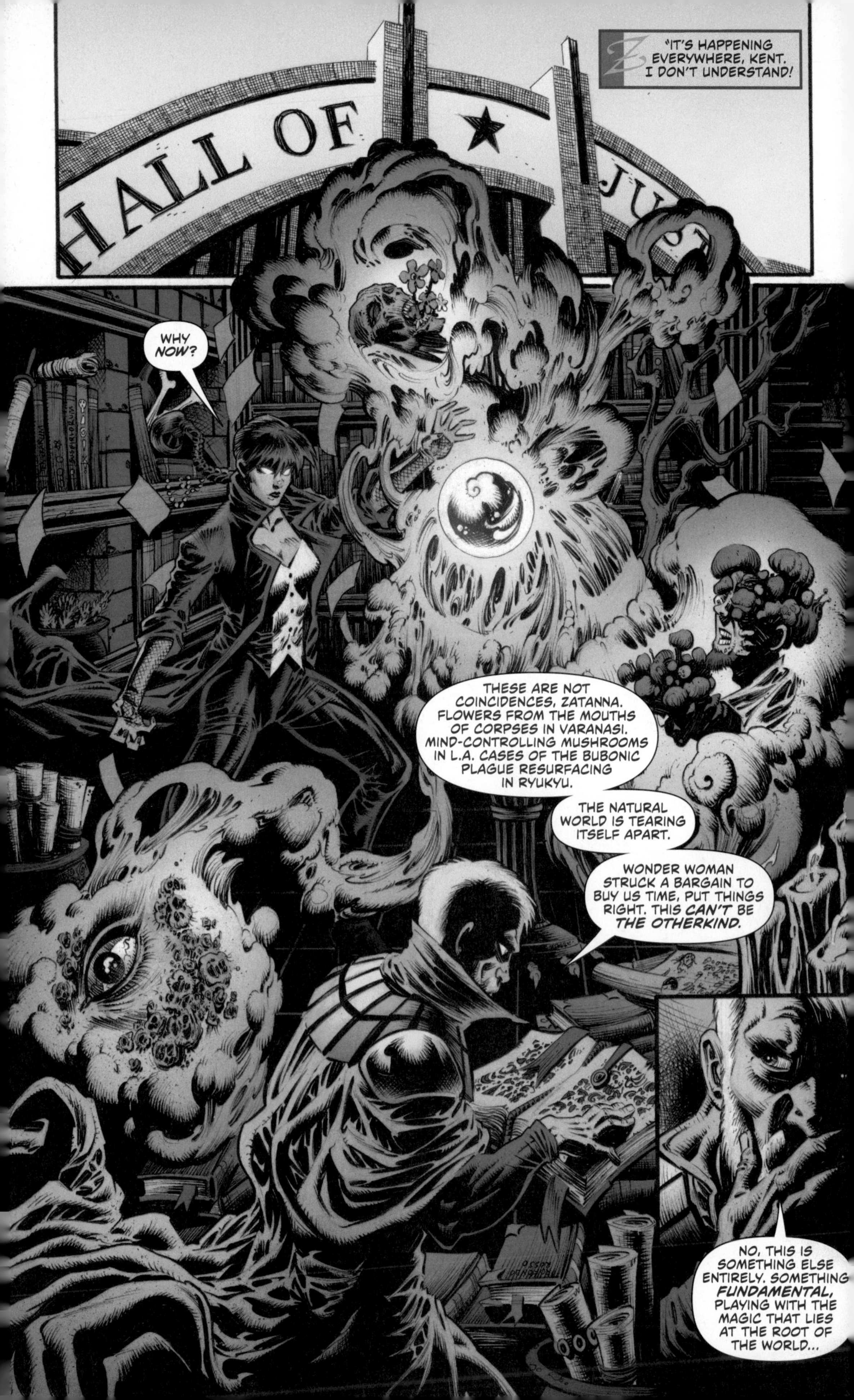
"IT'S HAPPENING EVERYWHERE, KENT. I DON'T UNDERSTAND!
WHY NOW?
THESE ARE NOT COINCIDENCES, ZATANNA. FLOWERS FROM THE MOUTHS OF CORPSES IN VARANASI. MIND-CONTROLLING MUSHROOMS IN L.A. CASES OF THE BUBONIC PLAGUE RESURFACING IN RYUKYU.
THE NATURAL WORLD IS TEARING ITSELF APART.
WONDER WOMAN STRUCK A BARGAIN TO BUY US TIME, PUT THINGS RIGHT. THIS CAN'T BE THE OTHERKIND.
NO, THIS IS SOMETHING ELSE ENTIRELY. SOMETHING FUNDAMENTAL, PLAYING WITH THE MAGIC THAT LIES AT THE ROOT OF THE WORLD...

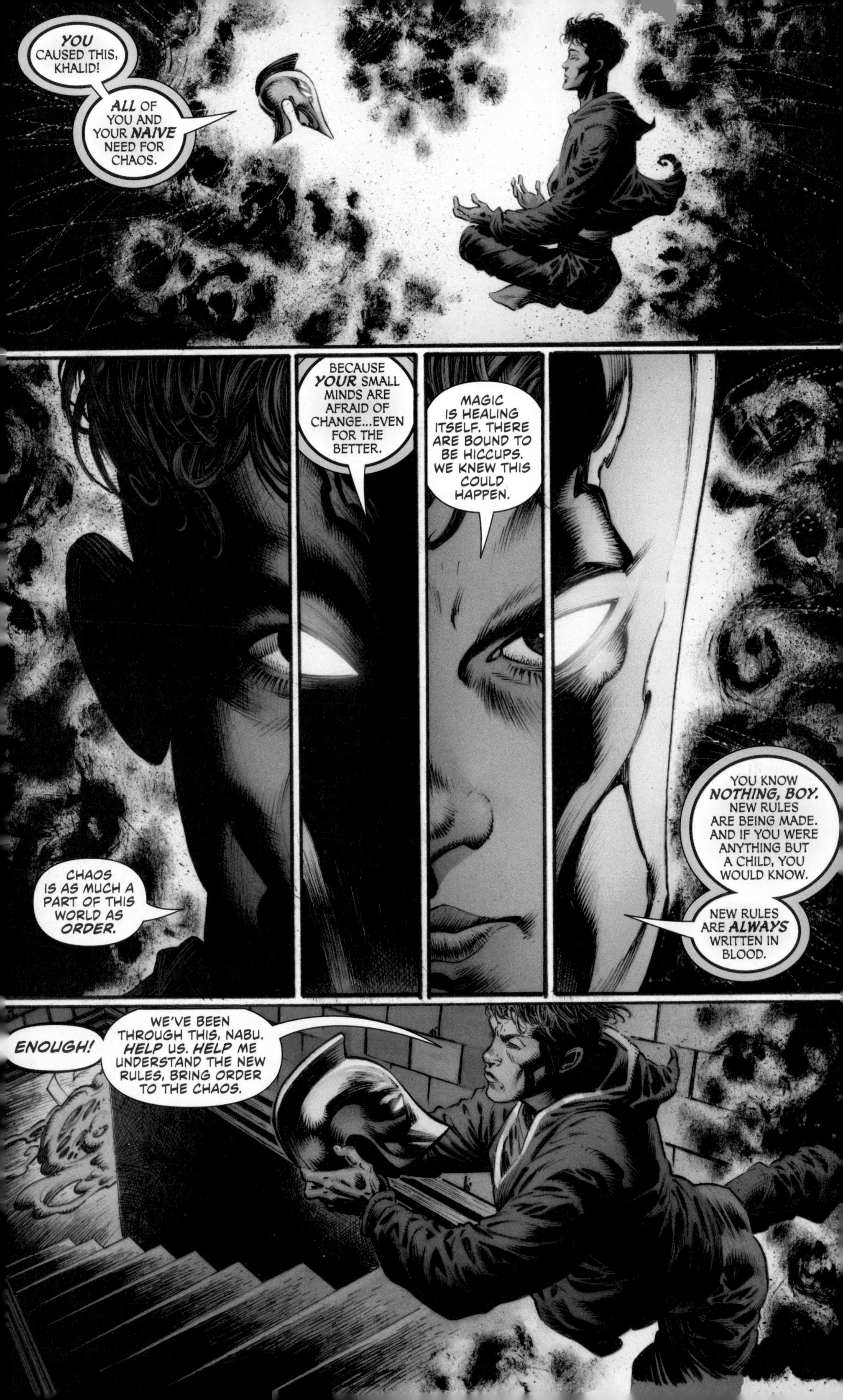
YOU CAUSED THIS, KHALID!
ALL OF YOU AND YOUR NAIVE NEED FOR CHAOS.
BECAUSE YOUR SMALL MINDS ARE AFRAID OF CHANGE...EVEN FOR THE BETTER.
MAGIC IS HEALING ITSELF. THERE ARE BOUND TO BE HICCUPS. WE KNEW THIS COULD HAPPEN.
CHAOS IS AS MUCH A PART OF THIS WORLD AS ORDER.
YOU KNOW NOTHING, BOY. NEW RULES ARE BEING MADE. AND IF YOU WERE ANYTHING BUT A CHILD, YOU WOULD KNOW.
NEW RULES ARE ALWAYS WRITTEN IN BLOOD.
ENOUGH!
WE'VE BEEN THROUGH THIS, NABU. HELP US. HELP ME UNDERSTAND THE NEW RULES, BRING ORDER TO THE CHAOS.

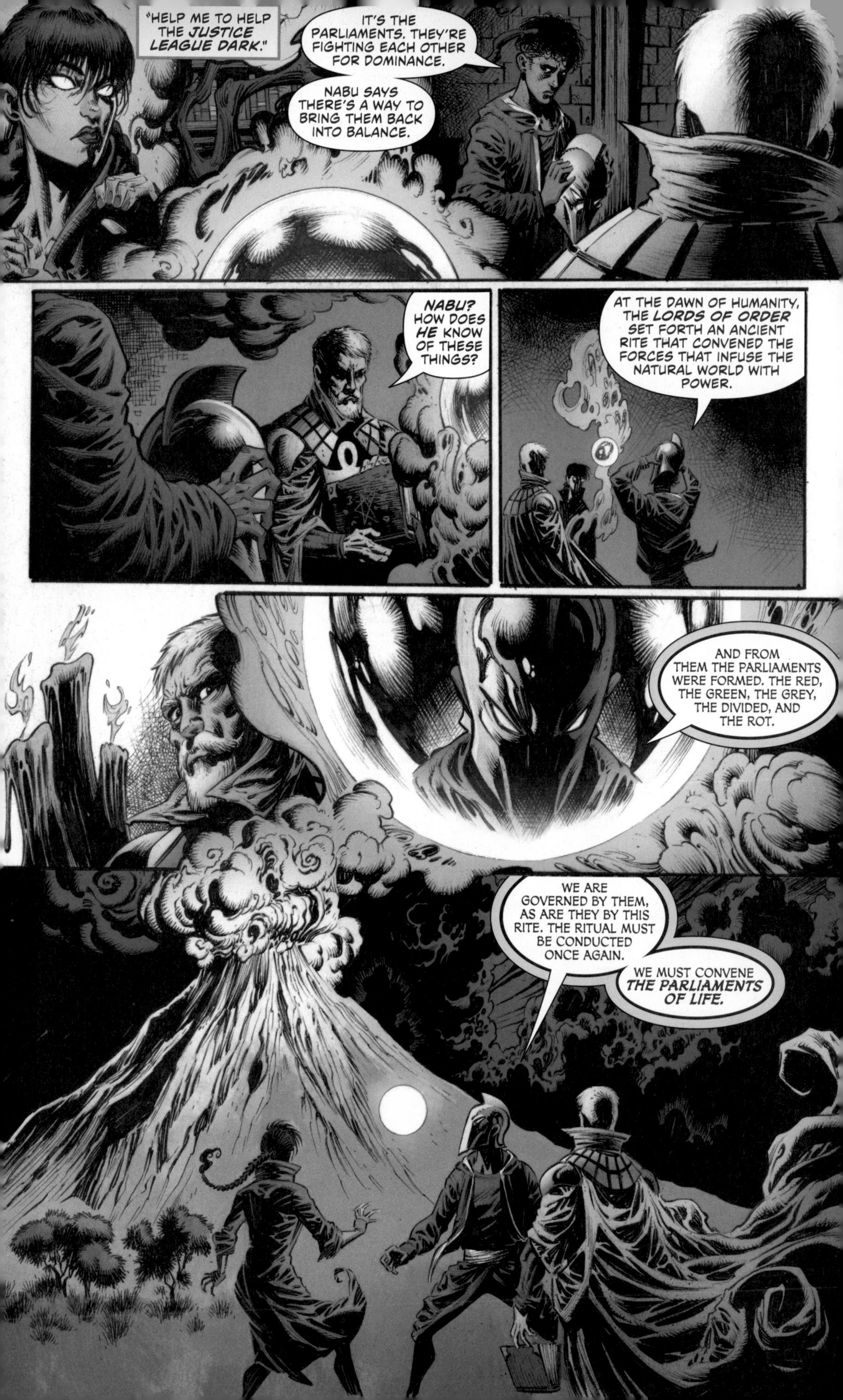
"HELP ME TO HELP THE *JUSTICE LEAGUE DARK*."
IT'S THE PARLIAMENTS. THEY'RE FIGHTING EACH OTHER FOR DOMINANCE.
NABU SAYS THERE'S A WAY TO BRING THEM BACK INTO BALANCE.
NABU? HOW DOES *HE* KNOW OF THESE THINGS?
AT THE DAWN OF HUMANITY, THE *LORDS OF ORDER* SET FORTH AN ANCIENT RITE THAT CONVENED THE FORCES THAT INFUSE THE NATURAL WORLD WITH POWER.
AND FROM THEM THE PARLIAMENTS WERE FORMED. THE RED, THE GREEN, THE GREY, THE DIVIDED, AND THE ROT.
WE ARE GOVERNED BY THEM, AS ARE THEY BY THIS RITE. THE RITUAL MUST BE CONDUCTED ONCE AGAIN.
WE MUST CONVENE ***THE PARLIAMENTS OF LIFE.***

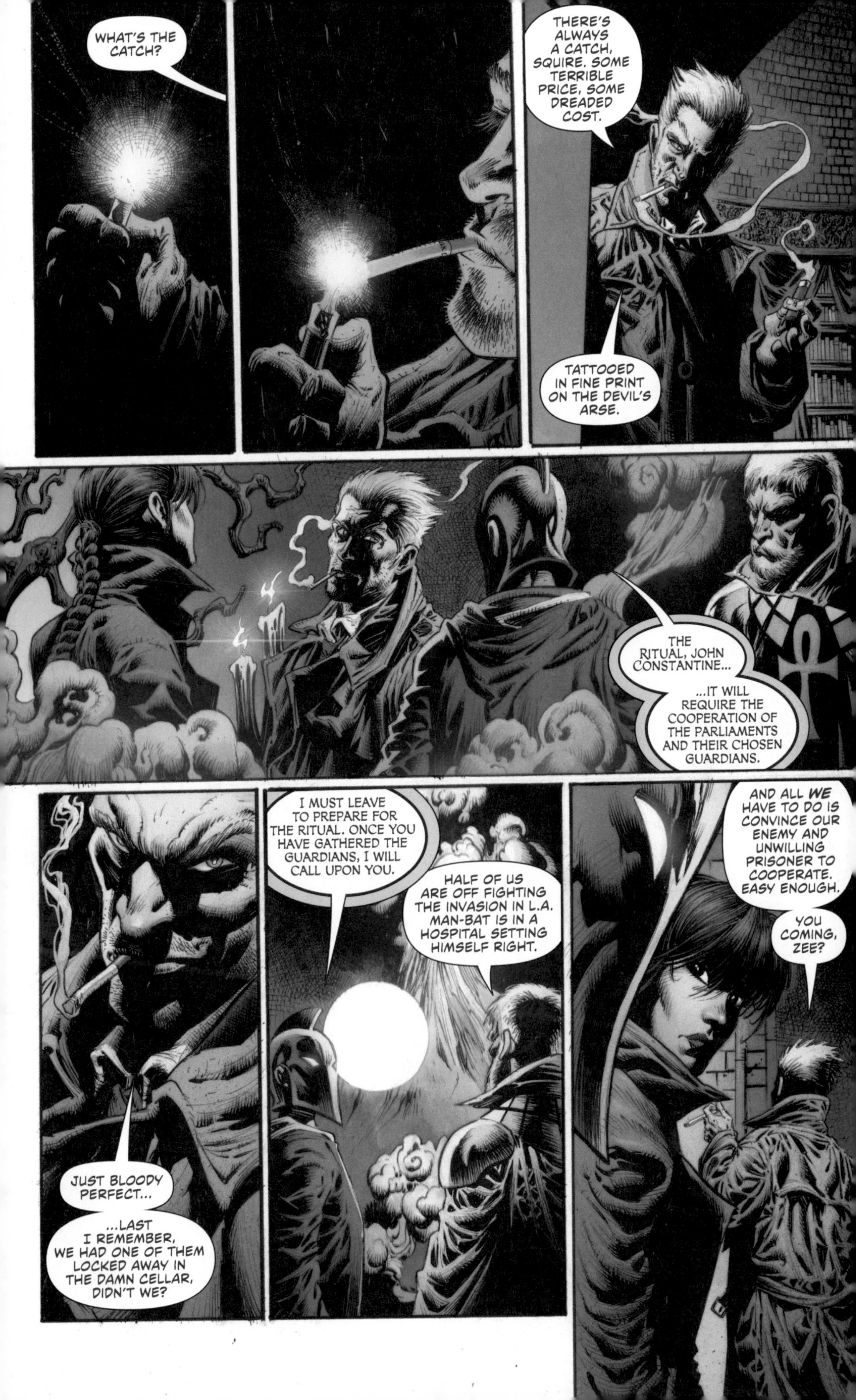
WHAT'S THE CATCH?
THERE'S ALWAYS A CATCH, SQUIRE. SOME TERRIBLE PRICE, SOME DREADED COST.
TATTOOED IN FINE PRINT ON THE DEVIL'S ARSE.
THE RITUAL, JOHN CONSTANTINE...
...IT WILL REQUIRE THE COOPERATION OF THE PARLIAMENTS AND THEIR CHOSEN GUARDIANS.
JUST BLOODY PERFECT...
...LAST I REMEMBER, WE HAD ONE OF THEM LOCKED AWAY IN THE DAMN CELLAR, DIDN'T WE?
I MUST LEAVE TO PREPARE FOR THE RITUAL. ONCE YOU HAVE GATHERED THE GUARDIANS, I WILL CALL UPON YOU.
HALF OF US ARE OFF FIGHTING THE INVASION IN L.A. MAN-BAT IS IN A HOSPITAL SETTING HIMSELF RIGHT.
AND ALL WE HAVE TO DO IS CONVINCE OUR ENEMY AND UNWILLING PRISONER TO COOPERATE. EASY ENOUGH.
YOU COMING, ZEE?

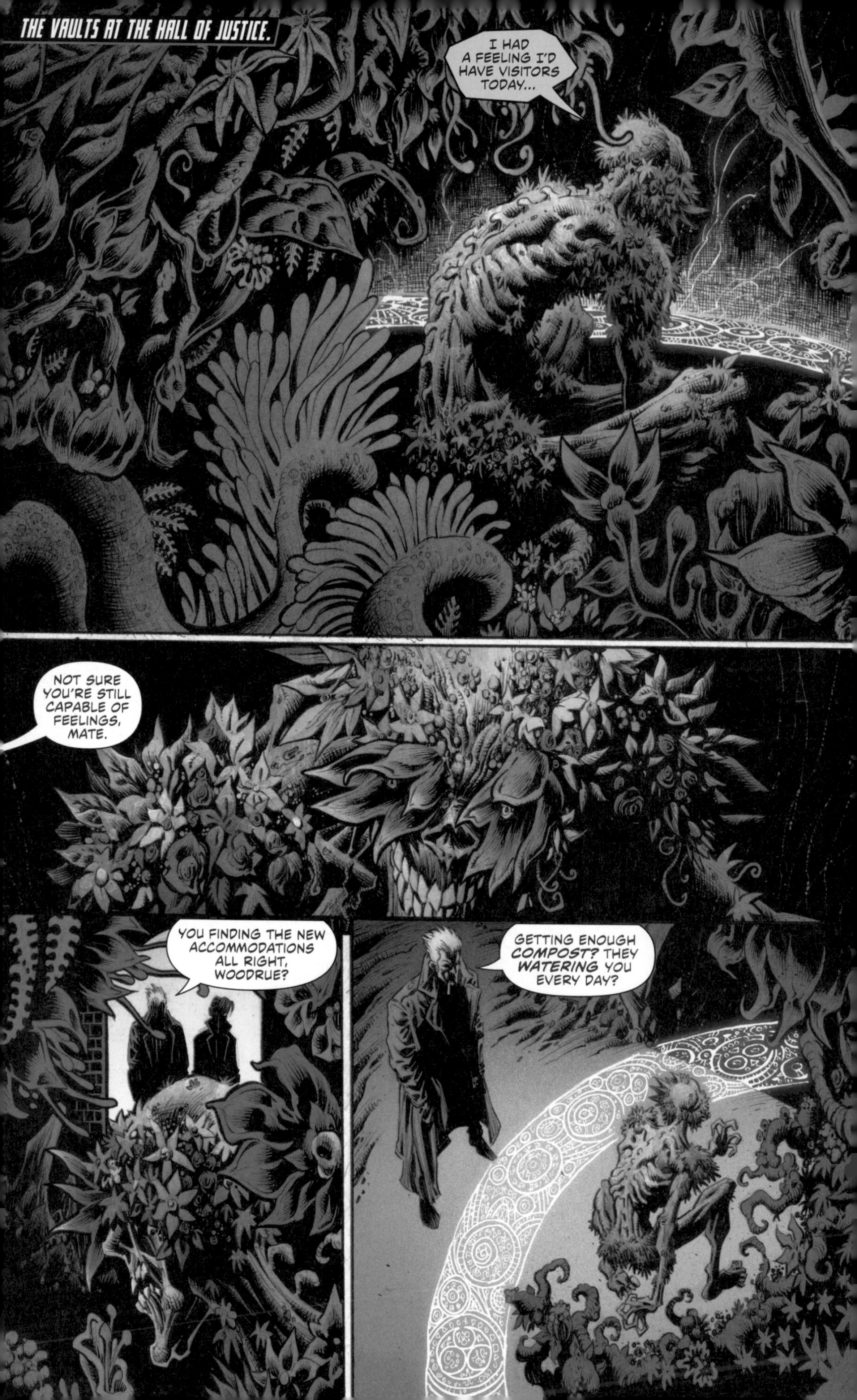
THE VAULTS AT THE HALL OF JUSTICE.
I HAD A FEELING I'D HAVE VISITORS TODAY...
NOT SURE YOU'RE STILL CAPABLE OF FEELINGS, MATE.
YOU FINDING THE NEW ACCOMMODATIONS ALL RIGHT, WOODRUE?
GETTING ENOUGH COMPOST? THEY WATERING YOU EVERY DAY?

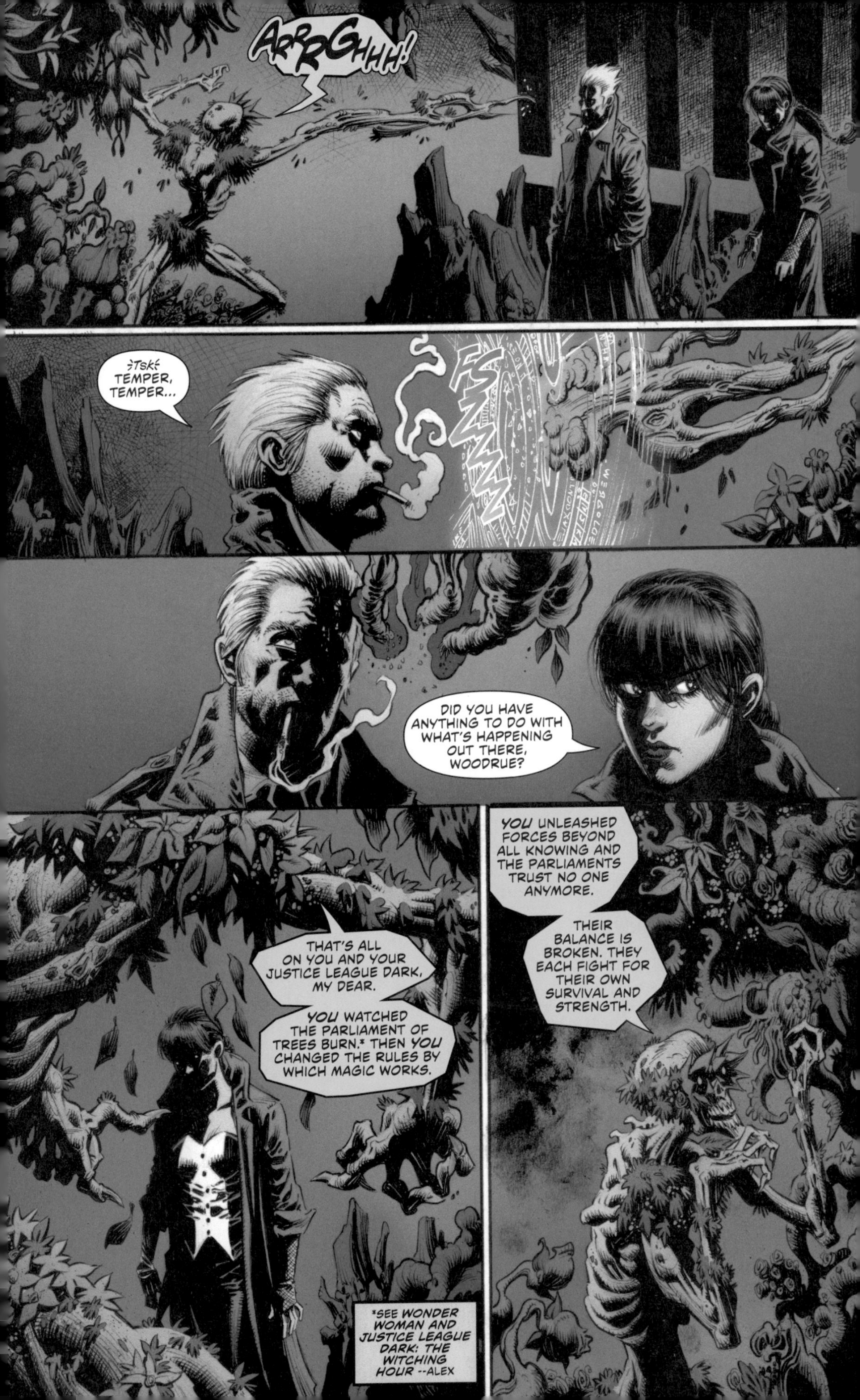
ARRRGHHH!
TSK TEMPER, TEMPER...
FSZZZZZ
DID YOU HAVE ANYTHING TO DO WITH WHAT'S HAPPENING OUT THERE, WOODRUE?
THAT'S ALL ON YOU AND YOUR JUSTICE LEAGUE DARK, MY DEAR.
YOU WATCHED THE PARLIAMENT OF TREES BURN.* THEN YOU CHANGED THE RULES BY WHICH MAGIC WORKS.
*SEE WONDER WOMAN AND JUSTICE LEAGUE DARK: THE WITCHING HOUR --ALEX
YOU UNLEASHED FORCES BEYOND ALL KNOWING AND THE PARLIAMENTS TRUST NO ONE ANYMORE.
THEIR BALANCE IS BROKEN. THEY EACH FIGHT FOR THEIR OWN SURVIVAL AND STRENGTH.

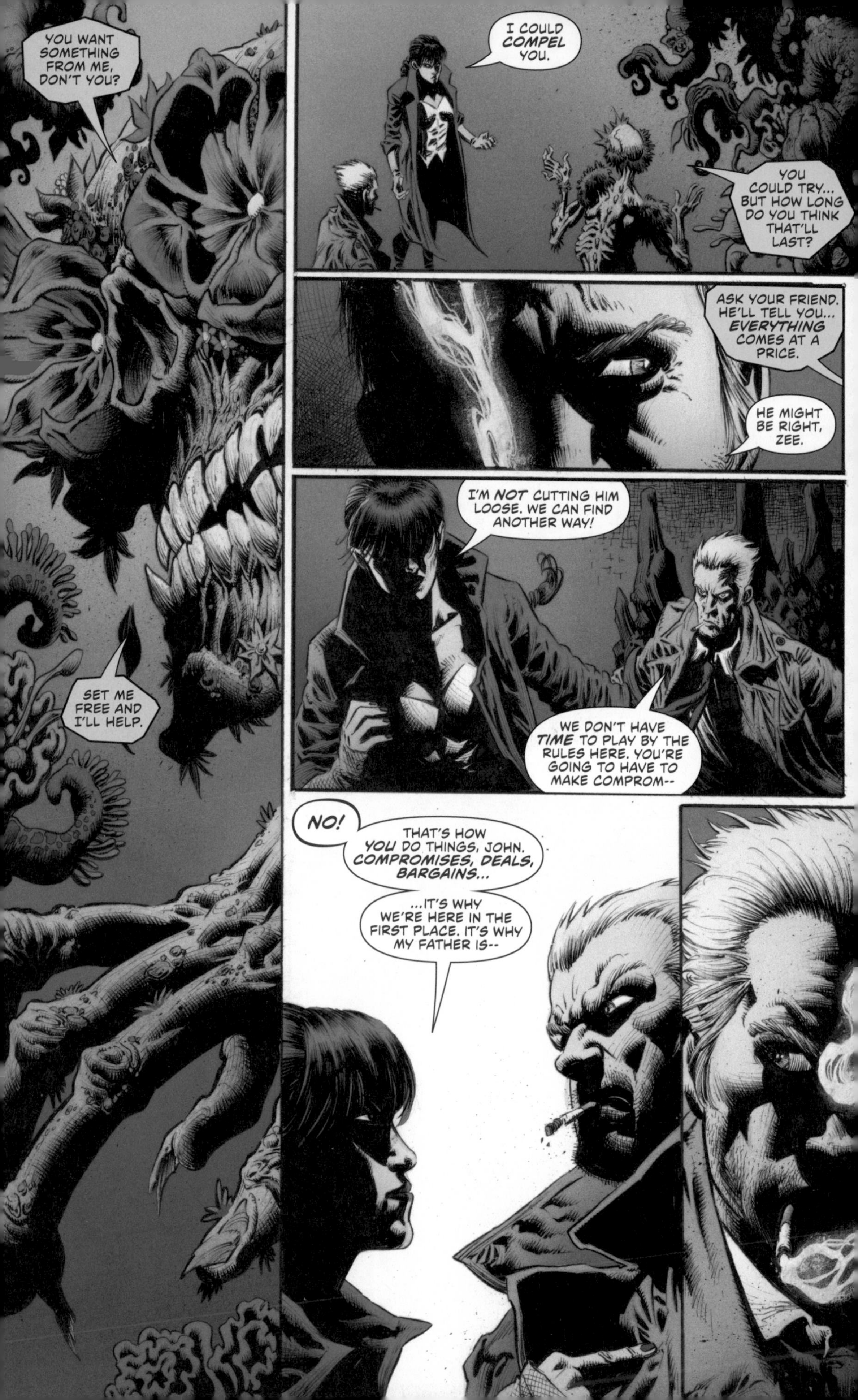
YOU WANT SOMETHING FROM ME, DON'T YOU?
I COULD COMPEL YOU.
YOU COULD TRY... BUT HOW LONG DO YOU THINK THAT'LL LAST?
ASK YOUR FRIEND. HE'LL TELL YOU... EVERYTHING COMES AT A PRICE.
HE MIGHT BE RIGHT, ZEE.
I'M NOT CUTTING HIM LOOSE. WE CAN FIND ANOTHER WAY!
WE DON'T HAVE TIME TO PLAY BY THE RULES HERE. YOU'RE GOING TO HAVE TO MAKE COMPROM--
SET ME FREE AND I'LL HELP.
NO!
THAT'S HOW YOU DO THINGS, JOHN. COMPROMISES, DEALS, BARGAINS...
...IT'S WHY WE'RE HERE IN THE FIRST PLACE. IT'S WHY MY FATHER IS--

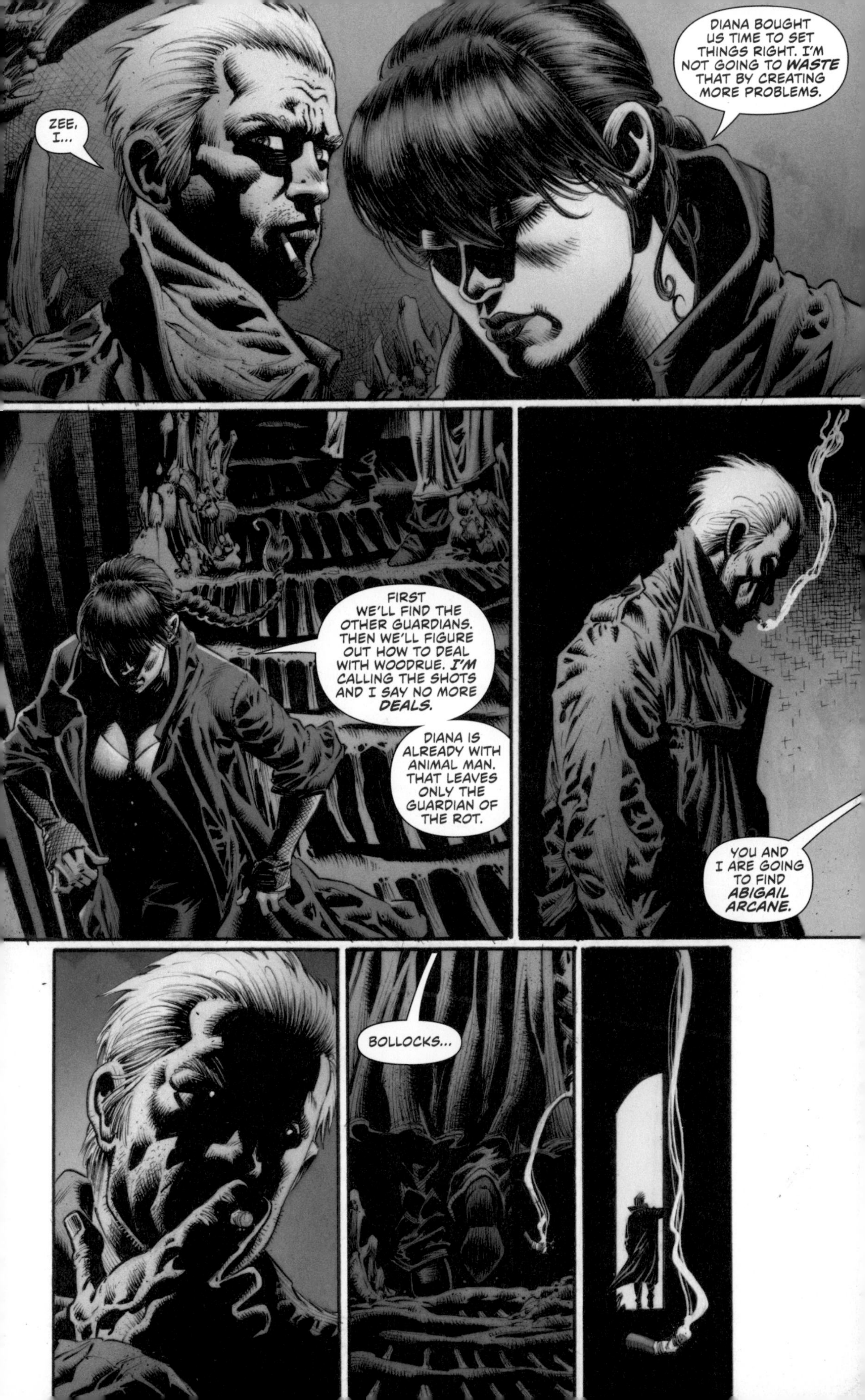
ZEE, I...
DIANA BOUGHT US TIME TO SET THINGS RIGHT. I'M NOT GOING TO WASTE THAT BY CREATING MORE PROBLEMS.
FIRST WE'LL FIND THE OTHER GUARDIANS. THEN WE'LL FIGURE OUT HOW TO DEAL WITH WOODRUE. I'M CALLING THE SHOTS AND I SAY NO MORE DEALS.
DIANA IS ALREADY WITH ANIMAL MAN. THAT LEAVES ONLY THE GUARDIAN OF THE ROT.
YOU AND I ARE GOING TO FIND ABIGAIL ARCANE.
BOLLOCKS...

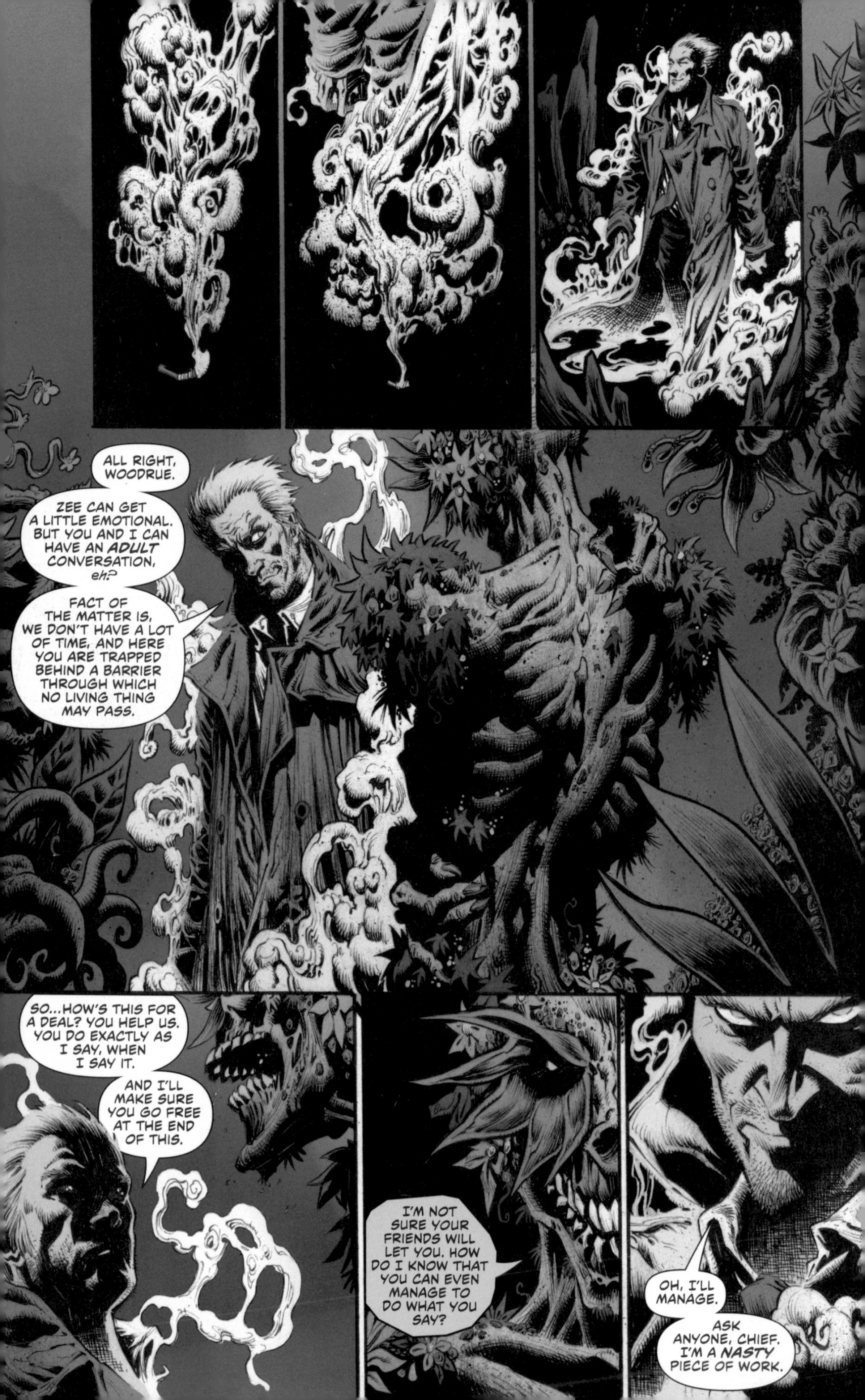
ALL RIGHT, WOODRUE.
ZEE CAN GET A LITTLE EMOTIONAL. BUT YOU AND I CAN HAVE AN *ADULT* CONVERSATION, *eh?*
FACT OF THE MATTER IS, WE DON'T HAVE A LOT OF TIME, AND HERE YOU ARE TRAPPED BEHIND A BARRIER THROUGH WHICH NO LIVING THING MAY PASS.
SO...HOW'S THIS FOR A DEAL? YOU HELP US. YOU DO EXACTLY AS I SAY, WHEN I SAY IT.
AND I'LL MAKE SURE YOU GO FREE AT THE END OF THIS.
I'M NOT SURE YOUR FRIENDS WILL LET YOU. HOW DO I KNOW THAT YOU CAN EVEN MANAGE TO DO WHAT YOU SAY?
OH, I'LL MANAGE.
ASK ANYONE, CHIEF. I'M A *NASTY* PIECE OF WORK.

AND SO IT STANDS.

ON THE ROOF OF THE WILSHIRE GRAND IN THE CITY OF ANGELS, BUDDY BAKER HAS A GROWING FEELING ON THE BACK OF HIS NECK THAT THINGS ARE GOING TO GET A LOT WORSE.

IN THE HALL OF JUSTICE, KHALID NASSOUR LEAVES TO CONVENE AN ANCIENT RITE. THE VOICE OF HIS MENTOR, KENT NELSON, TELLS HIM TO BE CAUTIOUS.

BUT THERE IS ANOTHER VOICE THAT LIVES WITHIN HIS HELM THAT MAY YET HAVE THINGS TO SAY, IN TIME.

ONE THAT GOES THROUGH THE BARRIER THAT NO LIVING THING MAY PASS.

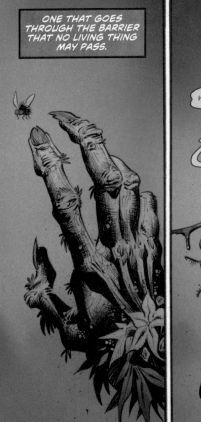

WOOOODRUUUUE...

AND BENEATH THE HALL, IN ITS MAGICAL VAULTS, IMPRISONED FOR HIS ACTIONS, JASON WOODRUE HAS A MOST **UNUSUAL** VISITOR.

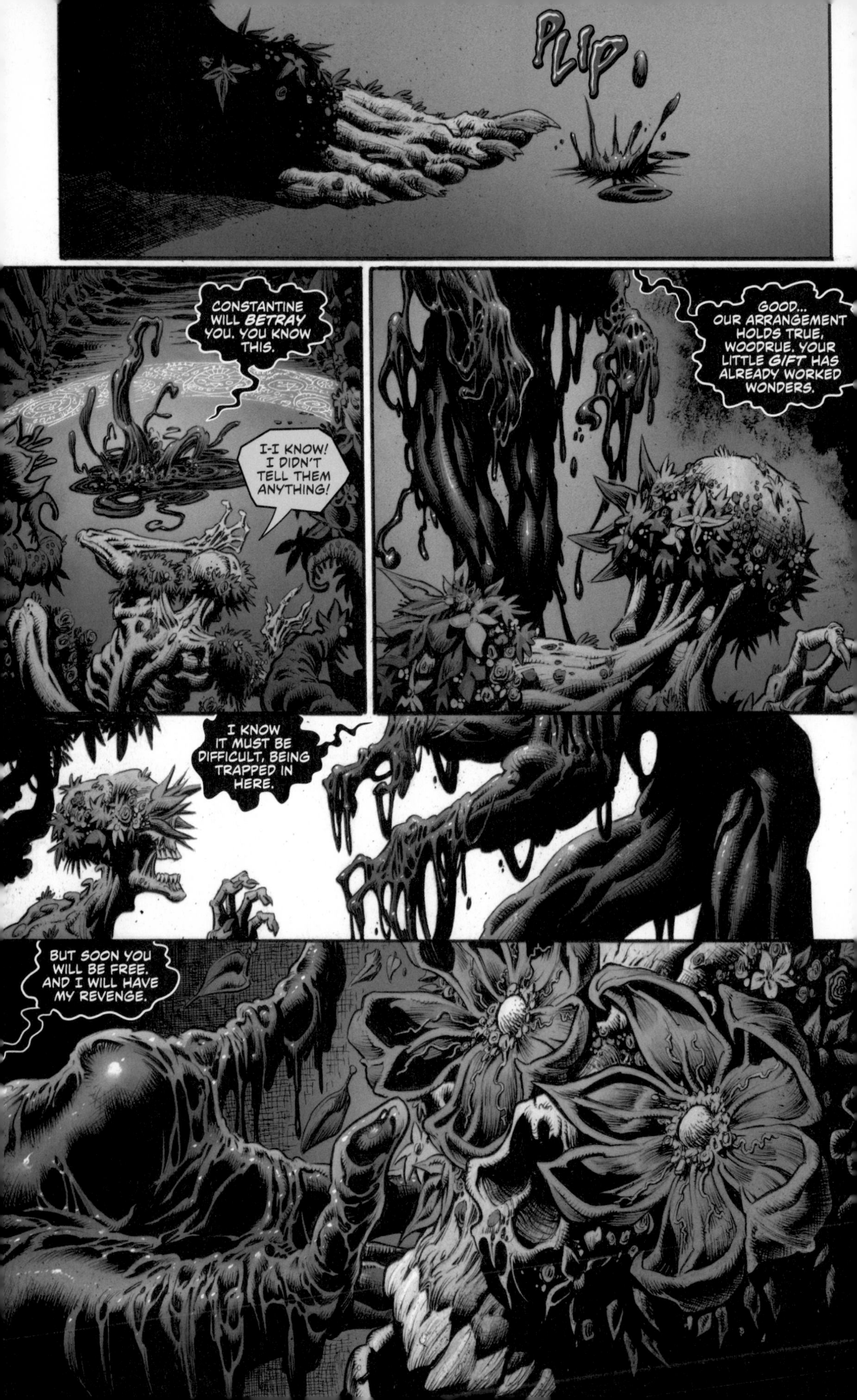
PLIP
CONSTANTINE WILL BETRAY YOU. YOU KNOW THIS.
I-I KNOW! I DIDN'T TELL THEM ANYTHING!
GOOD... OUR ARRANGEMENT HOLDS TRUE, WOODRUE. YOUR LITTLE GIFT HAS ALREADY WORKED WONDERS.
I KNOW IT MUST BE DIFFICULT, BEING TRAPPED IN HERE.
BUT SOON YOU WILL BE FREE. AND I WILL HAVE MY REVENGE.

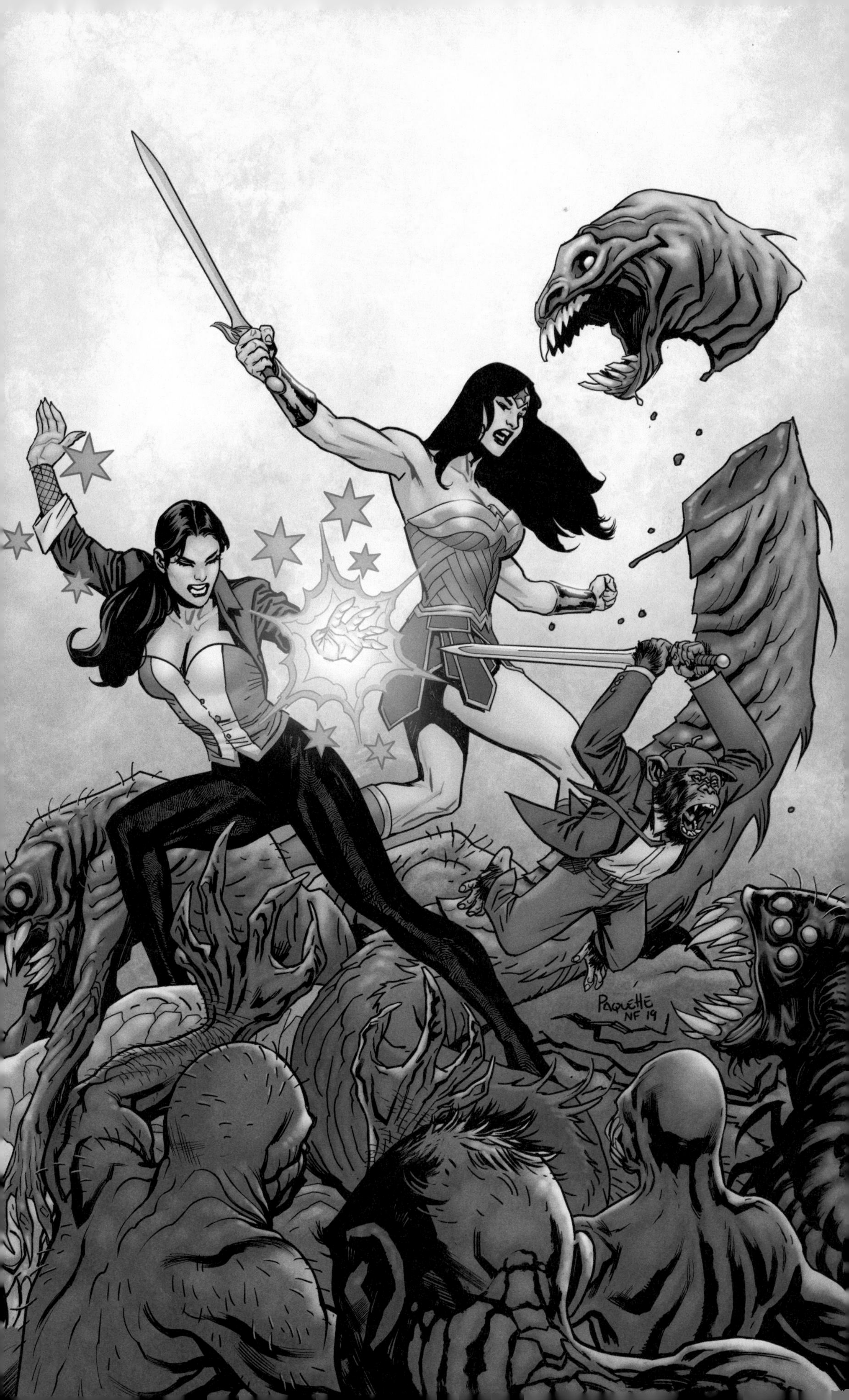
PAQUETTE
NF 19

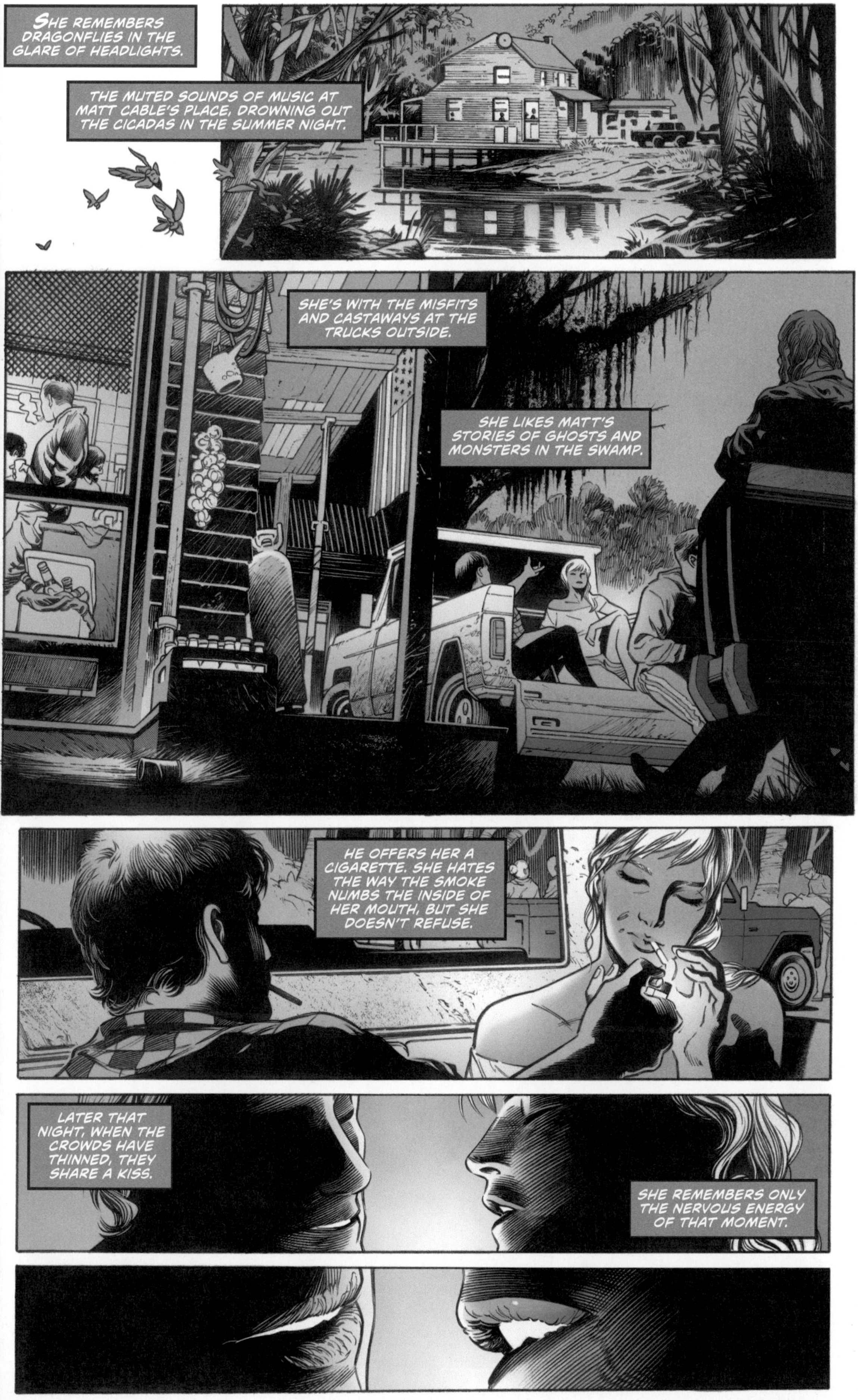

SHE REMEMBERS DRAGONFLIES IN THE GLARE OF HEADLIGHTS.
THE MUTED SOUNDS OF MUSIC AT MATT CABLE'S PLACE, DROWNING OUT THE CICADAS IN THE SUMMER NIGHT.
SHE'S WITH THE MISFITS AND CASTAWAYS AT THE TRUCKS OUTSIDE.
SHE LIKES MATT'S STORIES OF GHOSTS AND MONSTERS IN THE SWAMP.
HE OFFERS HER A CIGARETTE. SHE HATES THE WAY THE SMOKE NUMBS THE INSIDE OF HER MOUTH, BUT SHE DOESN'T REFUSE.
LATER THAT NIGHT, WHEN THE CROWDS HAVE THINNED, THEY SHARE A KISS.
SHE REMEMBERS ONLY THE NERVOUS ENERGY OF THAT MOMENT.

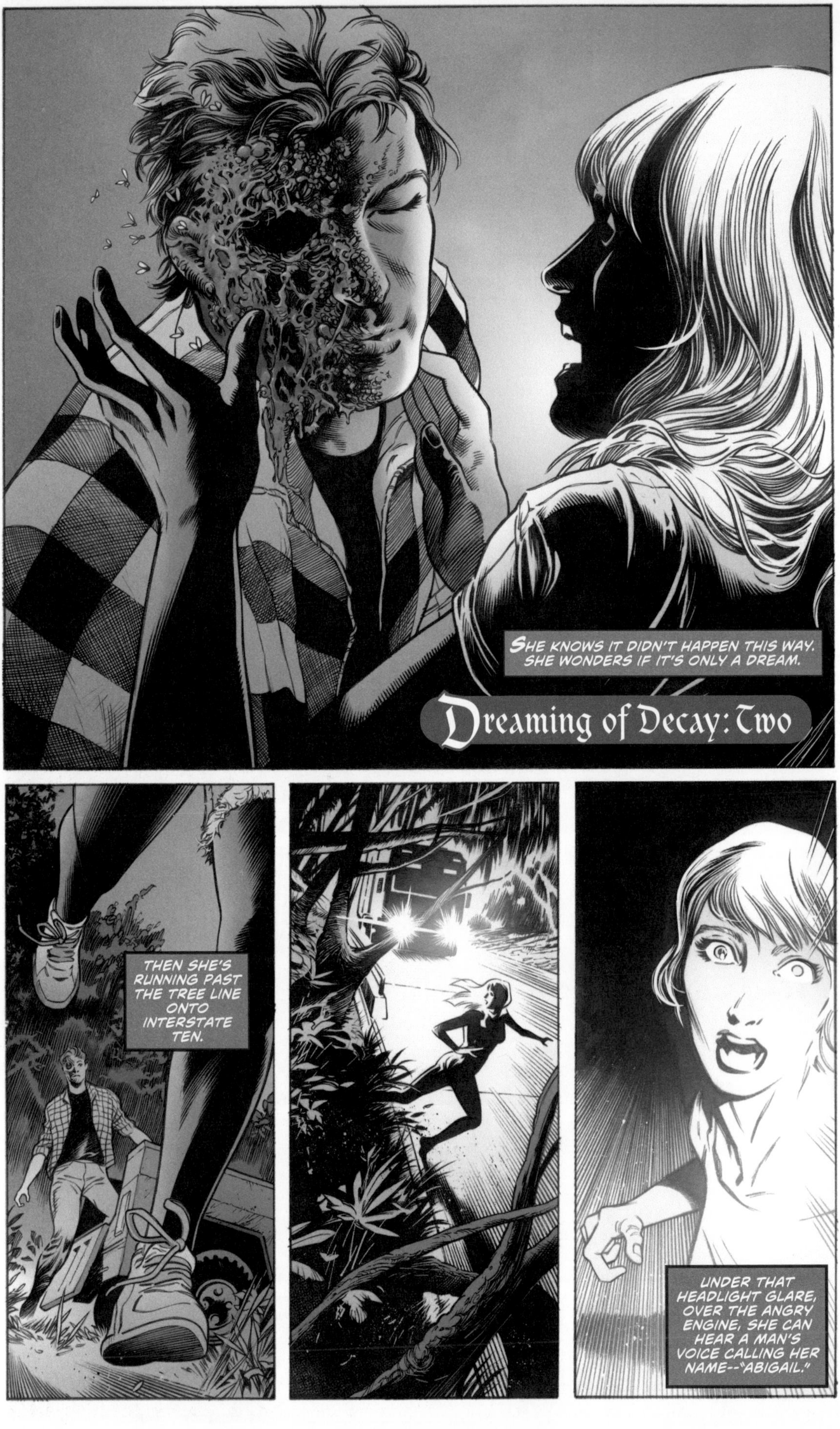
SHE KNOWS IT DIDN'T HAPPEN THIS WAY. SHE WONDERS IF IT'S ONLY A DREAM.
Dreaming of Decay: Two
THEN SHE'S RUNNING PAST THE TREE LINE ONTO INTERSTATE TEN.
UNDER THAT HEADLIGHT GLARE, OVER THE ANGRY ENGINE, SHE CAN HEAR A MAN'S VOICE CALLING HER NAME--"ABIGAIL."

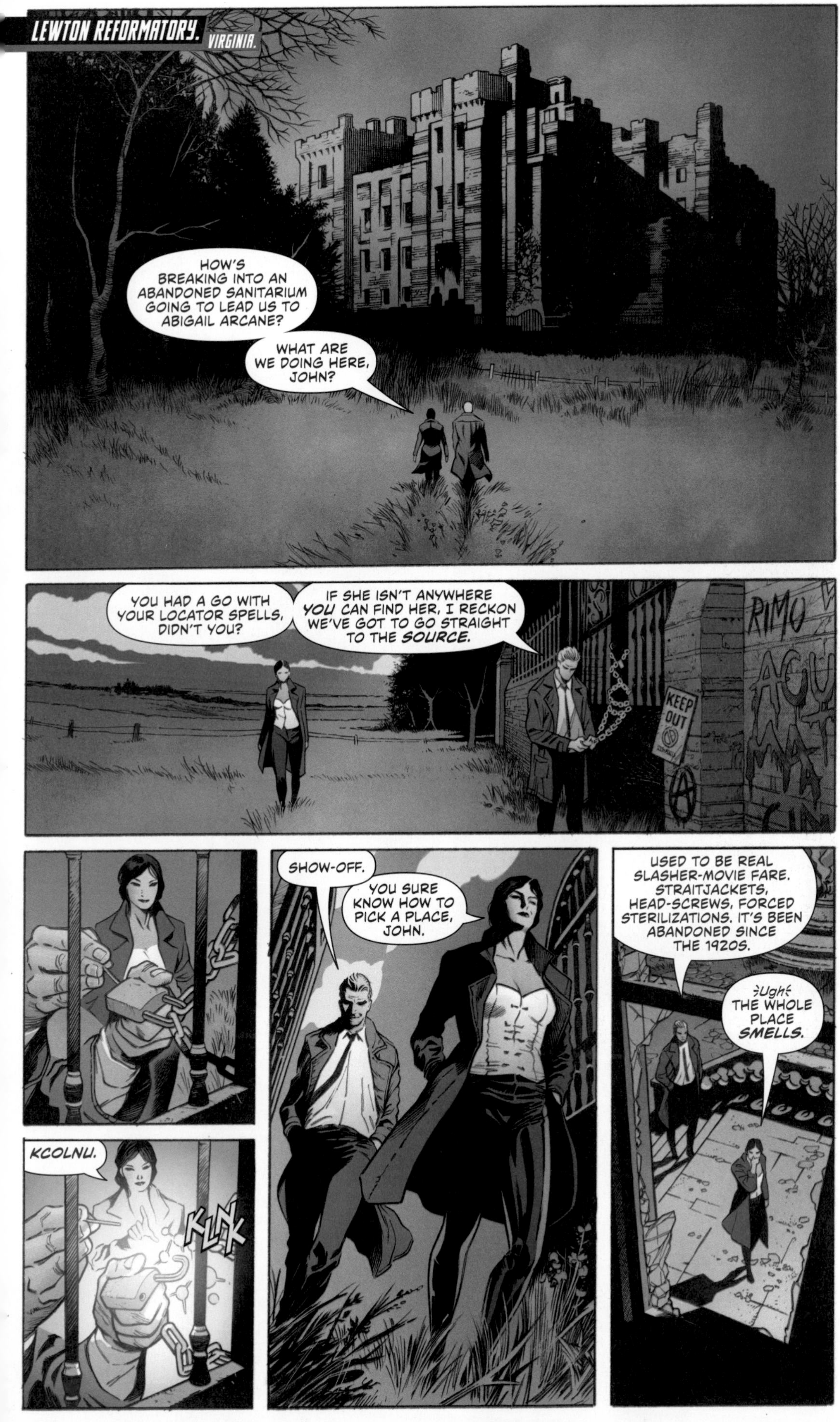
LEWTON REFORMATORY.
VIRGINIA.
HOW'S BREAKING INTO AN ABANDONED SANITARIUM GOING TO LEAD US TO ABIGAIL ARCANE?
WHAT ARE WE DOING HERE, JOHN?
YOU HAD A GO WITH YOUR LOCATOR SPELLS, DIDN'T YOU?
IF SHE ISN'T ANYWHERE YOU CAN FIND HER, I RECKON WE'VE GOT TO GO STRAIGHT TO THE SOURCE.
KEEP OUT
RIMO
KCOLNU.
KLNK
SHOW-OFF.
YOU SURE KNOW HOW TO PICK A PLACE, JOHN.
USED TO BE REAL SLASHER-MOVIE FARE. STRAITJACKETS, HEAD-SCREWS, FORCED STERILIZATIONS. IT'S BEEN ABANDONED SINCE THE 1920S.
Ugh THE WHOLE PLACE SMELLS.

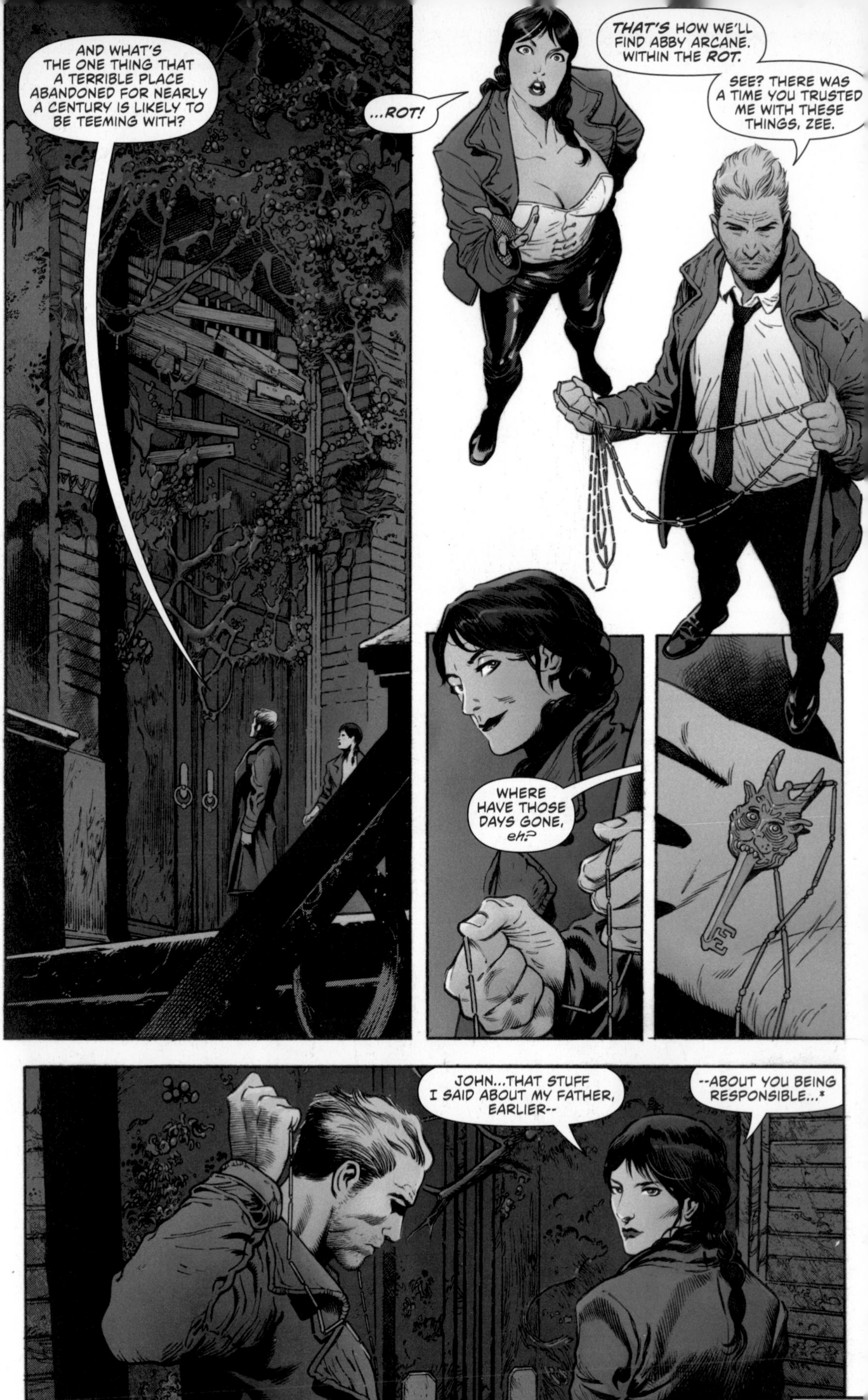
AND WHAT'S THE ONE THING THAT A TERRIBLE PLACE ABANDONED FOR NEARLY A CENTURY IS LIKELY TO BE TEEMING WITH?
...ROT!
THAT'S HOW WE'LL FIND ABBY ARCANE. WITHIN THE ROT.
SEE? THERE WAS A TIME YOU TRUSTED ME WITH THESE THINGS, ZEE.
WHERE HAVE THOSE DAYS GONE, eh?
JOHN...THAT STUFF I SAID ABOUT MY FATHER, EARLIER--
--ABOUT YOU BEING RESPONSIBLE...*
*SEE LAST ISSUE! --ALEX

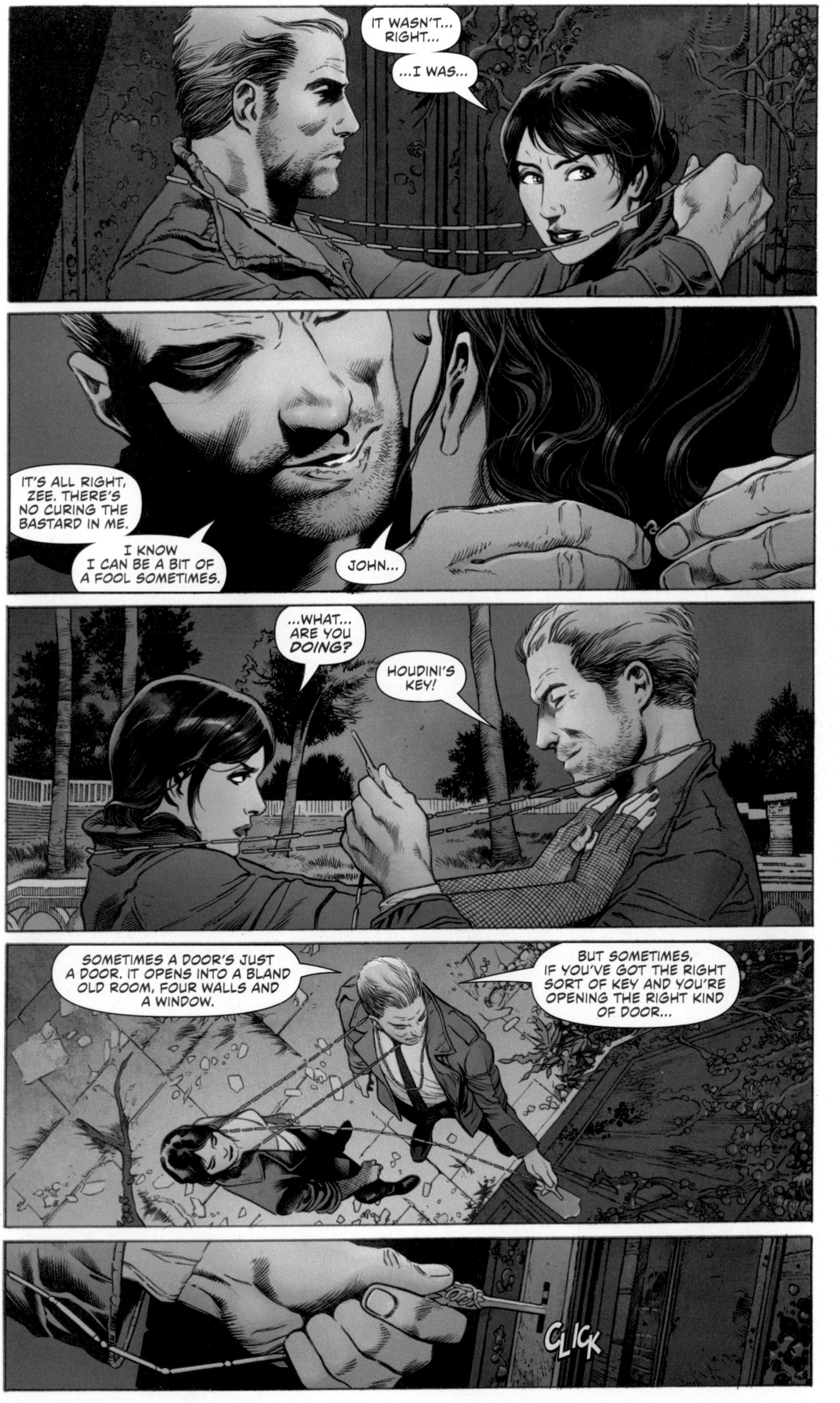
IT WASN'T... RIGHT...
...I WAS...
IT'S ALL RIGHT, ZEE. THERE'S NO CURING THE BASTARD IN ME.
I KNOW I CAN BE A BIT OF A FOOL SOMETIMES.
JOHN...
...WHAT... ARE YOU DOING?
HOUDINI'S KEY!
SOMETIMES A DOOR'S JUST A DOOR. IT OPENS INTO A BLAND OLD ROOM, FOUR WALLS AND A WINDOW.
BUT SOMETIMES, IF YOU'VE GOT THE RIGHT SORT OF KEY AND YOU'RE OPENING THE RIGHT KIND OF DOOR...
CLICK

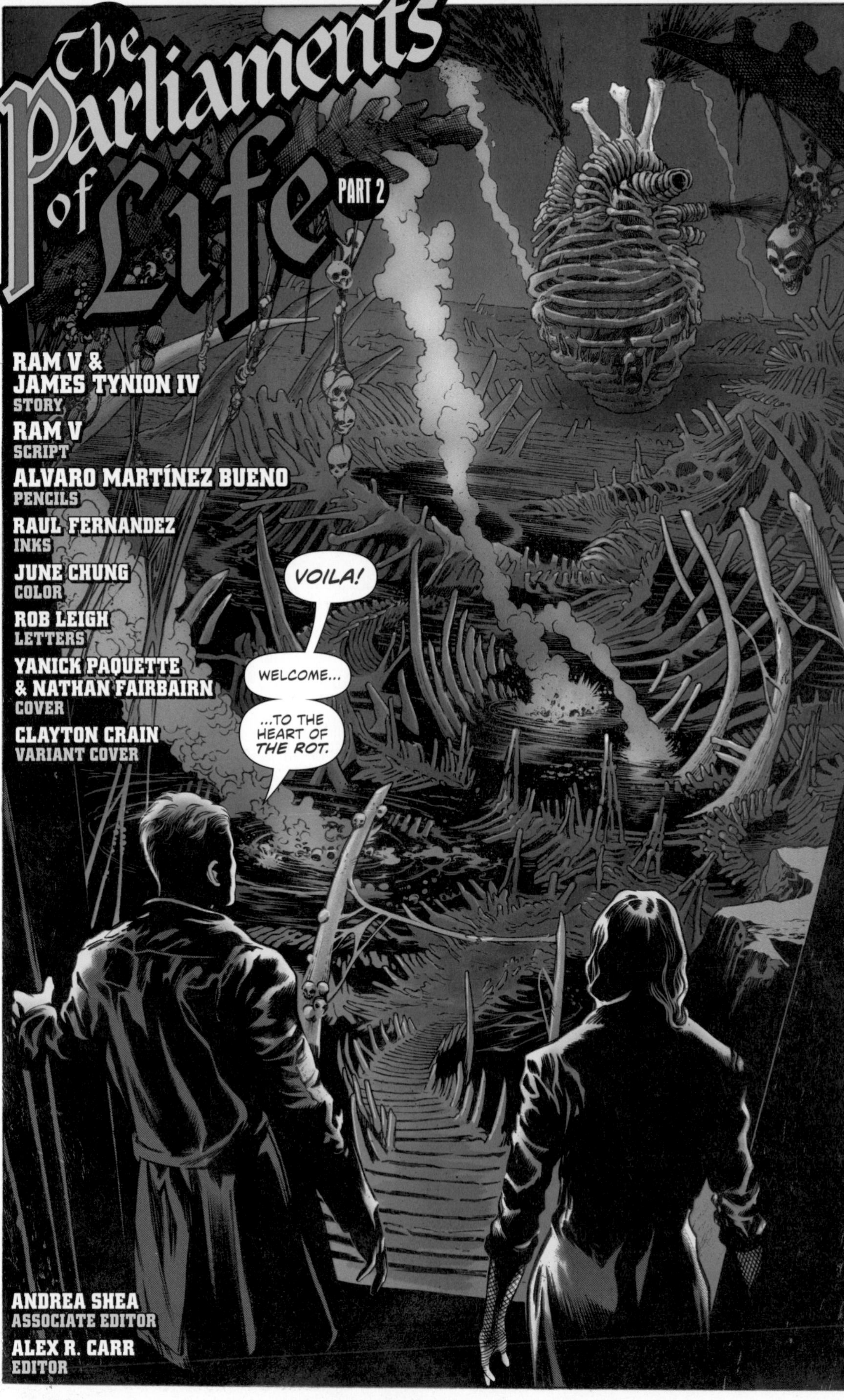
The Parliaments of Life
PART 2
RAM V & JAMES TYNION IV
STORY
RAM V
SCRIPT
ALVARO MARTÍNEZ BUENO
PENCILS
RAUL FERNANDEZ
INKS
JUNE CHUNG
COLOR
ROB LEIGH
LETTERS
YANICK PAQUETTE & NATHAN FAIRBAIRN
COVER
CLAYTON CRAIN
VARIANT COVER
VOILA!
WELCOME...
...TO THE HEART OF THE ROT.
ANDREA SHEA
ASSOCIATE EDITOR
ALEX R. CARR
EDITOR

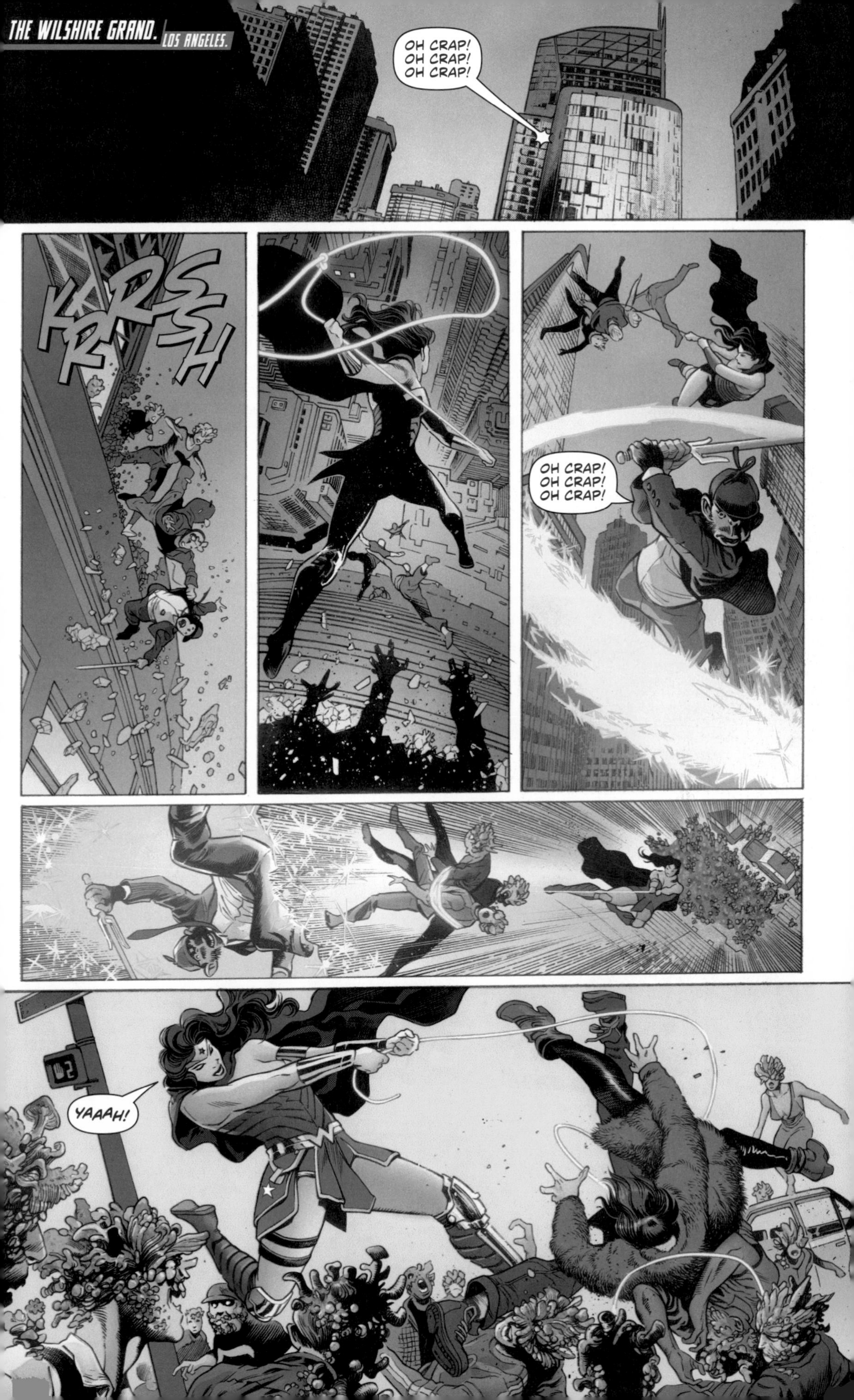
THE WILSHIRE GRAND.
LOS ANGELES.
OH CRAP! OH CRAP! OH CRAP!
KRRSSH
OH CRAP! OH CRAP! OH CRAP!
YAAAH!

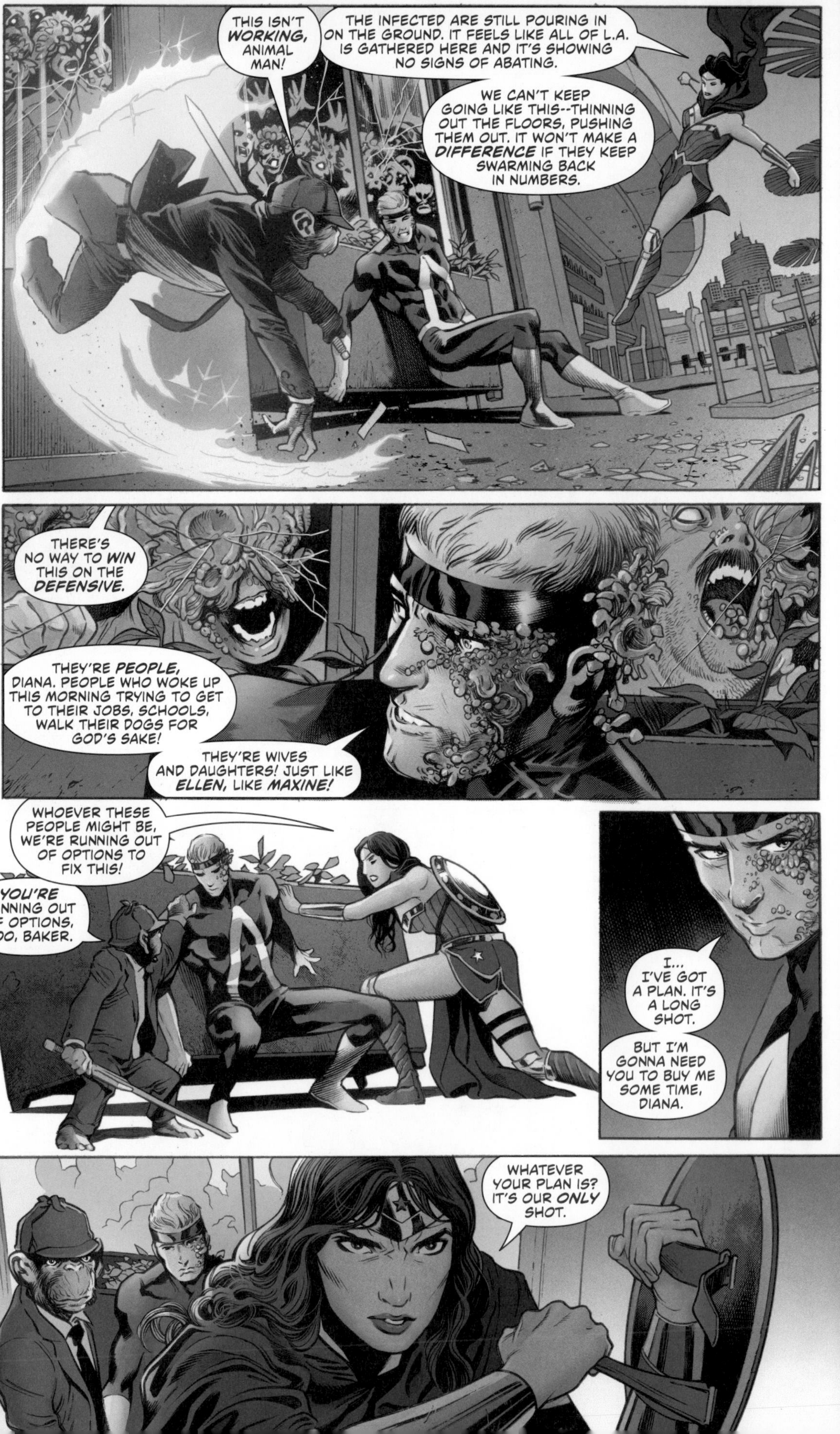

THIS ISN'T WORKING, ANIMAL MAN!
THE INFECTED ARE STILL POURING IN ON THE GROUND. IT FEELS LIKE ALL OF L.A. IS GATHERED HERE AND IT'S SHOWING NO SIGNS OF ABATING.
WE CAN'T KEEP GOING LIKE THIS--THINNING OUT THE FLOORS, PUSHING THEM OUT. IT WON'T MAKE A DIFFERENCE IF THEY KEEP SWARMING BACK IN NUMBERS.
THERE'S NO WAY TO WIN THIS ON THE DEFENSIVE.
THEY'RE PEOPLE, DIANA. PEOPLE WHO WOKE UP THIS MORNING TRYING TO GET TO THEIR JOBS, SCHOOLS, WALK THEIR DOGS FOR GOD'S SAKE!
THEY'RE WIVES AND DAUGHTERS! JUST LIKE ELLEN, LIKE MAXINE!
WHOEVER THESE PEOPLE MIGHT BE, WE'RE RUNNING OUT OF OPTIONS TO FIX THIS!
YOU'RE RUNNING OUT OF OPTIONS, TOO, BAKER.
I... I'VE GOT A PLAN. IT'S A LONG SHOT.
BUT I'M GONNA NEED YOU TO BUY ME SOME TIME, DIANA.
WHATEVER YOUR PLAN IS? IT'S OUR ONLY SHOT.

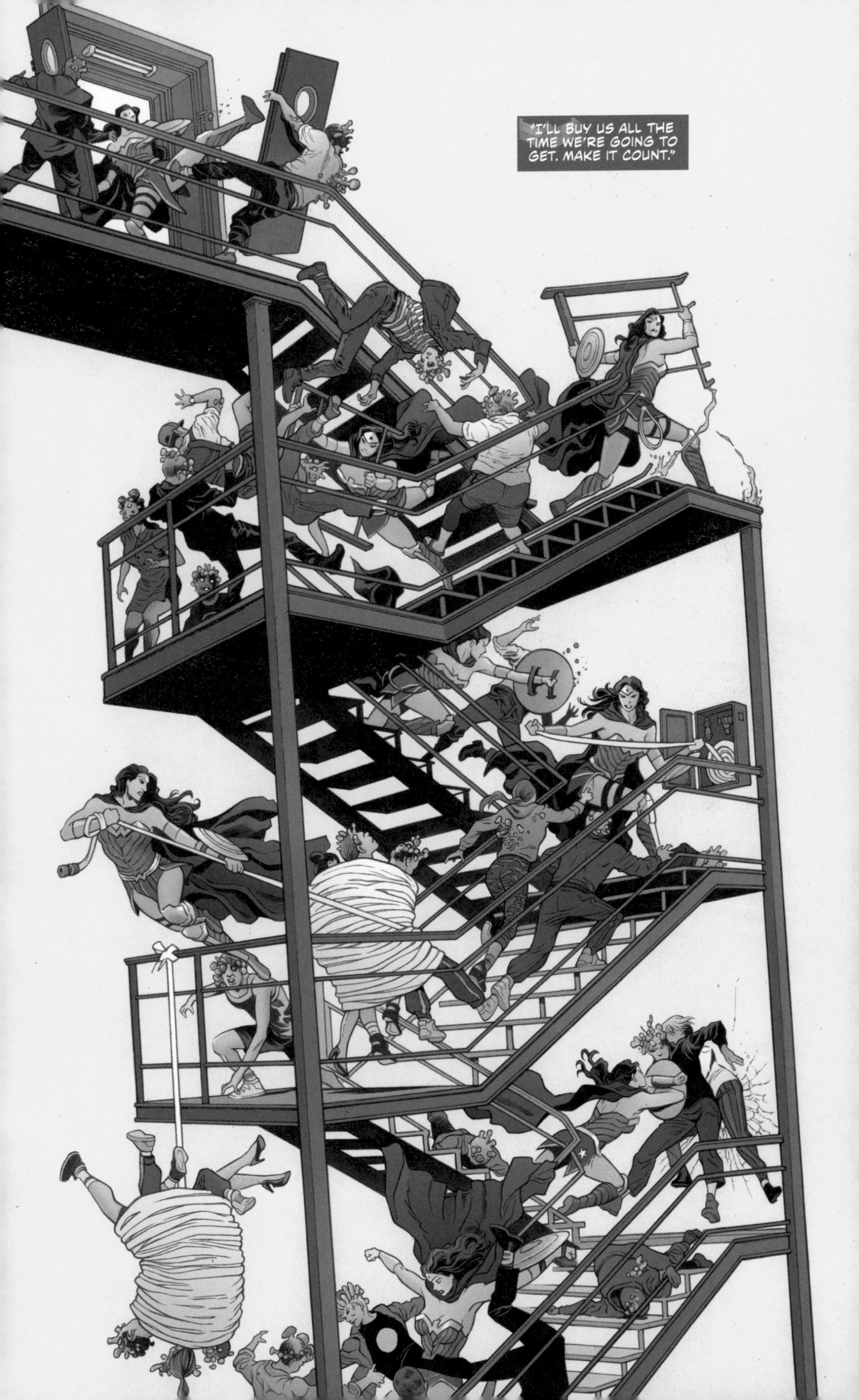
"I'LL BUY US ALL THE TIME WE'RE GOING TO GET. MAKE IT COUNT."

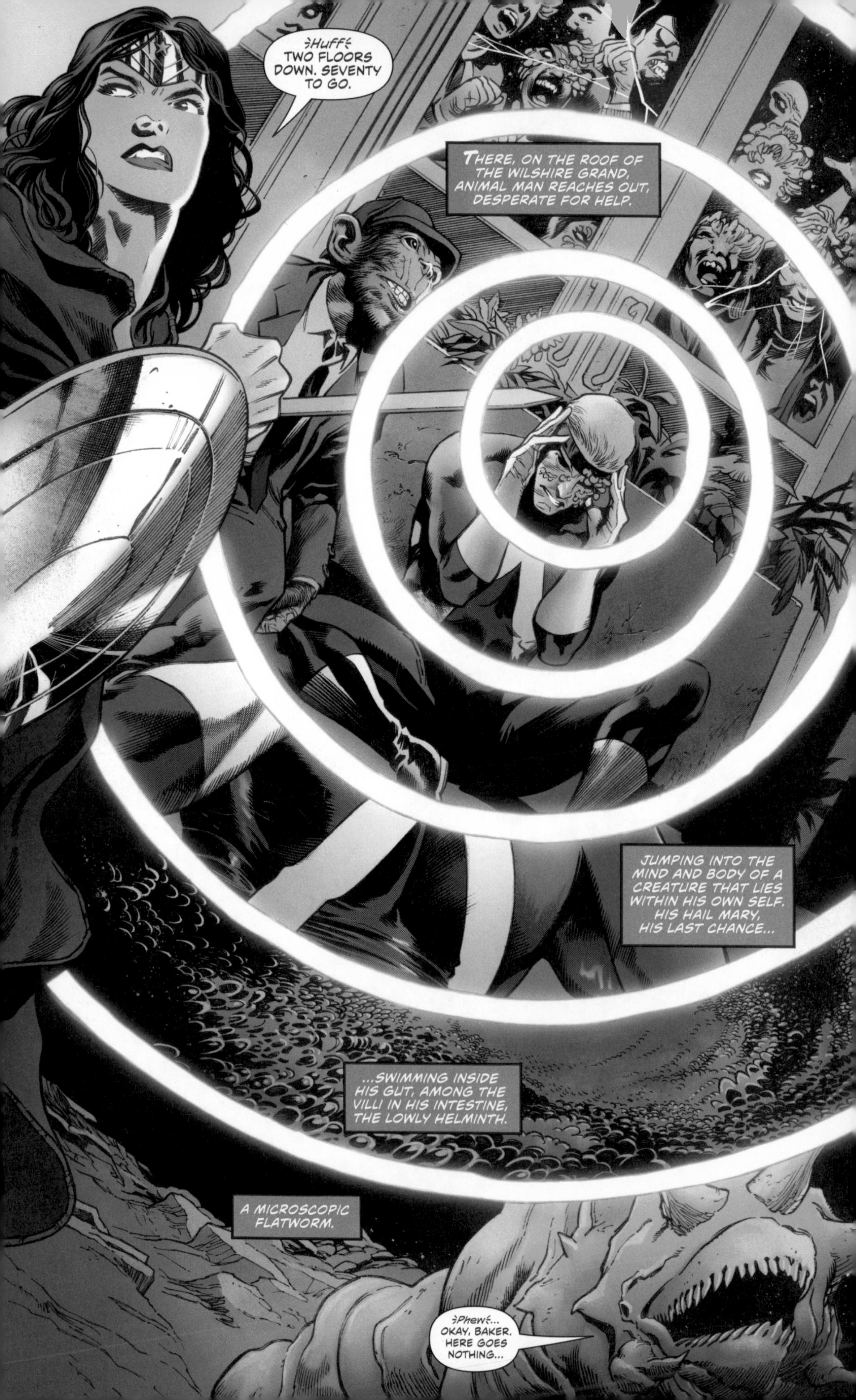

HUFF TWO FLOORS DOWN. SEVENTY TO GO.
THERE, ON THE ROOF OF THE WILSHIRE GRAND, ANIMAL MAN REACHES OUT, DESPERATE FOR HELP.
JUMPING INTO THE MIND AND BODY OF A CREATURE THAT LIES WITHIN HIS OWN SELF. HIS HAIL MARY, HIS LAST CHANCE...
...SWIMMING INSIDE HIS GUT, AMONG THE VILLI IN HIS INTESTINE, THE LOWLY HELMINTH.
A MICROSCOPIC FLATWORM.
PHEW... OKAY, BAKER. HERE GOES NOTHING...

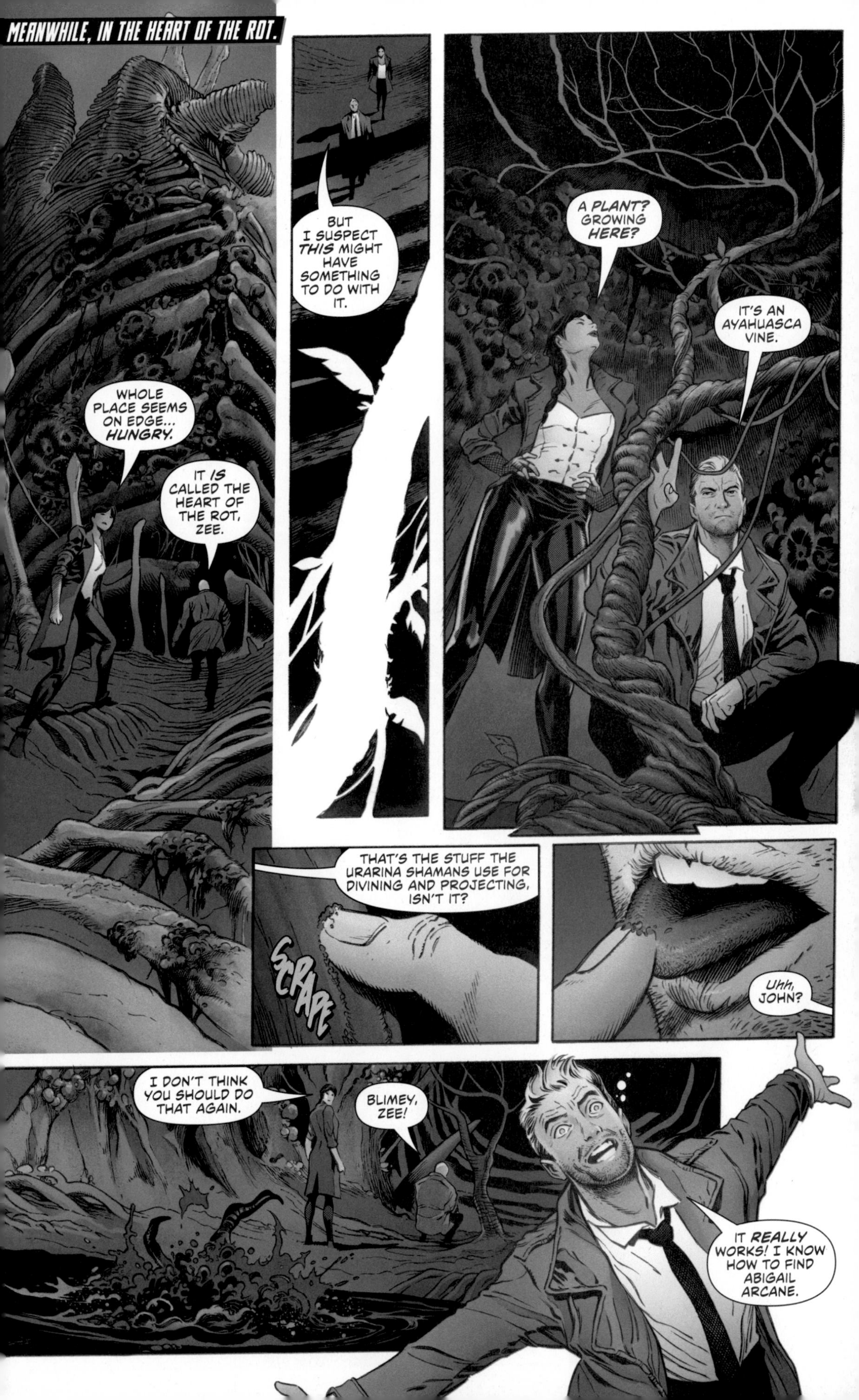
MEANWHILE, IN THE HEART OF THE ROT.
WHOLE PLACE SEEMS ON EDGE... HUNGRY.
IT IS CALLED THE HEART OF THE ROT, ZEE.
BUT I SUSPECT THIS MIGHT HAVE SOMETHING TO DO WITH IT.
A PLANT? GROWING HERE?
IT'S AN AYAHUASCA VINE.
THAT'S THE STUFF THE URARINA SHAMANS USE FOR DIVINING AND PROJECTING, ISN'T IT?
SCRAPE
Uhh, JOHN?
I DON'T THINK YOU SHOULD DO THAT AGAIN.
BLIMEY, ZEE!
IT REALLY WORKS! I KNOW HOW TO FIND ABIGAIL ARCANE.

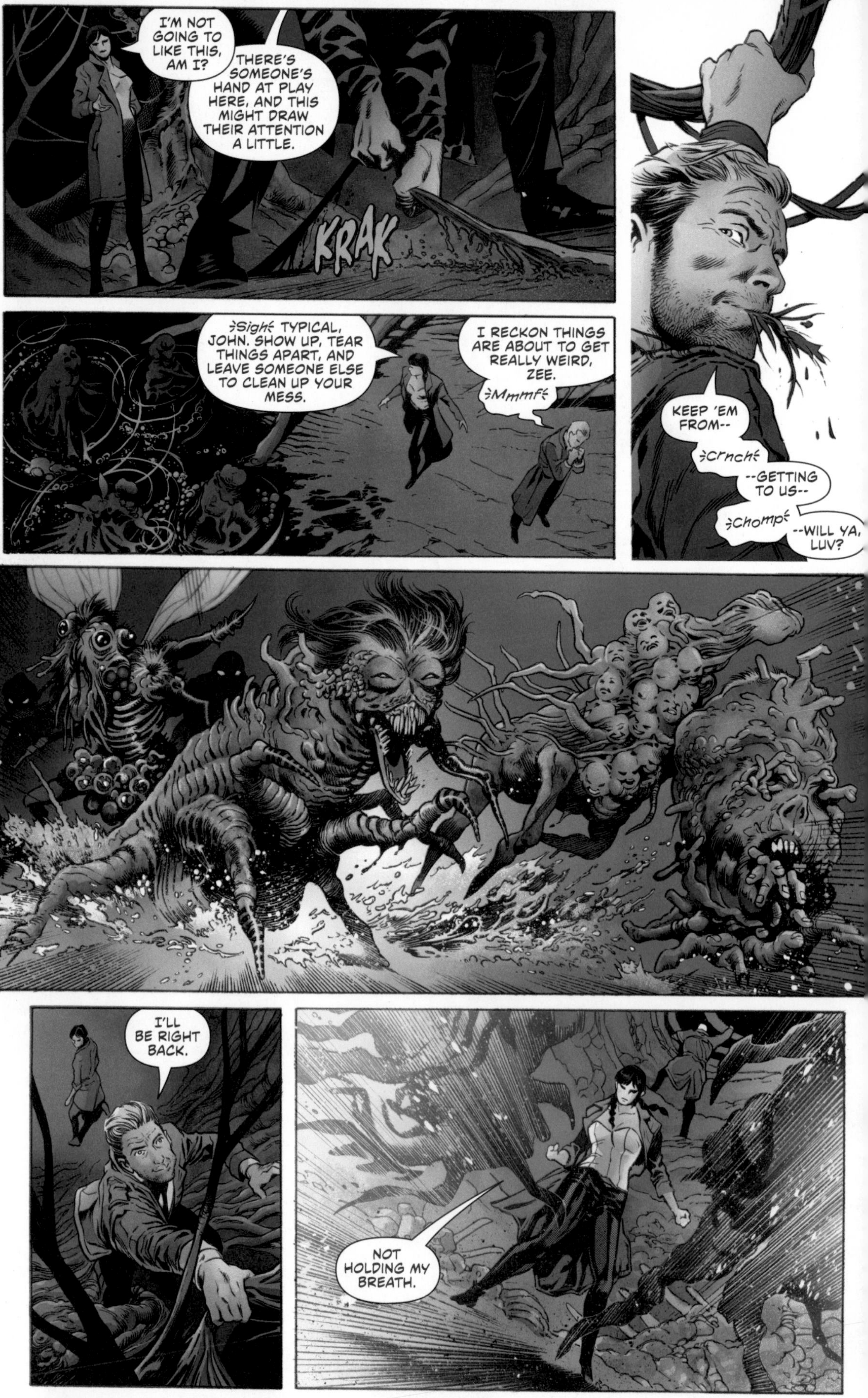
I'M NOT GOING TO LIKE THIS, AM I?
THERE'S SOMEONE'S HAND AT PLAY HERE, AND THIS MIGHT DRAW THEIR ATTENTION A LITTLE.
KRAK
Sigh TYPICAL, JOHN. SHOW UP, TEAR THINGS APART, AND LEAVE SOMEONE ELSE TO CLEAN UP YOUR MESS.
I RECKON THINGS ARE ABOUT TO GET REALLY WEIRD, ZEE.
Mmmf
KEEP 'EM FROM--
Crnch
--GETTING TO US--
Chomp
--WILL YA, LUV?
I'LL BE RIGHT BACK.
NOT HOLDING MY BREATH.

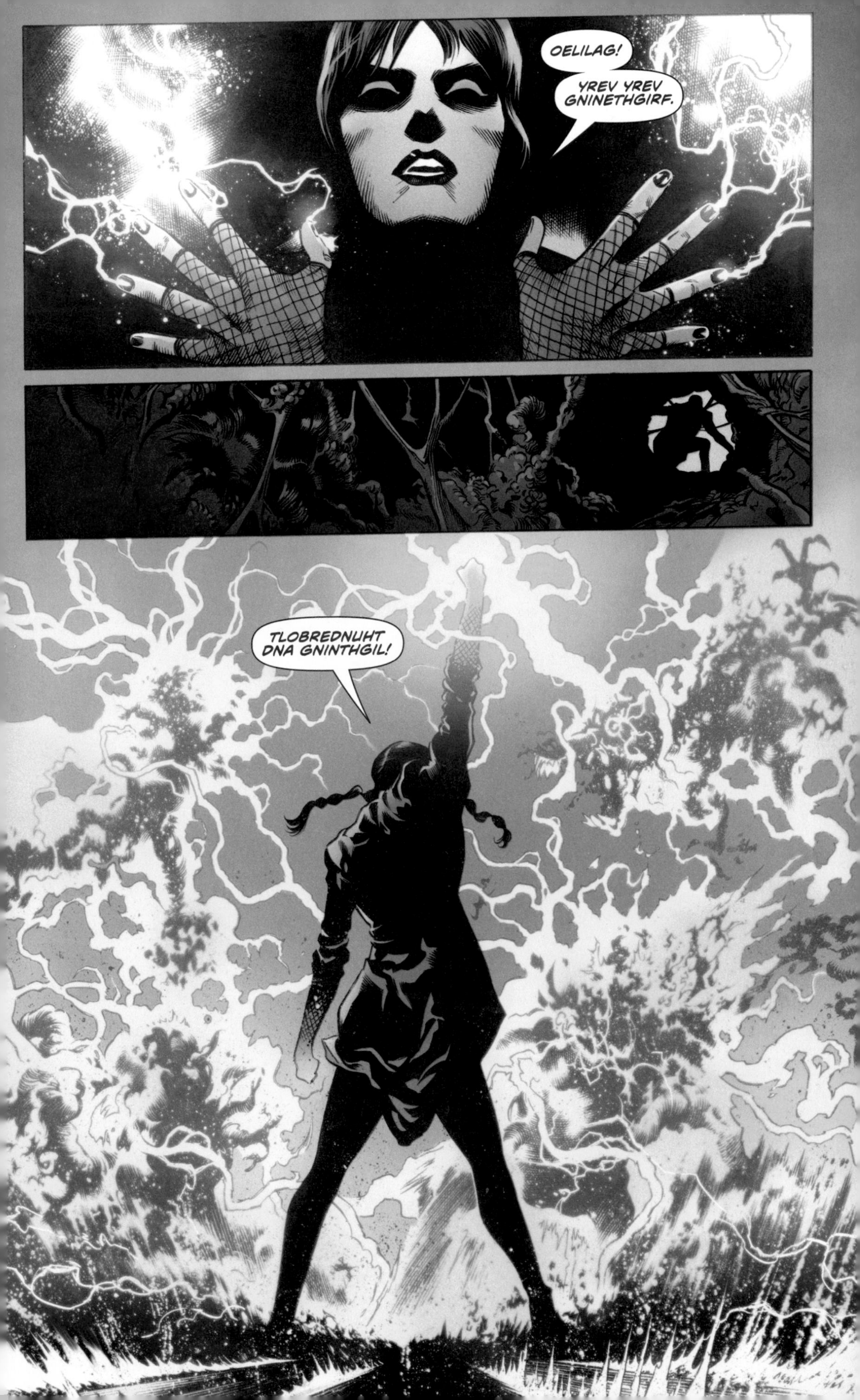
OELILAG!
YREV YREV GNINETHGIRF.
TLOBREDNUHT DNA GNINTHGIL!

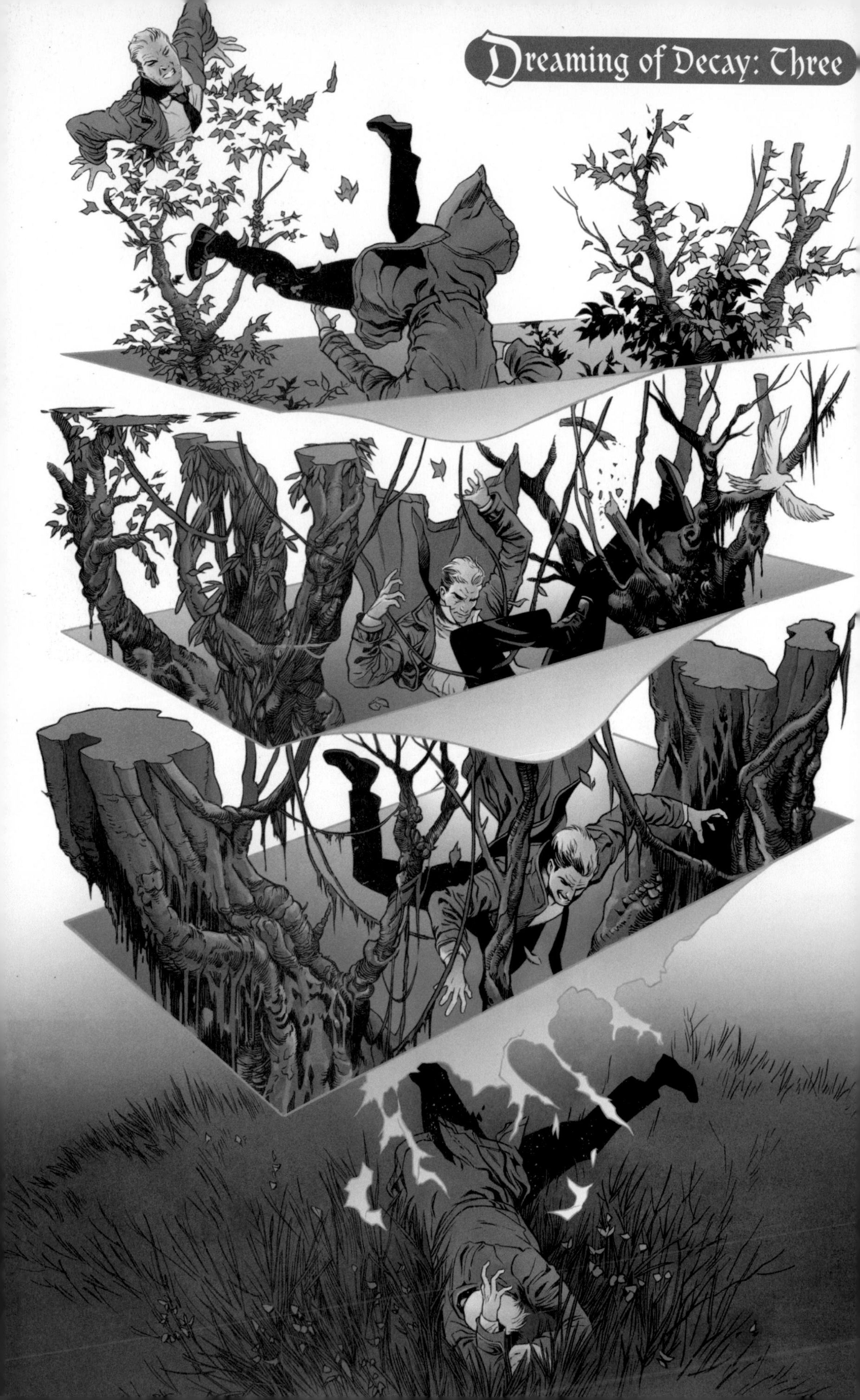
Dreaming of Decay: Three

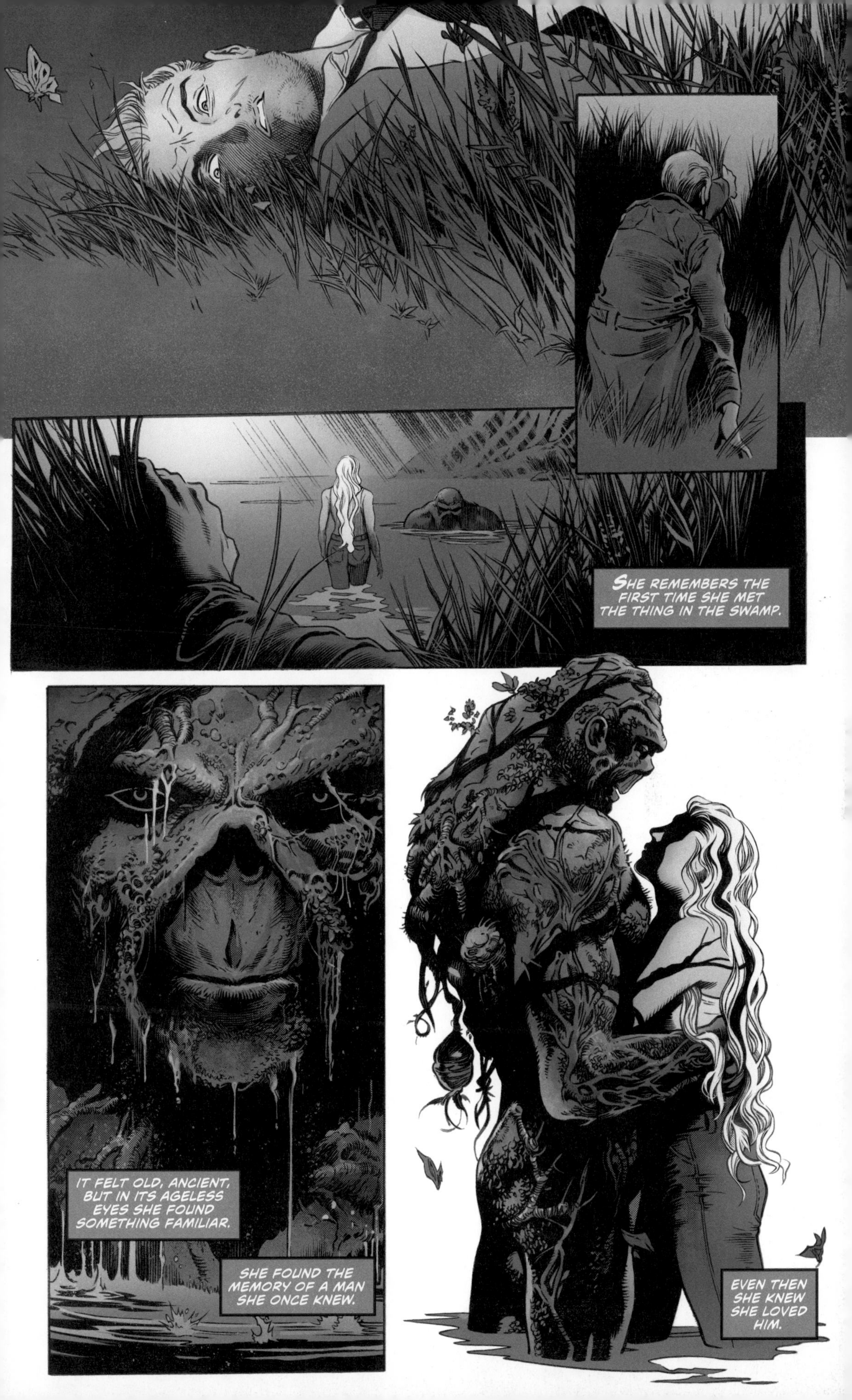
SHE REMEMBERS THE FIRST TIME SHE MET THE THING IN THE SWAMP.
IT FELT OLD, ANCIENT, BUT IN ITS AGELESS EYES SHE FOUND SOMETHING FAMILIAR.
SHE FOUND THE MEMORY OF A MAN SHE ONCE KNEW.
EVEN THEN SHE KNEW SHE LOVED HIM.

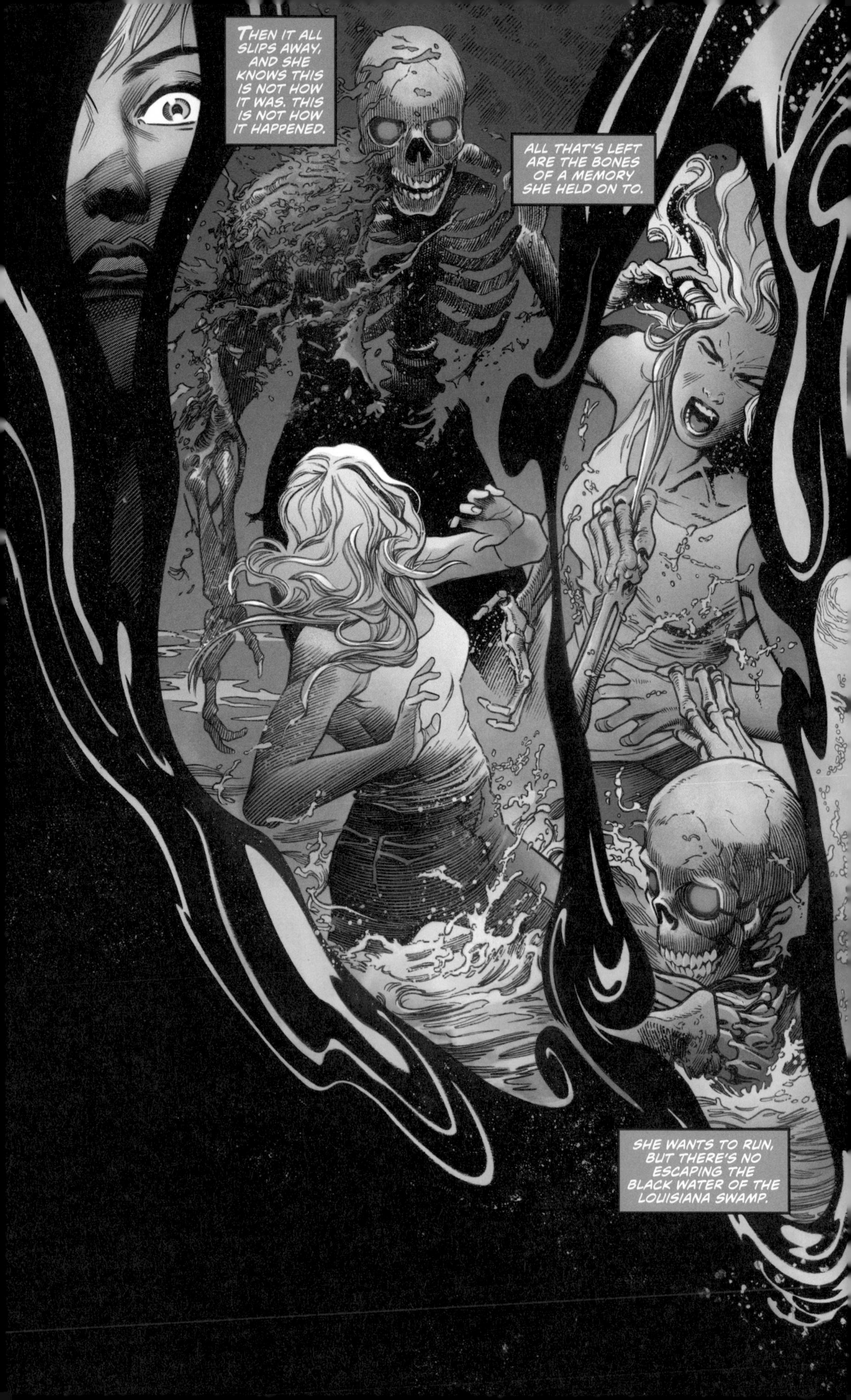
THEN IT ALL SLIPS AWAY, AND SHE KNOWS THIS IS NOT HOW IT WAS. THIS IS NOT HOW IT HAPPENED.
ALL THAT'S LEFT ARE THE BONES OF A MEMORY SHE HELD ON TO.
SHE WANTS TO RUN, BUT THERE'S NO ESCAPING THE BLACK WATER OF THE LOUISIANA SWAMP.

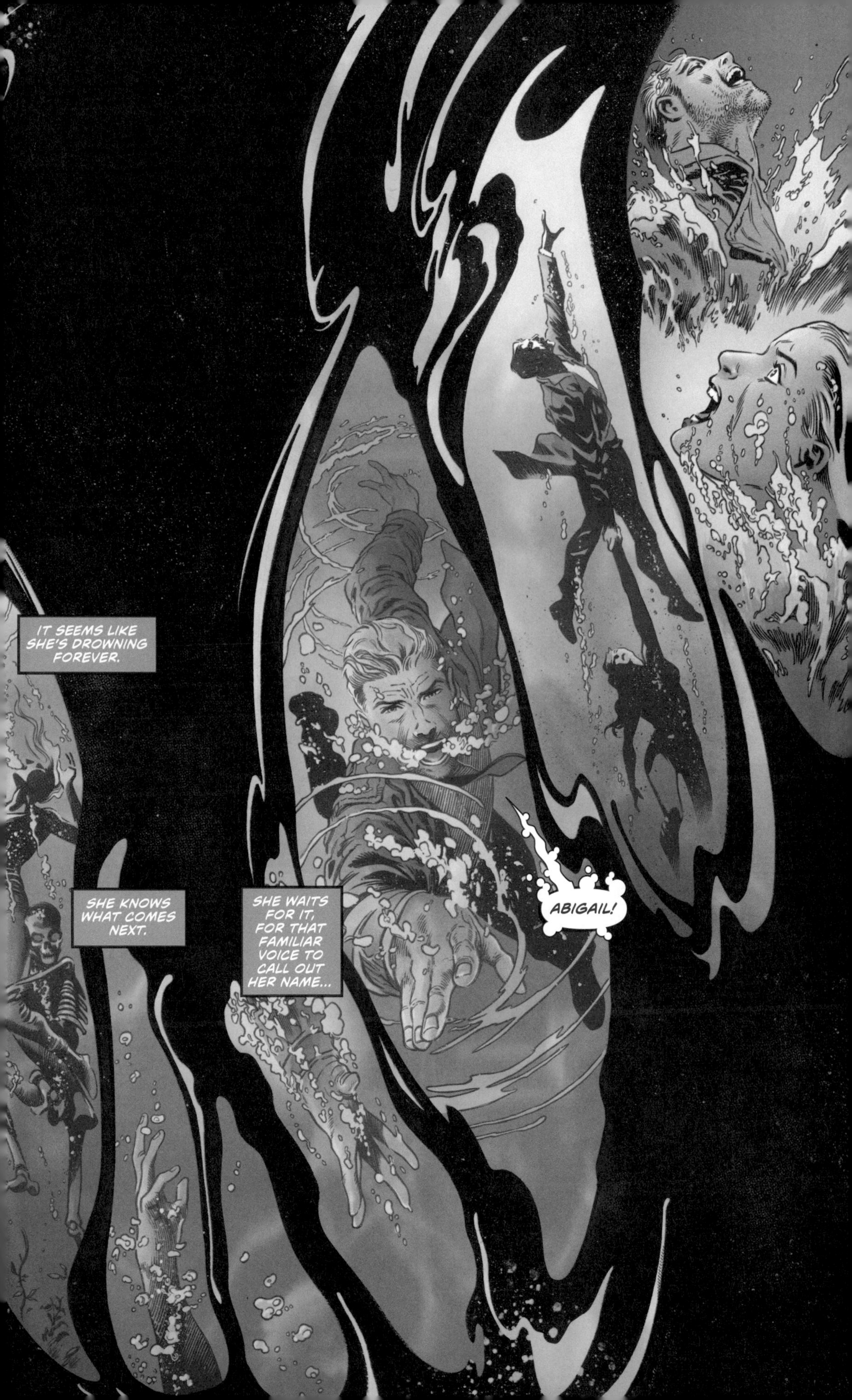
IT SEEMS LIKE SHE'S DROWNING FOREVER.
SHE KNOWS WHAT COMES NEXT.
SHE WAITS FOR IT, FOR THAT FAMILIAR VOICE TO CALL OUT HER NAME...
ABIGAIL!

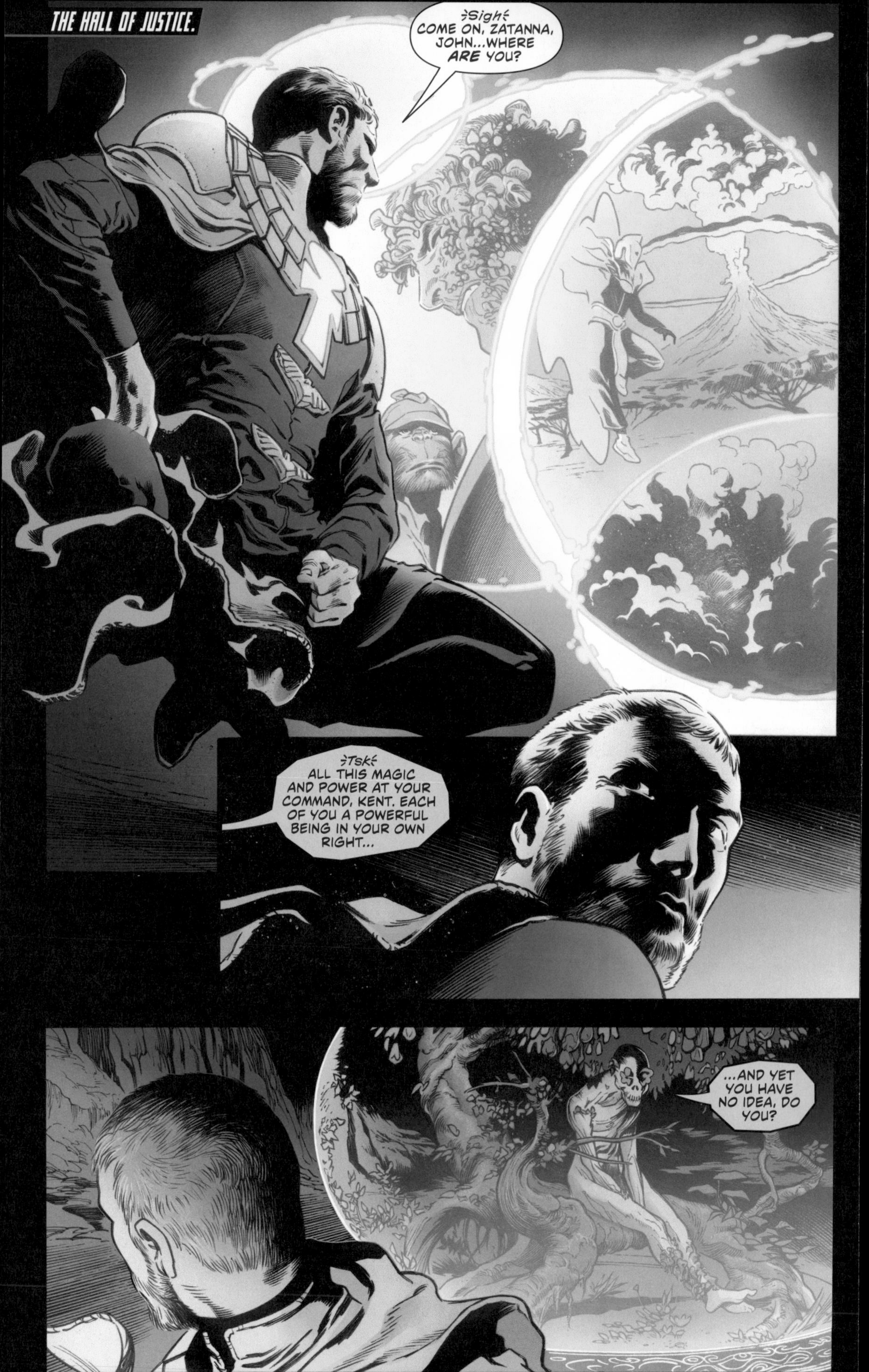
THE HALL OF JUSTICE.
Sigh
COME ON, ZATANNA, JOHN...WHERE ARE YOU?
Tsk
ALL THIS MAGIC AND POWER AT YOUR COMMAND, KENT. EACH OF YOU A POWERFUL BEING IN YOUR OWN RIGHT...
...AND YET YOU HAVE NO IDEA, DO YOU?

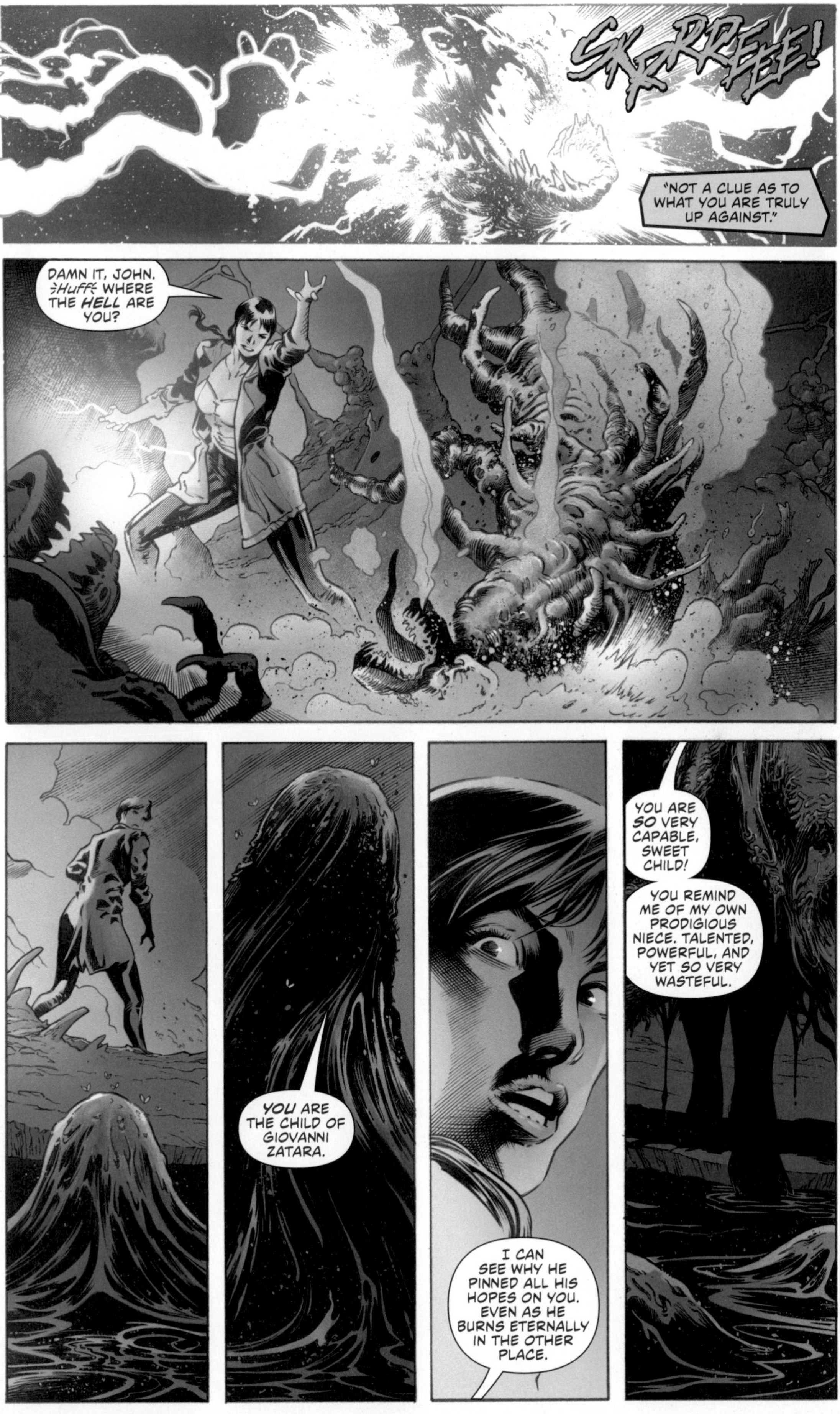
SKRRREEE!
"NOT A CLUE AS TO WHAT YOU ARE TRULY UP AGAINST."
DAMN IT, JOHN. *Huff* WHERE THE HELL ARE YOU?
YOU ARE THE CHILD OF GIOVANNI ZATARA.
I CAN SEE WHY HE PINNED ALL HIS HOPES ON YOU. EVEN AS HE BURNS ETERNALLY IN THE OTHER PLACE.
YOU ARE SO VERY CAPABLE, SWEET CHILD!
YOU REMIND ME OF MY OWN PRODIGIOUS NIECE. TALENTED, POWERFUL, AND YET SO VERY WASTEFUL.

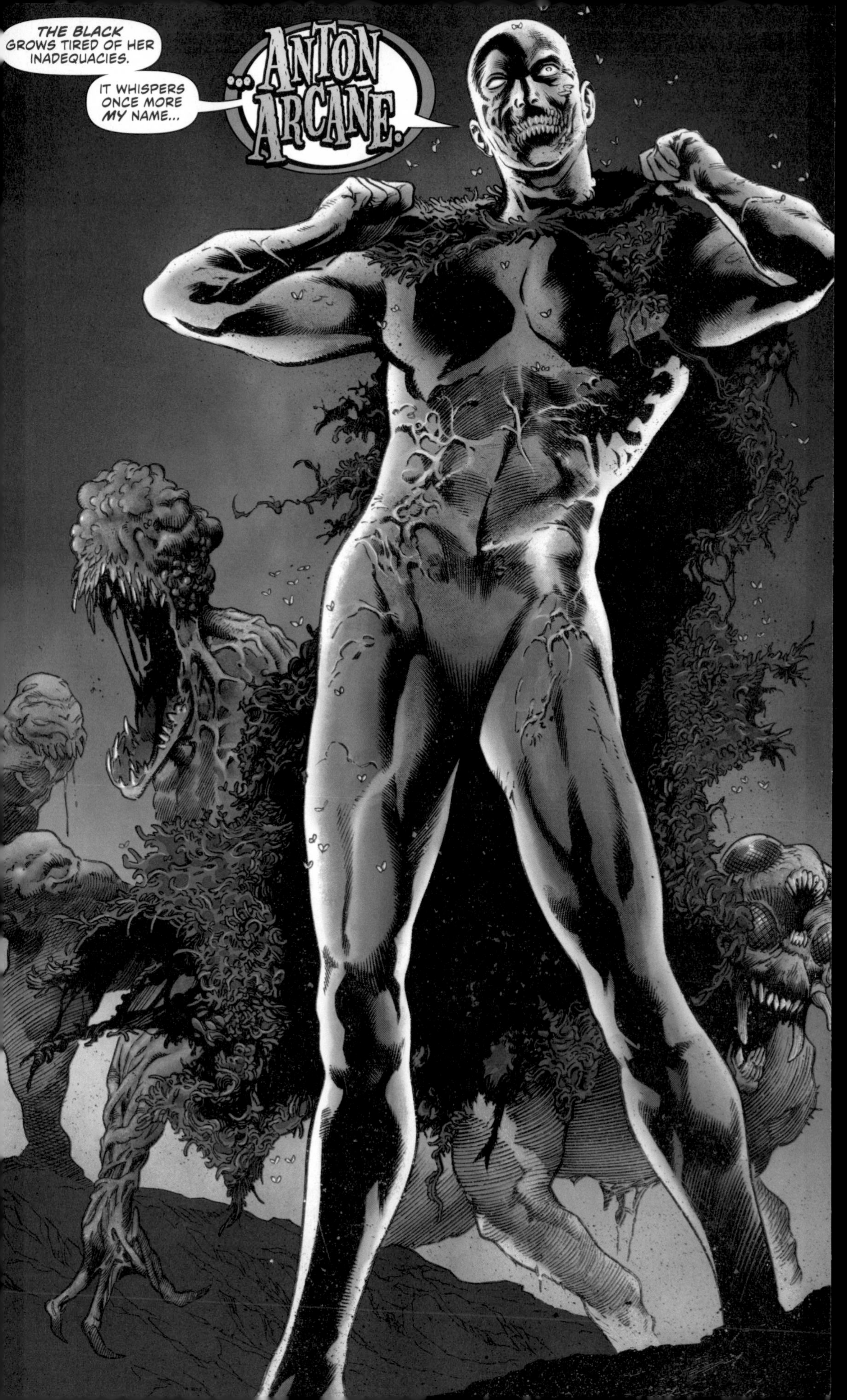
THE BLACK GROWS TIRED OF HER INADEQUACIES.
IT WHISPERS ONCE MORE MY NAME...
...ANTON ARCANE.

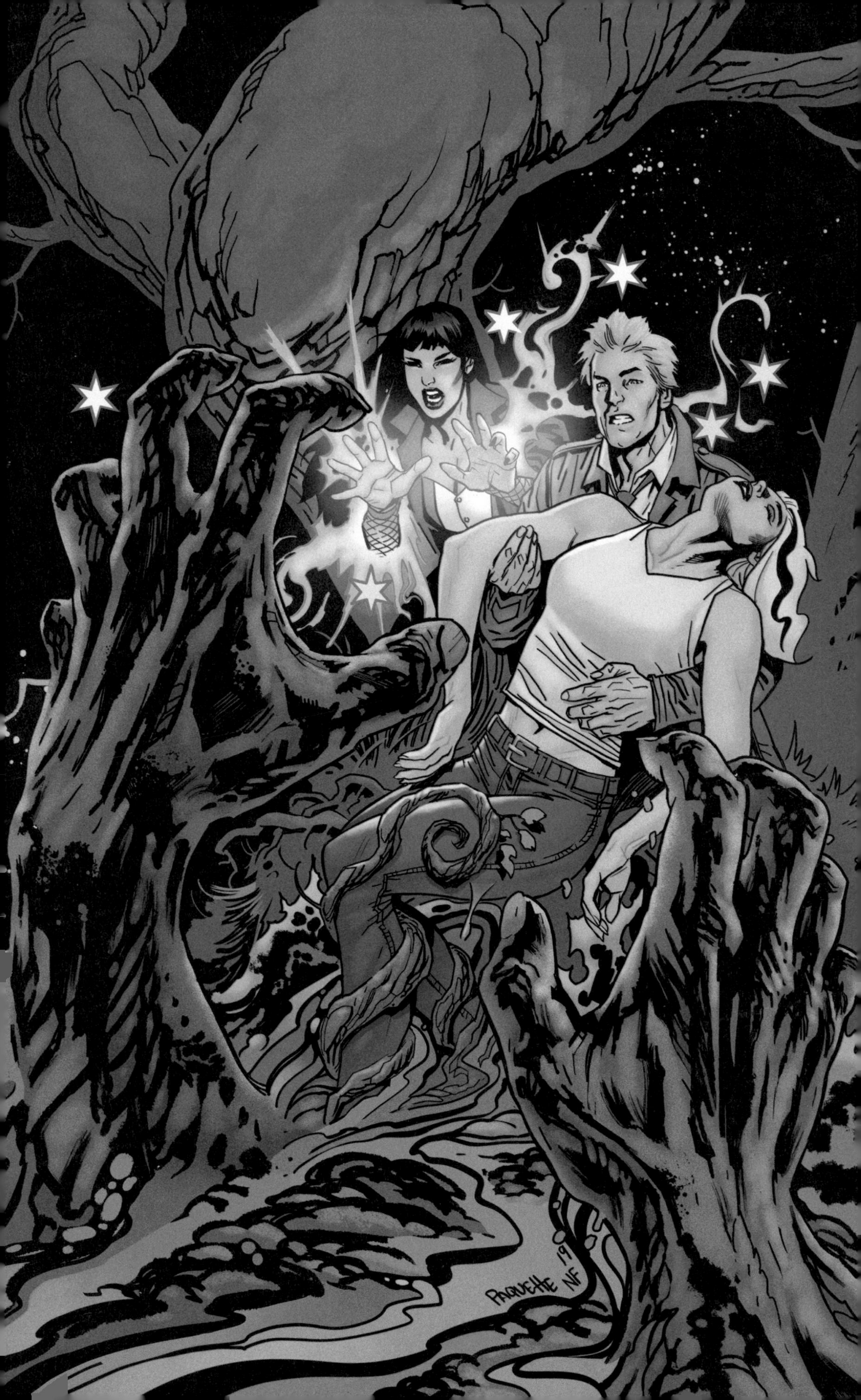
PAQUETTE '19
NF

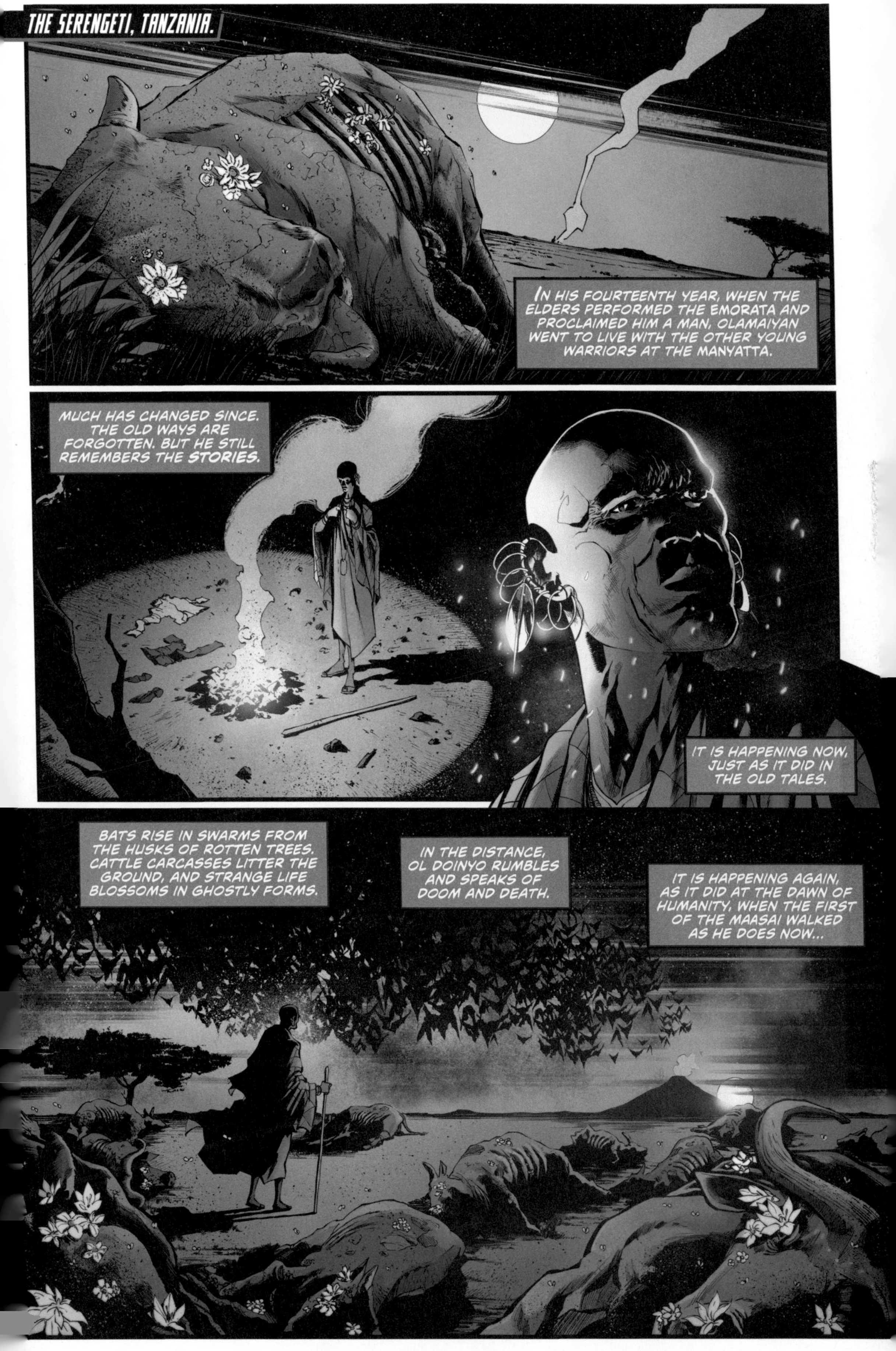
THE SERENGETI, TANZANIA.
IN HIS FOURTEENTH YEAR, WHEN THE ELDERS PERFORMED THE EMORATA AND PROCLAIMED HIM A MAN, OLAMAIYAN WENT TO LIVE WITH THE OTHER YOUNG WARRIORS AT THE MANYATTA.
MUCH HAS CHANGED SINCE. THE OLD WAYS ARE FORGOTTEN. BUT HE STILL REMEMBERS THE STORIES.
IT IS HAPPENING NOW, JUST AS IT DID IN THE OLD TALES.
BATS RISE IN SWARMS FROM THE HUSKS OF ROTTEN TREES. CATTLE CARCASSES LITTER THE GROUND, AND STRANGE LIFE BLOSSOMS IN GHOSTLY FORMS.
IN THE DISTANCE, OL DOINYO RUMBLES AND SPEAKS OF DOOM AND DEATH.
IT IS HAPPENING AGAIN, AS IT DID AT THE DAWN OF HUMANITY, WHEN THE FIRST OF THE MAASAI WALKED AS HE DOES NOW...

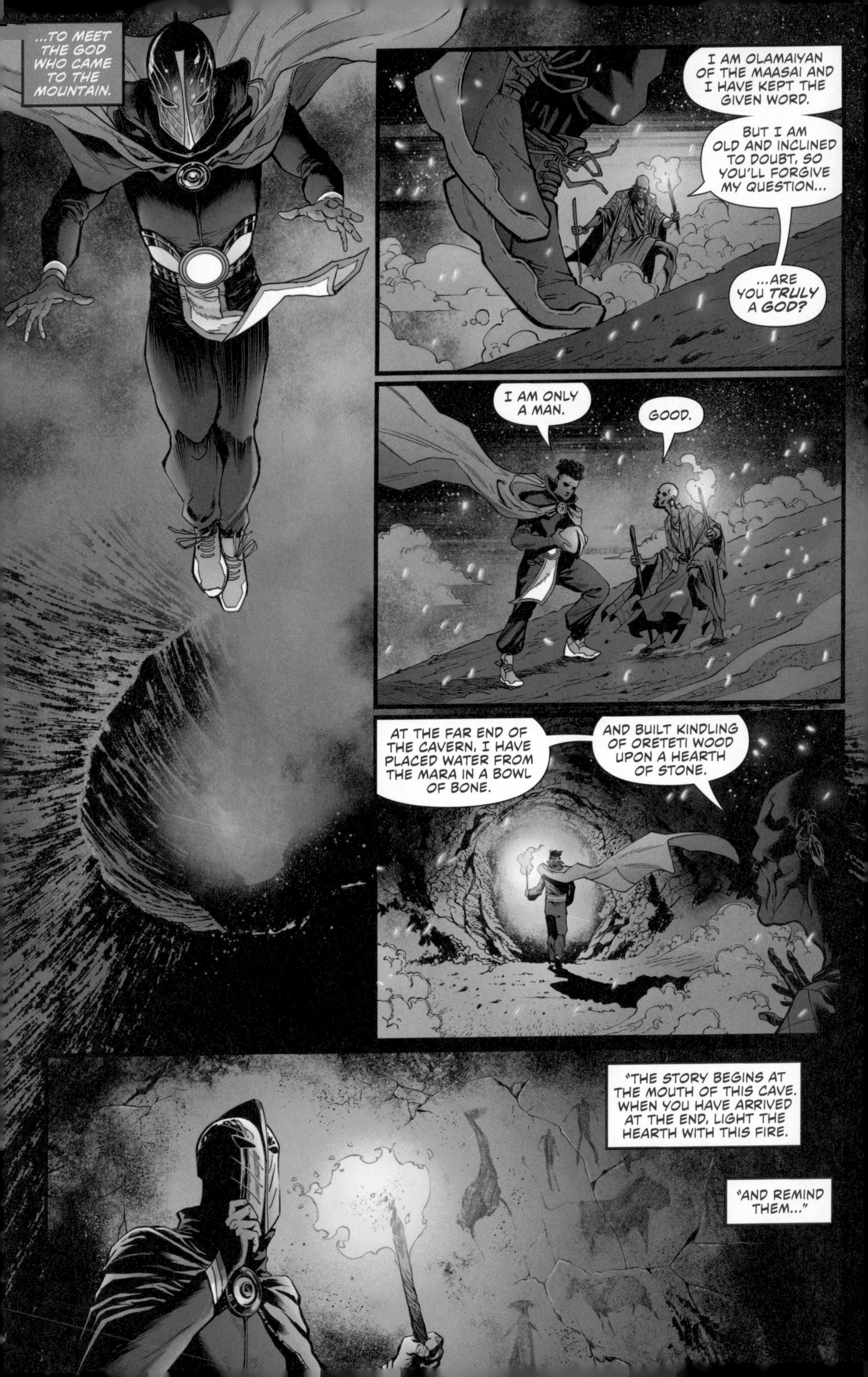
...TO MEET THE GOD WHO CAME TO THE MOUNTAIN.
I AM OLAMAIYAN OF THE MAASAI AND I HAVE KEPT THE GIVEN WORD.
BUT I AM OLD AND INCLINED TO DOUBT, SO YOU'LL FORGIVE MY QUESTION...
...ARE YOU TRULY A GOD?
I AM ONLY A MAN.
GOOD.
AT THE FAR END OF THE CAVERN, I HAVE PLACED WATER FROM THE MARA IN A BOWL OF BONE.
AND BUILT KINDLING OF ORETETI WOOD UPON A HEARTH OF STONE.
"THE STORY BEGINS AT THE MOUTH OF THIS CAVE. WHEN YOU HAVE ARRIVED AT THE END, LIGHT THE HEARTH WITH THIS FIRE.
"AND REMIND THEM..."

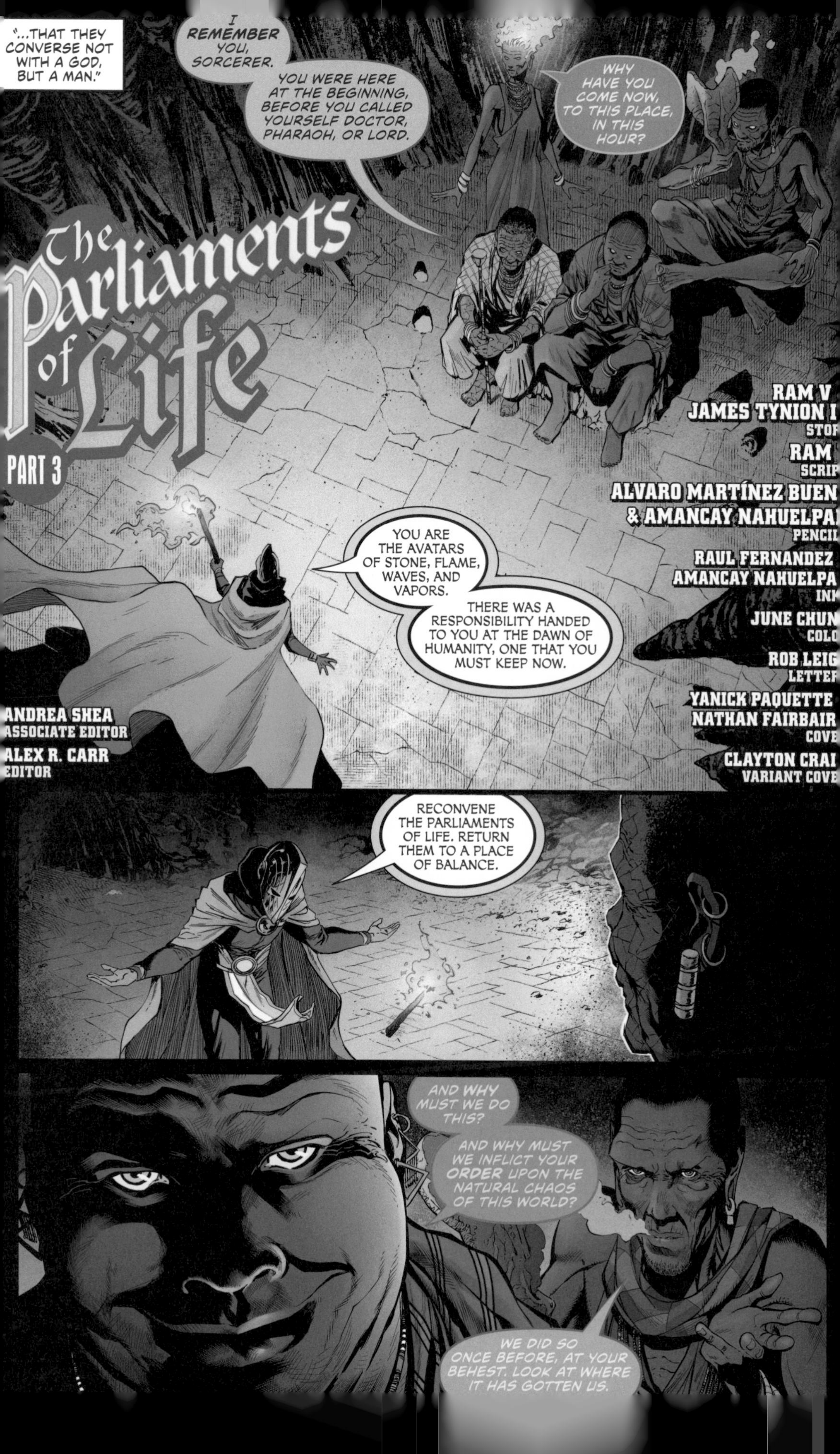
"...THAT THEY CONVERSE NOT WITH A GOD, BUT A MAN."
I REMEMBER YOU, SORCERER.
YOU WERE HERE AT THE BEGINNING, BEFORE YOU CALLED YOURSELF DOCTOR, PHARAOH, OR LORD.
WHY HAVE YOU COME NOW, TO THIS PLACE, IN THIS HOUR?
The Parliaments of Life
PART 3
RAM V
JAMES TYNION I
STOR
RAM
SCRIP
ALVARO MARTÍNEZ BUEN
& AMANCAY NAHUELPA
PENCIL
RAUL FERNANDEZ
AMANCAY NAHUELPA
INK
JUNE CHUN
COLO
ROB LEIG
LETTER
YANICK PAQUETTE
NATHAN FAIRBAIR
COVE
CLAYTON CRAI
VARIANT COVE
ANDREA SHEA
ASSOCIATE EDITOR
ALEX R. CARR
EDITOR
YOU ARE THE AVATARS OF STONE, FLAME, WAVES, AND VAPORS.
THERE WAS A RESPONSIBILITY HANDED TO YOU AT THE DAWN OF HUMANITY, ONE THAT YOU MUST KEEP NOW.
RECONVENE THE PARLIAMENTS OF LIFE. RETURN THEM TO A PLACE OF BALANCE.
AND WHY MUST WE DO THIS?
AND WHY MUST WE INFLICT YOUR ORDER UPON THE NATURAL CHAOS OF THIS WORLD?
WE DID SO ONCE BEFORE, AT YOUR BEHEST. LOOK AT WHERE IT HAS GOTTEN US.

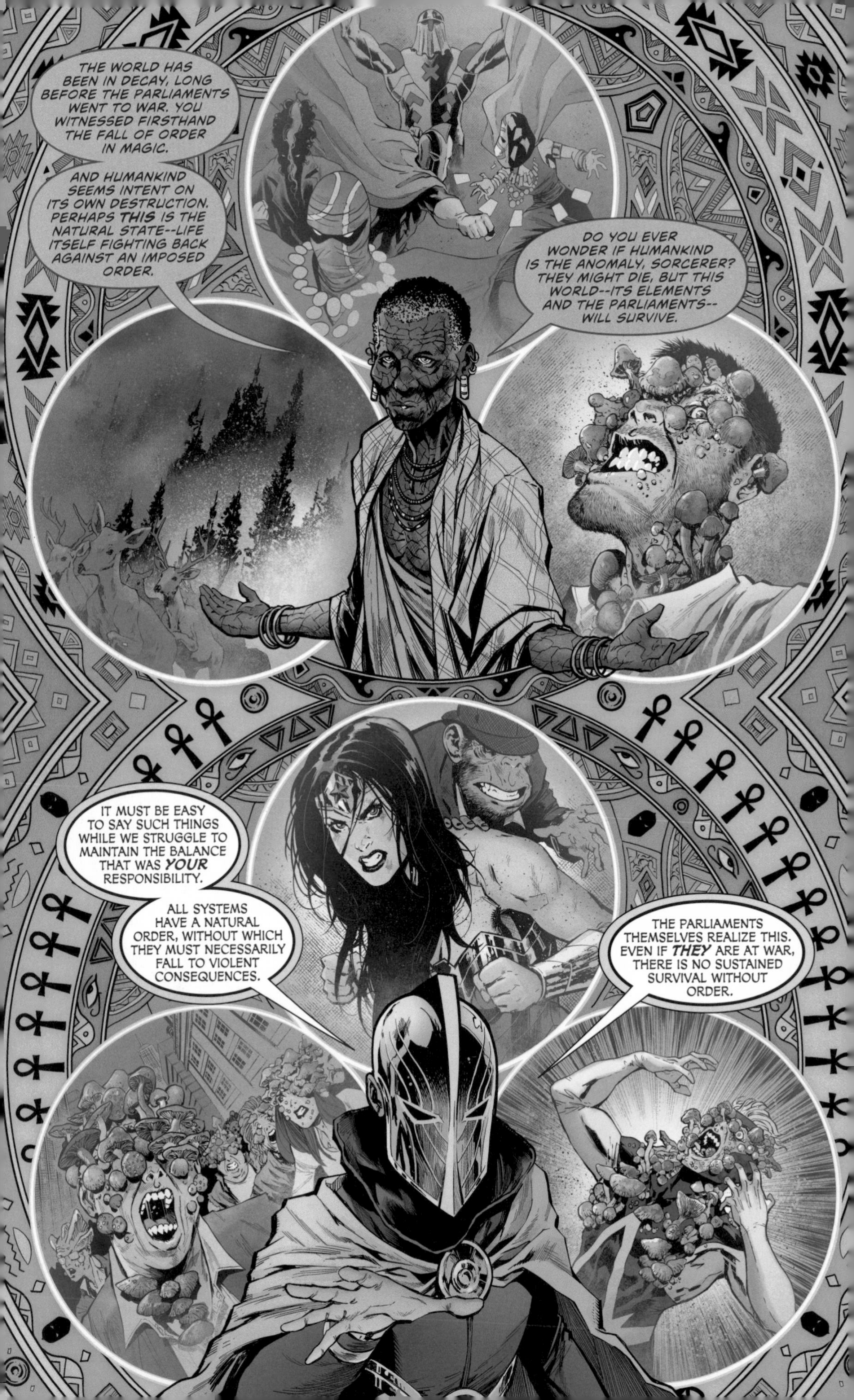
THE WORLD HAS BEEN IN DECAY, LONG BEFORE THE PARLIAMENTS WENT TO WAR. YOU WITNESSED FIRSTHAND THE FALL OF ORDER IN MAGIC.
AND HUMANKIND SEEMS INTENT ON ITS OWN DESTRUCTION. PERHAPS THIS IS THE NATURAL STATE--LIFE ITSELF FIGHTING BACK AGAINST AN IMPOSED ORDER.
DO YOU EVER WONDER IF HUMANKIND IS THE ANOMALY, SORCERER? THEY MIGHT DIE, BUT THIS WORLD--ITS ELEMENTS AND THE PARLIAMENTS--WILL SURVIVE.
IT MUST BE EASY TO SAY SUCH THINGS WHILE WE STRUGGLE TO MAINTAIN THE BALANCE THAT WAS YOUR RESPONSIBILITY.
ALL SYSTEMS HAVE A NATURAL ORDER, WITHOUT WHICH THEY MUST NECESSARILY FALL TO VIOLENT CONSEQUENCES.
THE PARLIAMENTS THEMSELVES REALIZE THIS. EVEN IF THEY ARE AT WAR, THERE IS NO SUSTAINED SURVIVAL WITHOUT ORDER.

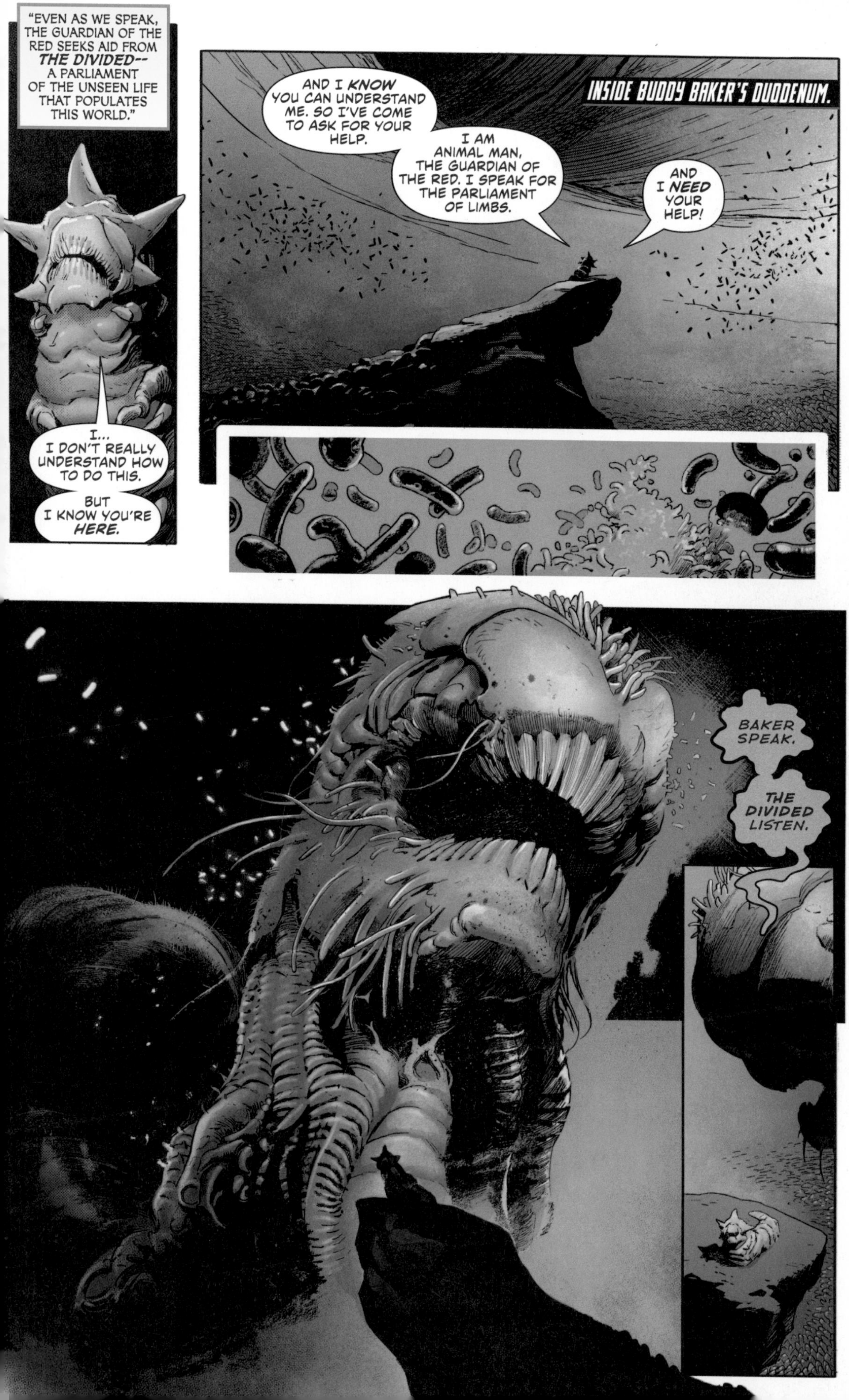
"EVEN AS WE SPEAK, THE GUARDIAN OF THE RED SEEKS AID FROM THE DIVIDED-- A PARLIAMENT OF THE UNSEEN LIFE THAT POPULATES THIS WORLD."
I... I DON'T REALLY UNDERSTAND HOW TO DO THIS.
BUT I KNOW YOU'RE HERE.
INSIDE BUDDY BAKER'S DUODENUM.
AND I KNOW YOU CAN UNDERSTAND ME. SO I'VE COME TO ASK FOR YOUR HELP.
I AM ANIMAL MAN, THE GUARDIAN OF THE RED. I SPEAK FOR THE PARLIAMENT OF LIMBS.
AND I NEED YOUR HELP!
BAKER SPEAK.
THE DIVIDED LISTEN.

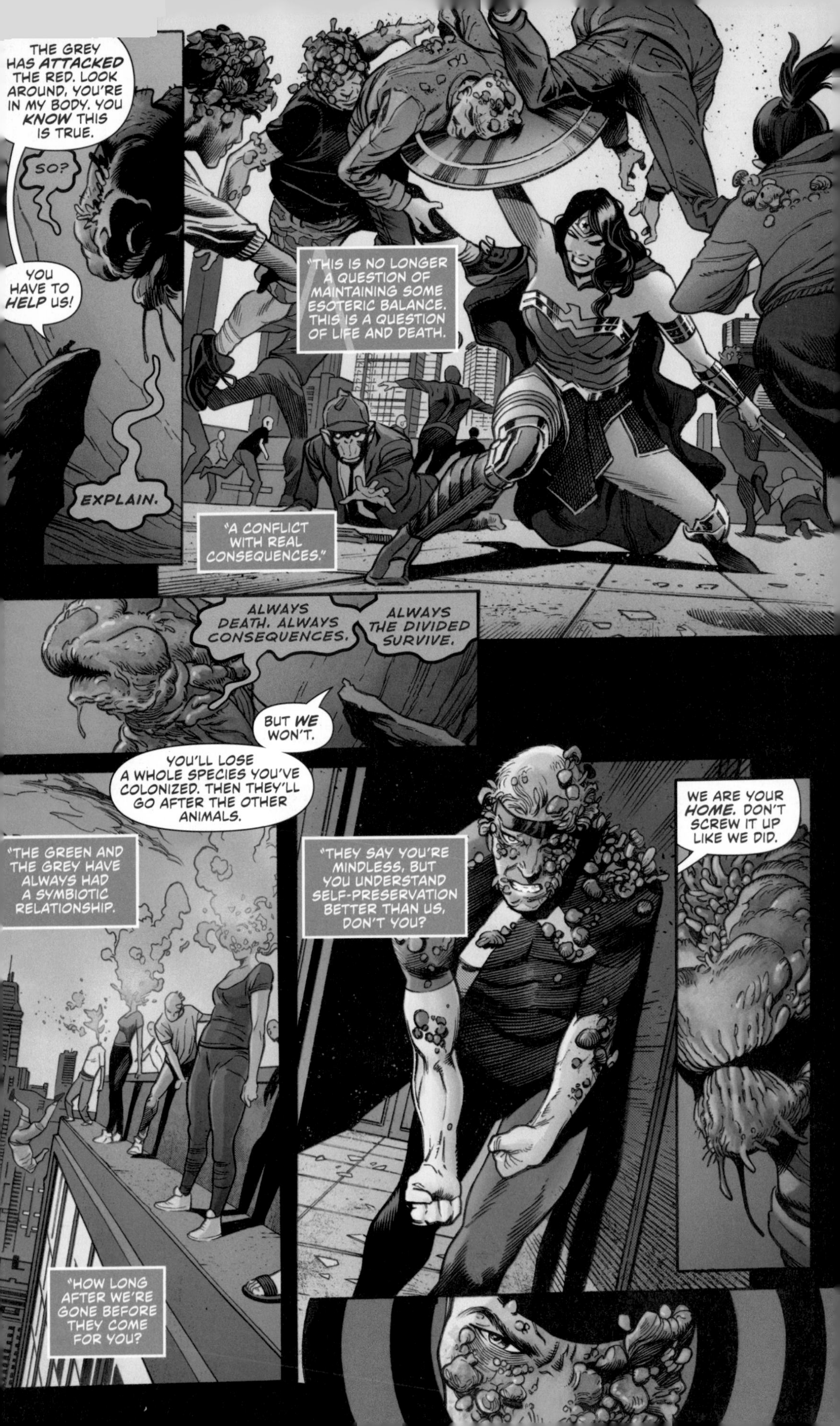

THE GREY HAS ATTACKED THE RED. LOOK AROUND, YOU'RE IN MY BODY. YOU KNOW THIS IS TRUE.
SO?
YOU HAVE TO HELP US!
EXPLAIN.
"THIS IS NO LONGER A QUESTION OF MAINTAINING SOME ESOTERIC BALANCE. THIS IS A QUESTION OF LIFE AND DEATH.
"A CONFLICT WITH REAL CONSEQUENCES."
ALWAYS DEATH. ALWAYS CONSEQUENCES.
ALWAYS THE DIVIDED SURVIVE.
BUT WE WON'T.
YOU'LL LOSE A WHOLE SPECIES YOU'VE COLONIZED. THEN THEY'LL GO AFTER THE OTHER ANIMALS.
"THE GREEN AND THE GREY HAVE ALWAYS HAD A SYMBIOTIC RELATIONSHIP.
"HOW LONG AFTER WE'RE GONE BEFORE THEY COME FOR YOU?
"THEY SAY YOU'RE MINDLESS, BUT YOU UNDERSTAND SELF-PRESERVATION BETTER THAN US, DON'T YOU?
WE ARE YOUR HOME. DON'T SCREW IT UP LIKE WE DID.

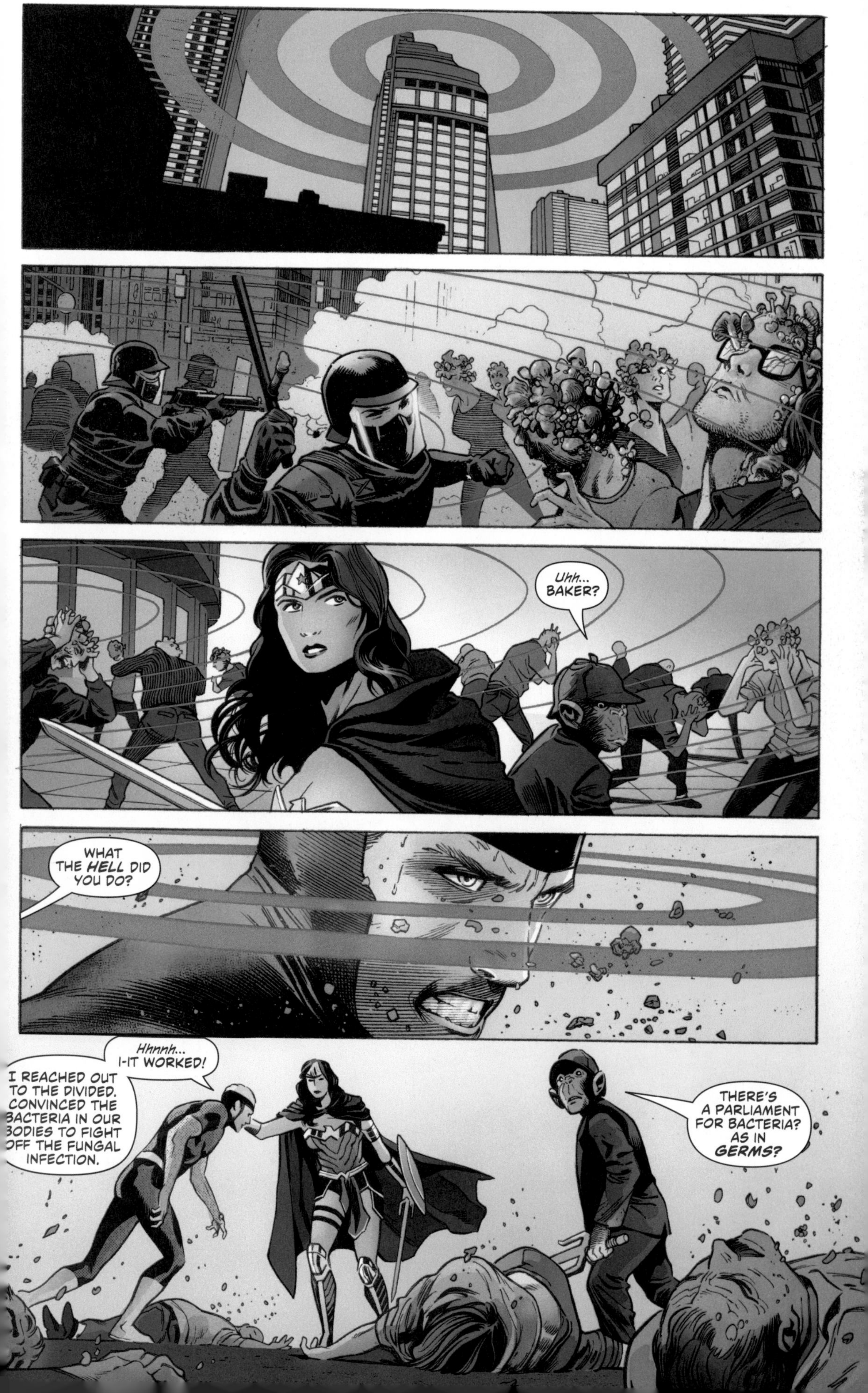
Uhh... BAKER?
WHAT THE HELL DID YOU DO?
Hhnnh... I-IT WORKED!
I REACHED OUT TO THE DIVIDED. CONVINCED THE BACTERIA IN OUR BODIES TO FIGHT OFF THE FUNGAL INFECTION.
THERE'S A PARLIAMENT FOR BACTERIA? AS IN GERMS?

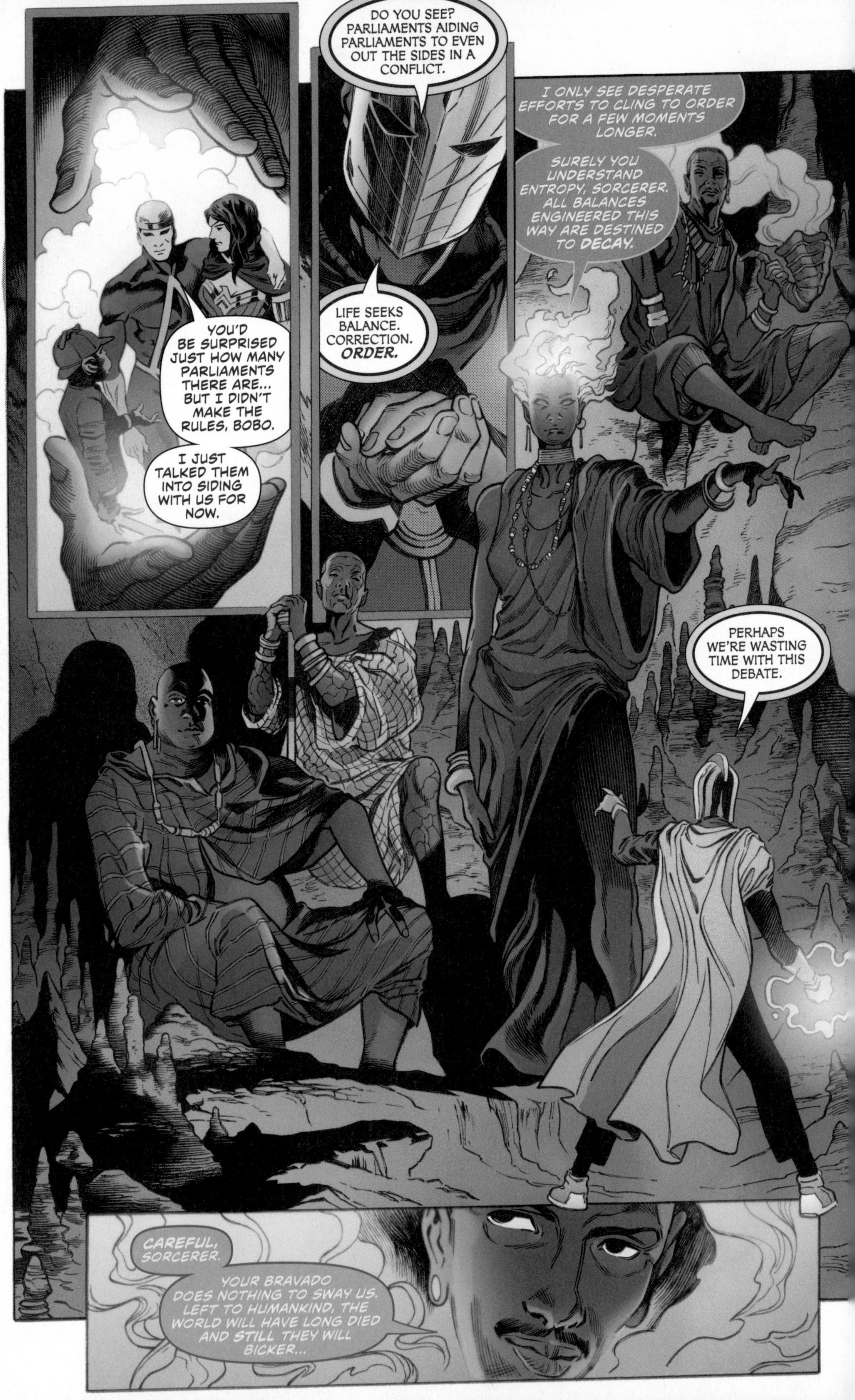
DO YOU SEE? PARLIAMENTS AIDING PARLIAMENTS TO EVEN OUT THE SIDES IN A CONFLICT.
YOU'D BE SURPRISED JUST HOW MANY PARLIAMENTS THERE ARE... BUT I DIDN'T MAKE THE RULES, BOBO.
I JUST TALKED THEM INTO SIDING WITH US FOR NOW.
LIFE SEEKS BALANCE. CORRECTION. ORDER.
I ONLY SEE DESPERATE EFFORTS TO CLING TO ORDER FOR A FEW MOMENTS LONGER.
SURELY YOU UNDERSTAND ENTROPY, SORCERER. ALL BALANCES ENGINEERED THIS WAY ARE DESTINED TO DECAY.
PERHAPS WE'RE WASTING TIME WITH THIS DEBATE.
CAREFUL, SORCERER.
YOUR BRAVADO DOES NOTHING TO SWAY US. LEFT TO HUMANKIND, THE WORLD WILL HAVE LONG DIED AND STILL THEY WILL BICKER...

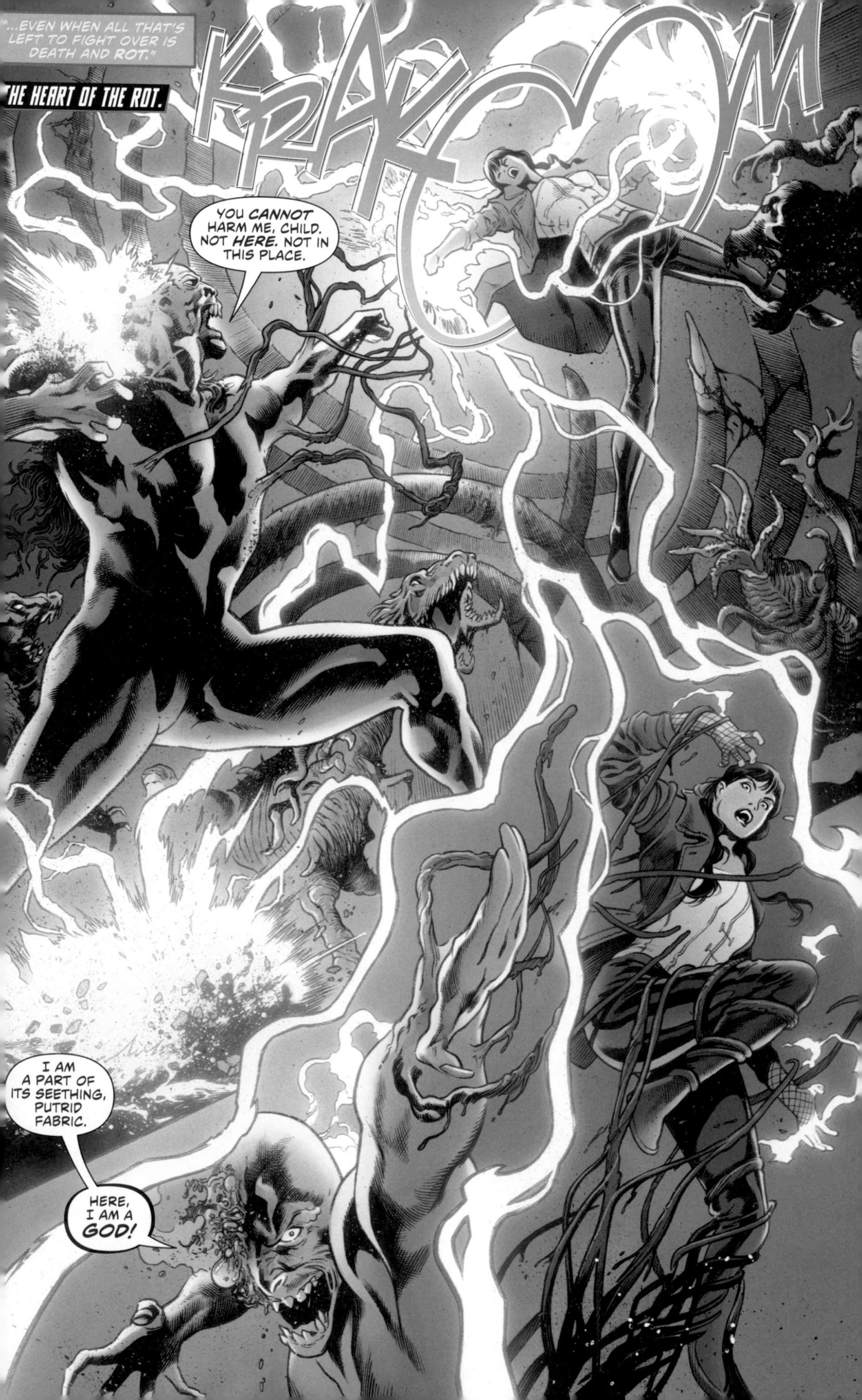
"...EVEN WHEN ALL THAT'S LEFT TO FIGHT OVER IS DEATH AND ROT."
THE HEART OF THE ROT.
KRAKOOM
YOU CANNOT HARM ME, CHILD. NOT HERE. NOT IN THIS PLACE.
I AM A PART OF ITS SEETHING, PUTRID FABRIC.
HERE, I AM A GOD!

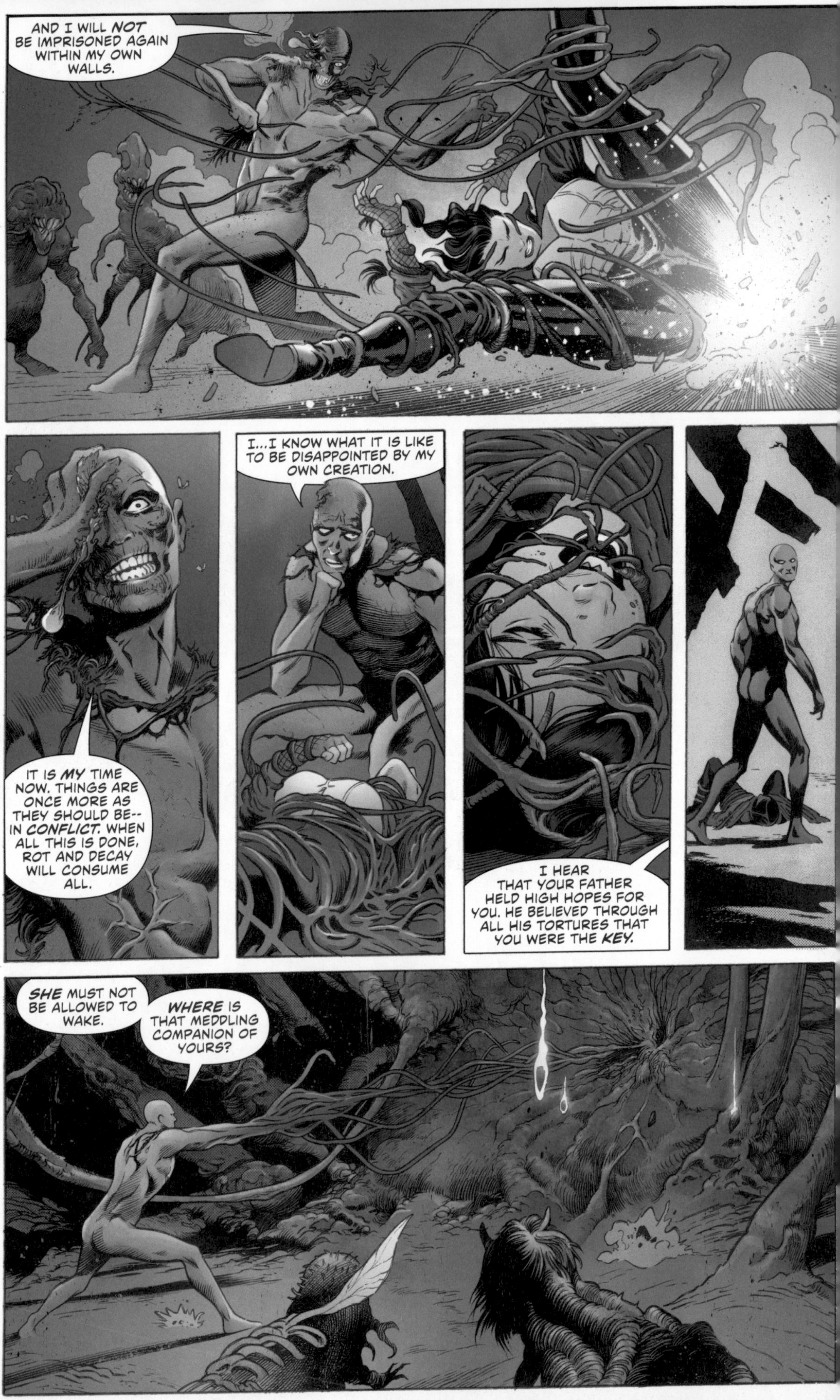

AND I WILL NOT BE IMPRISONED AGAIN WITHIN MY OWN WALLS.
IT IS MY TIME NOW. THINGS ARE ONCE MORE AS THEY SHOULD BE-- IN CONFLICT. WHEN ALL THIS IS DONE, ROT AND DECAY WILL CONSUME ALL.
I...I KNOW WHAT IT IS LIKE TO BE DISAPPOINTED BY MY OWN CREATION.
I HEAR THAT YOUR FATHER HELD HIGH HOPES FOR YOU. HE BELIEVED THROUGH ALL HIS TORTURES THAT YOU WERE THE KEY.
SHE MUST NOT BE ALLOWED TO WAKE.
WHERE IS THAT MEDDLING COMPANION OF YOURS?

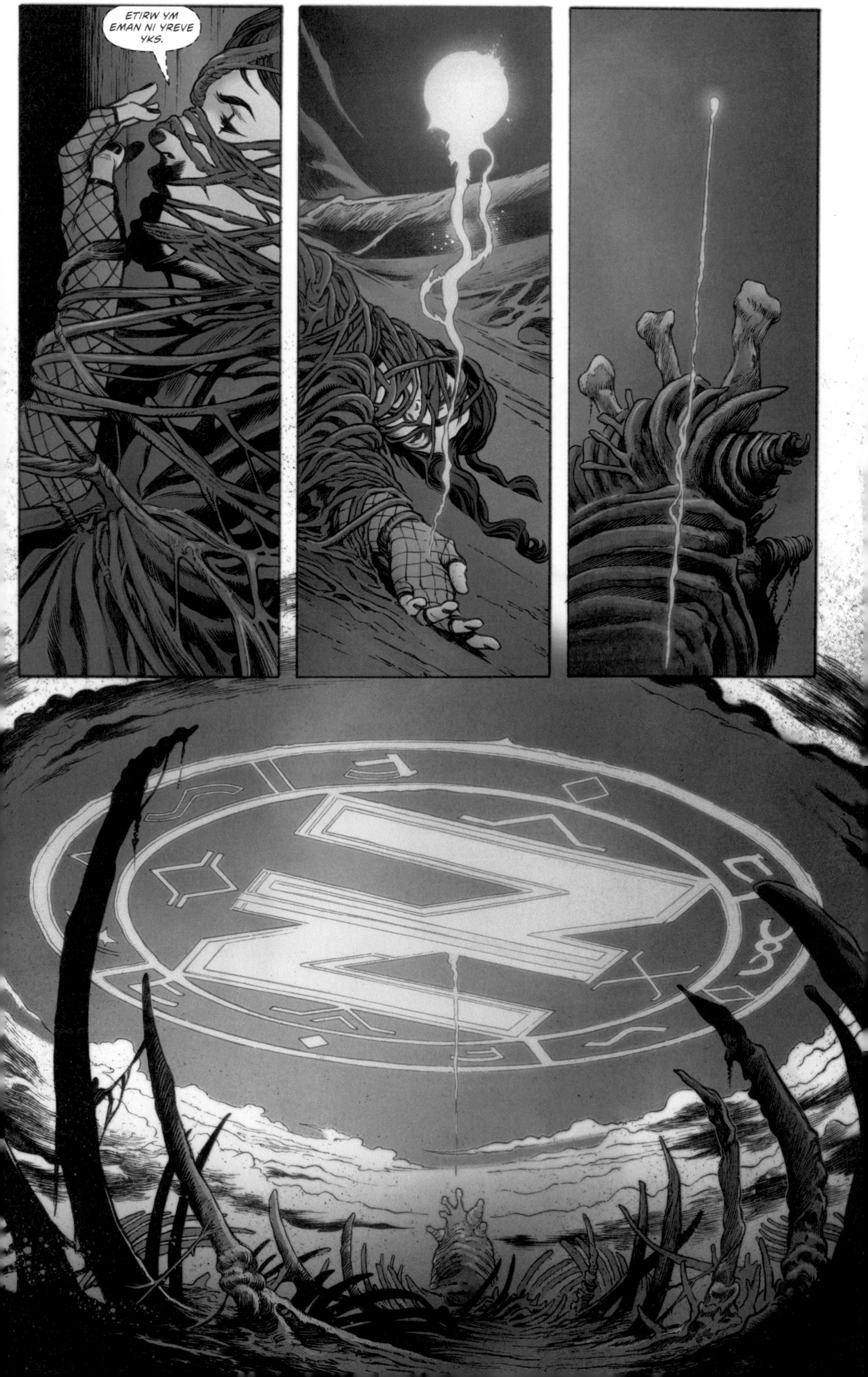
ETIRW YM EMAN NI YREVE YKS.

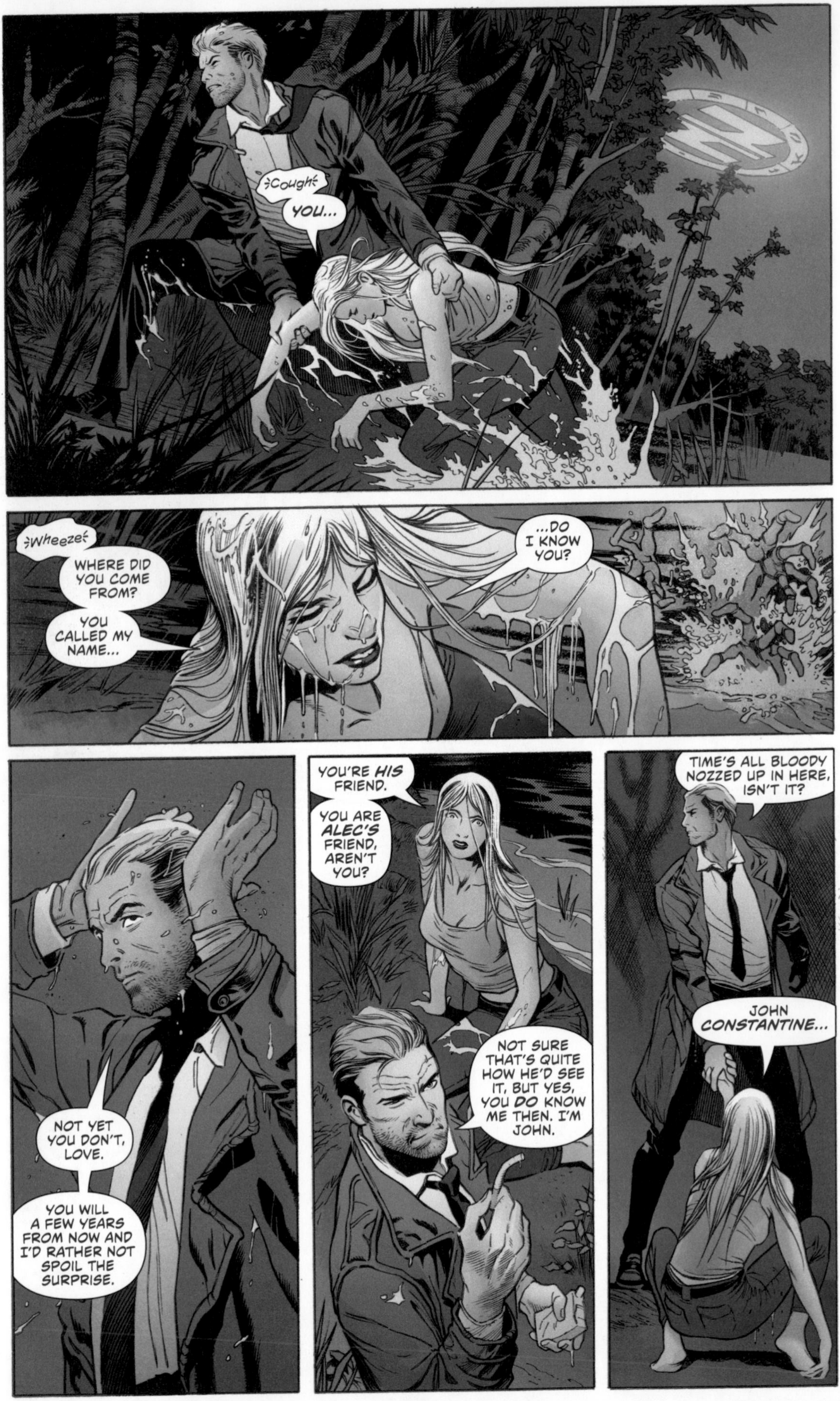

Cough
YOU...
Wheeze
WHERE DID YOU COME FROM?
YOU CALLED MY NAME...
...DO I KNOW YOU?
NOT YET YOU DON'T, LOVE.
YOU WILL A FEW YEARS FROM NOW AND I'D RATHER NOT SPOIL THE SURPRISE.
YOU'RE HIS FRIEND.
YOU ARE ALEC'S FRIEND, AREN'T YOU?
NOT SURE THAT'S QUITE HOW HE'D SEE IT, BUT YES, YOU DO KNOW ME THEN. I'M JOHN.
TIME'S ALL BLOODY NOZZED UP IN HERE, ISN'T IT?
JOHN CONSTANTINE...

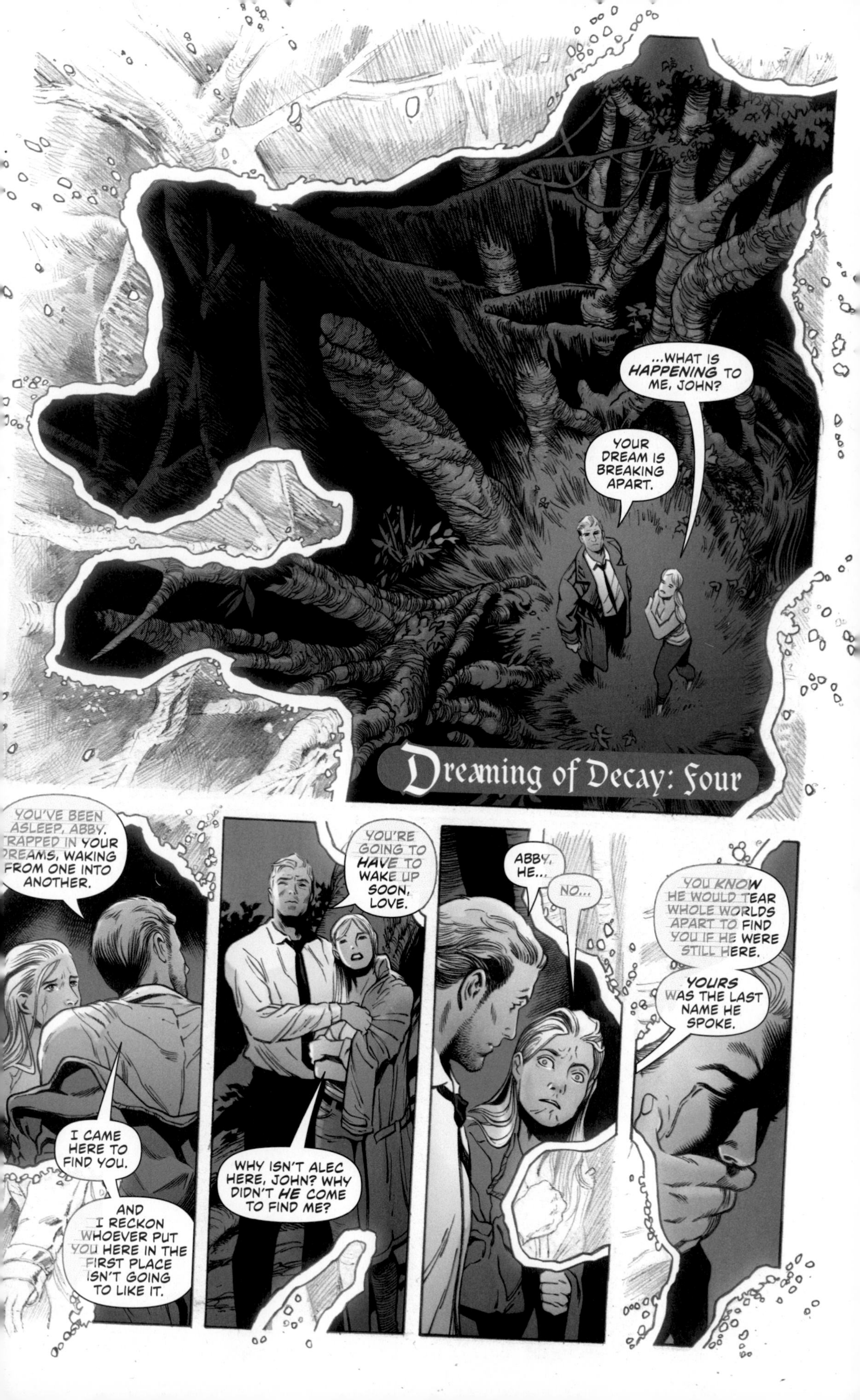

...WHAT IS HAPPENING TO ME, JOHN?
YOUR DREAM IS BREAKING APART.
Dreaming of Decay: Four
YOU'VE BEEN ASLEEP, ABBY. TRAPPED IN YOUR DREAMS, WAKING FROM ONE INTO ANOTHER.
I CAME HERE TO FIND YOU.
AND I RECKON WHOEVER PUT YOU HERE IN THE FIRST PLACE ISN'T GOING TO LIKE IT.
YOU'RE GOING TO HAVE TO WAKE UP SOON, LOVE.
WHY ISN'T ALEC HERE, JOHN? WHY DIDN'T HE COME TO FIND ME?
ABBY, HE...
NO...
YOU KNOW HE WOULD TEAR WHOLE WORLDS APART TO FIND YOU IF HE WERE STILL HERE.
YOURS WAS THE LAST NAME HE SPOKE.

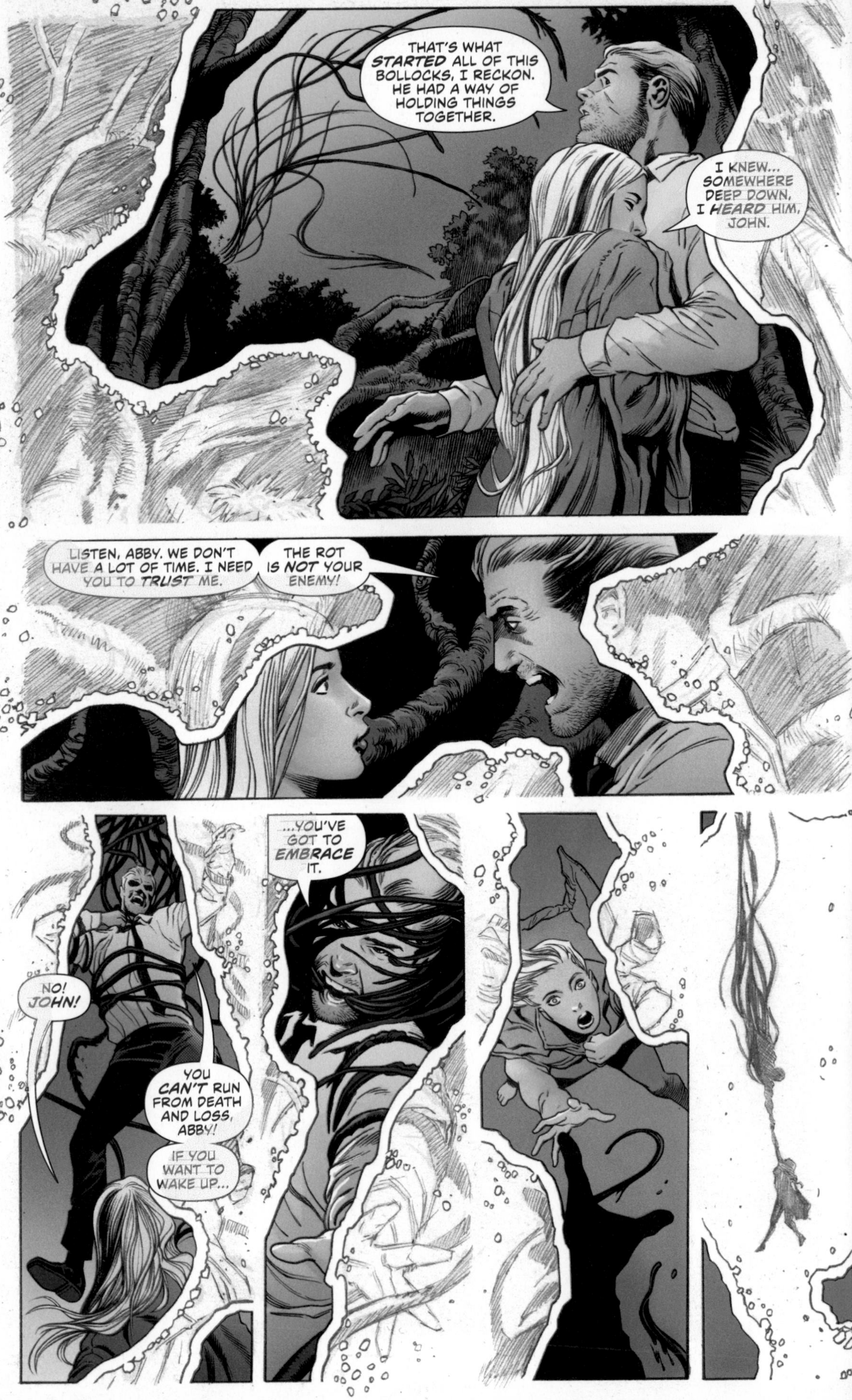
THAT'S WHAT STARTED ALL OF THIS BOLLOCKS, I RECKON. HE HAD A WAY OF HOLDING THINGS TOGETHER.
I KNEW... SOMEWHERE DEEP DOWN, I HEARD HIM, JOHN.
LISTEN, ABBY. WE DON'T HAVE A LOT OF TIME. I NEED YOU TO TRUST ME.
THE ROT IS NOT YOUR ENEMY!
NO! JOHN!
YOU CAN'T RUN FROM DEATH AND LOSS, ABBY!
IF YOU WANT TO WAKE UP...
...YOU'VE GOT TO EMBRACE IT.

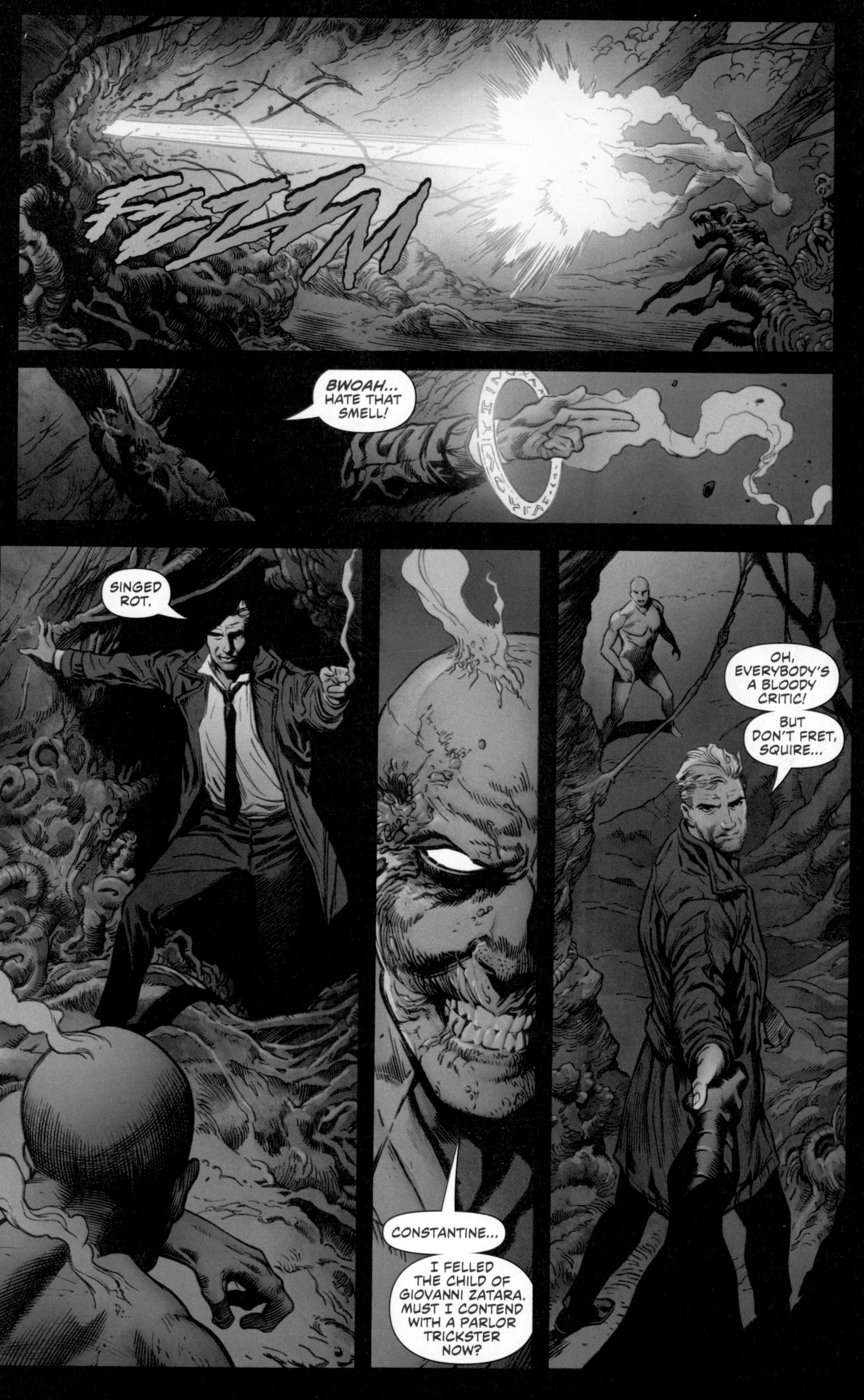
FZZAM
BWOAH... HATE THAT SMELL!
SINGED ROT.
CONSTANTINE...
I FELLED THE CHILD OF GIOVANNI ZATARA. MUST I CONTEND WITH A PARLOR TRICKSTER NOW?
OH, EVERYBODY'S A BLOODY CRITIC!
BUT DON'T FRET, SQUIRE...

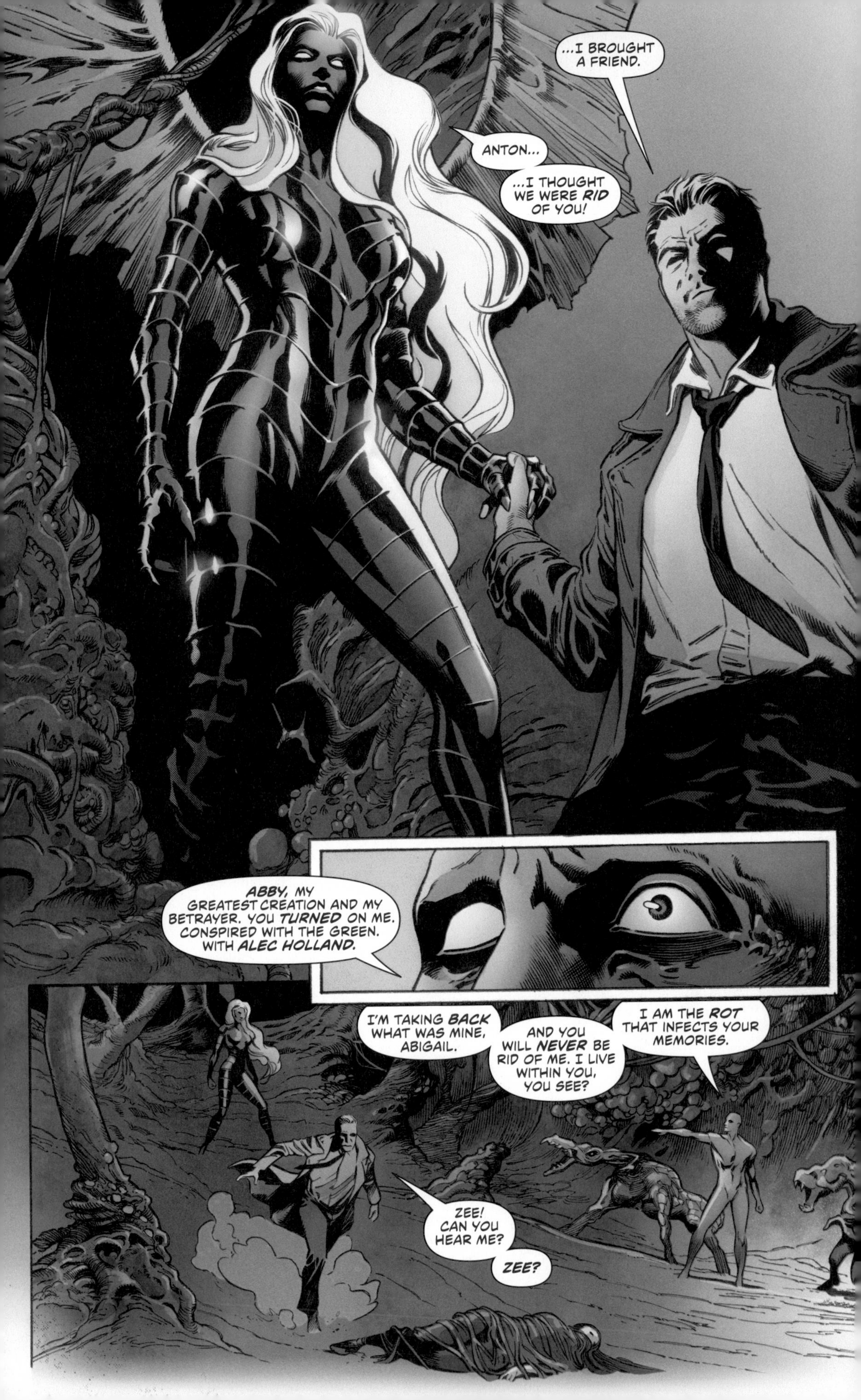
...I BROUGHT A FRIEND.
ANTON...
...I THOUGHT WE WERE RID OF YOU!
ABBY, MY GREATEST CREATION AND MY BETRAYER. YOU TURNED ON ME. CONSPIRED WITH THE GREEN. WITH ALEC HOLLAND.
I'M TAKING BACK WHAT WAS MINE, ABIGAIL.
AND YOU WILL NEVER BE RID OF ME. I LIVE WITHIN YOU, YOU SEE?
I AM THE ROT THAT INFECTS YOUR MEMORIES.
ZEE! CAN YOU HEAR ME?
ZEE?

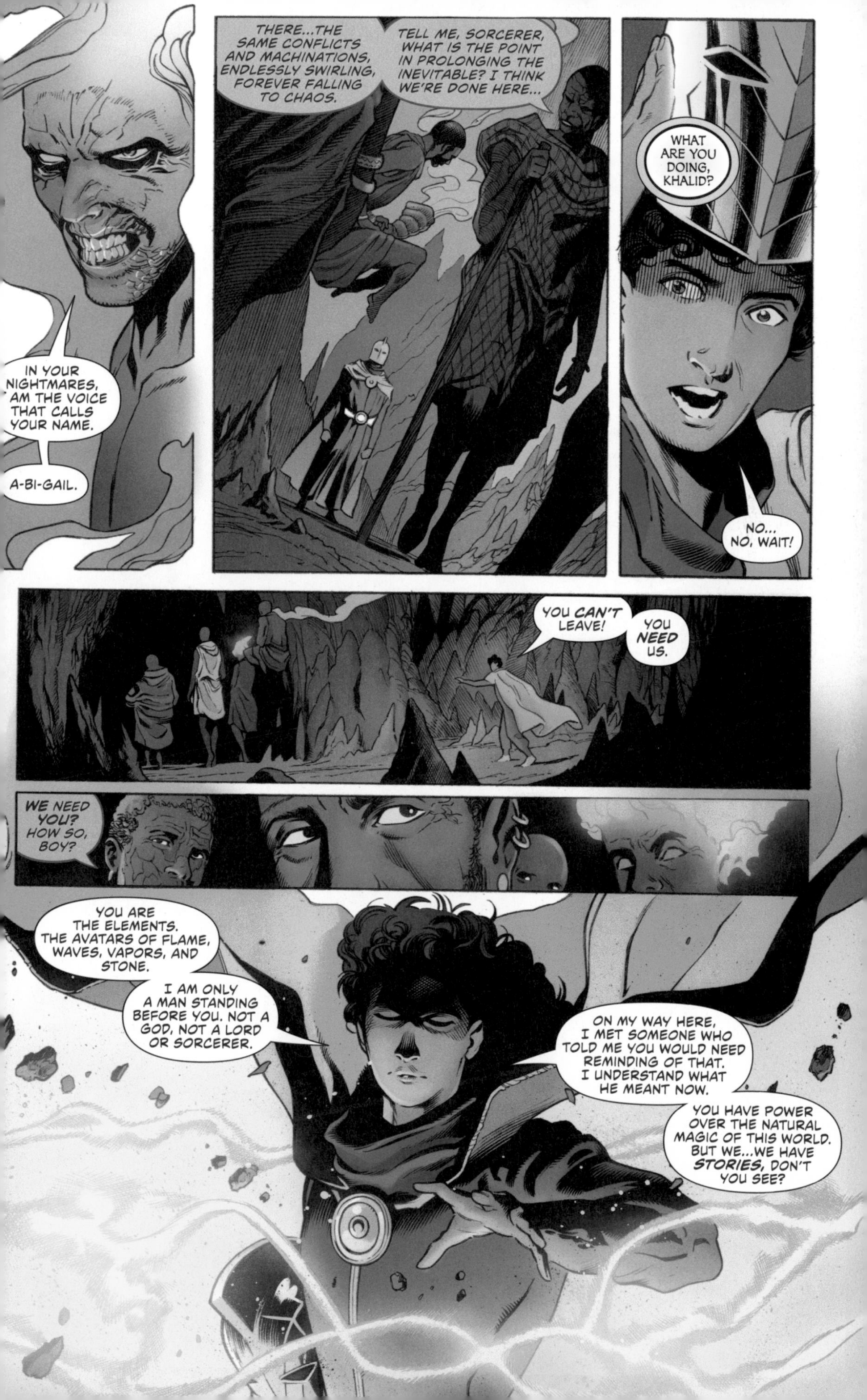
IN YOUR NIGHTMARES, I AM THE VOICE THAT CALLS YOUR NAME.
A-BI-GAIL.
THERE...THE SAME CONFLICTS AND MACHINATIONS, ENDLESSLY SWIRLING, FOREVER FALLING TO CHAOS.
TELL ME, SORCERER, WHAT IS THE POINT IN PROLONGING THE INEVITABLE? I THINK WE'RE DONE HERE...
WHAT ARE YOU DOING, KHALID?
NO... NO, WAIT!
YOU CAN'T LEAVE!
YOU NEED US.
WE NEED YOU? HOW SO, BOY?
YOU ARE THE ELEMENTS. THE AVATARS OF FLAME, WAVES, VAPORS, AND STONE.
I AM ONLY A MAN STANDING BEFORE YOU. NOT A GOD, NOT A LORD OR SORCERER.
ON MY WAY HERE, I MET SOMEONE WHO TOLD ME YOU WOULD NEED REMINDING OF THAT. I UNDERSTAND WHAT HE MEANT NOW.
YOU HAVE POWER OVER THE NATURAL MAGIC OF THIS WORLD. BUT WE...WE HAVE STORIES, DON'T YOU SEE?

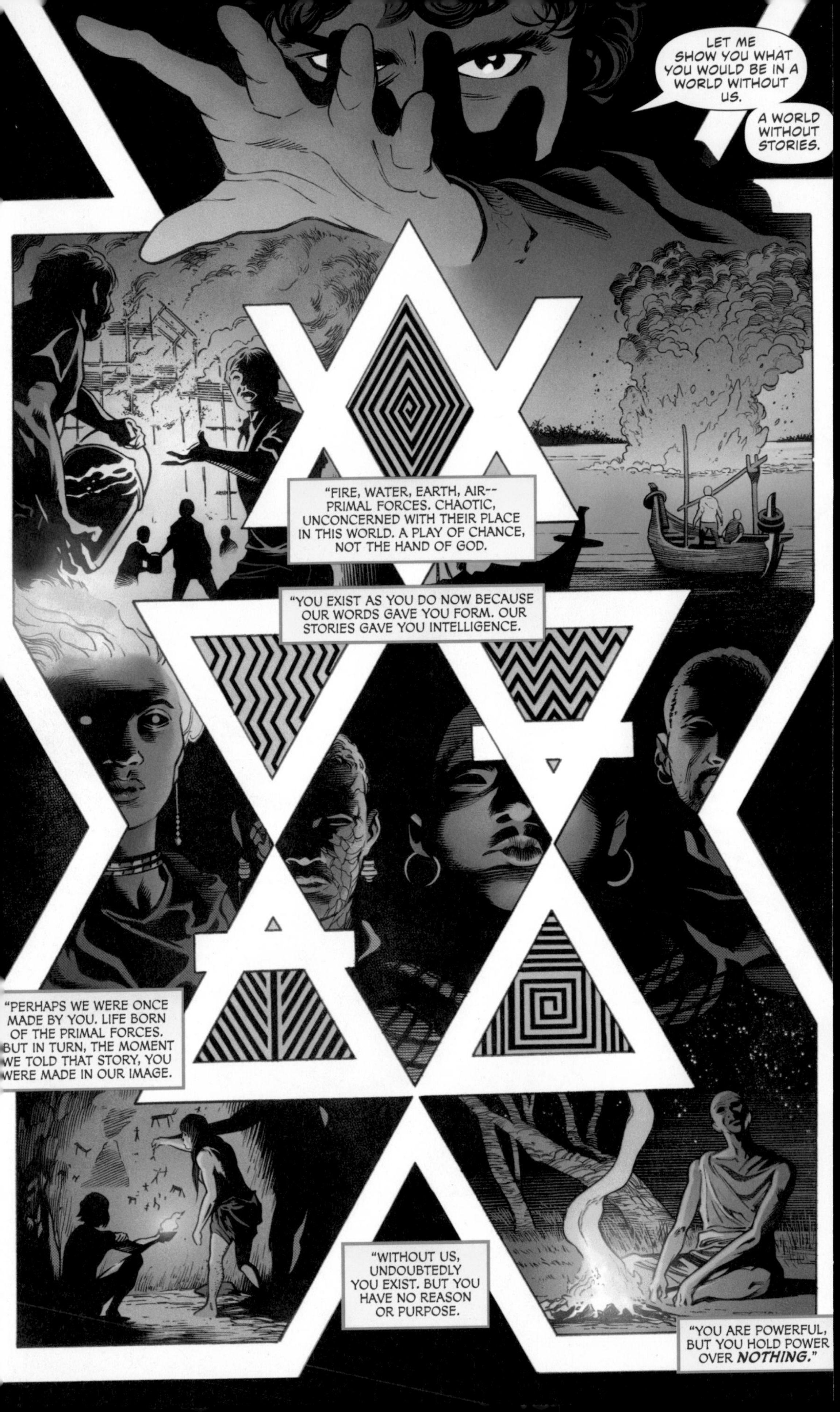
LET ME SHOW YOU WHAT YOU WOULD BE IN A WORLD WITHOUT US.
A WORLD WITHOUT STORIES.
"FIRE, WATER, EARTH, AIR--PRIMAL FORCES. CHAOTIC, UNCONCERNED WITH THEIR PLACE IN THIS WORLD. A PLAY OF CHANCE, NOT THE HAND OF GOD.
"YOU EXIST AS YOU DO NOW BECAUSE OUR WORDS GAVE YOU FORM. OUR STORIES GAVE YOU INTELLIGENCE.
"PERHAPS WE WERE ONCE MADE BY YOU. LIFE BORN OF THE PRIMAL FORCES. BUT IN TURN, THE MOMENT WE TOLD THAT STORY, YOU WERE MADE IN OUR IMAGE.
"WITHOUT US, UNDOUBTEDLY YOU EXIST. BUT YOU HAVE NO REASON OR PURPOSE.
"YOU ARE POWERFUL, BUT YOU HOLD POWER OVER *NOTHING.*"

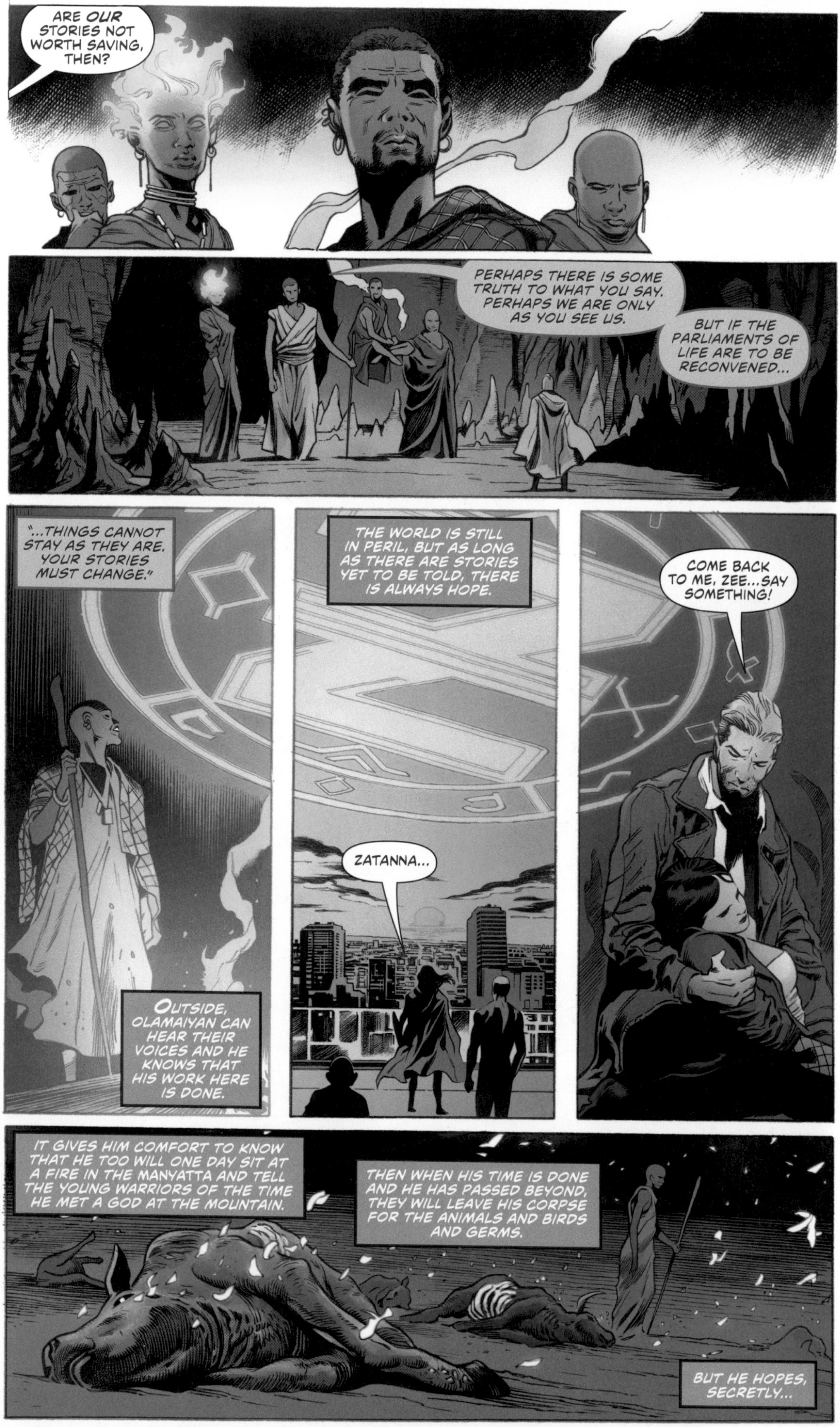
ARE OUR STORIES NOT WORTH SAVING, THEN?
PERHAPS THERE IS SOME TRUTH TO WHAT YOU SAY. PERHAPS WE ARE ONLY AS YOU SEE US.
BUT IF THE PARLIAMENTS OF LIFE ARE TO BE RECONVENED...
"...THINGS CANNOT STAY AS THEY ARE. YOUR STORIES MUST CHANGE."
OUTSIDE, OLAMAIYAN CAN HEAR THEIR VOICES AND HE KNOWS THAT HIS WORK HERE IS DONE.
THE WORLD IS STILL IN PERIL, BUT AS LONG AS THERE ARE STORIES YET TO BE TOLD, THERE IS ALWAYS HOPE.
ZATANNA...
COME BACK TO ME, ZEE...SAY SOMETHING!
IT GIVES HIM COMFORT TO KNOW THAT HE TOO WILL ONE DAY SIT AT A FIRE IN THE MANYATTA AND TELL THE YOUNG WARRIORS OF THE TIME HE MET A GOD AT THE MOUNTAIN.
THEN WHEN HIS TIME IS DONE AND HE HAS PASSED BEYOND, THEY WILL LEAVE HIS CORPSE FOR THE ANIMALS AND BIRDS AND GERMS.
BUT HE HOPES, SECRETLY...

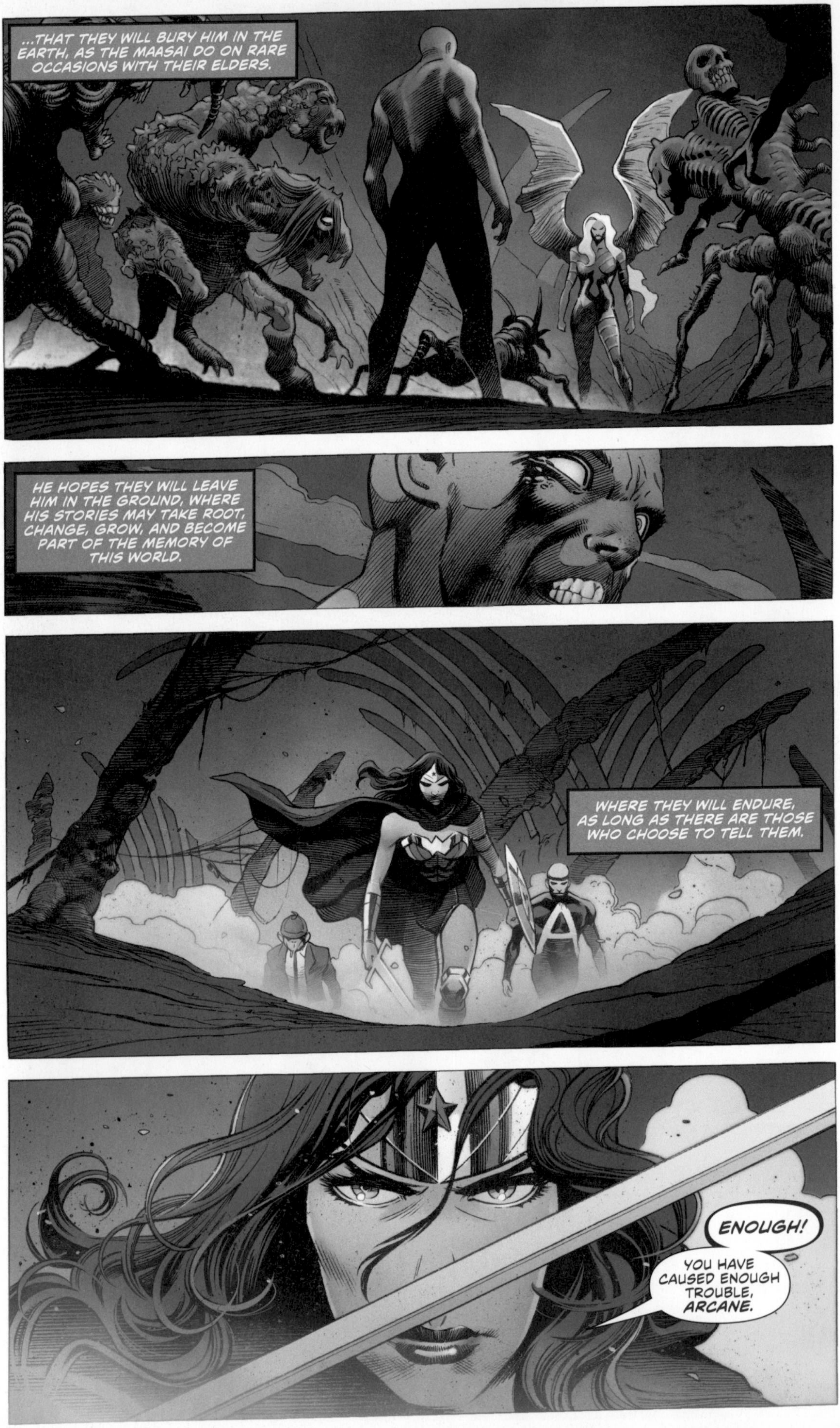
...THAT THEY WILL BURY HIM IN THE EARTH, AS THE MAASAI DO ON RARE OCCASIONS WITH THEIR ELDERS.
HE HOPES THEY WILL LEAVE HIM IN THE GROUND, WHERE HIS STORIES MAY TAKE ROOT, CHANGE, GROW, AND BECOME PART OF THE MEMORY OF THIS WORLD.
WHERE THEY WILL ENDURE, AS LONG AS THERE ARE THOSE WHO CHOOSE TO TELL THEM.
ENOUGH!
YOU HAVE CAUSED ENOUGH TROUBLE, ARCANE.

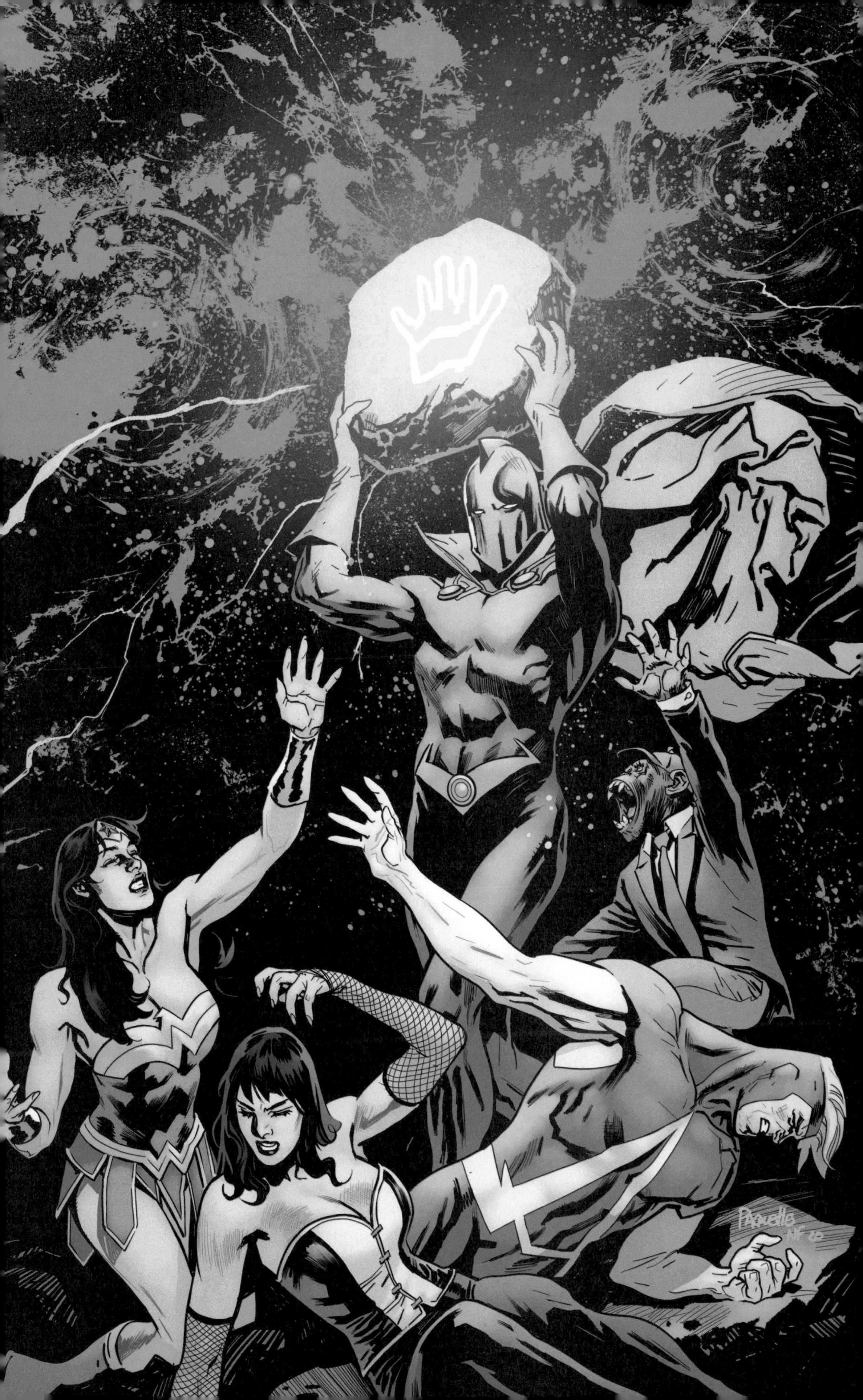

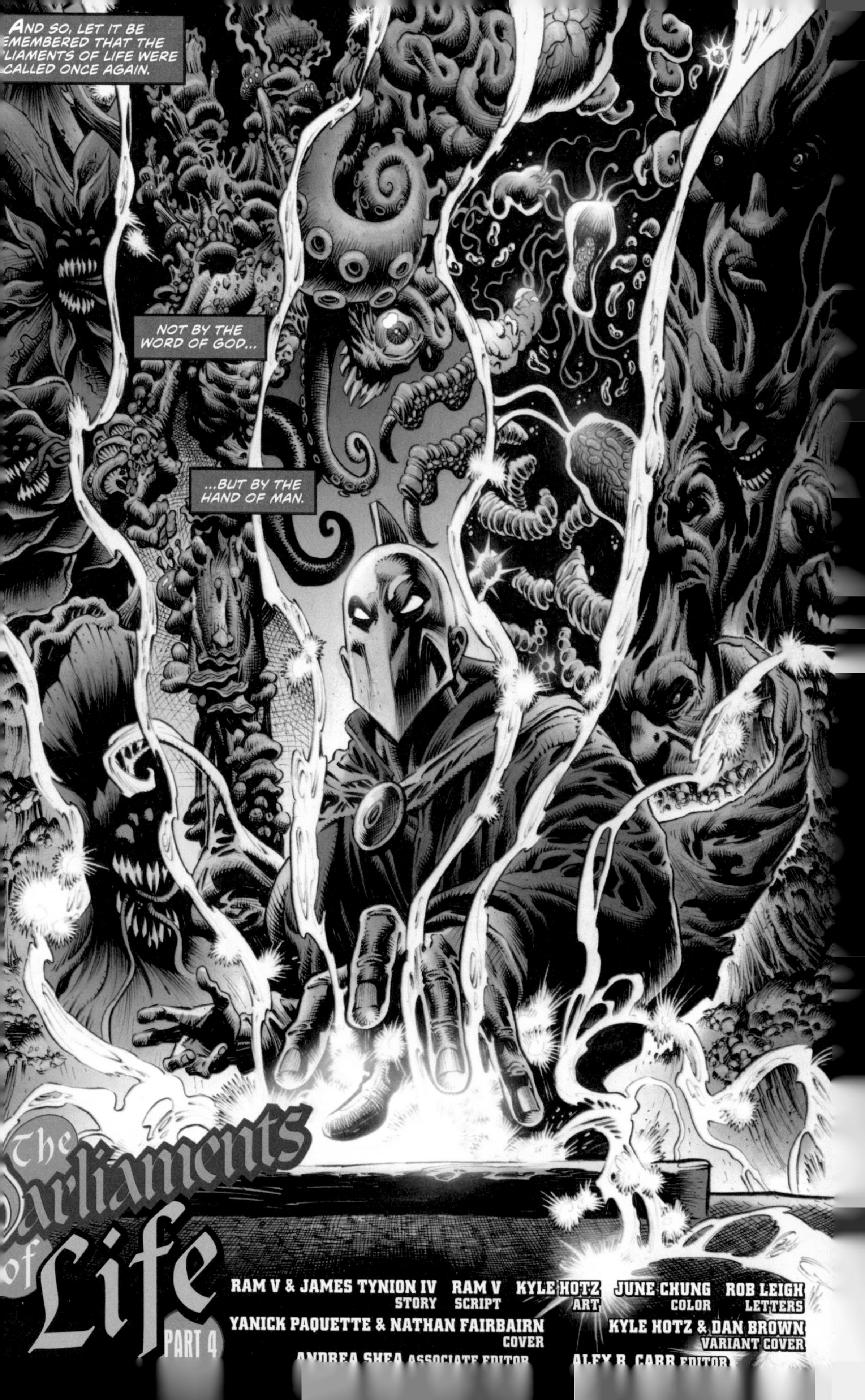
AND SO, LET IT BE
EMEMBERED THAT THE
LIAMENTS OF LIFE WERE
CALLED ONCE AGAIN.
NOT BY THE
WORD OF GOD...
...BUT BY THE
HAND OF MAN.
The
arliaments
of
Life
PART 4
RAM V & JAMES TYNION IV STORY
RAM V SCRIPT
KYLE HOTZ ART
JUNE CHUNG COLOR
ROB LEIGH LETTERS
YANICK PAQUETTE & NATHAN FAIRBAIRN COVER
KYLE HOTZ & DAN BROWN VARIANT COVER
ANDREA SHEA ASSOCIATE EDITOR
ALEX R. CARR EDITOR

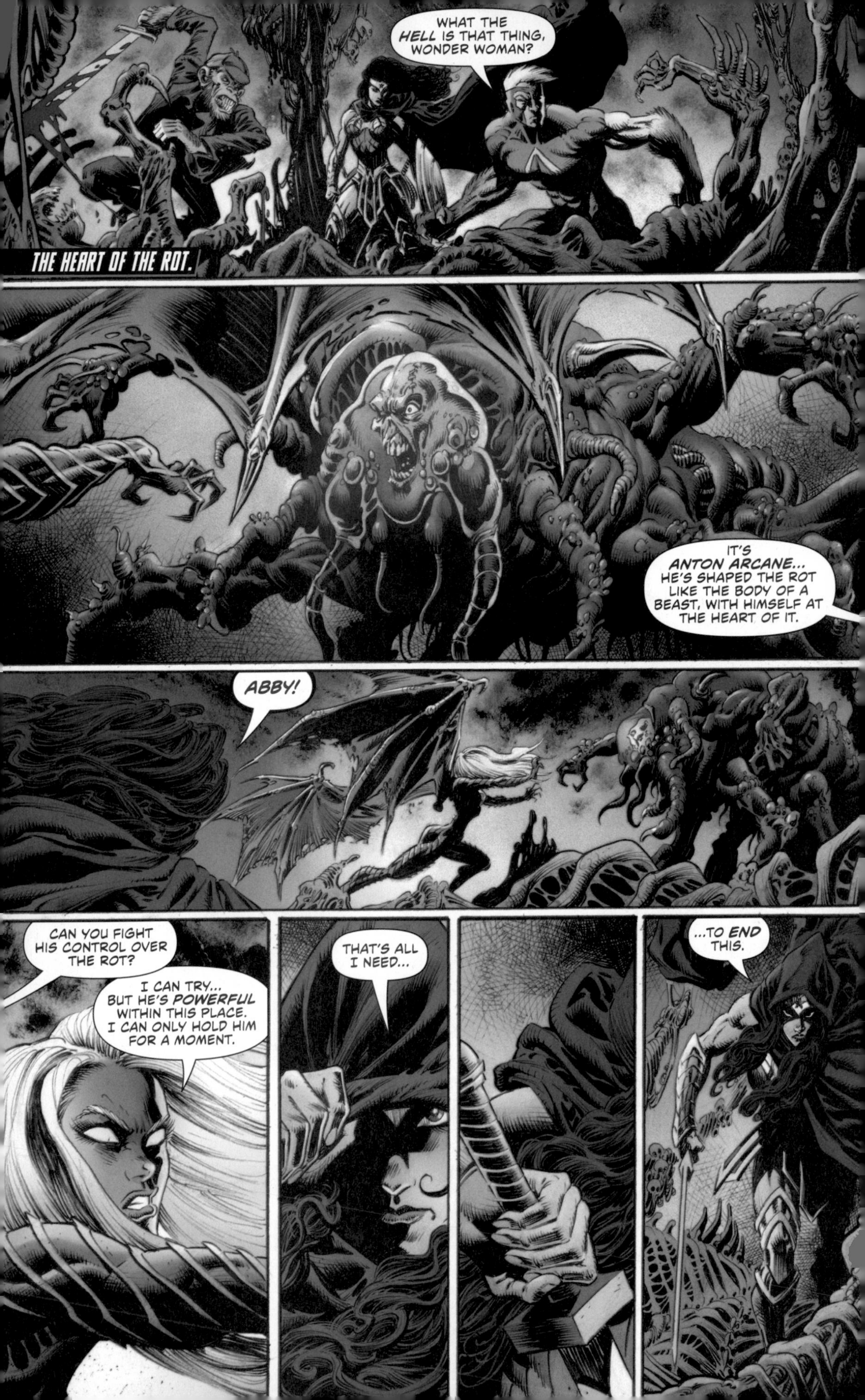

WHAT THE HELL IS THAT THING, WONDER WOMAN?
THE HEART OF THE ROT.
IT'S ANTON ARCANE... HE'S SHAPED THE ROT LIKE THE BODY OF A BEAST, WITH HIMSELF AT THE HEART OF IT.
ABBY!
CAN YOU FIGHT HIS CONTROL OVER THE ROT?
I CAN TRY... BUT HE'S POWERFUL WITHIN THIS PLACE. I CAN ONLY HOLD HIM FOR A MOMENT.
THAT'S ALL I NEED...
...TO END THIS.

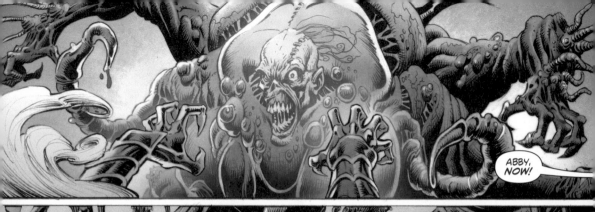

ABBY, NOW!

SHDRRKKT

I KNOW I CANNOT KILL YOU IN THIS PLACE, ARCANE.

BUT AT THE VERY LEAST, THIS IS GOING TO HURT.

YOU DON'T KNOW WHAT I AM CAPABLE OF, PRINCESS.

AND OF WHAT IS TO COME, YOU KNOW EVEN LESS.

BLINDLY YOU HAVE THRUST YOUR HAND...

...INTO THE HEART OF THE SWARM.

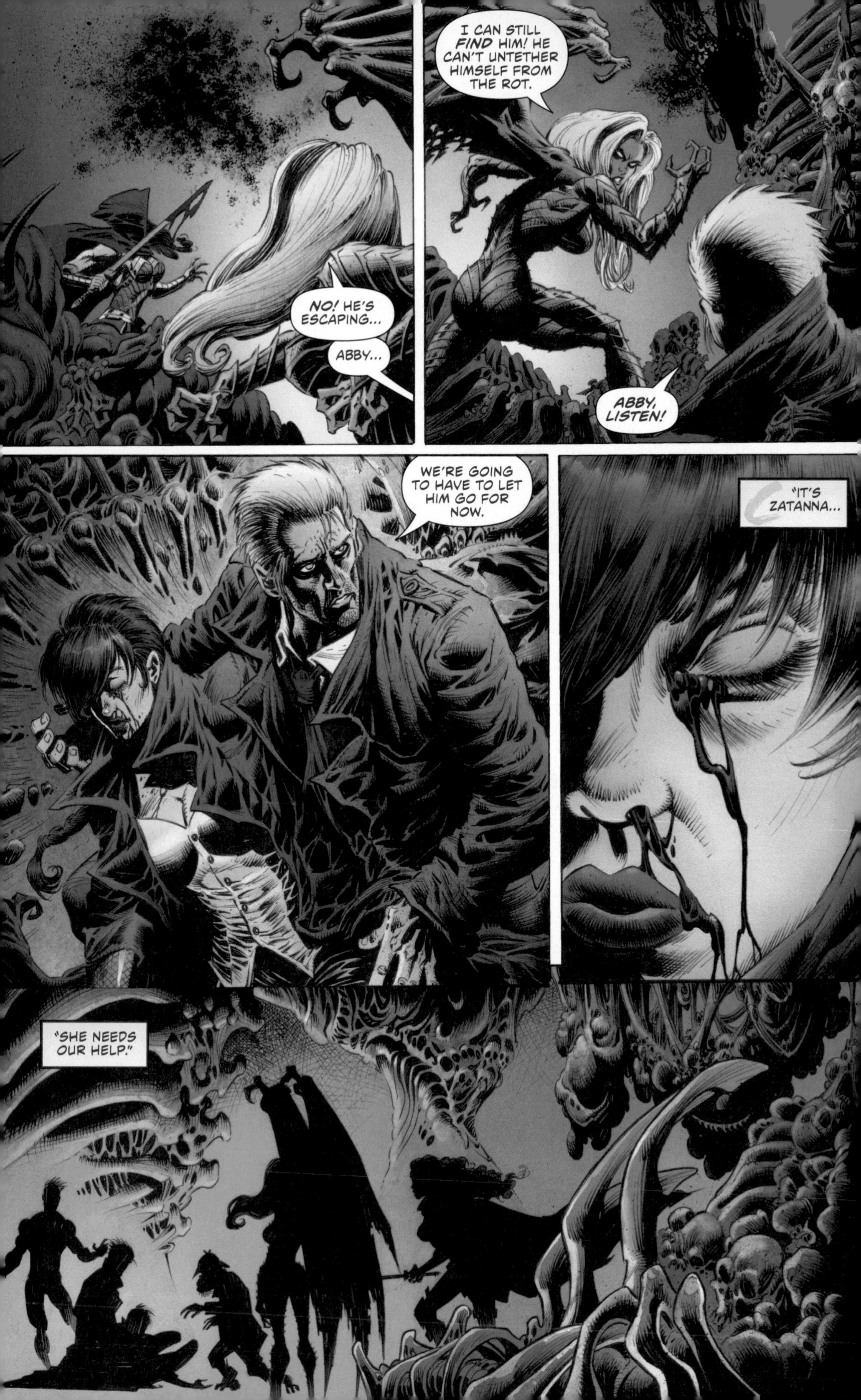

NO! HE'S ESCAPING...
ABBY...
I CAN STILL FIND HIM! HE CAN'T UNTETHER HIMSELF FROM THE ROT.
ABBY, LISTEN!
WE'RE GOING TO HAVE TO LET HIM GO FOR NOW.
"IT'S ZATANNA...
"SHE NEEDS OUR HELP."

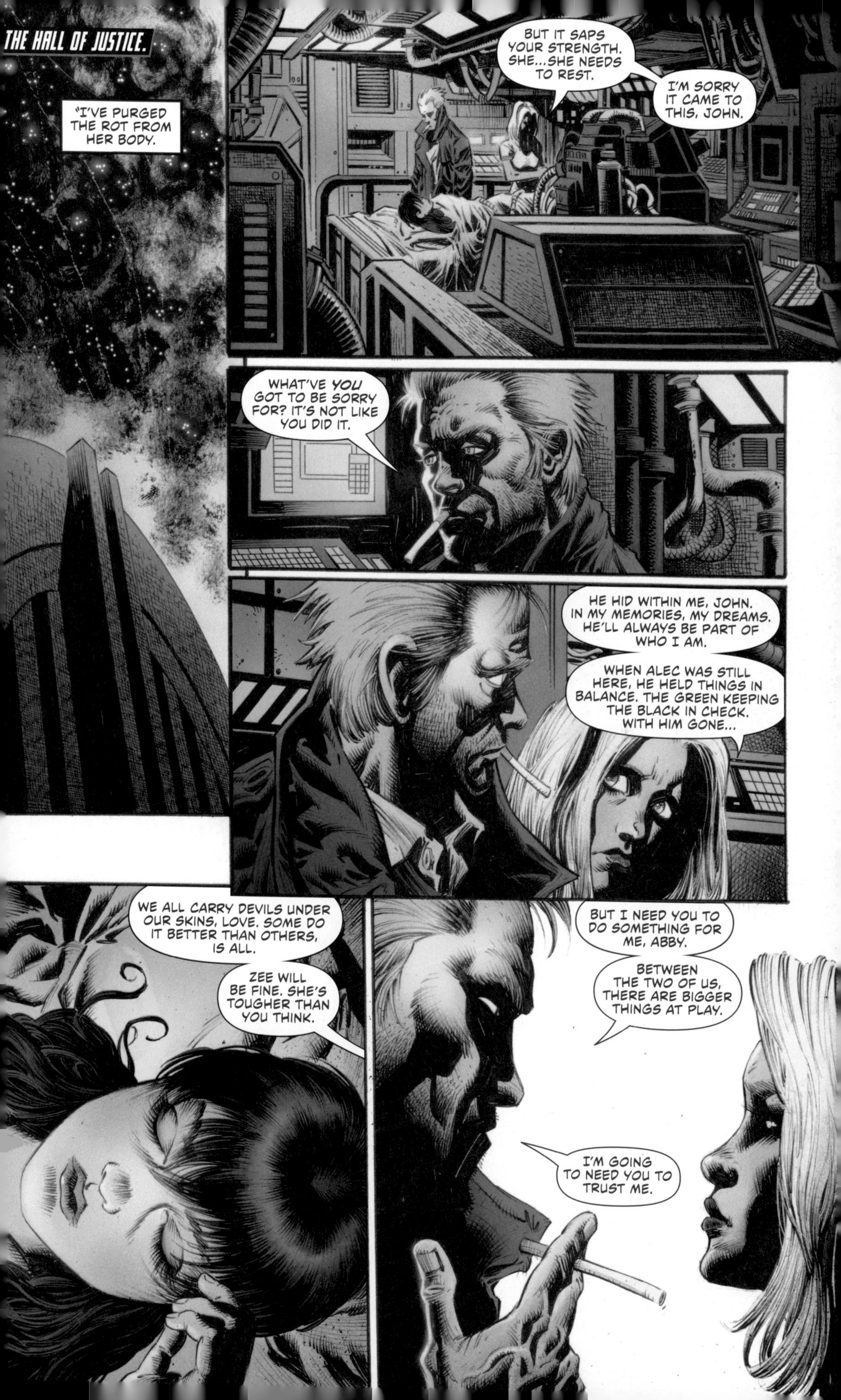
THE HALL OF JUSTICE.
"I'VE PURGED THE ROT FROM HER BODY.
BUT IT SAPS YOUR STRENGTH. SHE...SHE NEEDS TO REST.
I'M SORRY IT CAME TO THIS, JOHN.
WHAT'VE YOU GOT TO BE SORRY FOR? IT'S NOT LIKE YOU DID IT.
HE HID WITHIN ME, JOHN. IN MY MEMORIES, MY DREAMS. HE'LL ALWAYS BE PART OF WHO I AM.
WHEN ALEC WAS STILL HERE, HE HELD THINGS IN BALANCE. THE GREEN KEEPING THE BLACK IN CHECK. WITH HIM GONE...
WE ALL CARRY DEVILS UNDER OUR SKINS, LOVE. SOME DO IT BETTER THAN OTHERS, IS ALL.
ZEE WILL BE FINE. SHE'S TOUGHER THAN YOU THINK.
BUT I NEED YOU TO DO SOMETHING FOR ME, ABBY.
BETWEEN THE TWO OF US, THERE ARE BIGGER THINGS AT PLAY.
I'M GOING TO NEED YOU TO TRUST ME.

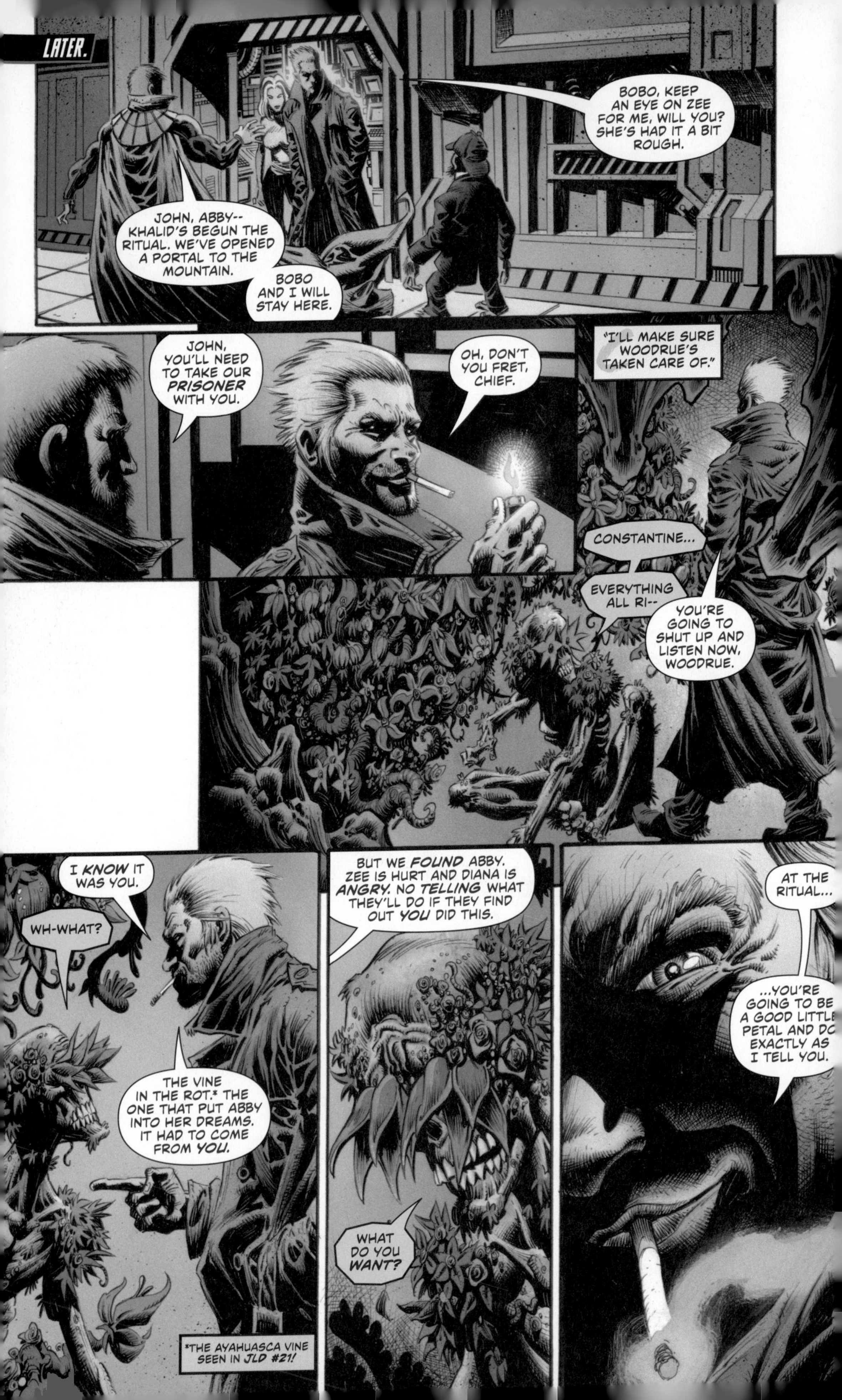
LATER.
BOBO, KEEP AN EYE ON ZEE FOR ME, WILL YOU? SHE'S HAD IT A BIT ROUGH.
JOHN, ABBY-- KHALID'S BEGUN THE RITUAL. WE'VE OPENED A PORTAL TO THE MOUNTAIN.
BOBO AND I WILL STAY HERE.
JOHN, YOU'LL NEED TO TAKE OUR PRISONER WITH YOU.
OH, DON'T YOU FRET, CHIEF.
"I'LL MAKE SURE WOODRUE'S TAKEN CARE OF."
CONSTANTINE...
EVERYTHING ALL RI--
YOU'RE GOING TO SHUT UP AND LISTEN NOW, WOODRUE.
I KNOW IT WAS YOU.
WH-WHAT?
THE VINE IN THE ROT.* THE ONE THAT PUT ABBY INTO HER DREAMS. IT HAD TO COME FROM YOU.
*THE AYAHUASCA VINE SEEN IN JLD #21!
BUT WE FOUND ABBY. ZEE IS HURT AND DIANA IS ANGRY. NO TELLING WHAT THEY'LL DO IF THEY FIND OUT YOU DID THIS.
WHAT DO YOU WANT?
AT THE RITUAL...
...YOU'RE GOING TO BE A GOOD LITTLE PETAL AND DO EXACTLY AS I TELL YOU.

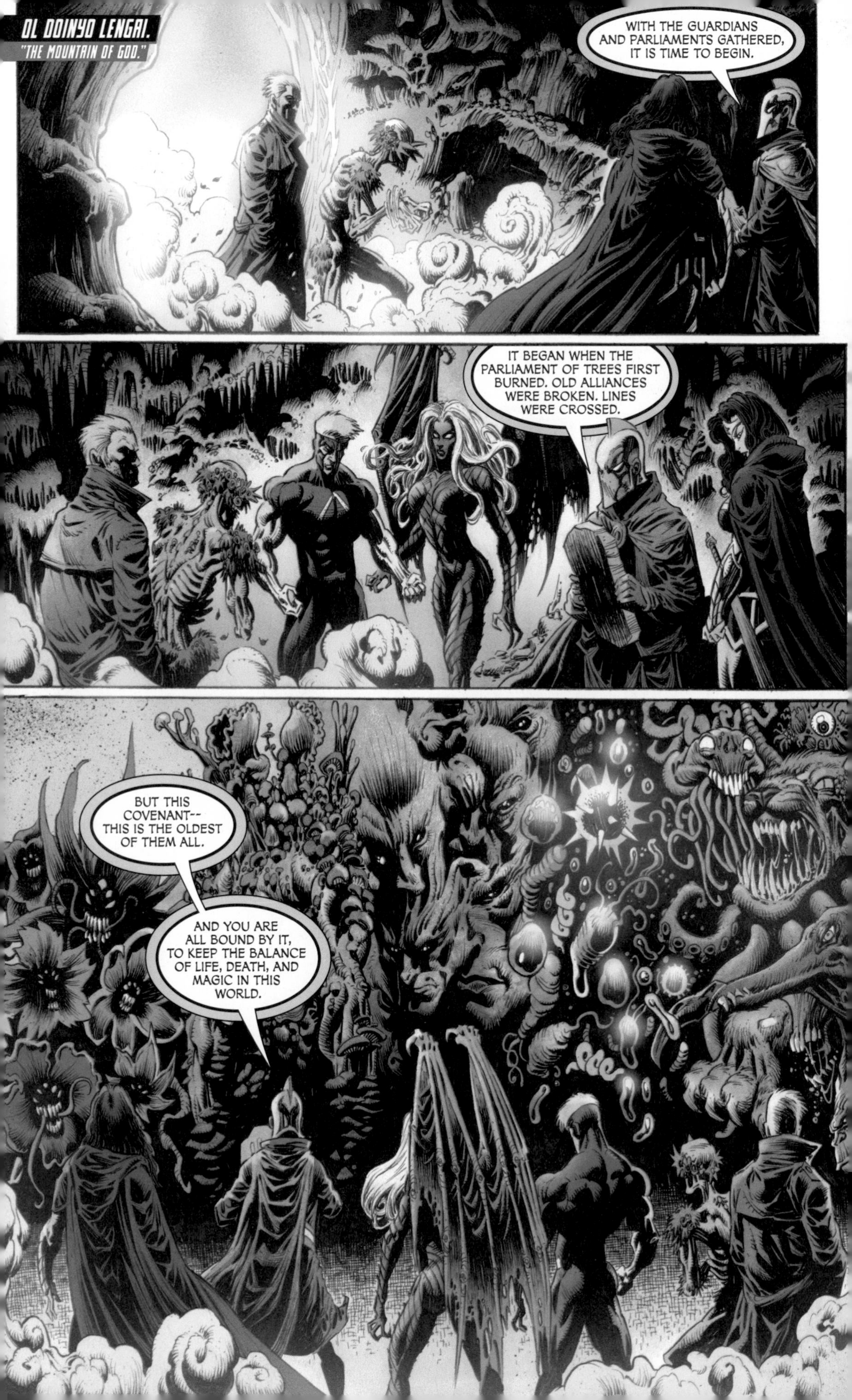
OL DOINYO LENGAI.
"THE MOUNTAIN OF GOD."
WITH THE GUARDIANS AND PARLIAMENTS GATHERED, IT IS TIME TO BEGIN.
IT BEGAN WHEN THE PARLIAMENT OF TREES FIRST BURNED. OLD ALLIANCES WERE BROKEN. LINES WERE CROSSED.
BUT THIS COVENANT-- THIS IS THE OLDEST OF THEM ALL.
AND YOU ARE ALL BOUND BY IT, TO KEEP THE BALANCE OF LIFE, DEATH, AND MAGIC IN THIS WORLD.

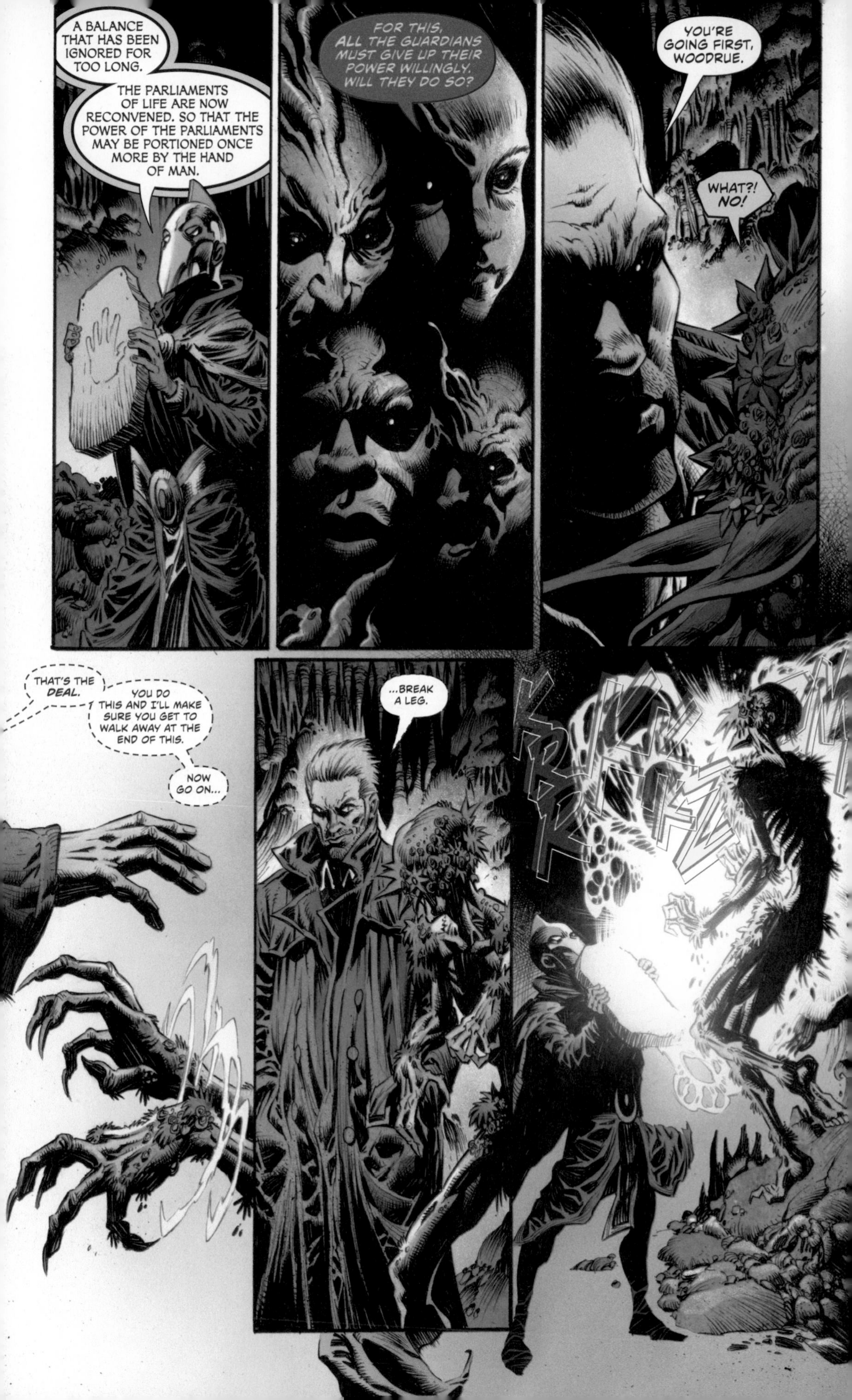
A BALANCE THAT HAS BEEN IGNORED FOR TOO LONG.
THE PARLIAMENTS OF LIFE ARE NOW RECONVENED. SO THAT THE POWER OF THE PARLIAMENTS MAY BE PORTIONED ONCE MORE BY THE HAND OF MAN.
FOR THIS, ALL THE GUARDIANS MUST GIVE UP THEIR POWER WILLINGLY. WILL THEY DO SO?
YOU'RE GOING FIRST, WOODRUE.
WHAT?! NO!
THAT'S THE DEAL.
YOU DO THIS AND I'LL MAKE SURE YOU GET TO WALK AWAY AT THE END OF THIS.
NOW GO ON...
...BREAK A LEG.
KRRZZK

I'LL GO NEXT...

NNNGUH!

≶HUFF≶

≶HUFF≶

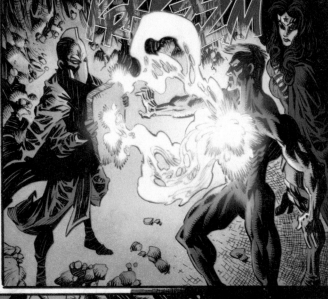

FRKSSZM

I'VE GOT YOU, BAKER.

ABIGAIL, THE ROT IS NEXT.

I...I'M SORRY.

BUT THIS IS--

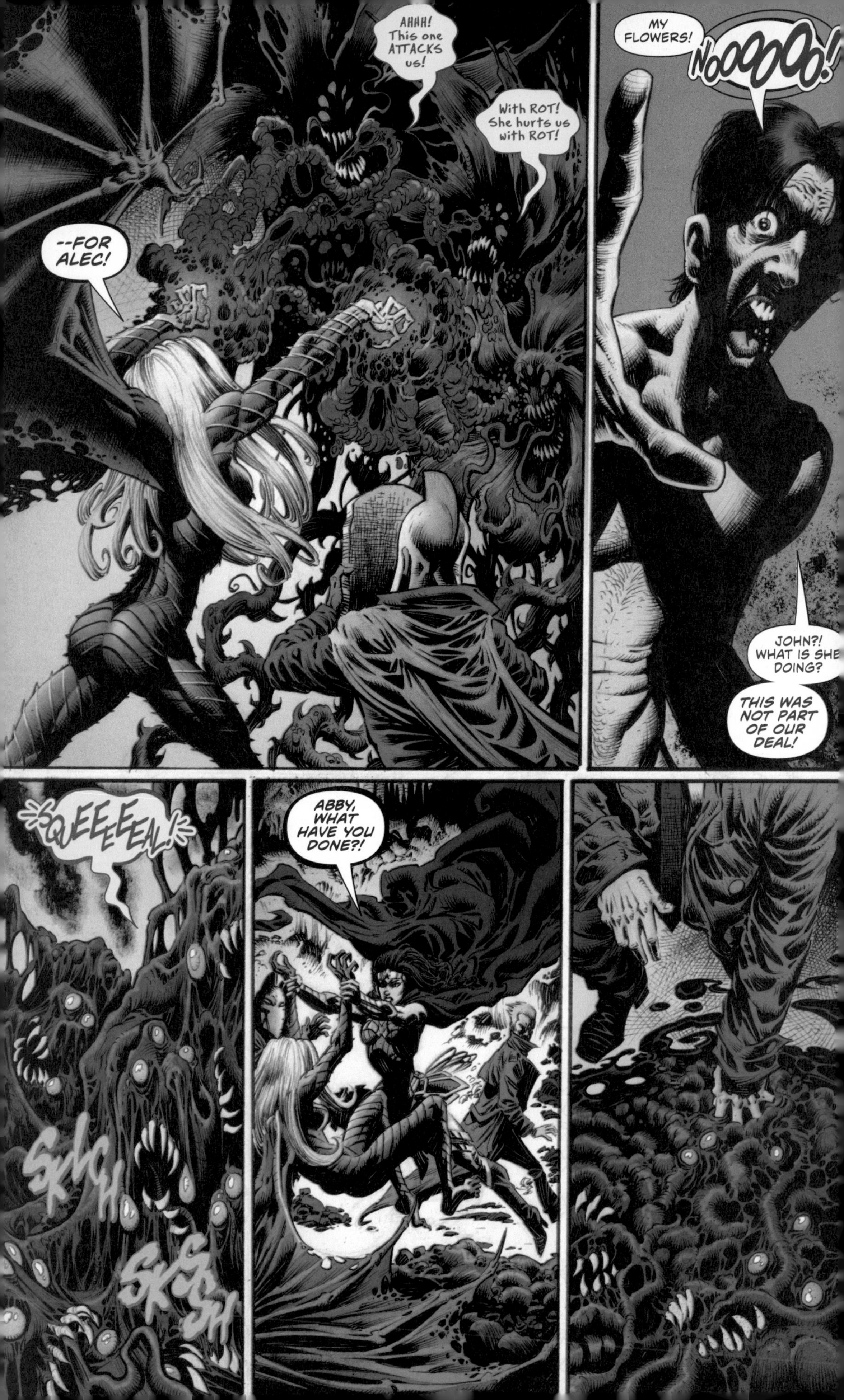
AHHH! This one ATTACKS us!
With ROT! She hurts us with ROT!
--FOR ALEC!
MY FLOWERS!
NOOOOOO!
JOHN?! WHAT IS SHE DOING?
THIS WAS NOT PART OF OUR DEAL!
SQUEEEEEAL!
SKLCH
SKSSH
ABBY, WHAT HAVE YOU DONE?!

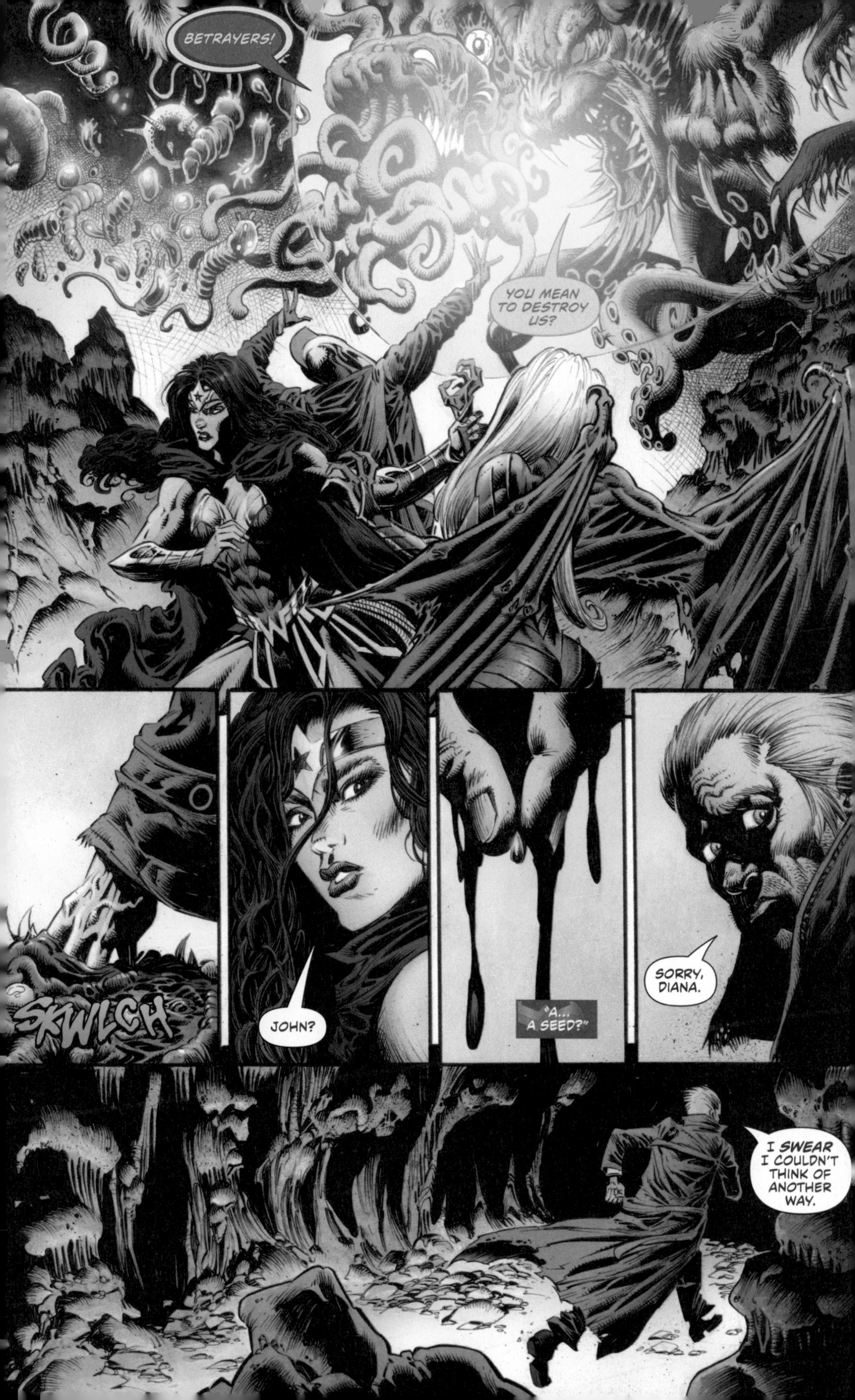
BETRAYERS!
YOU MEAN TO DESTROY US?
SKWLCH
JOHN?
"A... A SEED?"
SORRY, DIANA.
I SWEAR I COULDN'T THINK OF ANOTHER WAY.

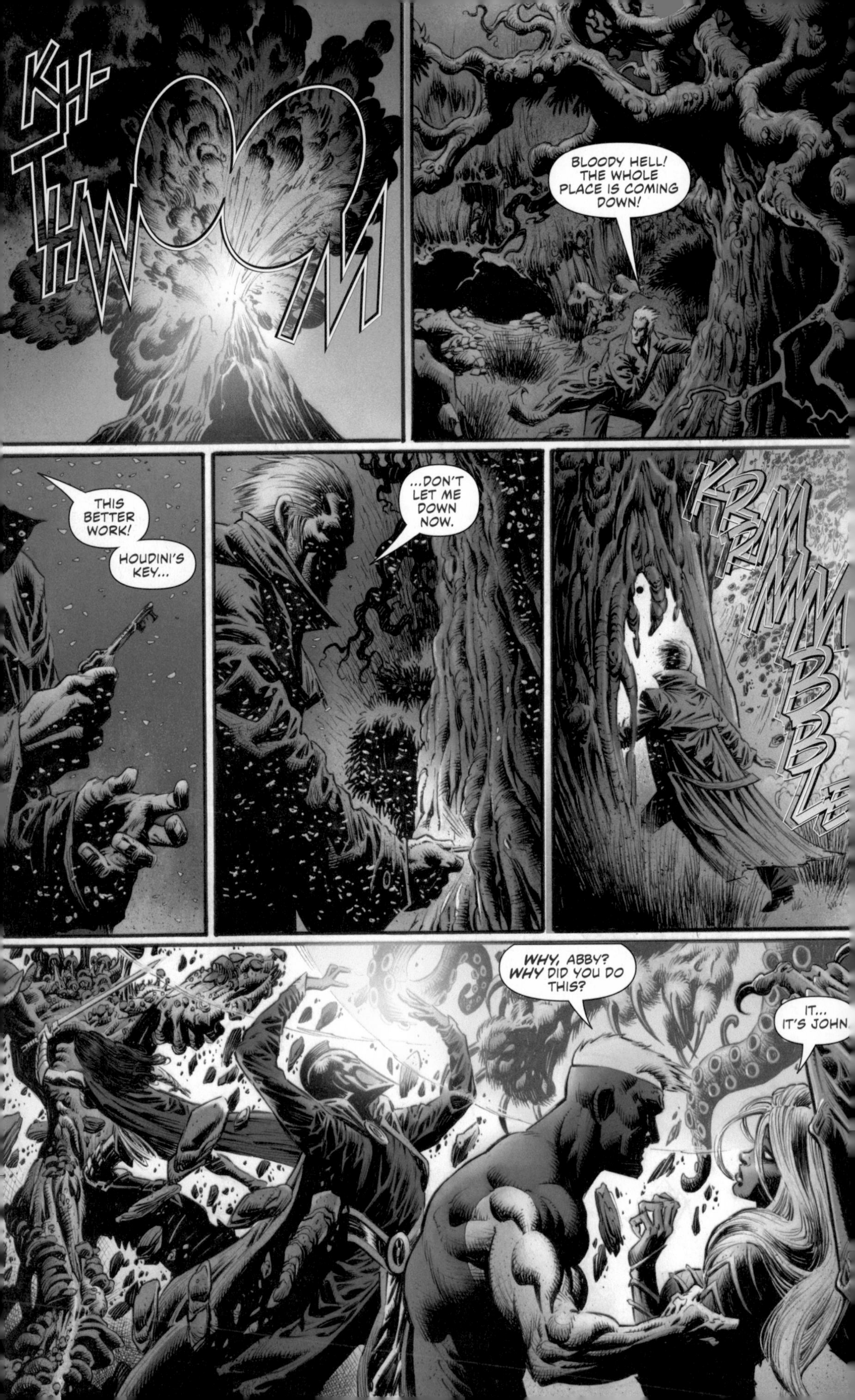
KH-THWOOM
BLOODY HELL! THE WHOLE PLACE IS COMING DOWN!
THIS BETTER WORK!
HOUDINI'S KEY...
...DON'T LET ME DOWN NOW.
KRRMMMBBLE
WHY, ABBY? WHY DID YOU DO THIS?
IT... IT'S JOHN

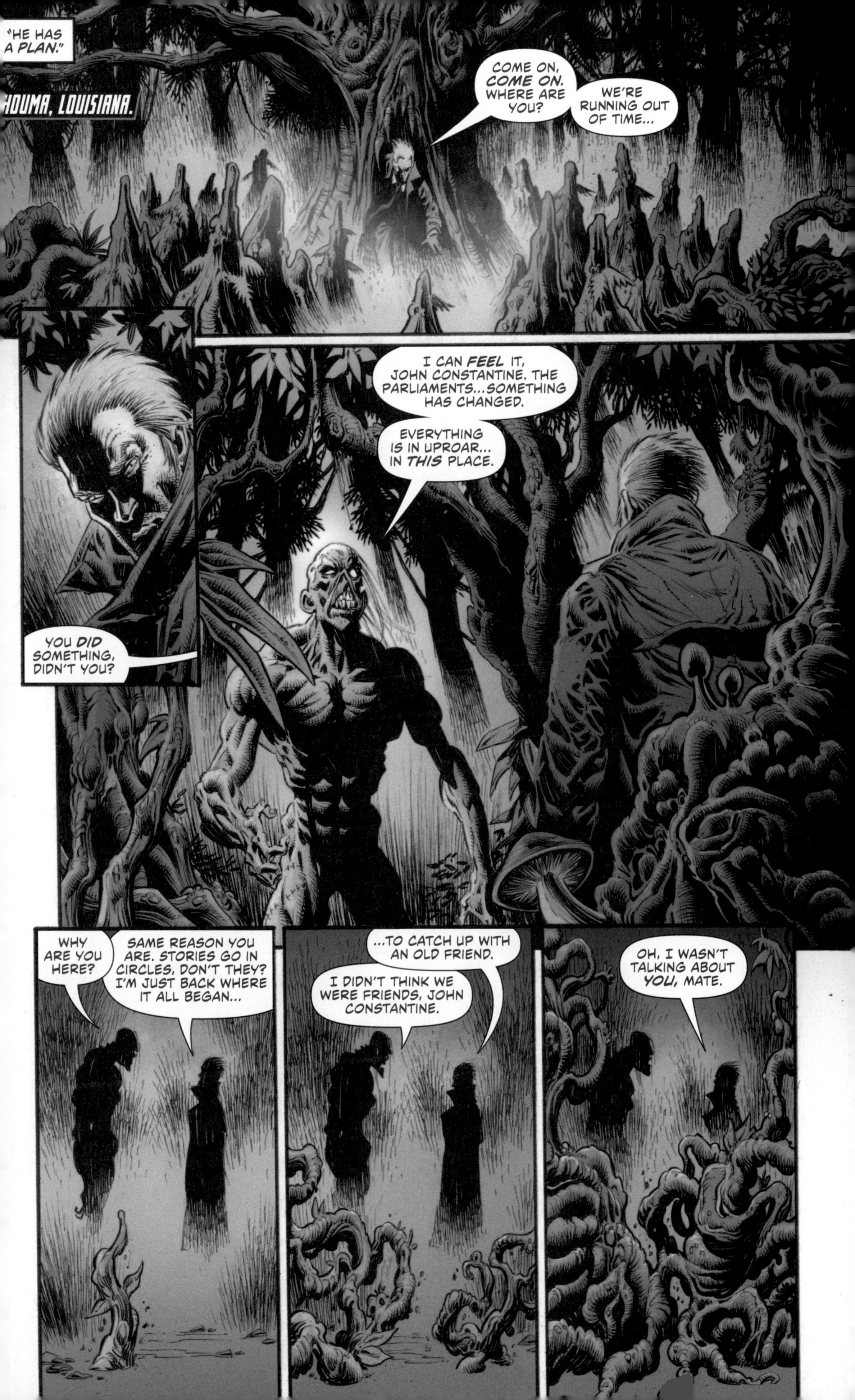
"HE HAS A PLAN."
HOUMA, LOUISIANA.
COME ON, COME ON. WHERE ARE YOU?
WE'RE RUNNING OUT OF TIME...
I CAN FEEL IT, JOHN CONSTANTINE. THE PARLIAMENTS...SOMETHING HAS CHANGED.
EVERYTHING IS IN UPROAR... IN THIS PLACE.
YOU DID SOMETHING, DIDN'T YOU?
WHY ARE YOU HERE?
SAME REASON YOU ARE. STORIES GO IN CIRCLES, DON'T THEY? I'M JUST BACK WHERE IT ALL BEGAN...
...TO CATCH UP WITH AN OLD FRIEND.
I DIDN'T THINK WE WERE FRIENDS, JOHN CONSTANTINE.
OH, I WASN'T TALKING ABOUT YOU, MATE.

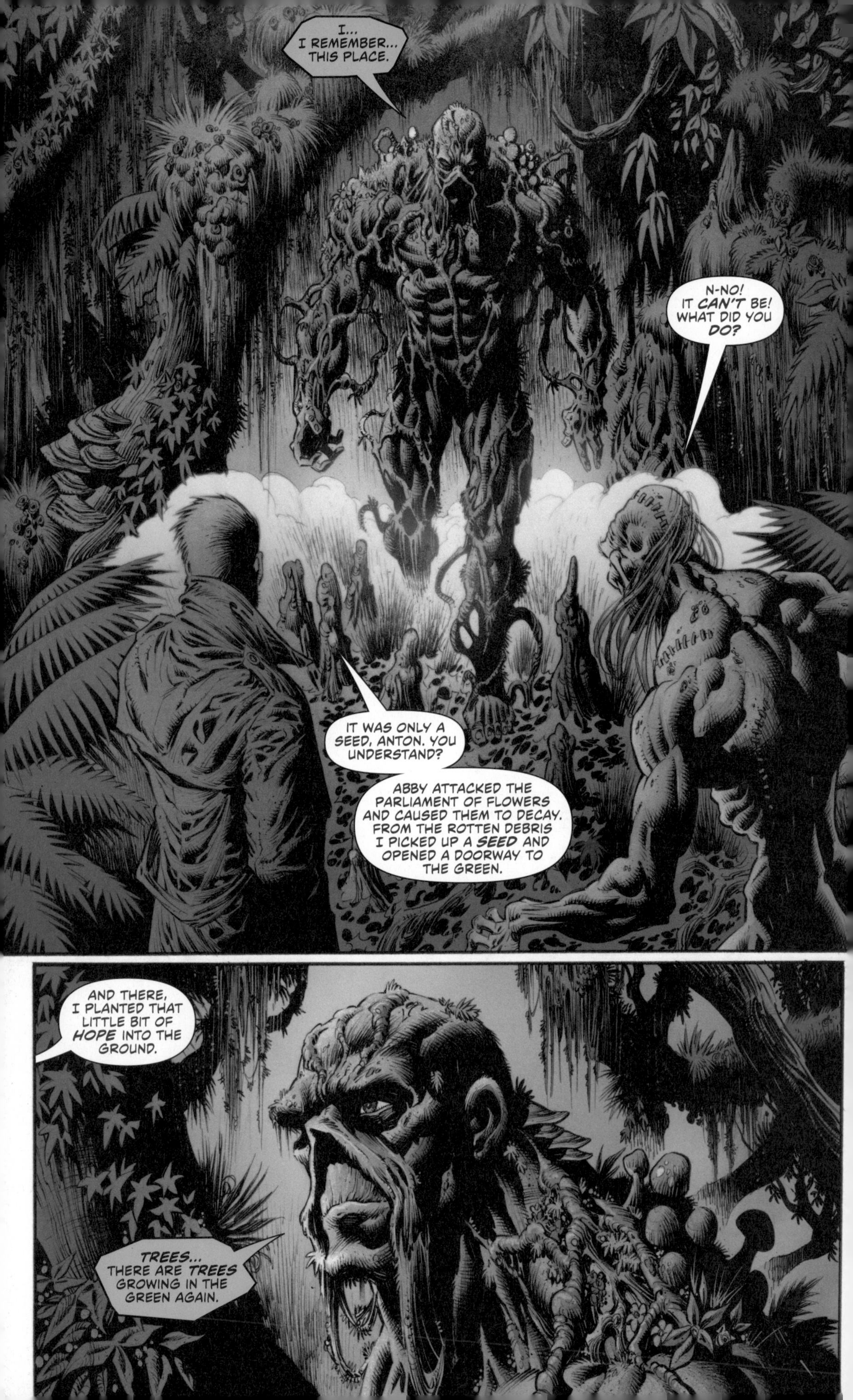
I...
I REMEMBER...
THIS PLACE.
N-NO!
IT CAN'T BE!
WHAT DID YOU
DO?
IT WAS ONLY A
SEED, ANTON. YOU
UNDERSTAND?
ABBY ATTACKED THE
PARLIAMENT OF FLOWERS
AND CAUSED THEM TO DECAY.
FROM THE ROTTEN DEBRIS
I PICKED UP A SEED AND
OPENED A DOORWAY TO
THE GREEN.
AND THERE,
I PLANTED THAT
LITTLE BIT OF
HOPE INTO THE
GROUND.
TREES...
THERE ARE TREES
GROWING IN THE
GREEN AGAIN.

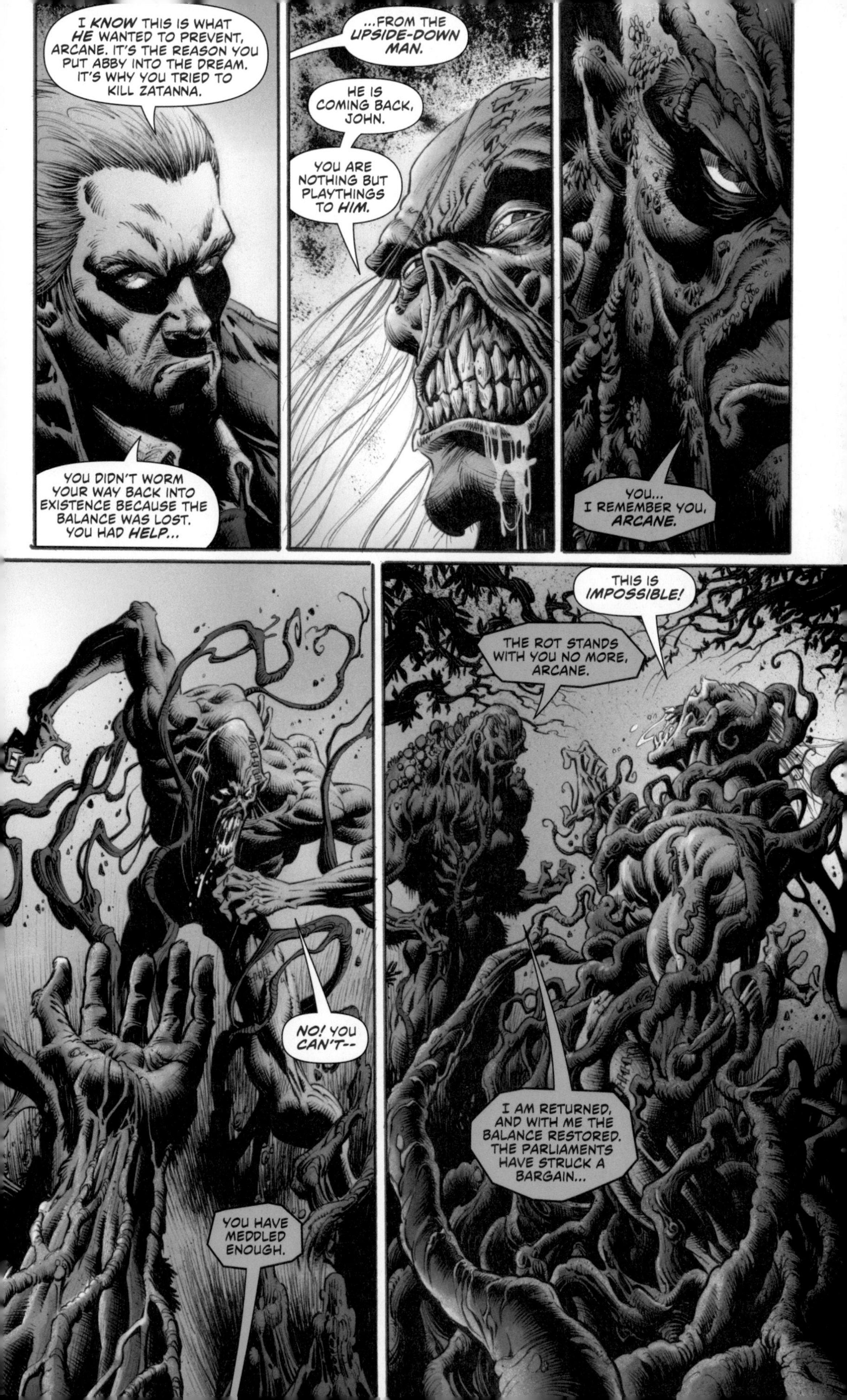

I KNOW THIS IS WHAT HE WANTED TO PREVENT, ARCANE. IT'S THE REASON YOU PUT ABBY INTO THE DREAM. IT'S WHY YOU TRIED TO KILL ZATANNA.
YOU DIDN'T WORM YOUR WAY BACK INTO EXISTENCE BECAUSE THE BALANCE WAS LOST. YOU HAD HELP...
...FROM THE UPSIDE-DOWN MAN.
HE IS COMING BACK, JOHN.
YOU ARE NOTHING BUT PLAYTHINGS TO HIM.
YOU... I REMEMBER YOU, ARCANE.
NO! YOU CAN'T--
YOU HAVE MEDDLED ENOUGH.
THIS IS IMPOSSIBLE!
THE ROT STANDS WITH YOU NO MORE, ARCANE.
I AM RETURNED, AND WITH ME THE BALANCE RESTORED. THE PARLIAMENTS HAVE STRUCK A BARGAIN...

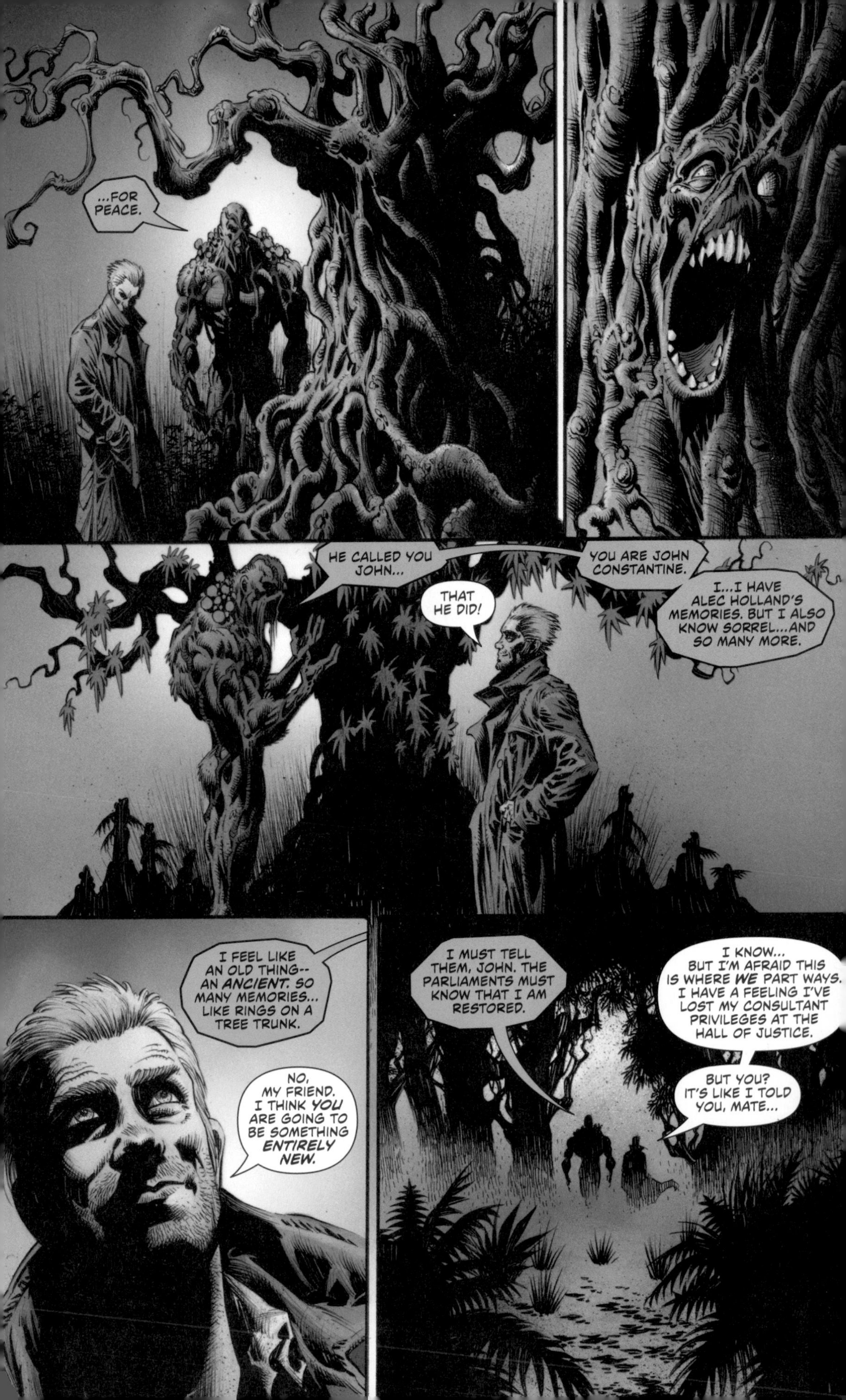
...FOR PEACE.
HE CALLED YOU JOHN...
YOU ARE JOHN CONSTANTINE.
THAT HE DID!
I...I HAVE ALEC HOLLAND'S MEMORIES. BUT I ALSO KNOW SORREL...AND SO MANY MORE.
I FEEL LIKE AN OLD THING-- AN ANCIENT. SO MANY MEMORIES... LIKE RINGS ON A TREE TRUNK.
NO, MY FRIEND. I THINK YOU ARE GOING TO BE SOMETHING ENTIRELY NEW.
I MUST TELL THEM, JOHN. THE PARLIAMENTS MUST KNOW THAT I AM RESTORED.
I KNOW... BUT I'M AFRAID THIS IS WHERE WE PART WAYS. I HAVE A FEELING I'VE LOST MY CONSULTANT PRIVILEGES AT THE HALL OF JUSTICE.
BUT YOU? IT'S LIKE I TOLD YOU, MATE...

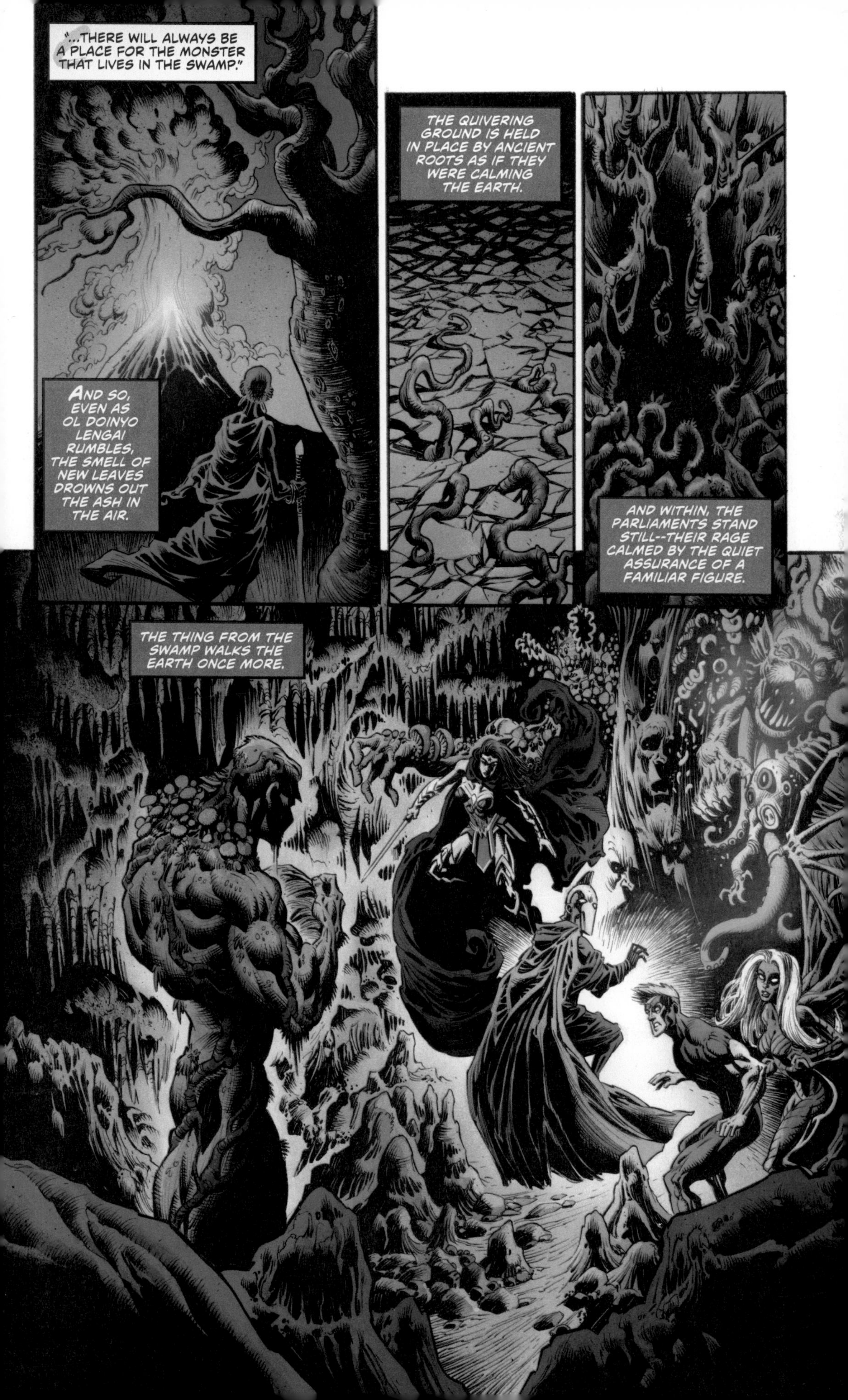
"...THERE WILL ALWAYS BE A PLACE FOR THE MONSTER THAT LIVES IN THE SWAMP."
AND SO, EVEN AS OL DOINYO LENGAI RUMBLES, THE SMELL OF NEW LEAVES DROWNS OUT THE ASH IN THE AIR.
THE QUIVERING GROUND IS HELD IN PLACE BY ANCIENT ROOTS AS IF THEY WERE CALMING THE EARTH.
AND WITHIN, THE PARLIAMENTS STAND STILL--THEIR RAGE CALMED BY THE QUIET ASSURANCE OF A FAMILIAR FIGURE.
THE THING FROM THE SWAMP WALKS THE EARTH ONCE MORE.

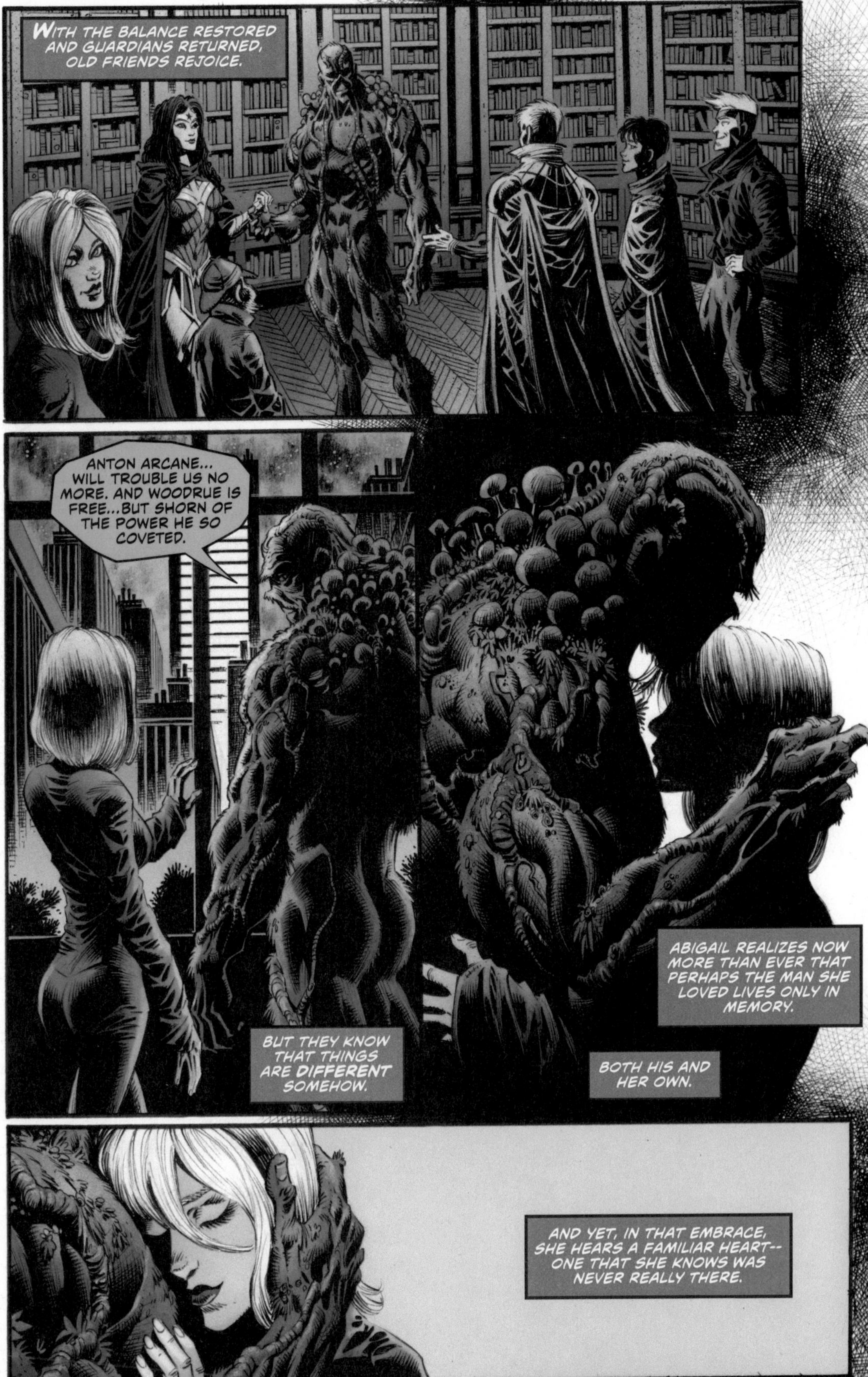
WITH THE BALANCE RESTORED AND GUARDIANS RETURNED, OLD FRIENDS REJOICE.
ANTON ARCANE... WILL TROUBLE US NO MORE. AND WOODRUE IS FREE...BUT SHORN OF THE POWER HE SO COVETED.
BUT THEY KNOW THAT THINGS ARE DIFFERENT SOMEHOW.
ABIGAIL REALIZES NOW MORE THAN EVER THAT PERHAPS THE MAN SHE LOVED LIVES ONLY IN MEMORY.
BOTH HIS AND HER OWN.
AND YET, IN THAT EMBRACE, SHE HEARS A FAMILIAR HEART-- ONE THAT SHE KNOWS WAS NEVER REALLY THERE.

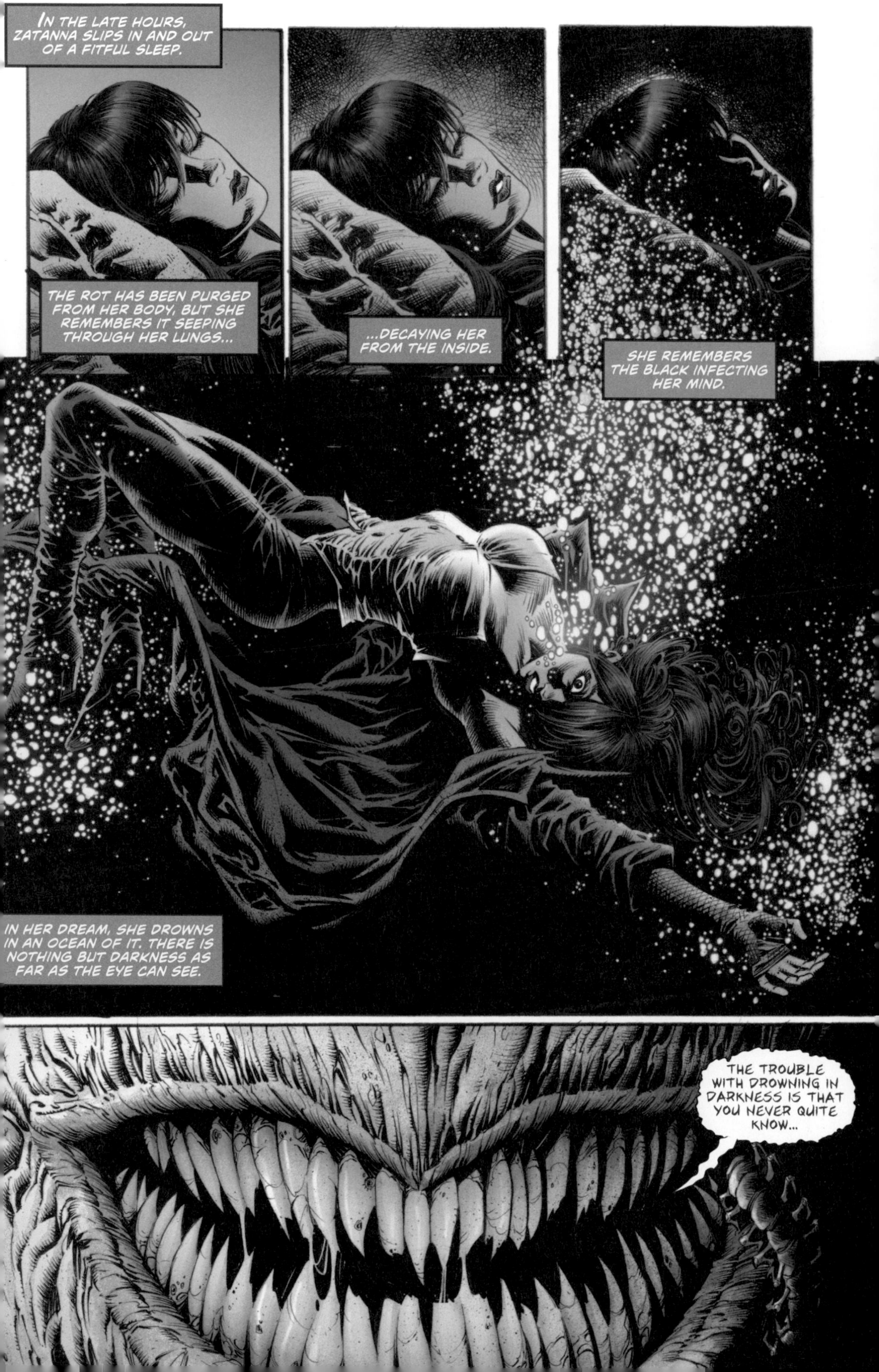
IN THE LATE HOURS, ZATANNA SLIPS IN AND OUT OF A FITFUL SLEEP.
THE ROT HAS BEEN PURGED FROM HER BODY, BUT SHE REMEMBERS IT SEEPING THROUGH HER LUNGS...
...DECAYING HER FROM THE INSIDE.
SHE REMEMBERS THE BLACK INFECTING HER MIND.
IN HER DREAM, SHE DROWNS IN AN OCEAN OF IT. THERE IS NOTHING BUT DARKNESS AS FAR AS THE EYE CAN SEE.
THE TROUBLE WITH DROWNING IN DARKNESS IS THAT YOU NEVER QUITE KNOW...

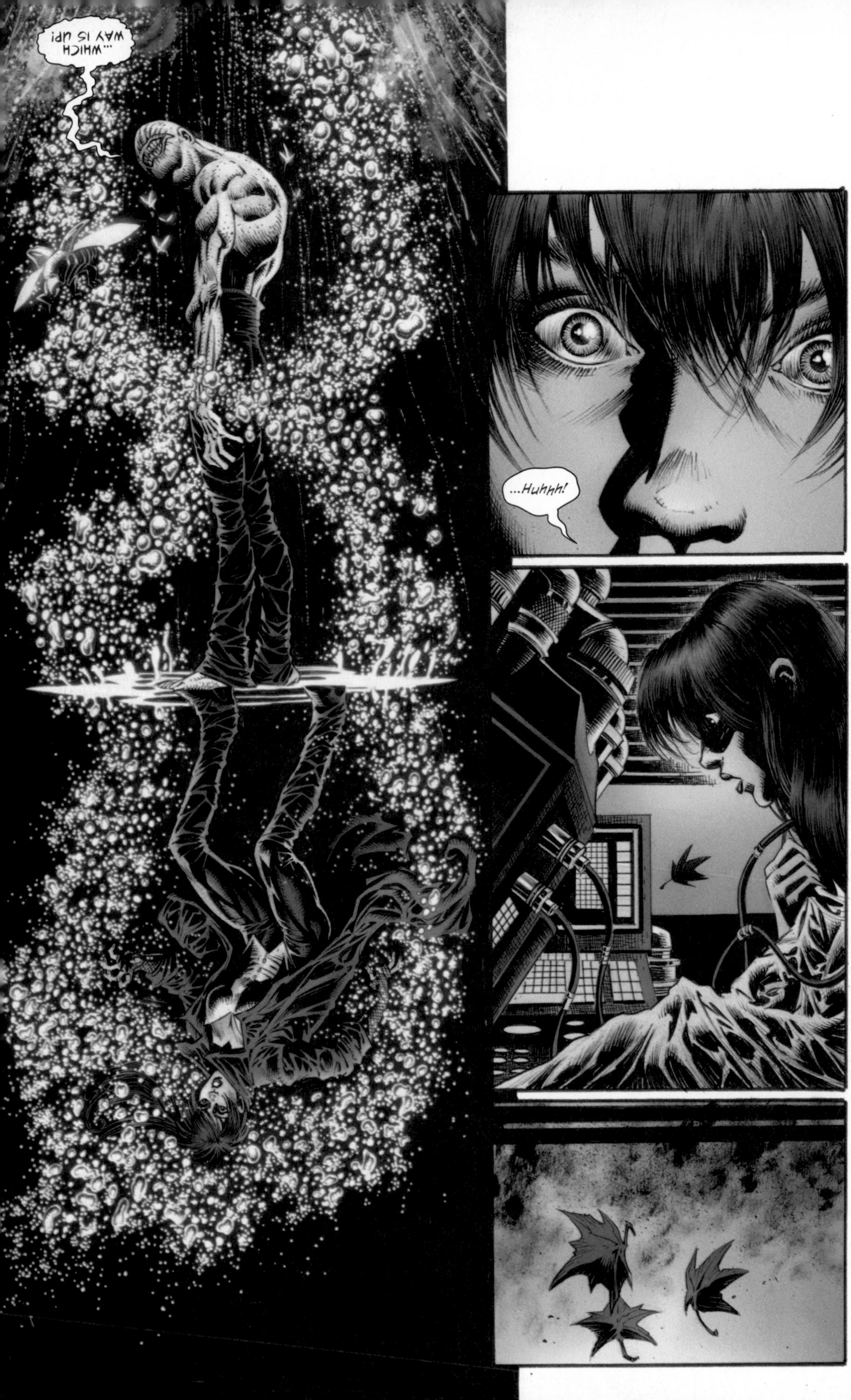
...WHICH WAY IS UP!
...Huhhh!

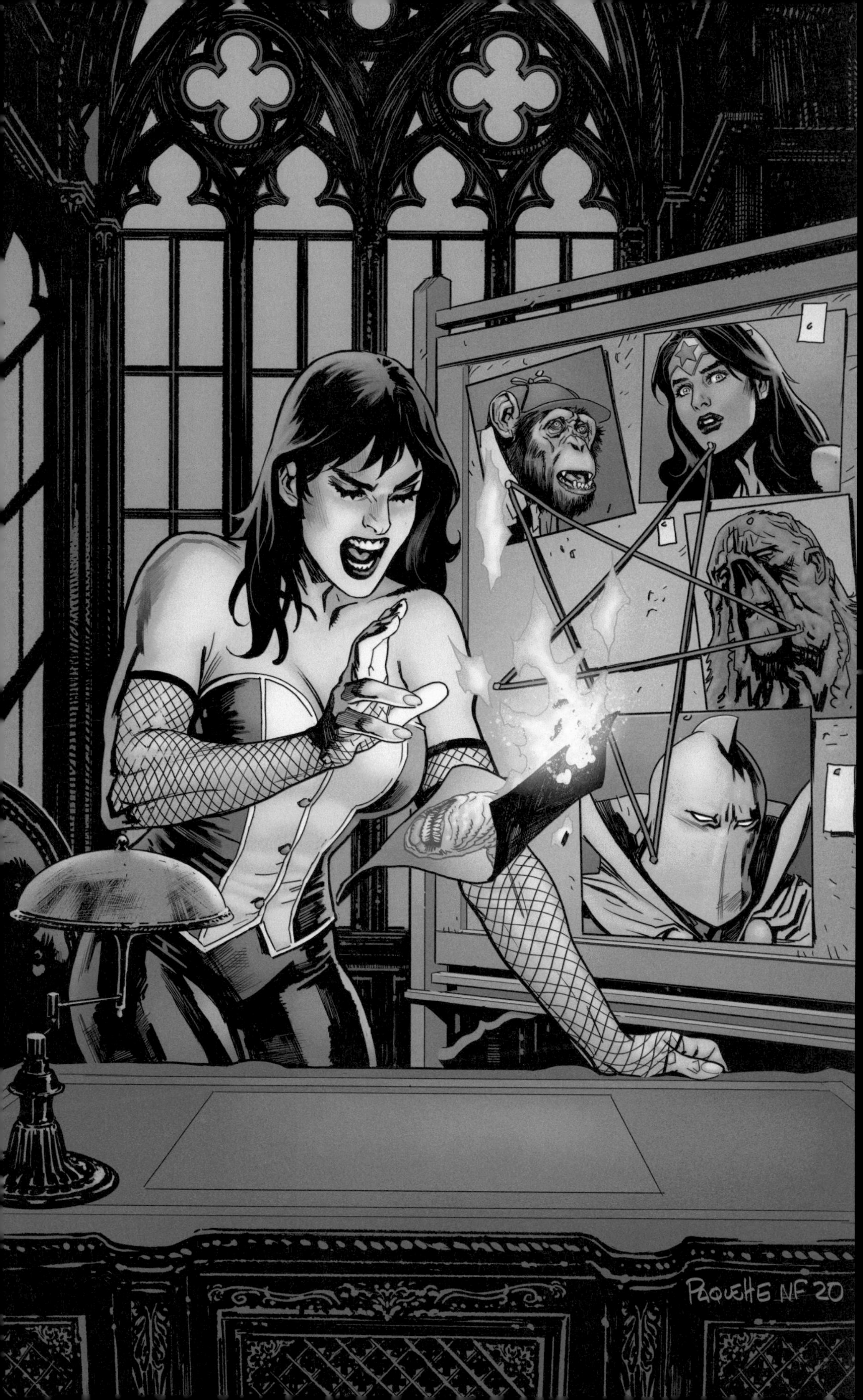
PAQUETTE NF 20

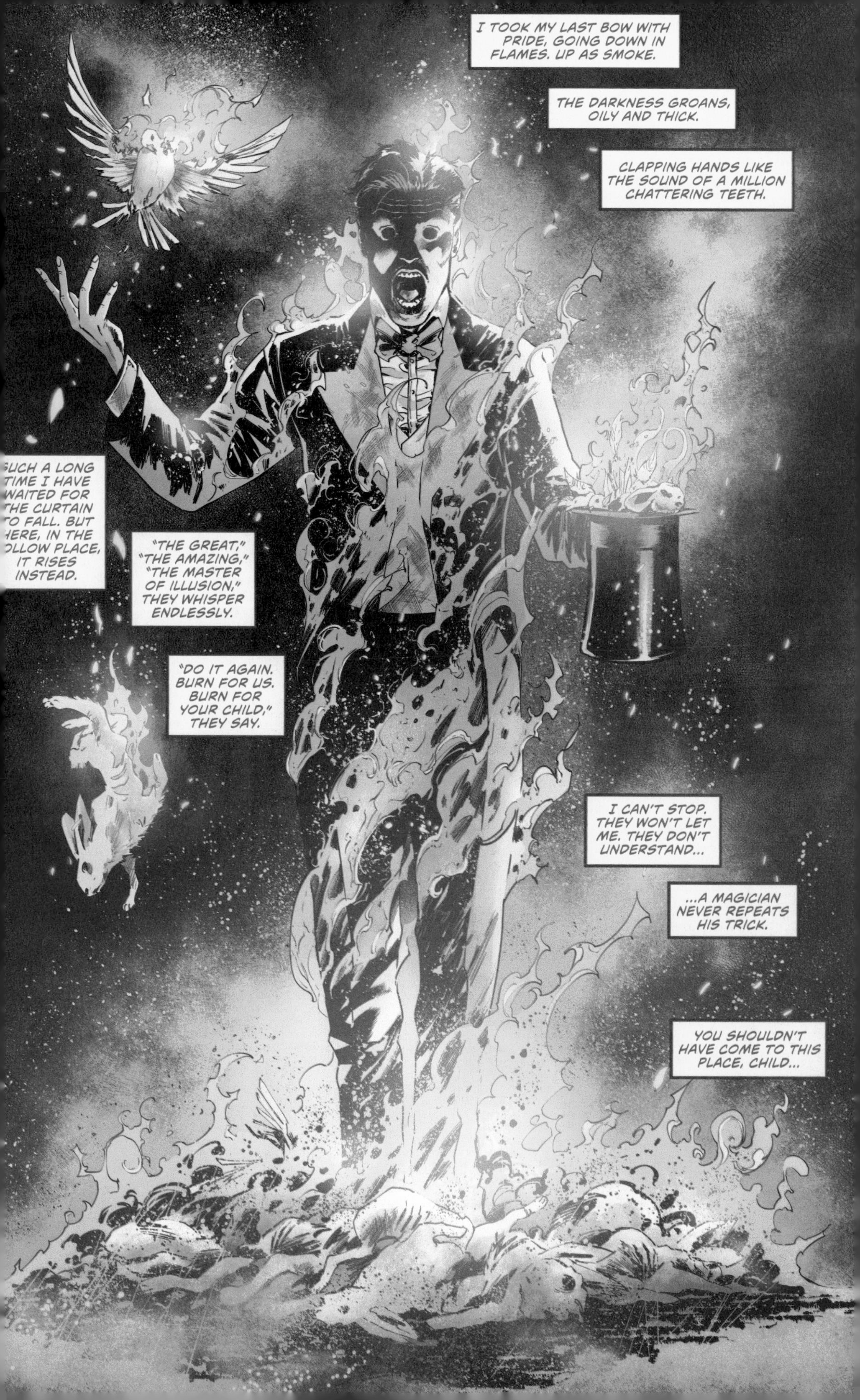

I TOOK MY LAST BOW WITH PRIDE, GOING DOWN IN FLAMES. UP AS SMOKE.
THE DARKNESS GROANS, OILY AND THICK.
CLAPPING HANDS LIKE THE SOUND OF A MILLION CHATTERING TEETH.
SUCH A LONG TIME I HAVE WAITED FOR THE CURTAIN TO FALL. BUT HERE, IN THE OLLOW PLACE, IT RISES INSTEAD.
"THE GREAT," "THE AMAZING," "THE MASTER OF ILLUSION," THEY WHISPER ENDLESSLY.
"DO IT AGAIN. BURN FOR US. BURN FOR YOUR CHILD," THEY SAY.
I CAN'T STOP. THEY WON'T LET ME. THEY DON'T UNDERSTAND...
...A MAGICIAN NEVER REPEATS HIS TRICK.
YOU SHOULDN'T HAVE COME TO THIS PLACE, CHILD...

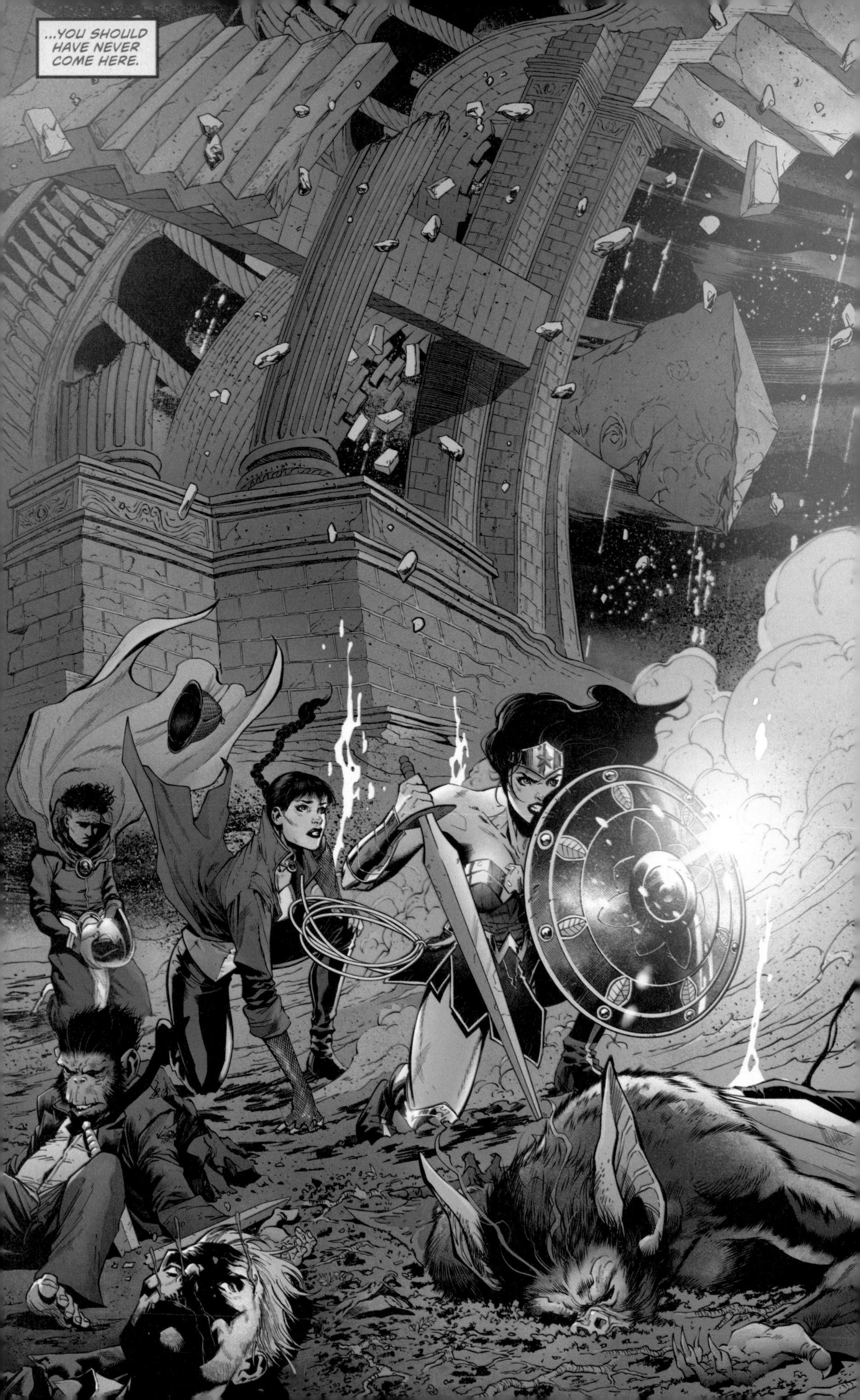
...YOU SHOULD HAVE NEVER COME HERE.

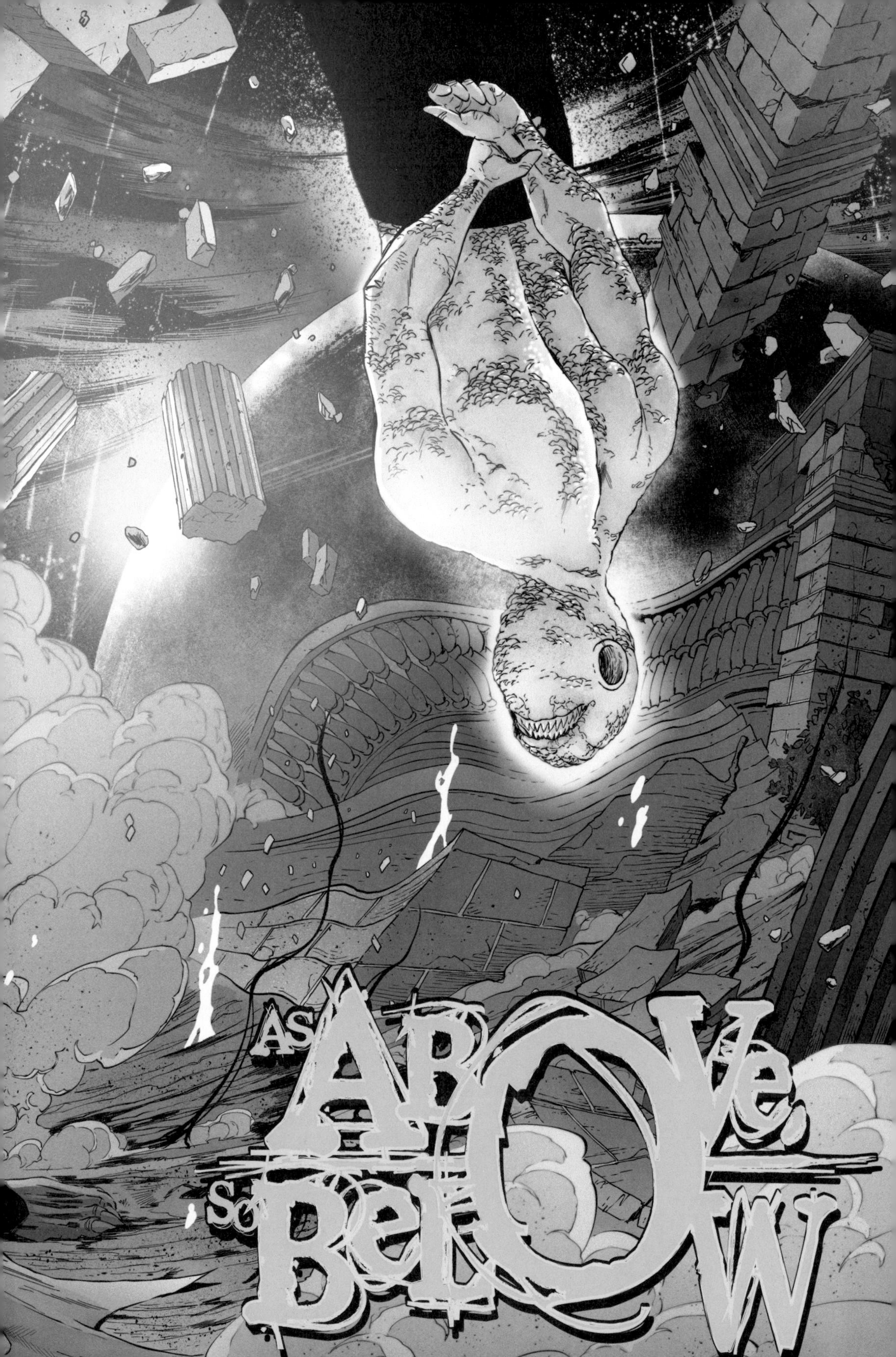
As Above So Below

RAM V WRITER • AMANCAY NAHUELPAN ARTIST • JUNE CHUNG COLORIST • ROB LEIGH LETTERER
YANICK PAQUETTE AND NATHAN FAIRBAIRN COVER • JOHN GIANG VARIANT COVER
ANDREA SHEA ASSOCIATE EDITOR • ALEX R. CARR EDITOR

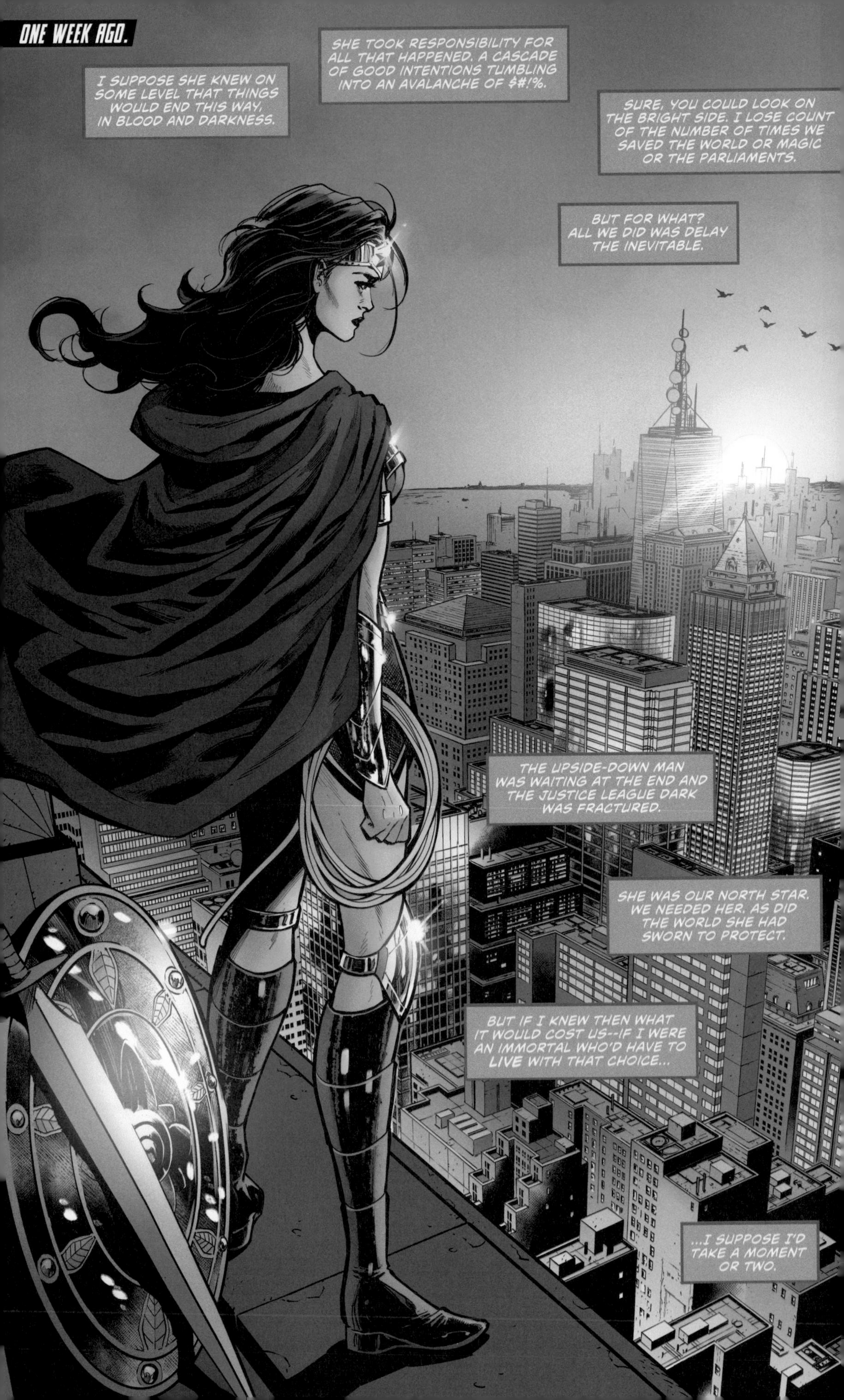
ONE WEEK AGO.
I SUPPOSE SHE KNEW ON SOME LEVEL THAT THINGS WOULD END THIS WAY, IN BLOOD AND DARKNESS.
SHE TOOK RESPONSIBILITY FOR ALL THAT HAPPENED. A CASCADE OF GOOD INTENTIONS TUMBLING INTO AN AVALANCHE OF $#!%.
SURE, YOU COULD LOOK ON THE BRIGHT SIDE. I LOSE COUNT OF THE NUMBER OF TIMES WE SAVED THE WORLD OR MAGIC OR THE PARLIAMENTS.
BUT FOR WHAT? ALL WE DID WAS DELAY THE INEVITABLE.
THE UPSIDE-DOWN MAN WAS WAITING AT THE END AND THE JUSTICE LEAGUE DARK WAS FRACTURED.
SHE WAS OUR NORTH STAR. WE NEEDED HER. AS DID THE WORLD SHE HAD SWORN TO PROTECT.
BUT IF I KNEW THEN WHAT IT WOULD COST US--IF I WERE AN IMMORTAL WHO'D HAVE TO LIVE WITH THAT CHOICE...
...I SUPPOSE I'D TAKE A MOMENT OR TWO.

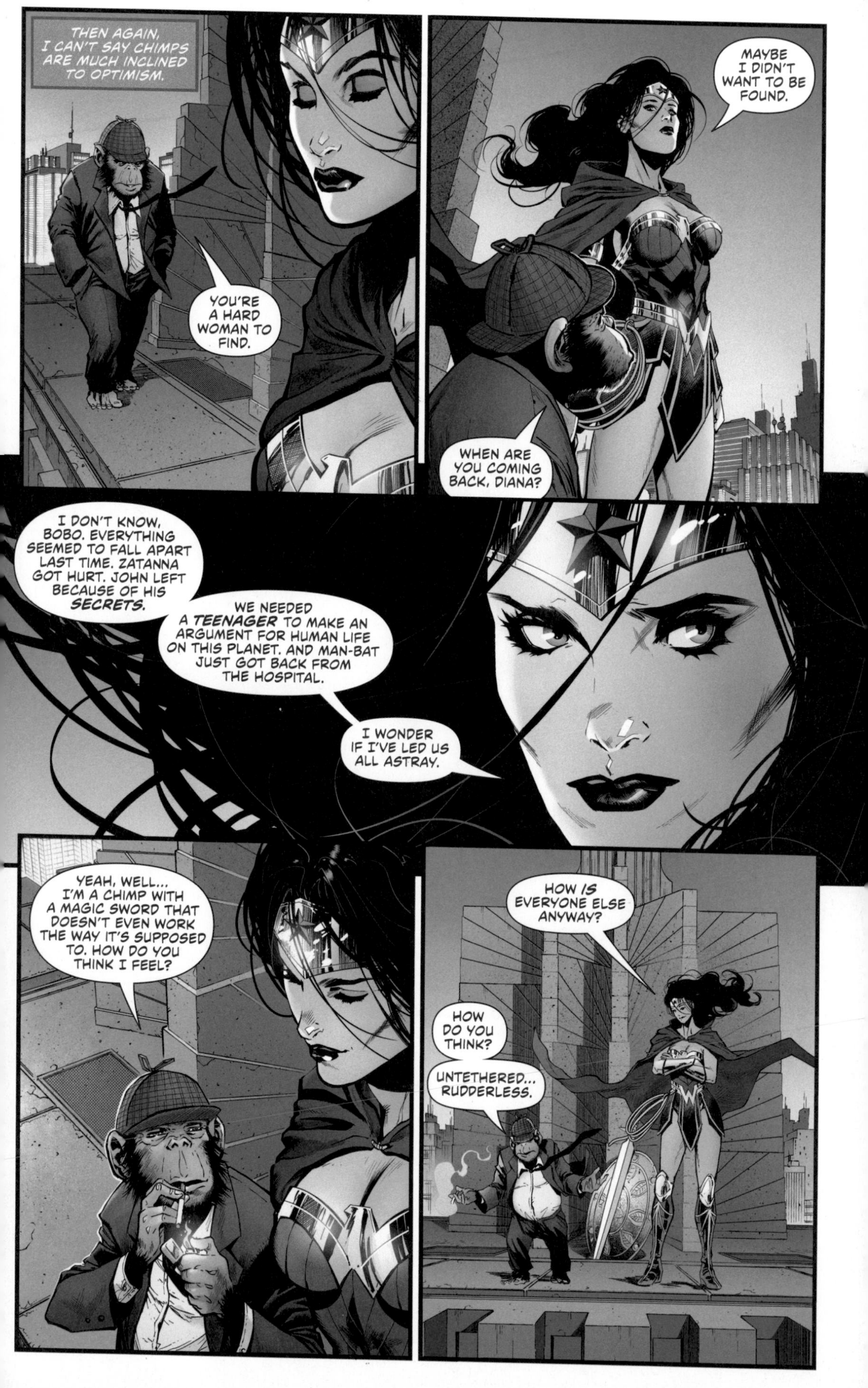
THEN AGAIN, I CAN'T SAY CHIMPS ARE MUCH INCLINED TO OPTIMISM.
YOU'RE A HARD WOMAN TO FIND.
MAYBE I DIDN'T WANT TO BE FOUND.
WHEN ARE YOU COMING BACK, DIANA?
I DON'T KNOW, BOBO. EVERYTHING SEEMED TO FALL APART LAST TIME. ZATANNA GOT HURT. JOHN LEFT BECAUSE OF HIS SECRETS.
WE NEEDED A TEENAGER TO MAKE AN ARGUMENT FOR HUMAN LIFE ON THIS PLANET. AND MAN-BAT JUST GOT BACK FROM THE HOSPITAL.
I WONDER IF I'VE LED US ALL ASTRAY.
YEAH, WELL... I'M A CHIMP WITH A MAGIC SWORD THAT DOESN'T EVEN WORK THE WAY IT'S SUPPOSED TO. HOW DO YOU THINK I FEEL?
HOW IS EVERYONE ELSE ANYWAY?
HOW DO YOU THINK?
UNTETHERED... RUDDERLESS.

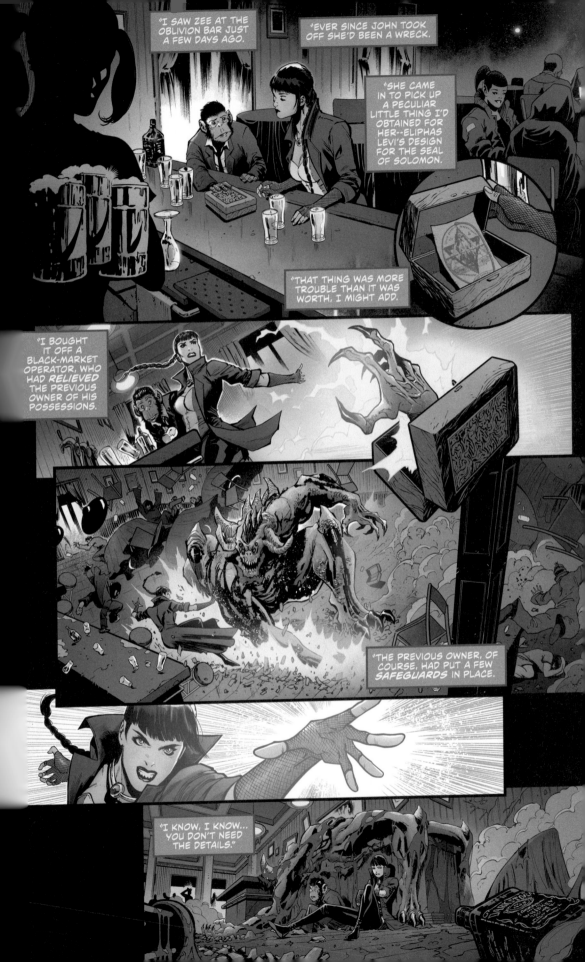

"I SAW ZEE AT THE OBLIVION BAR JUST A FEW DAYS AGO.

"EVER SINCE JOHN TOOK OFF SHE'D BEEN A WRECK.

"SHE CAME IN TO PICK UP A PECULIAR LITTLE THING I'D OBTAINED FOR HER--ELIPHAS LEVI'S DESIGN FOR THE SEAL OF SOLOMON.

"THAT THING WAS MORE TROUBLE THAN IT WAS WORTH, I MIGHT ADD.

"I BOUGHT IT OFF A BLACK-MARKET OPERATOR, WHO HAD *RELIEVED* THE PREVIOUS OWNER OF HIS POSSESSIONS.

"THE PREVIOUS OWNER, OF COURSE, HAD PUT A FEW *SAFEGUARDS* IN PLACE.

"I KNOW, I KNOW... YOU DON'T NEED THE DETAILS."

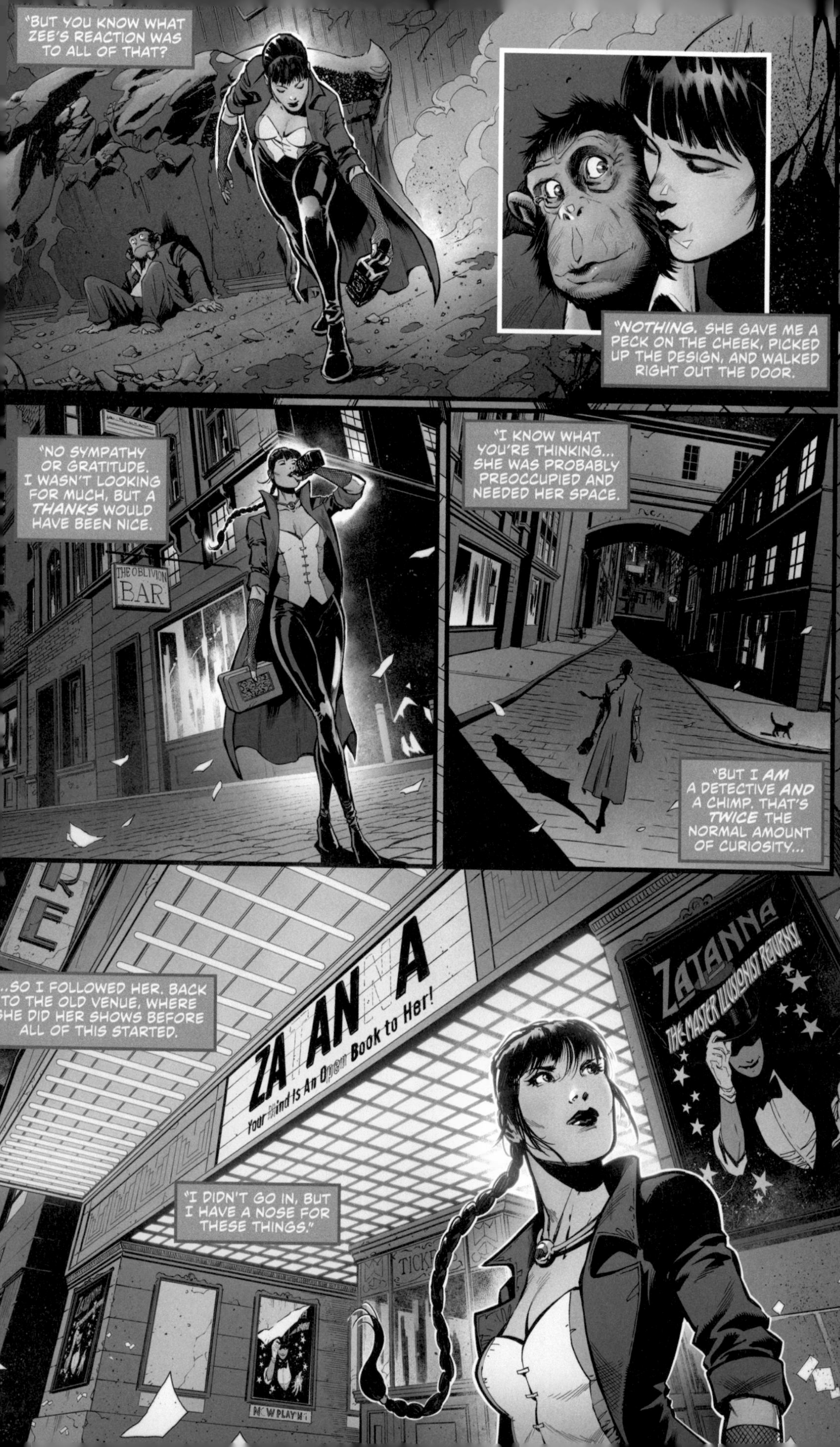
"BUT YOU KNOW WHAT ZEE'S REACTION WAS TO ALL OF THAT?
"NOTHING. SHE GAVE ME A PECK ON THE CHEEK, PICKED UP THE DESIGN, AND WALKED RIGHT OUT THE DOOR.
"NO SYMPATHY OR GRATITUDE. I WASN'T LOOKING FOR MUCH, BUT A THANKS WOULD HAVE BEEN NICE.
THE OBLIVION BAR
"I KNOW WHAT YOU'RE THINKING... SHE WAS PROBABLY PREOCCUPIED AND NEEDED HER SPACE.
"BUT I AM A DETECTIVE AND A CHIMP. THAT'S TWICE THE NORMAL AMOUNT OF CURIOSITY...
...SO I FOLLOWED HER. BACK TO THE OLD VENUE, WHERE SHE DID HER SHOWS BEFORE ALL OF THIS STARTED.
ZA AN A
Your Is An Open Book to Her!
ZATANNA
THE MASTER ILLUSIONIST RETURNS!
"I DIDN'T GO IN, BUT I HAVE A NOSE FOR THESE THINGS."

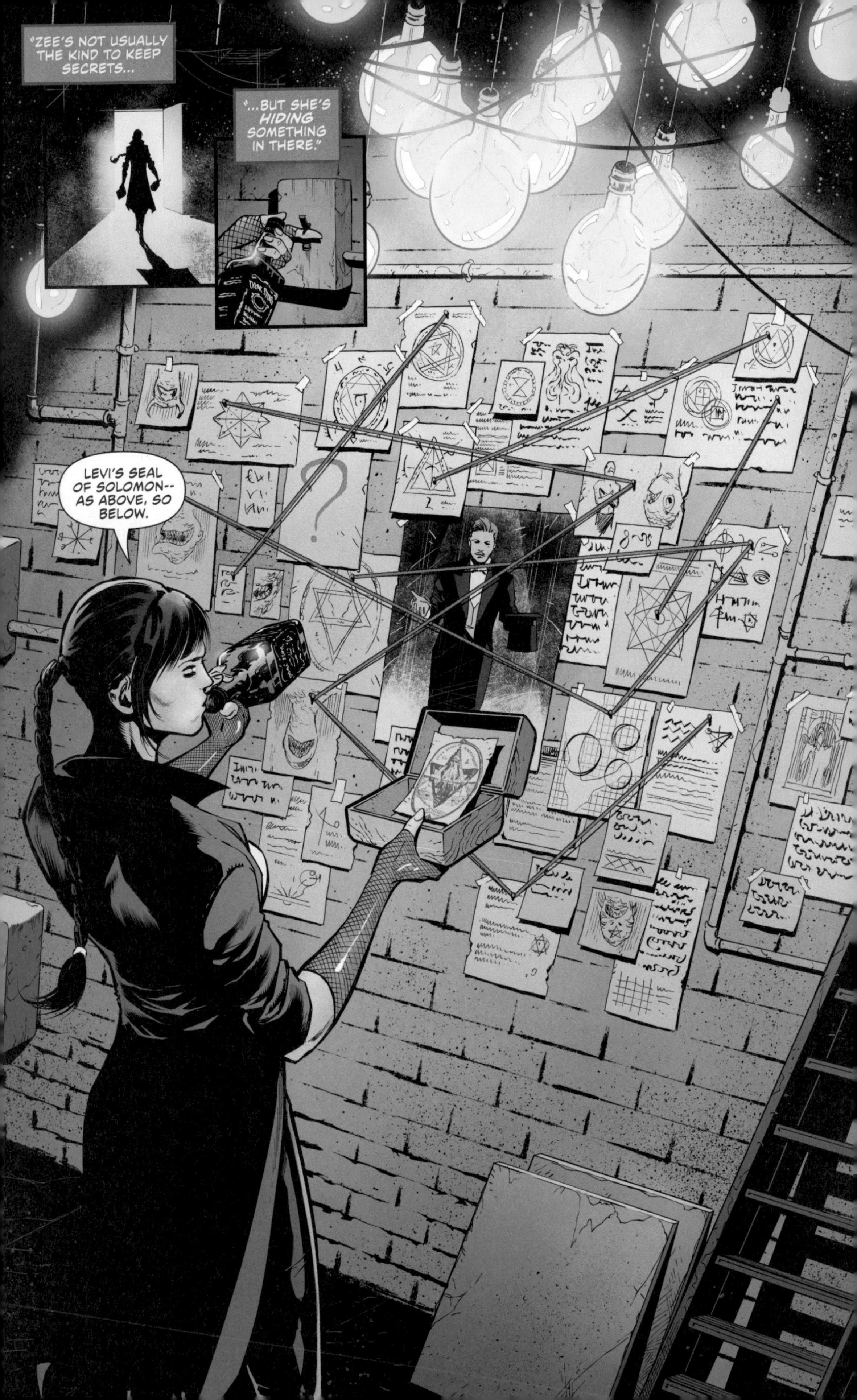
"ZEE'S NOT USUALLY THE KIND TO KEEP SECRETS...
"...BUT SHE'S HIDING SOMETHING IN THERE."
LEVI'S SEAL OF SOLOMON-- AS ABOVE, SO BELOW.

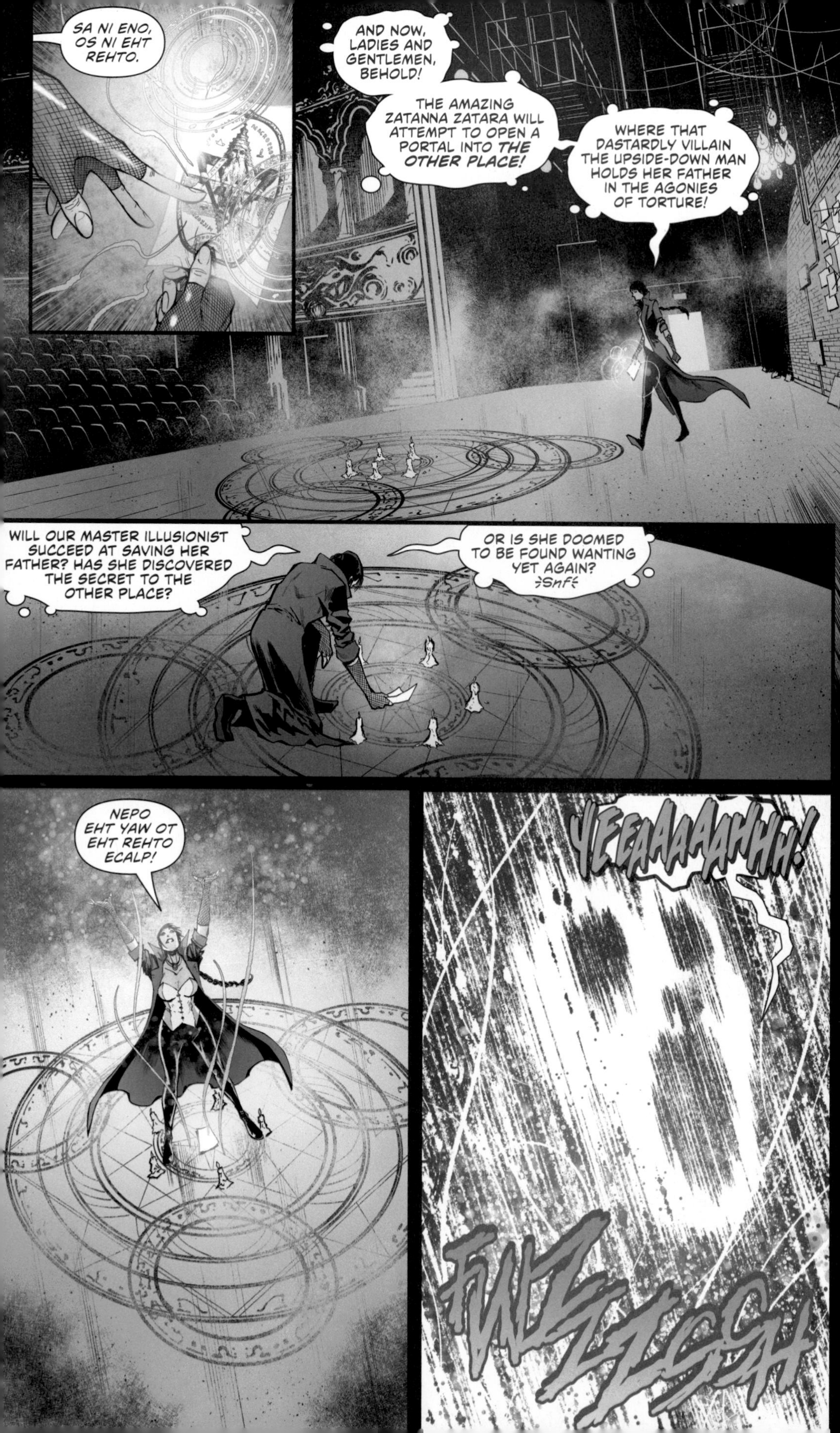
SA NI ENO, OS NI EHT REHTO.
AND NOW, LADIES AND GENTLEMEN, BEHOLD!
THE AMAZING ZATANNA ZATARA WILL ATTEMPT TO OPEN A PORTAL INTO *THE OTHER PLACE!*
WHERE THAT DASTARDLY VILLAIN THE UPSIDE-DOWN MAN HOLDS HER FATHER IN THE AGONIES OF TORTURE!
WILL OUR MASTER ILLUSIONIST SUCCEED AT SAVING HER FATHER? HAS SHE DISCOVERED THE SECRET TO THE OTHER PLACE?
OR IS SHE DOOMED TO BE FOUND WANTING YET AGAIN? *Snf*
NEPO EHT YAW OT EHT REHTO ECALP!
YEEAAAAAHHHH!

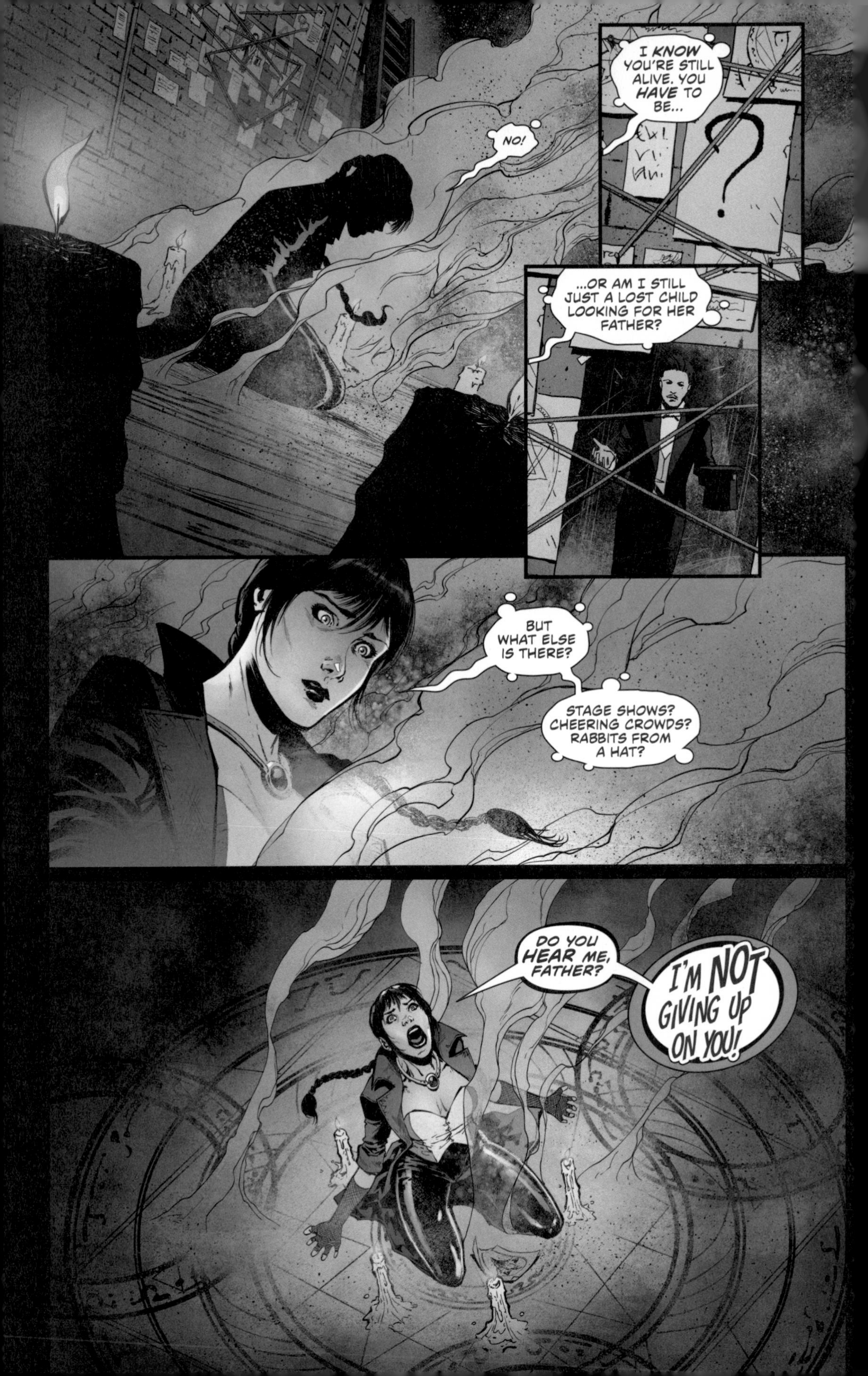
NO!
I KNOW YOU'RE STILL ALIVE. YOU HAVE TO BE...
...OR AM I STILL JUST A LOST CHILD LOOKING FOR HER FATHER?
BUT WHAT ELSE IS THERE?
STAGE SHOWS? CHEERING CROWDS? RABBITS FROM A HAT?
DO YOU HEAR ME, FATHER?
I'M NOT GIVING UP ON YOU!

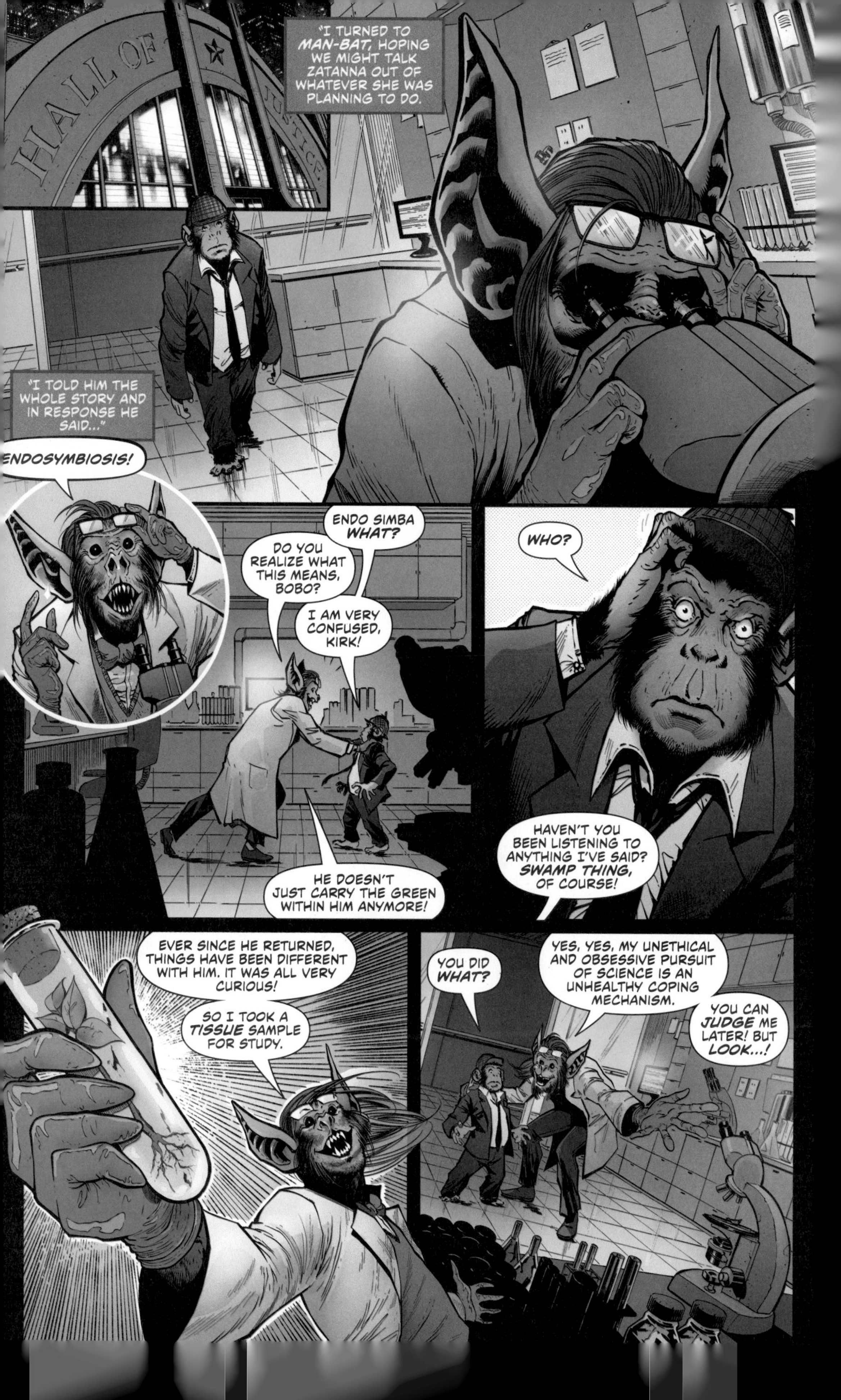

HALL OF JUSTICE
"I TURNED TO MAN-BAT, HOPING WE MIGHT TALK ZATANNA OUT OF WHATEVER SHE WAS PLANNING TO DO.
"I TOLD HIM THE WHOLE STORY AND IN RESPONSE HE SAID..."
ENDOSYMBIOSIS!
ENDO SIMBA WHAT?
DO YOU REALIZE WHAT THIS MEANS, BOBO?
I AM VERY CONFUSED, KIRK!
HE DOESN'T JUST CARRY THE GREEN WITHIN HIM ANYMORE!
WHO?
HAVEN'T YOU BEEN LISTENING TO ANYTHING I'VE SAID? SWAMP THING, OF COURSE!
EVER SINCE HE RETURNED, THINGS HAVE BEEN DIFFERENT WITH HIM. IT WAS ALL VERY CURIOUS!
SO I TOOK A TISSUE SAMPLE FOR STUDY.
YOU DID WHAT?
YES, YES, MY UNETHICAL AND OBSESSIVE PURSUIT OF SCIENCE IS AN UNHEALTHY COPING MECHANISM.
YOU CAN JUDGE ME LATER! BUT LOOK...!

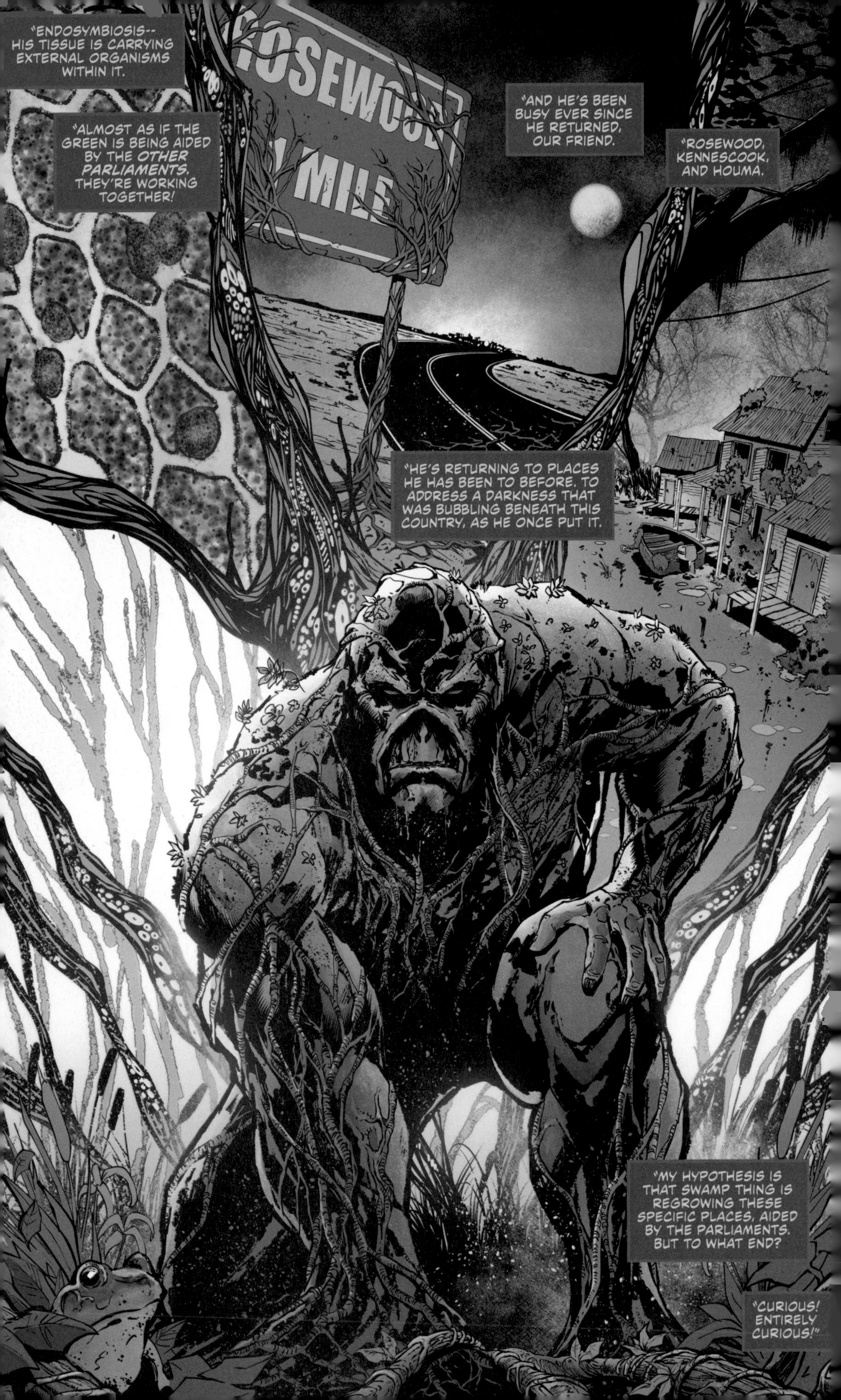
"ENDOSYMBIOSIS--
HIS TISSUE IS CARRYING EXTERNAL ORGANISMS WITHIN IT.
"ALMOST AS IF THE GREEN IS BEING AIDED BY THE *OTHER PARLIAMENTS*. THEY'RE WORKING TOGETHER!
ROSEWOOD
MILE
"AND HE'S BEEN BUSY EVER SINCE HE RETURNED, OUR FRIEND.
"ROSEWOOD, KENNESCOOK, AND HOUMA.
"HE'S RETURNING TO PLACES HE HAS BEEN TO BEFORE, TO ADDRESS A DARKNESS THAT WAS BUBBLING BENEATH THIS COUNTRY, AS HE ONCE PUT IT.
"MY HYPOTHESIS IS THAT SWAMP THING IS REGROWING THESE SPECIFIC PLACES, AIDED BY THE PARLIAMENTS. BUT TO WHAT END?
"CURIOUS! ENTIRELY CURIOUS!"

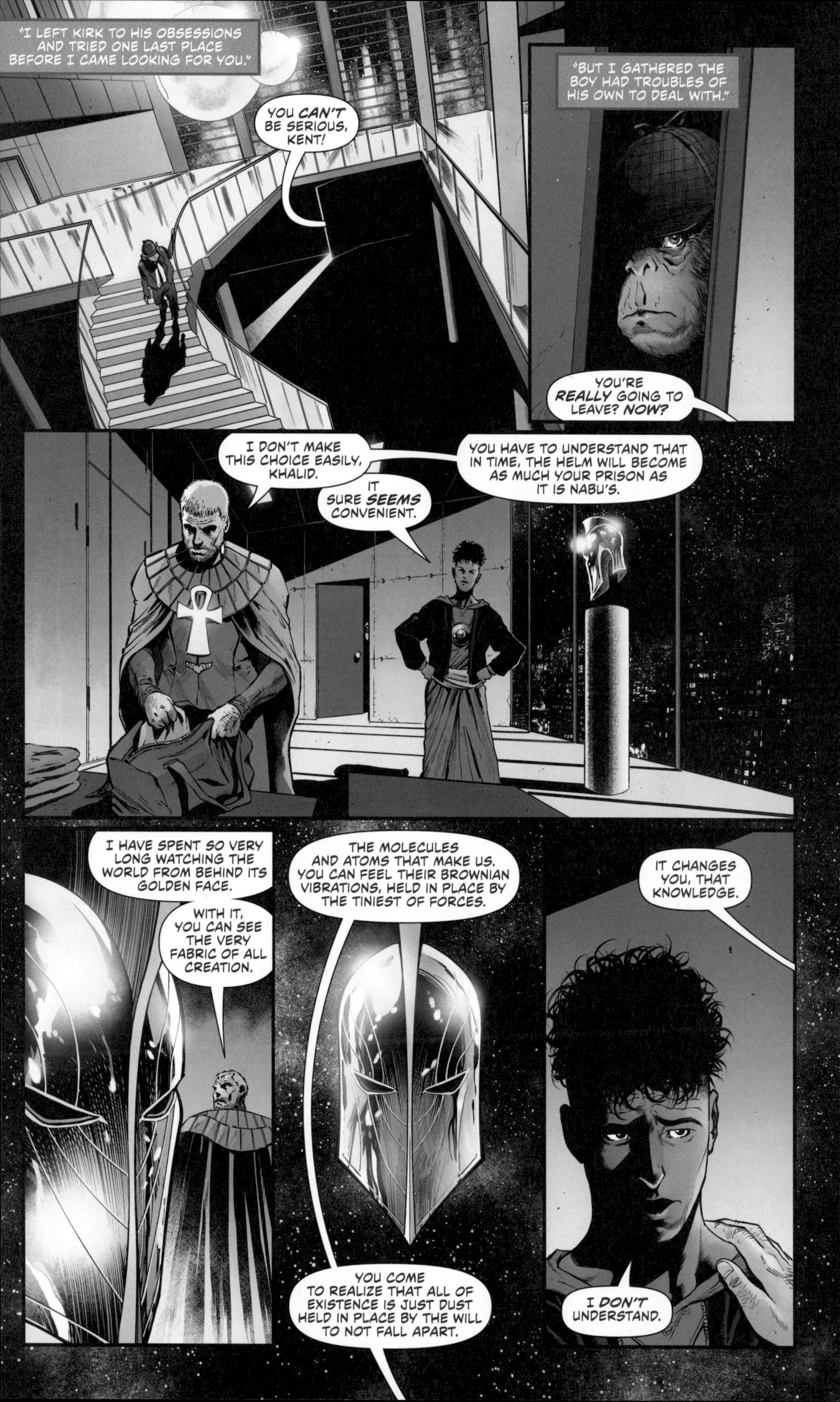
"I LEFT KIRK TO HIS OBSESSIONS AND TRIED ONE LAST PLACE BEFORE I CAME LOOKING FOR YOU."
YOU CAN'T BE SERIOUS, KENT!
"BUT I GATHERED THE BOY HAD TROUBLES OF HIS OWN TO DEAL WITH."
YOU'RE REALLY GOING TO LEAVE? NOW?
I DON'T MAKE THIS CHOICE EASILY, KHALID.
YOU HAVE TO UNDERSTAND THAT IN TIME, THE HELM WILL BECOME AS MUCH YOUR PRISON AS IT IS NABU'S.
IT SURE SEEMS CONVENIENT.
I HAVE SPENT SO VERY LONG WATCHING THE WORLD FROM BEHIND ITS GOLDEN FACE.
WITH IT, YOU CAN SEE THE VERY FABRIC OF ALL CREATION.
THE MOLECULES AND ATOMS THAT MAKE US. YOU CAN FEEL THEIR BROWNIAN VIBRATIONS, HELD IN PLACE BY THE TINIEST OF FORCES.
YOU COME TO REALIZE THAT ALL OF EXISTENCE IS JUST DUST HELD IN PLACE BY THE WILL TO NOT FALL APART.
IT CHANGES YOU, THAT KNOWLEDGE.
I DON'T UNDERSTAND.

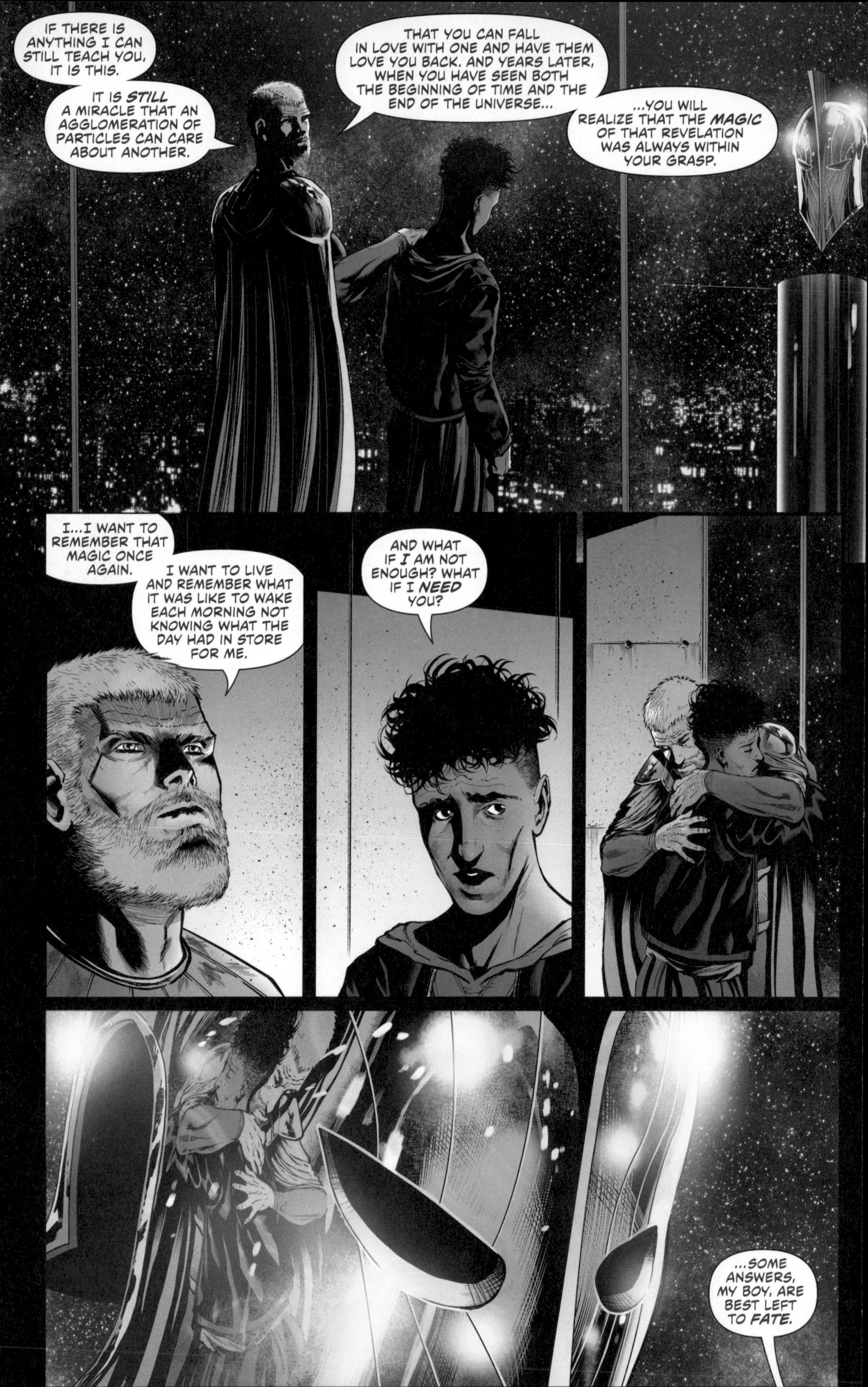
IF THERE IS ANYTHING I CAN STILL TEACH YOU, IT IS THIS.
IT IS STILL A MIRACLE THAT AN AGGLOMERATION OF PARTICLES CAN CARE ABOUT ANOTHER.
THAT YOU CAN FALL IN LOVE WITH ONE AND HAVE THEM LOVE YOU BACK. AND YEARS LATER, WHEN YOU HAVE SEEN BOTH THE BEGINNING OF TIME AND THE END OF THE UNIVERSE...
...YOU WILL REALIZE THAT THE MAGIC OF THAT REVELATION WAS ALWAYS WITHIN YOUR GRASP.
I...I WANT TO REMEMBER THAT MAGIC ONCE AGAIN.
I WANT TO LIVE AND REMEMBER WHAT IT WAS LIKE TO WAKE EACH MORNING NOT KNOWING WHAT THE DAY HAD IN STORE FOR ME.
AND WHAT IF I AM NOT ENOUGH? WHAT IF I NEED YOU?
...SOME ANSWERS, MY BOY, ARE BEST LEFT TO FATE.

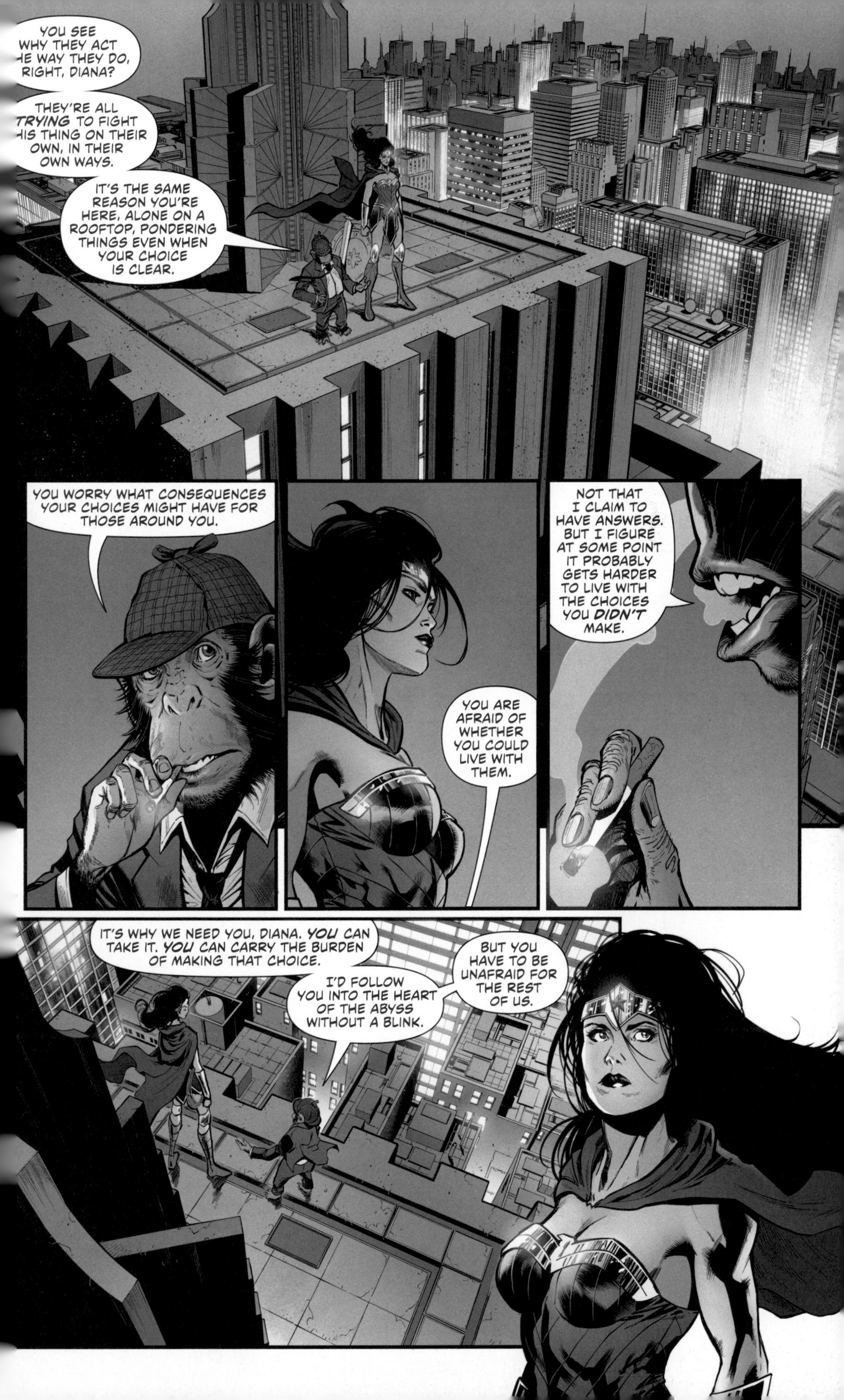
YOU SEE WHY THEY ACT THE WAY THEY DO, RIGHT, DIANA?
THEY'RE ALL *TRYING* TO FIGHT THIS THING ON THEIR OWN, IN THEIR OWN WAYS.
IT'S THE SAME REASON YOU'RE HERE, ALONE ON A ROOFTOP, PONDERING THINGS EVEN WHEN YOUR CHOICE IS CLEAR.
YOU WORRY WHAT CONSEQUENCES YOUR CHOICES MIGHT HAVE FOR THOSE AROUND YOU.
YOU ARE AFRAID OF WHETHER YOU COULD LIVE WITH THEM.
NOT THAT I CLAIM TO HAVE ANSWERS. BUT I FIGURE AT SOME POINT IT PROBABLY GETS HARDER TO LIVE WITH THE CHOICES YOU *DIDN'T* MAKE.
IT'S WHY WE NEED YOU, DIANA. *YOU* CAN TAKE IT. *YOU* CAN CARRY THE BURDEN OF MAKING THAT CHOICE.
I'D FOLLOW YOU INTO THE HEART OF THE ABYSS WITHOUT A BLINK.
BUT YOU HAVE TO BE UNAFRAID FOR THE REST OF US.

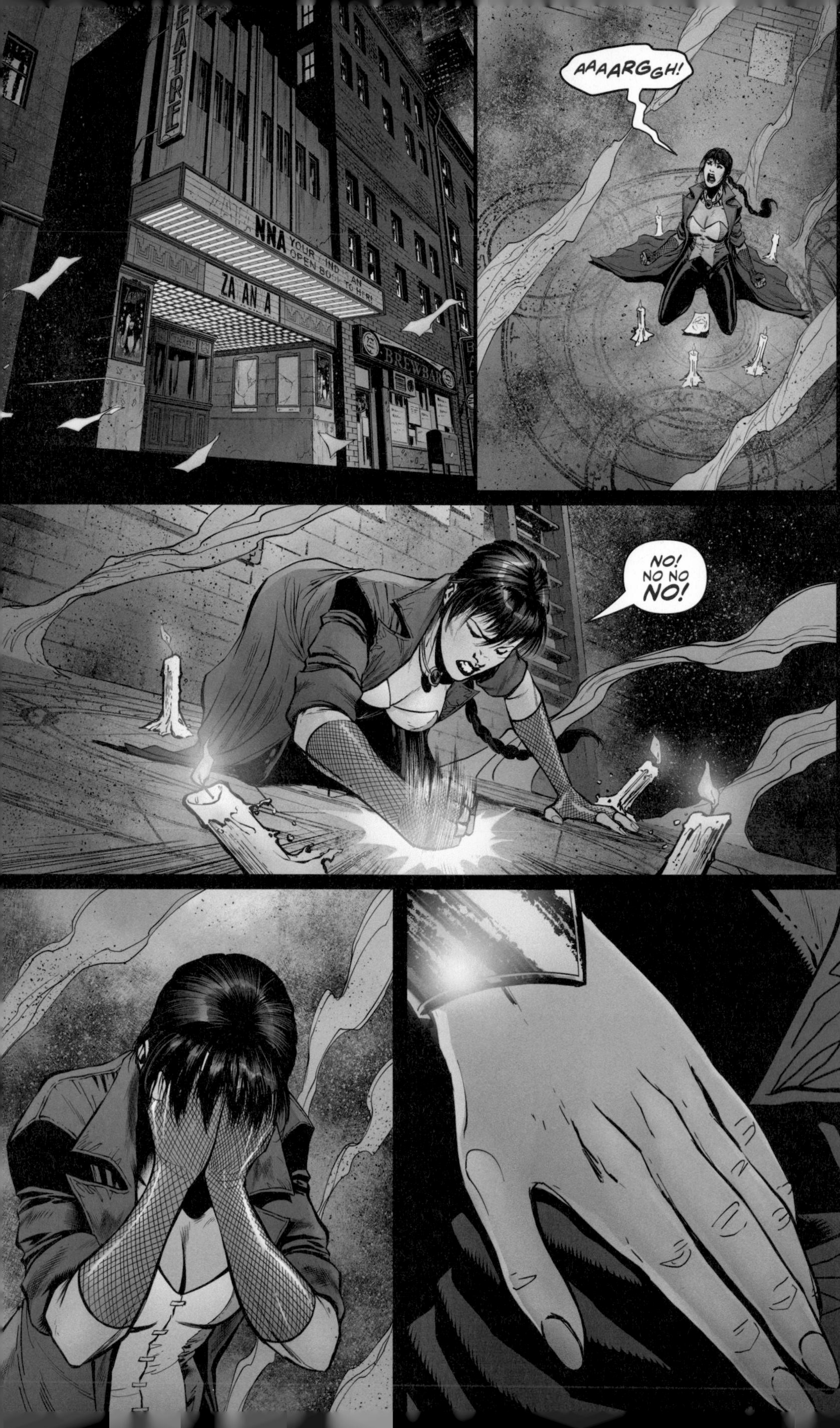

BREWBAR
AAAARGGH!
NO! NO NO NO!

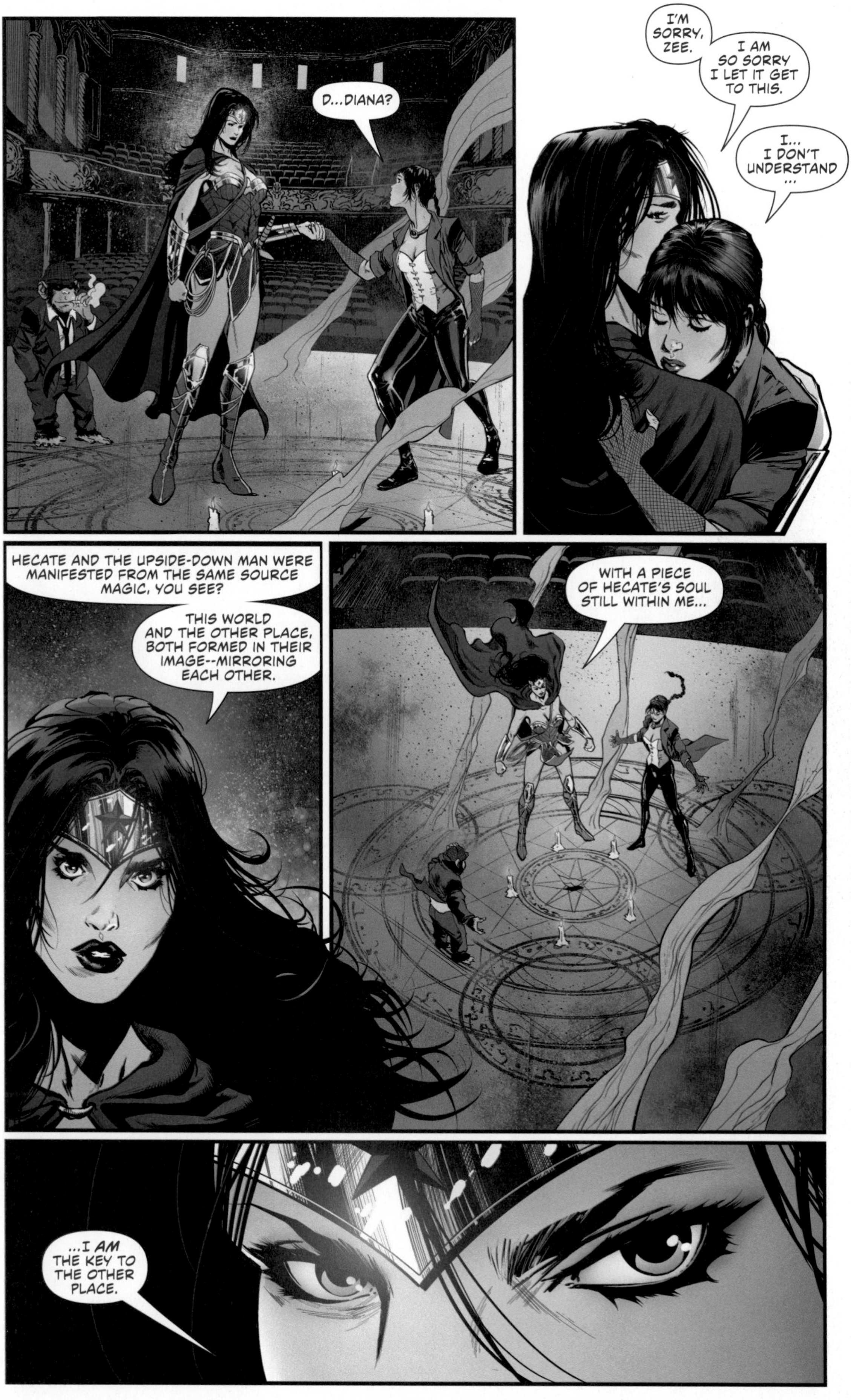
D...DIANA?
I'M SORRY, ZEE.
I AM SO SORRY I LET IT GET TO THIS.
I... I DON'T UNDERSTAND ...
HECATE AND THE UPSIDE-DOWN MAN WERE MANIFESTED FROM THE SAME SOURCE MAGIC, YOU SEE?
THIS WORLD AND THE OTHER PLACE, BOTH FORMED IN THEIR IMAGE--MIRRORING EACH OTHER.
WITH A PIECE OF HECATE'S SOUL STILL WITHIN ME...
...I AM THE KEY TO THE OTHER PLACE.

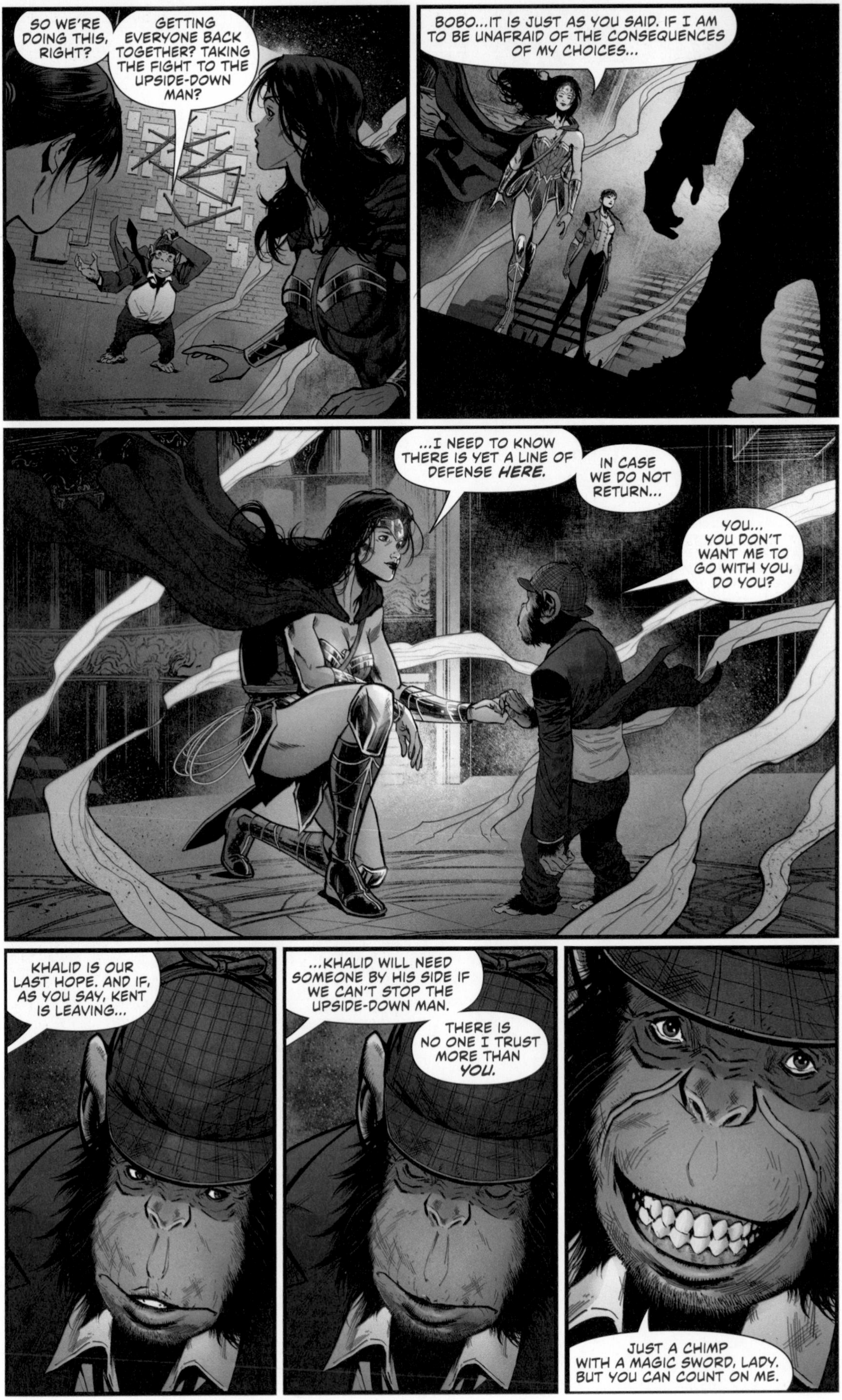
SO WE'RE DOING THIS, RIGHT?
GETTING EVERYONE BACK TOGETHER? TAKING THE FIGHT TO THE UPSIDE-DOWN MAN?
BOBO...IT IS JUST AS YOU SAID. IF I AM TO BE UNAFRAID OF THE CONSEQUENCES OF MY CHOICES...
...I NEED TO KNOW THERE IS YET A LINE OF DEFENSE HERE.
IN CASE WE DO NOT RETURN...
YOU... YOU DON'T WANT ME TO GO WITH YOU, DO YOU?
KHALID IS OUR LAST HOPE. AND IF, AS YOU SAY, KENT IS LEAVING...
...KHALID WILL NEED SOMEONE BY HIS SIDE IF WE CAN'T STOP THE UPSIDE-DOWN MAN.
THERE IS NO ONE I TRUST MORE THAN YOU.
JUST A CHIMP WITH A MAGIC SWORD, LADY. BUT YOU CAN COUNT ON ME.

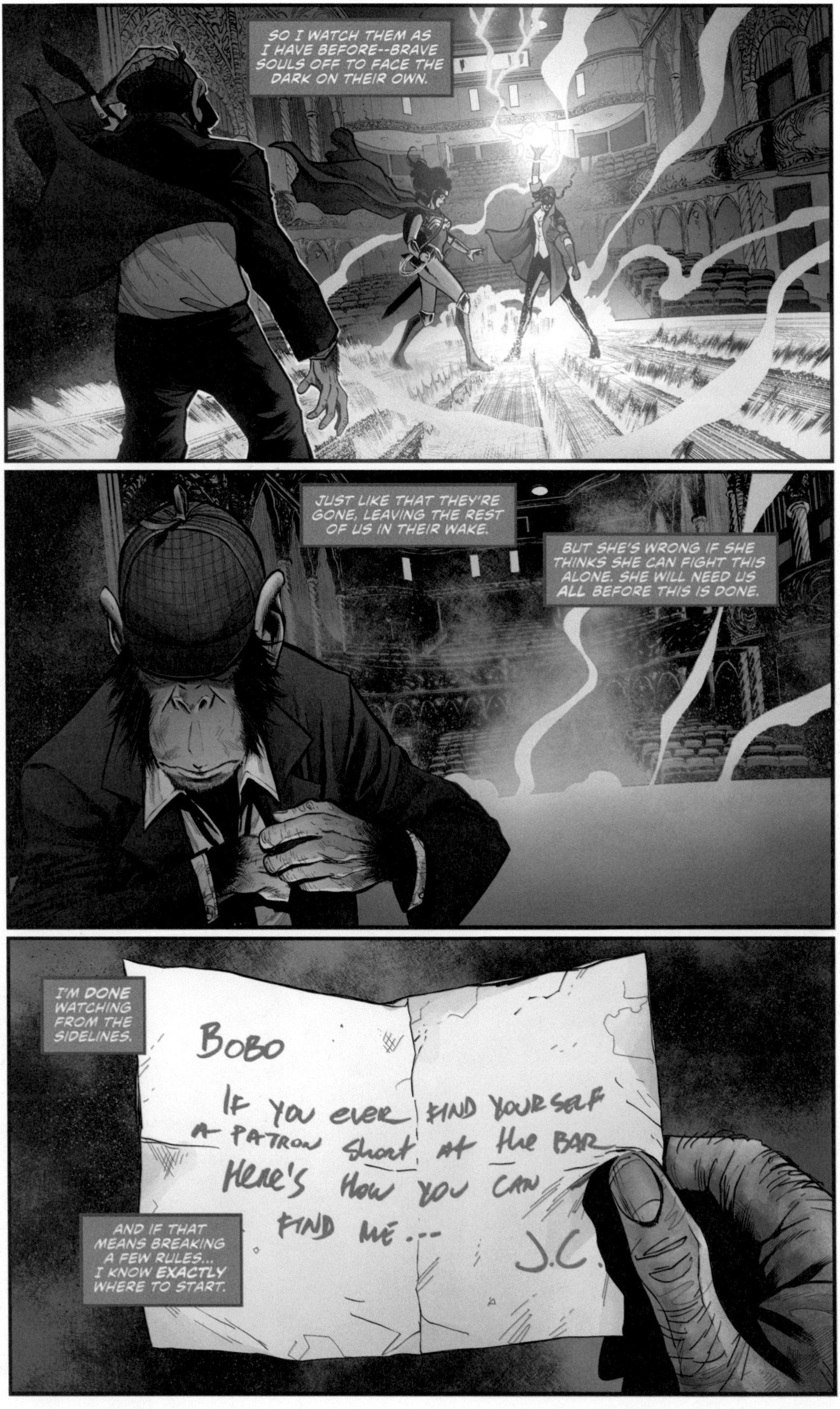
SO I WATCH THEM AS I HAVE BEFORE--BRAVE SOULS OFF TO FACE THE DARK ON THEIR OWN.
JUST LIKE THAT THEY'RE GONE, LEAVING THE REST OF US IN THEIR WAKE.
BUT SHE'S WRONG IF SHE THINKS SHE CAN FIGHT THIS ALONE. SHE WILL NEED US ALL BEFORE THIS IS DONE.
I'M DONE WATCHING FROM THE SIDELINES.
BOBO
IF YOU EVER FIND YOURSELF A PATRON SHORT AT THE BAR HERE'S HOW YOU CAN FIND ME...
J.C.
AND IF THAT MEANS BREAKING A FEW RULES... I KNOW EXACTLY WHERE TO START.

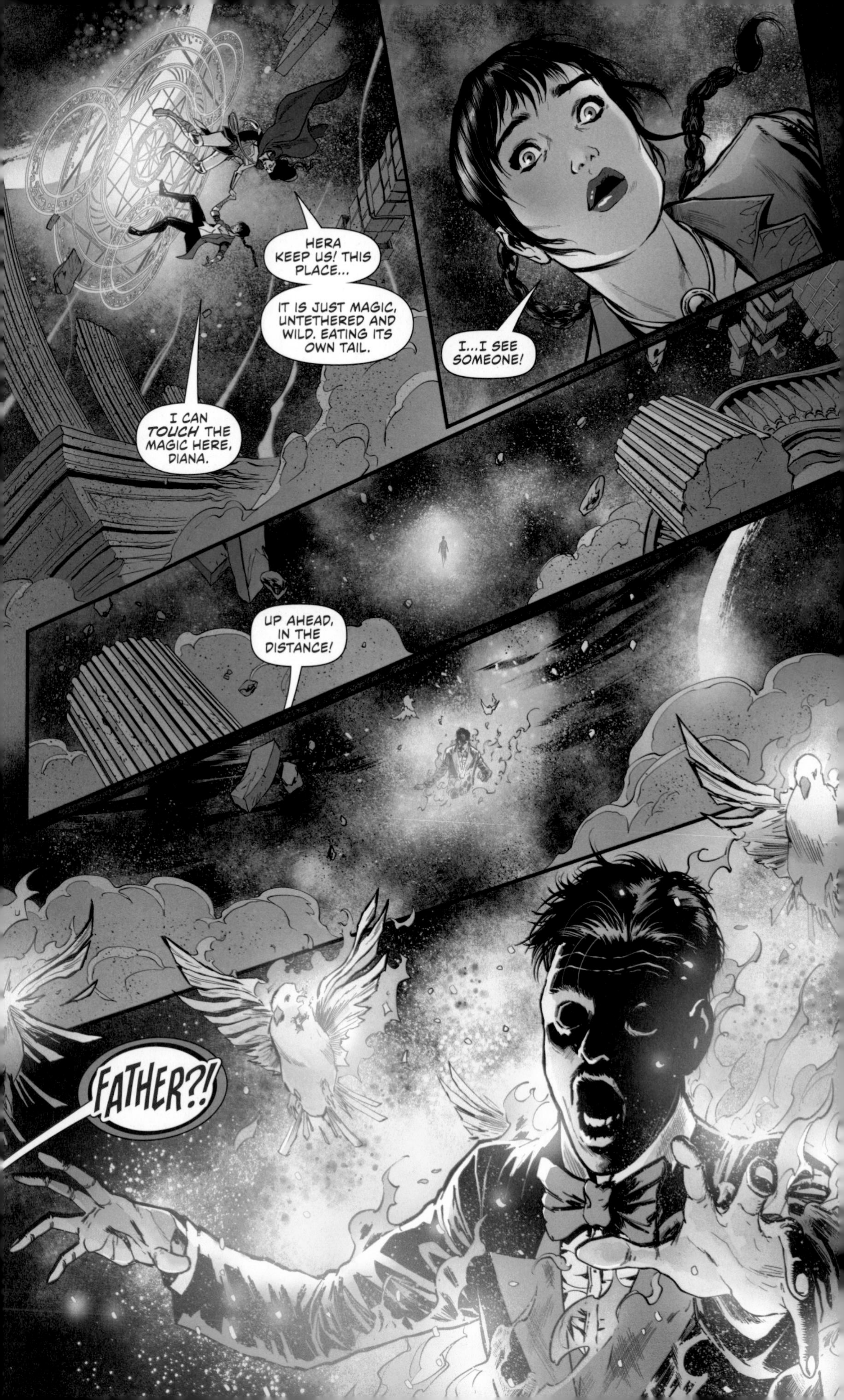
HERA KEEP US! THIS PLACE...
IT IS JUST MAGIC, UNTETHERED AND WILD. EATING ITS OWN TAIL.
I CAN *TOUCH* THE MAGIC HERE, DIANA.
I...I SEE SOMEONE!
UP AHEAD, IN THE DISTANCE!
FATHER?!

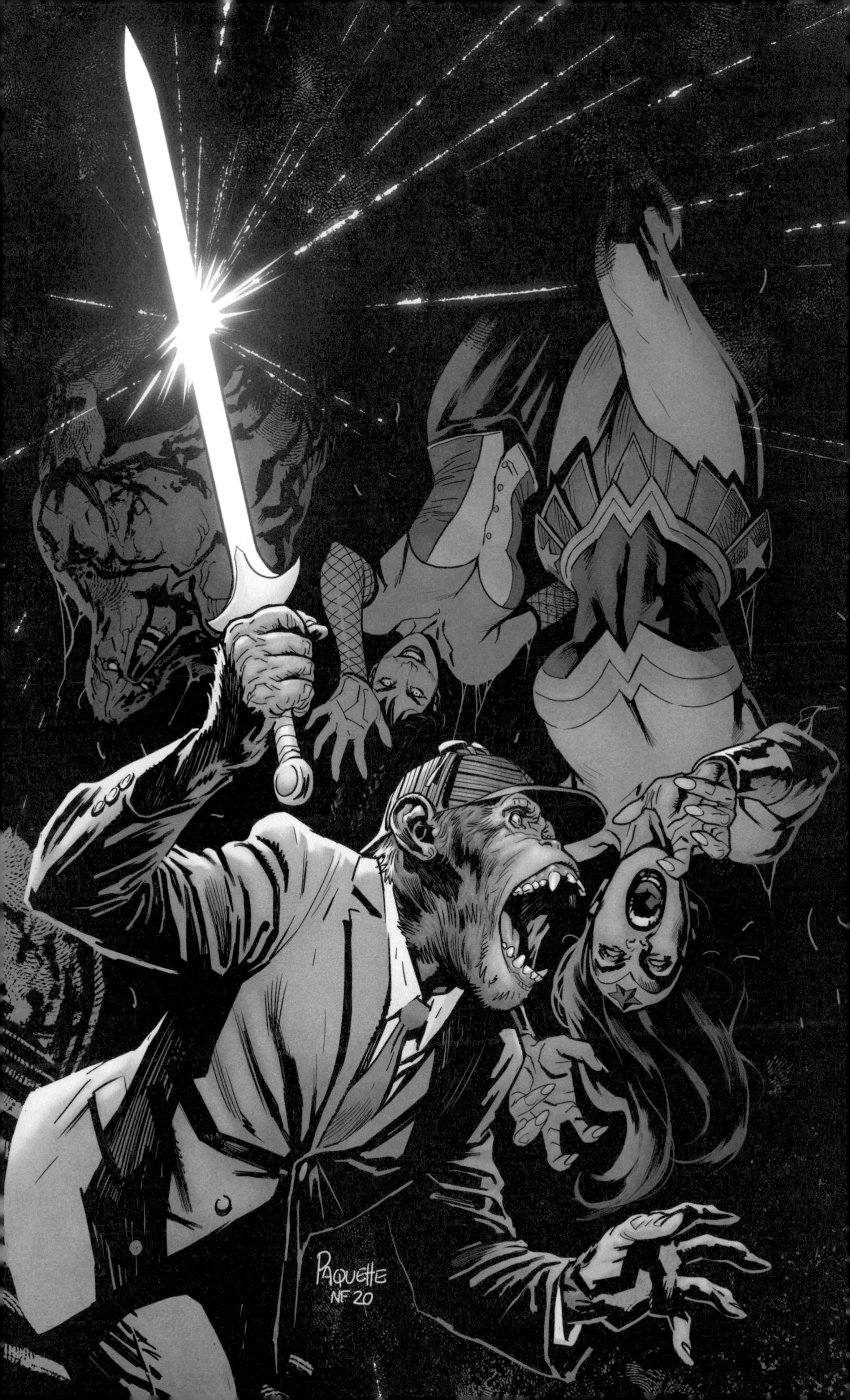
PAQUETTE
NF 20

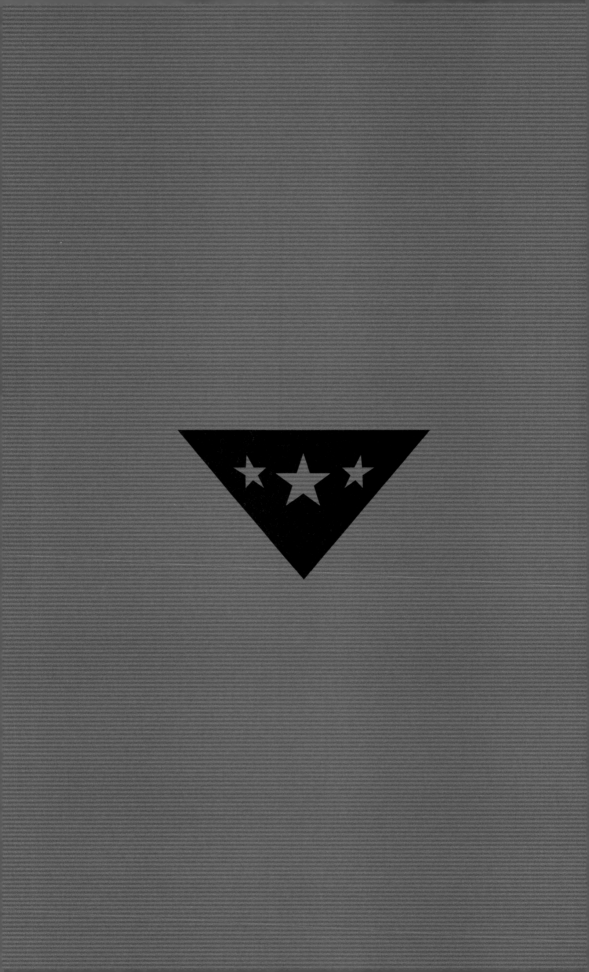

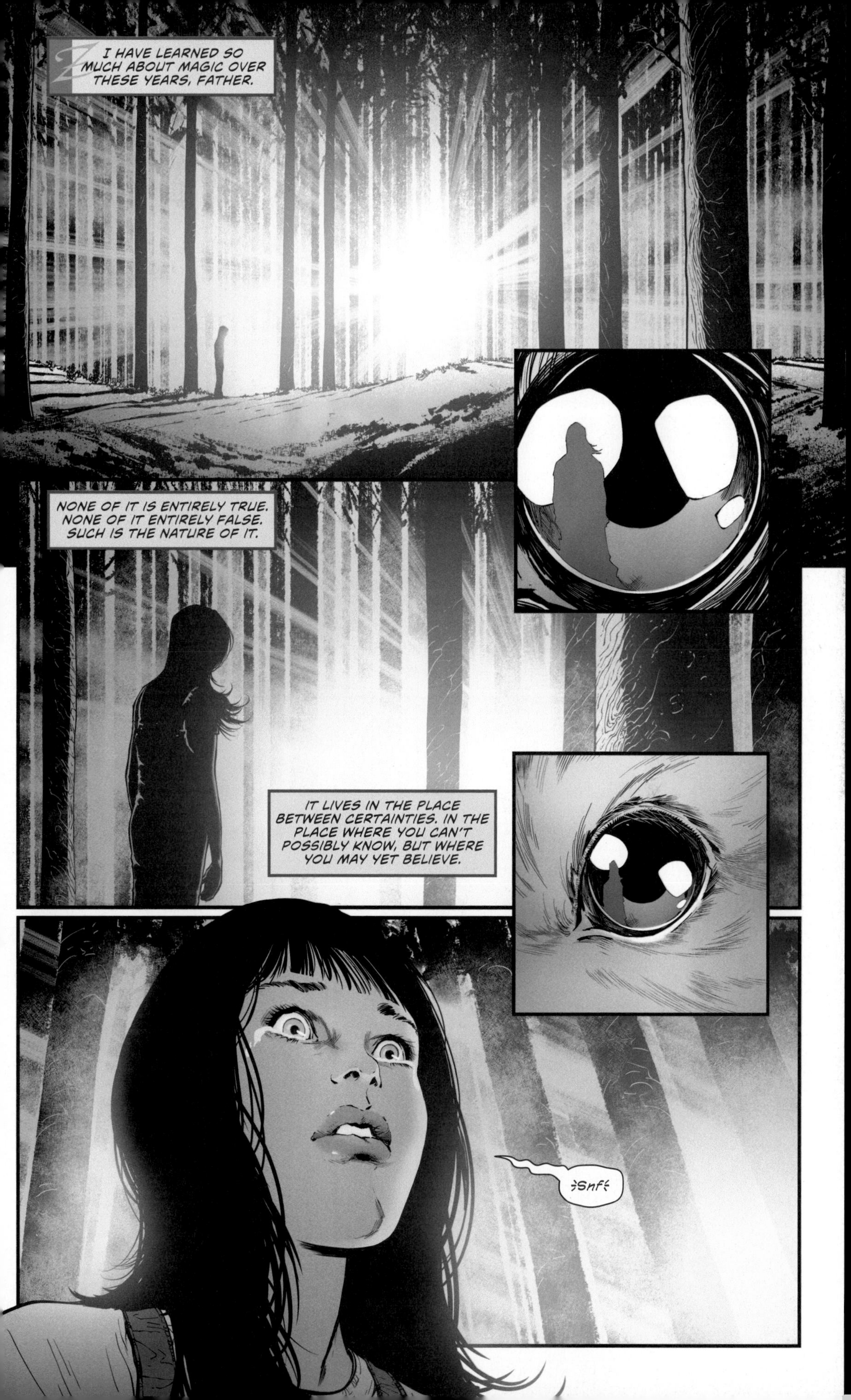
I HAVE LEARNED SO MUCH ABOUT MAGIC OVER THESE YEARS, FATHER.
NONE OF IT IS ENTIRELY TRUE. NONE OF IT ENTIRELY FALSE. SUCH IS THE NATURE OF IT.
IT LIVES IN THE PLACE BETWEEN CERTAINTIES. IN THE PLACE WHERE YOU CAN'T POSSIBLY KNOW, BUT WHERE YOU MAY YET BELIEVE.
Snf

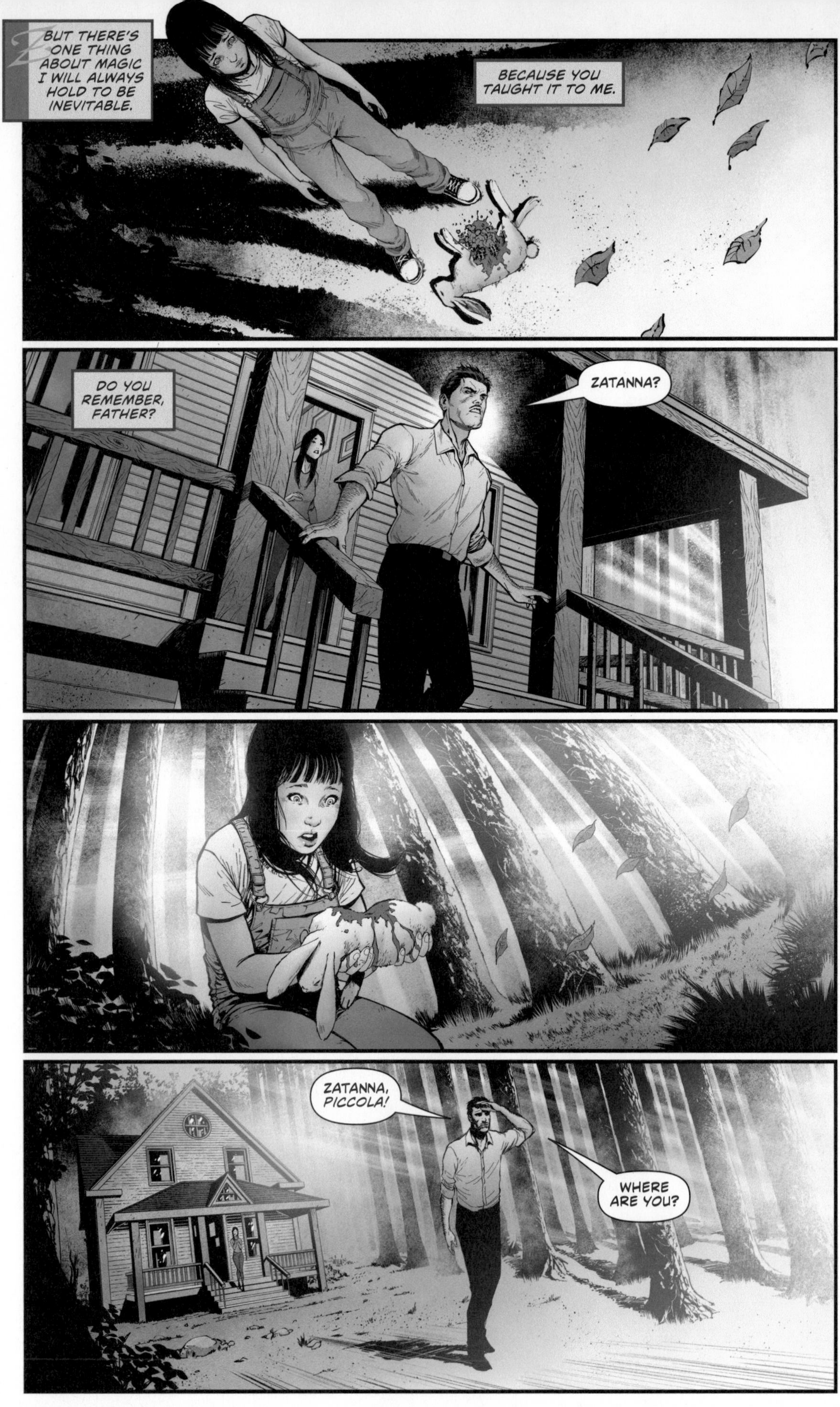
BUT THERE'S ONE THING ABOUT MAGIC I WILL ALWAYS HOLD TO BE INEVITABLE.
BECAUSE YOU TAUGHT IT TO ME.
DO YOU REMEMBER, FATHER?
ZATANNA?
ZATANNA, PICCOLA!
WHERE ARE YOU?

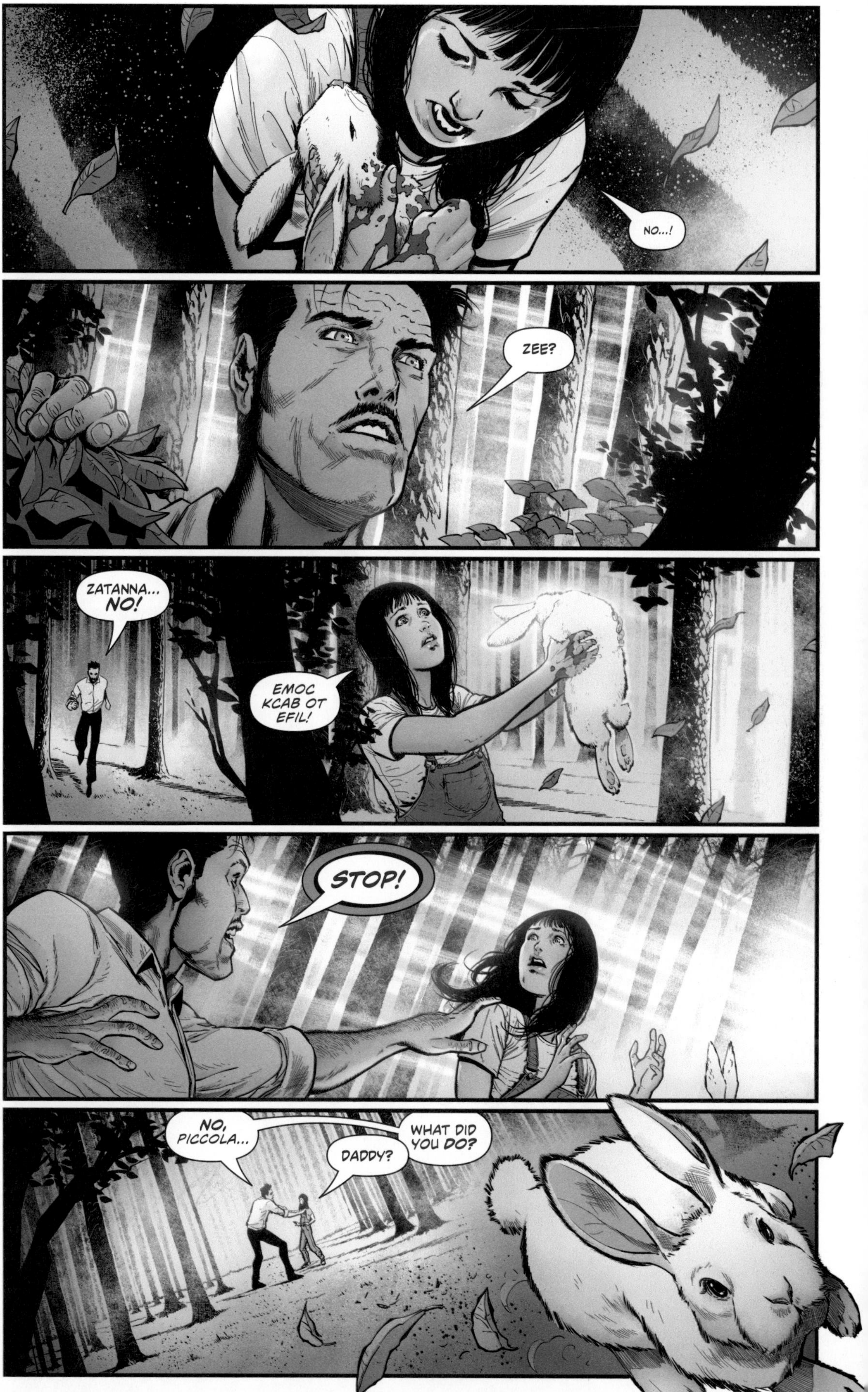
NO...!
ZEE?
ZATANNA... NO!
EMOC KCAB OT EFIL!
STOP!
NO, PICCOLA...
WHAT DID YOU DO?
DADDY?

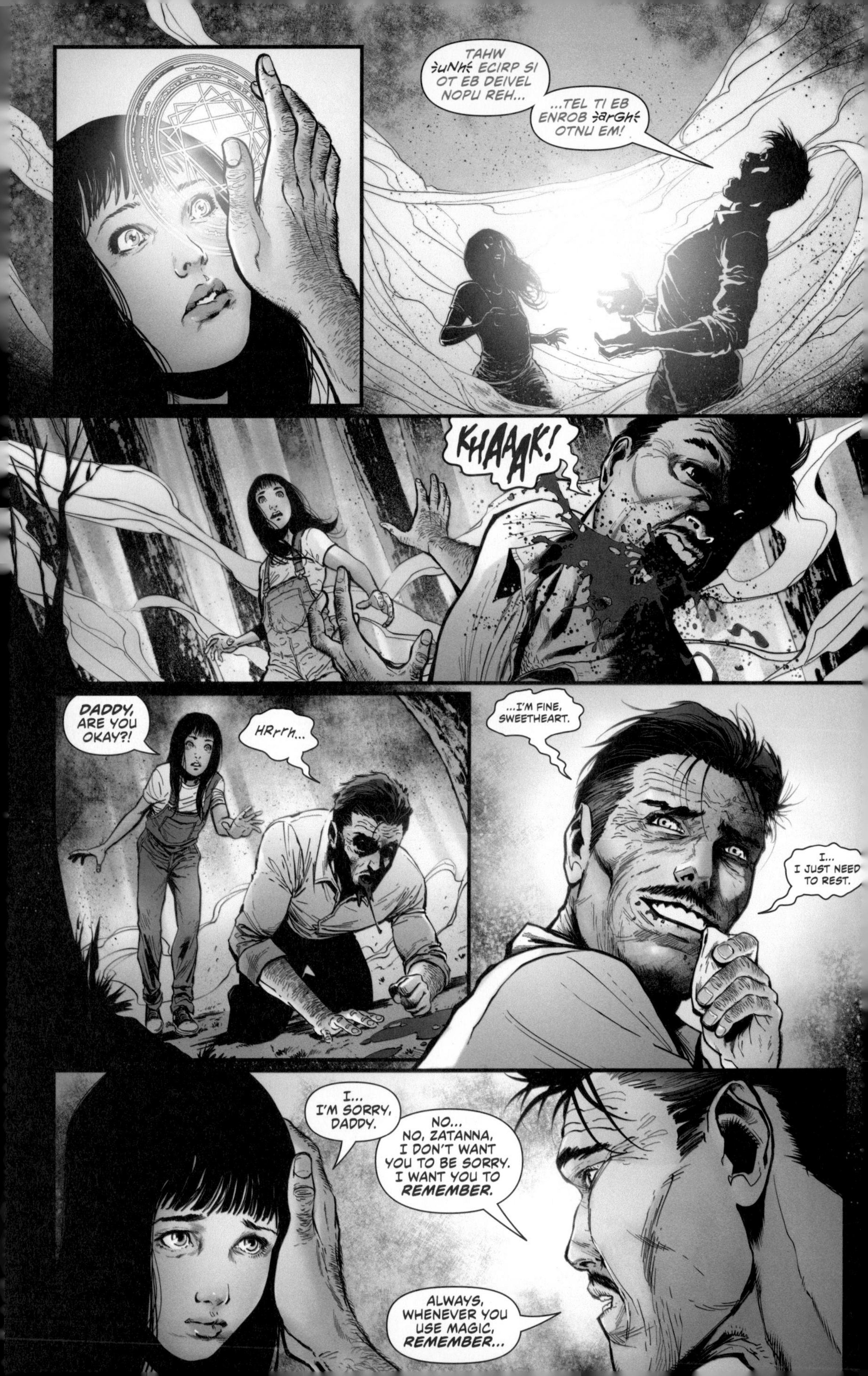
TAHW ⸮uNh⸮ ECIRP SI OT EB DEIVEL NOPU REH...
...TEL TI EB ENROB ⸮arGh⸮ OTNU EM!
KHAAAK!
DADDY, ARE YOU OKAY?!
HRrrh...
...I'M FINE, SWEETHEART.
I... I JUST NEED TO REST.
I... I'M SORRY, DADDY.
NO... NO, ZATANNA, I DON'T WANT YOU TO BE SORRY. I WANT YOU TO REMEMBER.
ALWAYS, WHENEVER YOU USE MAGIC, REMEMBER...

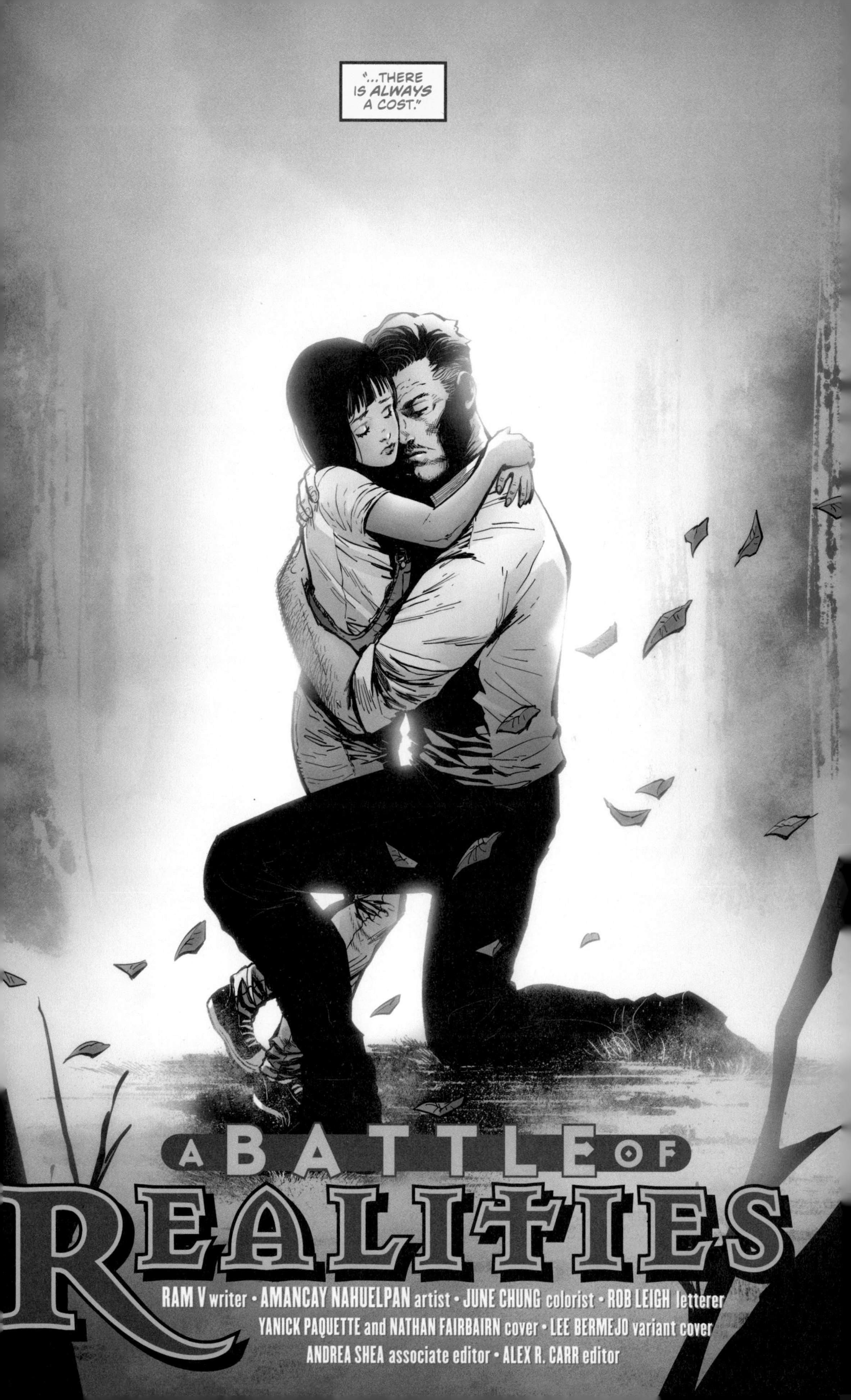
"...THERE IS ALWAYS A COST."
A BATTLE OF REALITIES
RAM V writer • AMANCAY NAHUELPAN artist • JUNE CHUNG colorist • ROB LEIGH letterer
YANICK PAQUETTE and NATHAN FAIRBAIRN cover • LEE BERMEJO variant cover
ANDREA SHEA associate editor • ALEX R. CARR editor

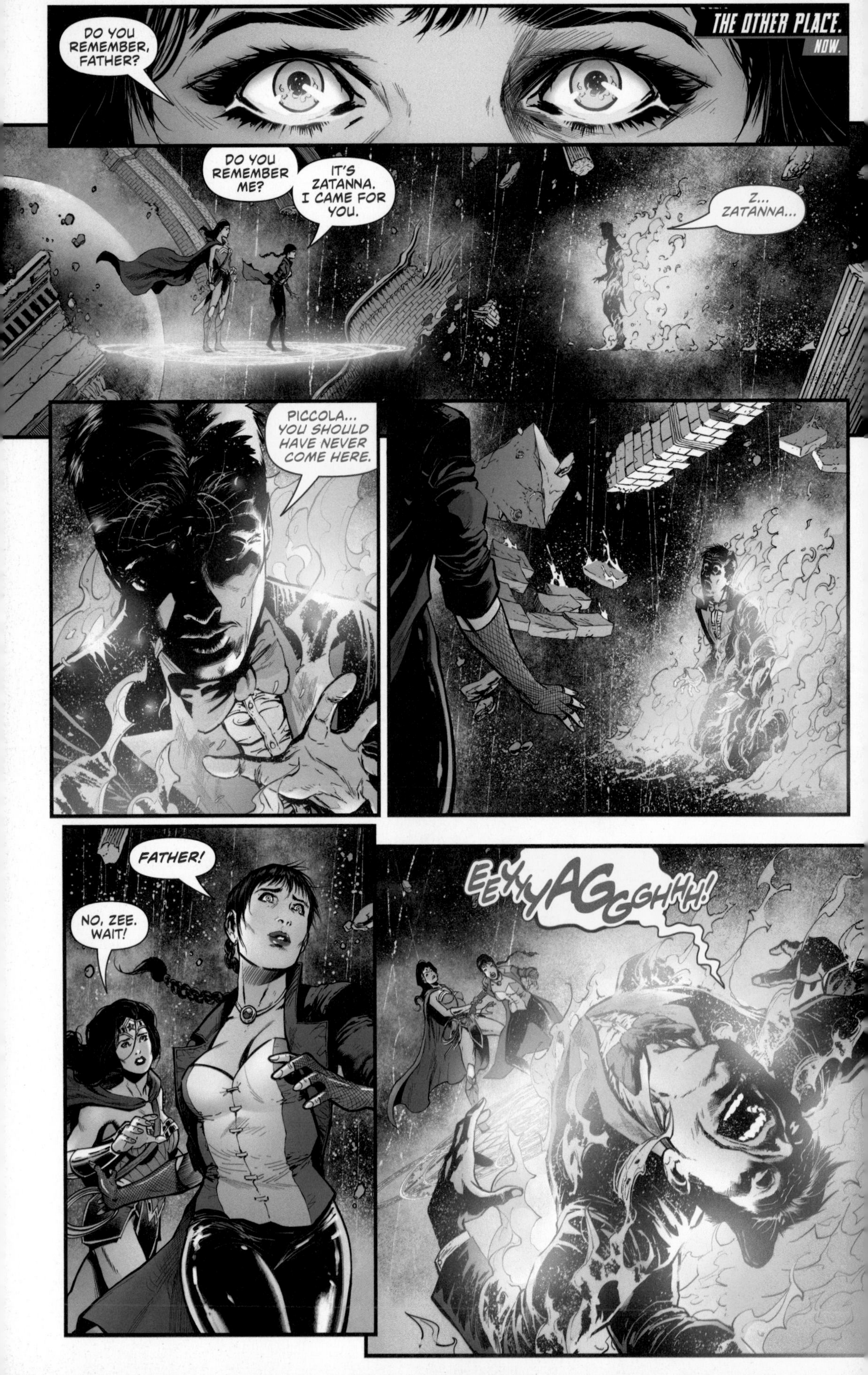
THE OTHER PLACE.
NOW.
DO YOU REMEMBER, FATHER?
DO YOU REMEMBER ME?
IT'S ZATANNA. I CAME FOR YOU.
Z... ZATANNA...
PICCOLA... YOU SHOULD HAVE NEVER COME HERE.
FATHER!
NO, ZEE. WAIT!
EEYYYAGGGHHH!

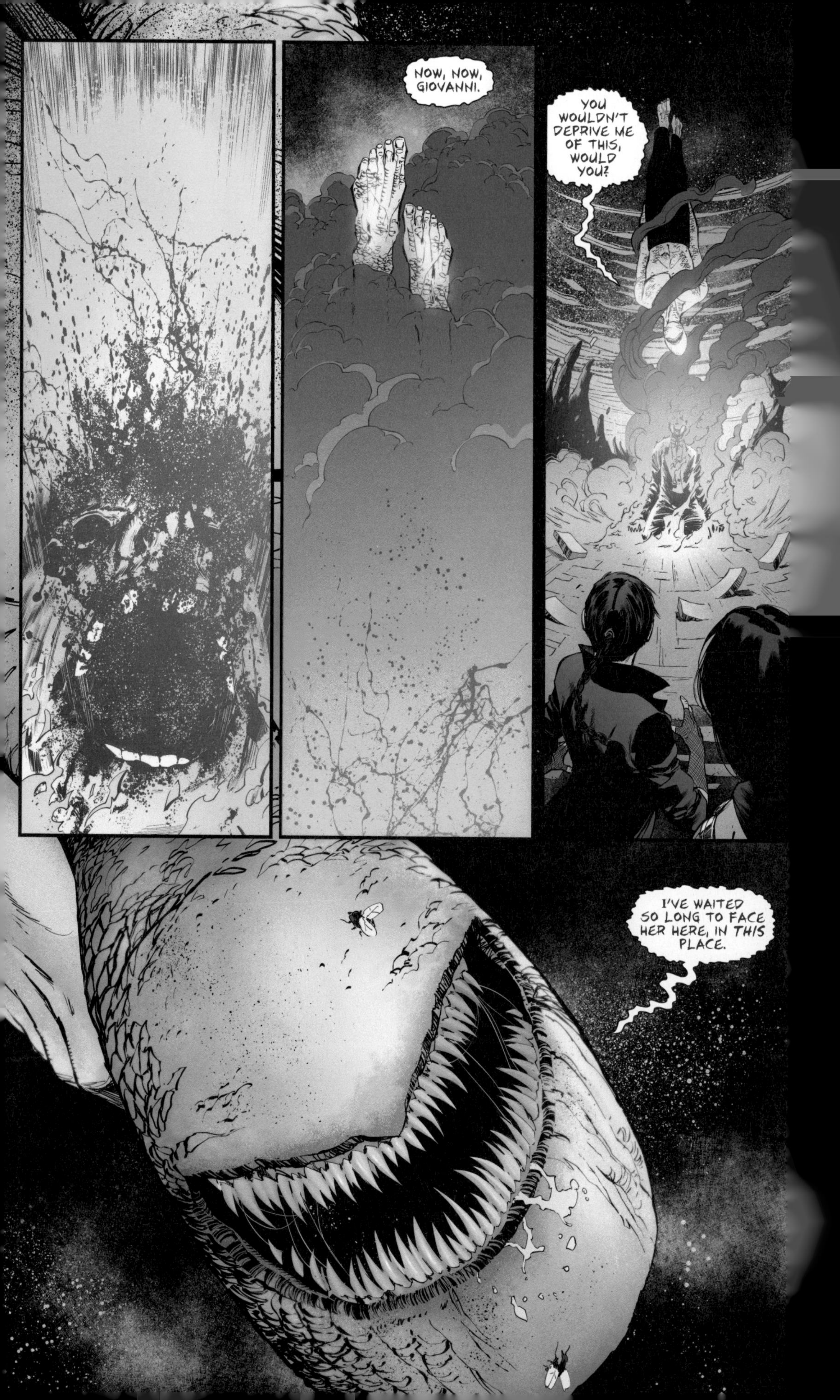
NOW, NOW, GIOVANNI.
YOU WOULDN'T DEPRIVE ME OF THIS, WOULD YOU?
I'VE WAITED SO LONG TO FACE HER HERE, IN THIS PLACE.

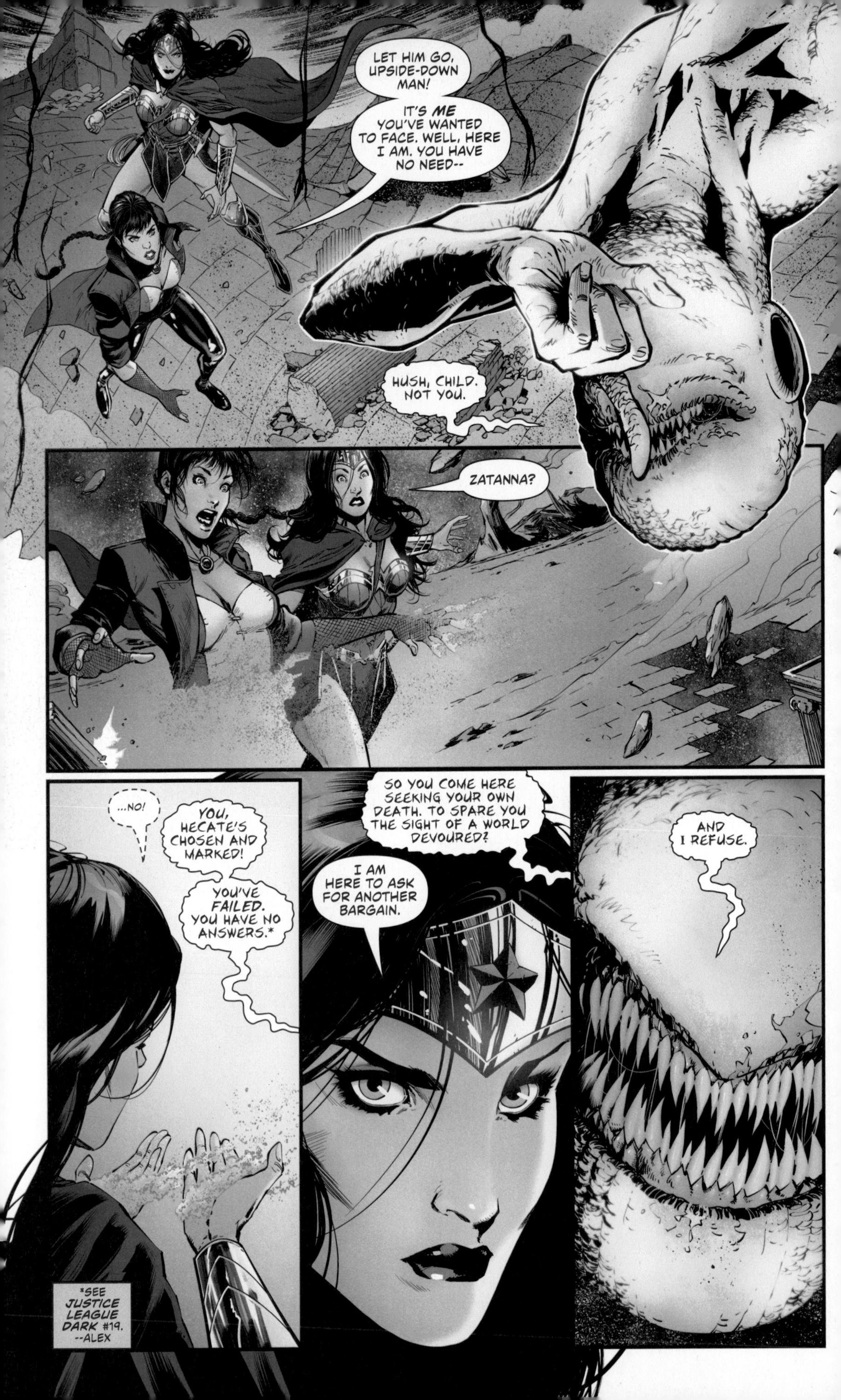
LET HIM GO, UPSIDE-DOWN MAN!
IT'S ME YOU'VE WANTED TO FACE. WELL, HERE I AM. YOU HAVE NO NEED--
HUSH, CHILD. NOT YOU.
ZATANNA?
...NO!
YOU, HECATE'S CHOSEN AND MARKED!
YOU'VE FAILED. YOU HAVE NO ANSWERS.*
SO YOU COME HERE SEEKING YOUR OWN DEATH. TO SPARE YOU THE SIGHT OF A WORLD DEVOURED?
I AM HERE TO ASK FOR ANOTHER BARGAIN.
AND I REFUSE.
*SEE JUSTICE LEAGUE DARK #19. --ALEX

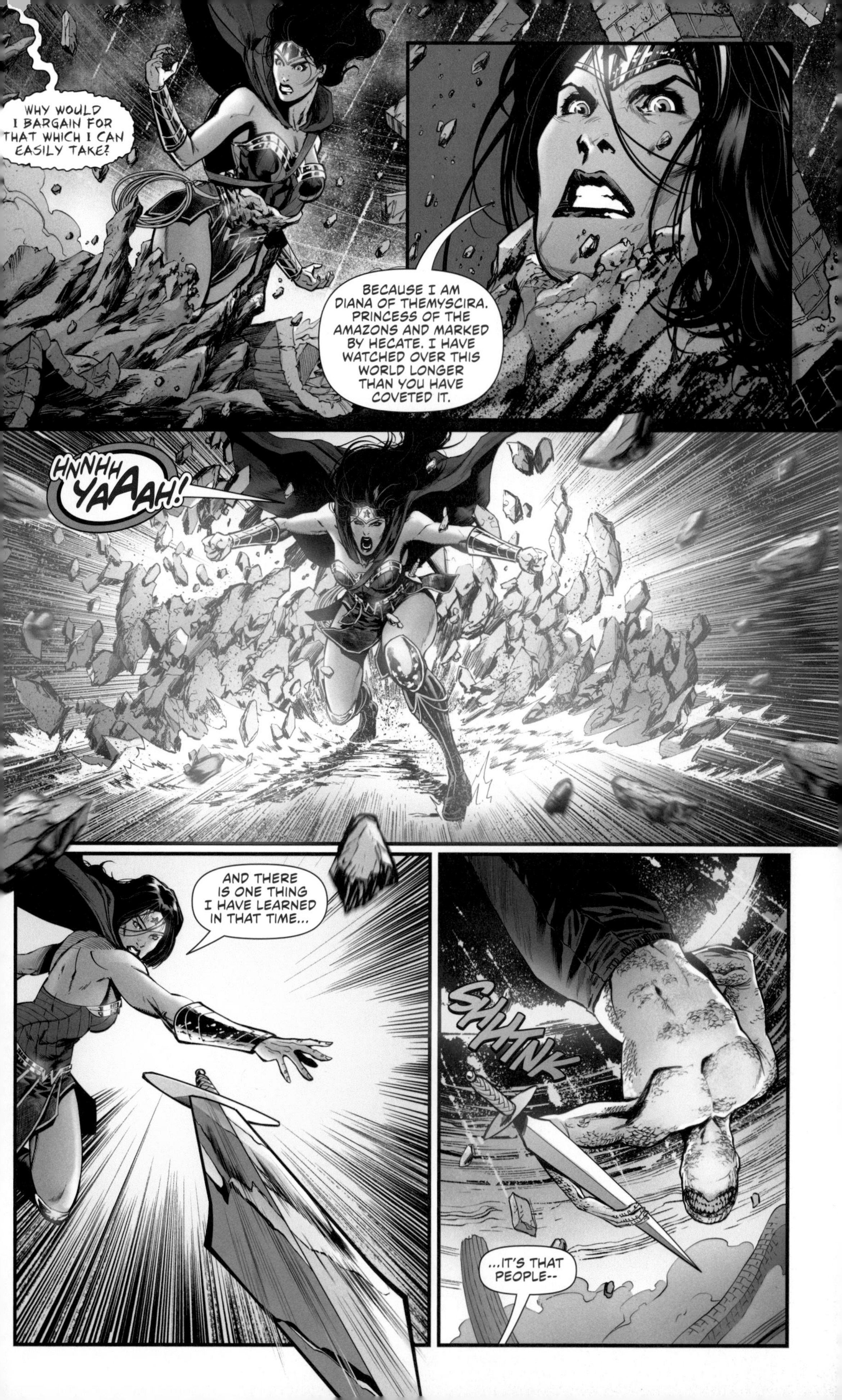
WHY WOULD I BARGAIN FOR THAT WHICH I CAN EASILY TAKE?
BECAUSE I AM DIANA OF THEMYSCIRA. PRINCESS OF THE AMAZONS AND MARKED BY HECATE. I HAVE WATCHED OVER THIS WORLD LONGER THAN YOU HAVE COVETED IT.
HNNHH YAAAH!
AND THERE IS ONE THING I HAVE LEARNED IN THAT TIME...
SHHHNK
...IT'S THAT PEOPLE--

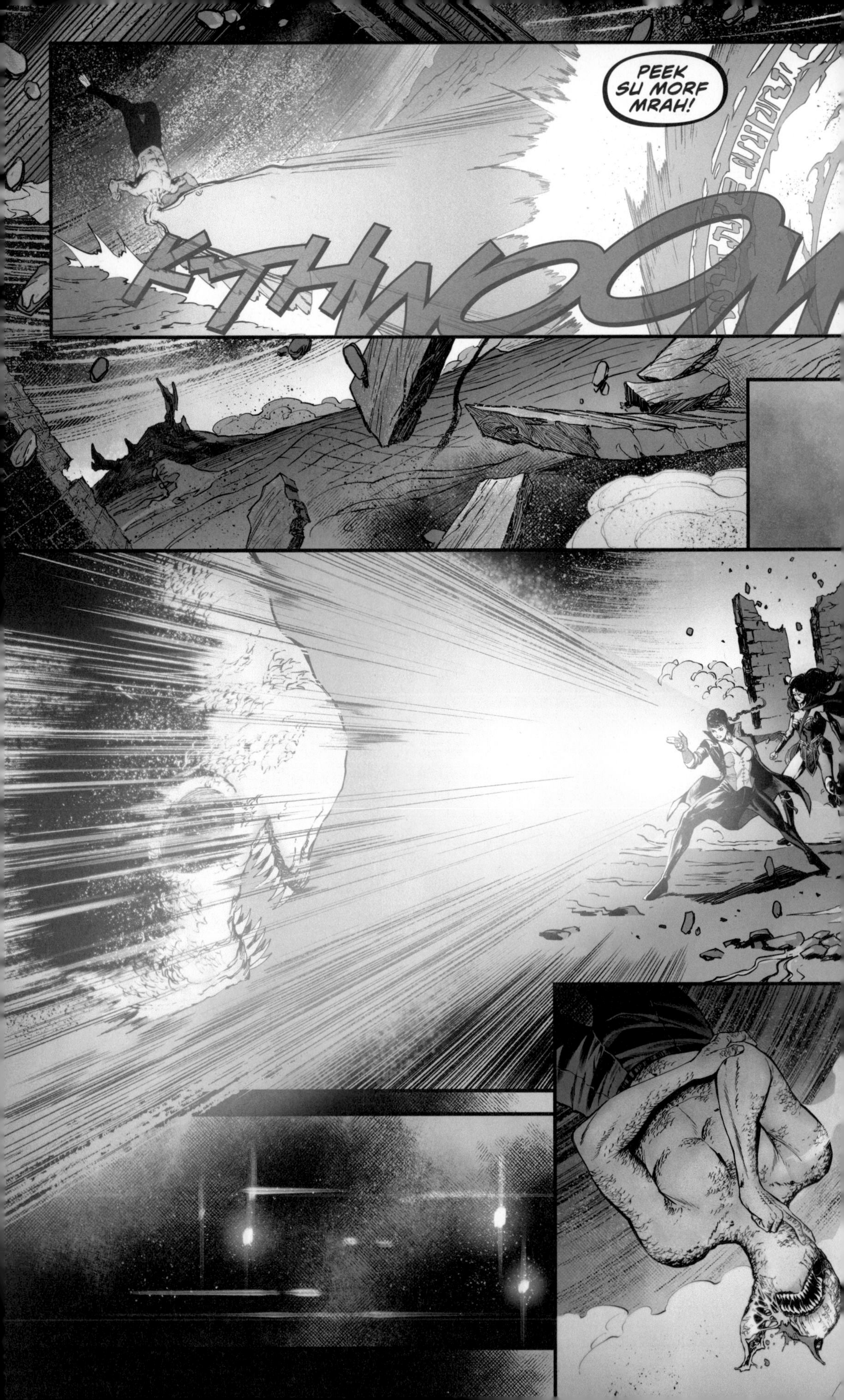
PEEK SU MORF MRAH!
K-THWOOM

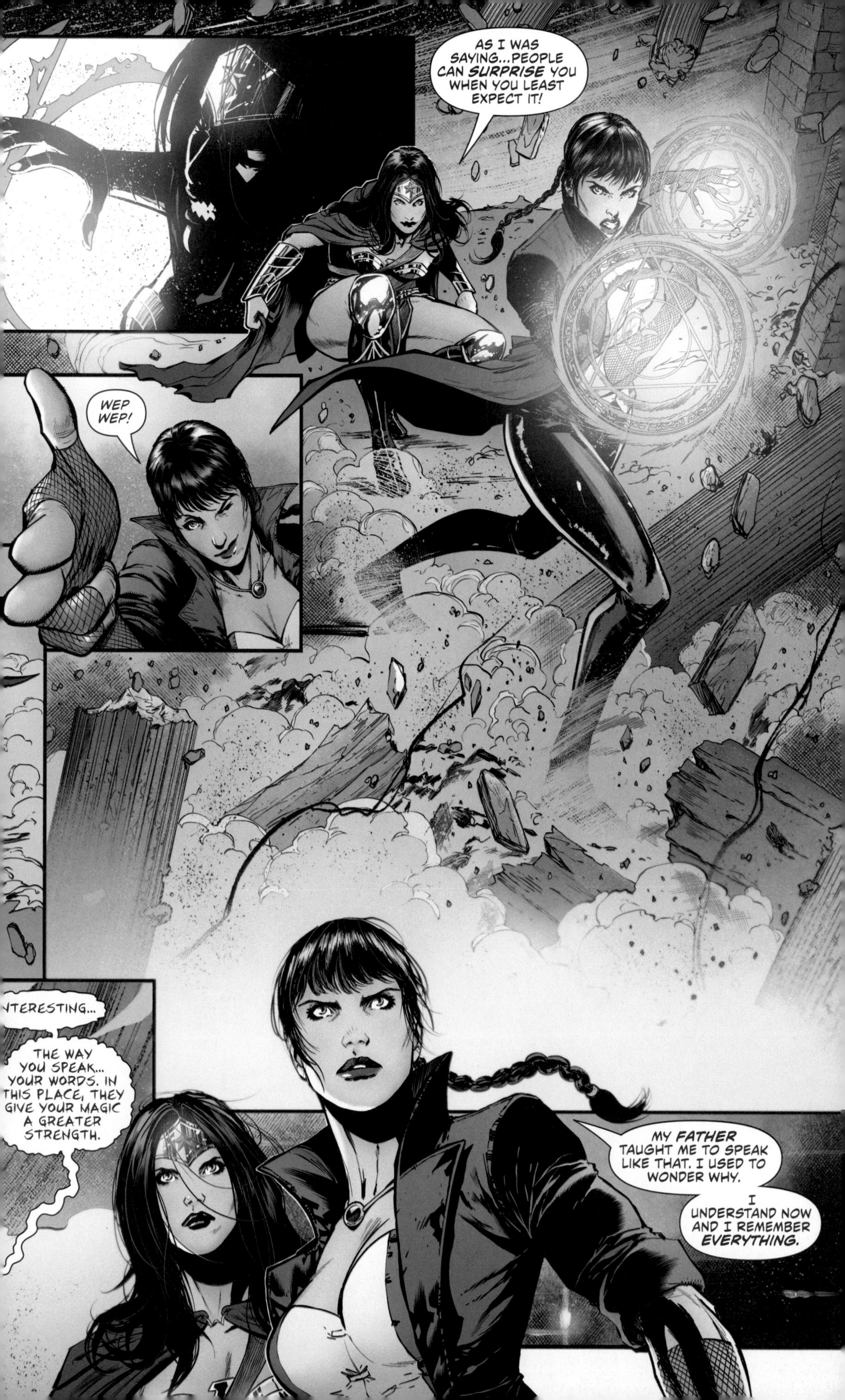
AS I WAS SAYING...PEOPLE CAN SURPRISE YOU WHEN YOU LEAST EXPECT IT!
WEP WEP!
NTERESTING...
THE WAY YOU SPEAK... YOUR WORDS. IN THIS PLACE, THEY GIVE YOUR MAGIC A GREATER STRENGTH.
MY FATHER TAUGHT ME TO SPEAK LIKE THAT. I USED TO WONDER WHY.
I UNDERSTAND NOW AND I REMEMBER EVERYTHING.

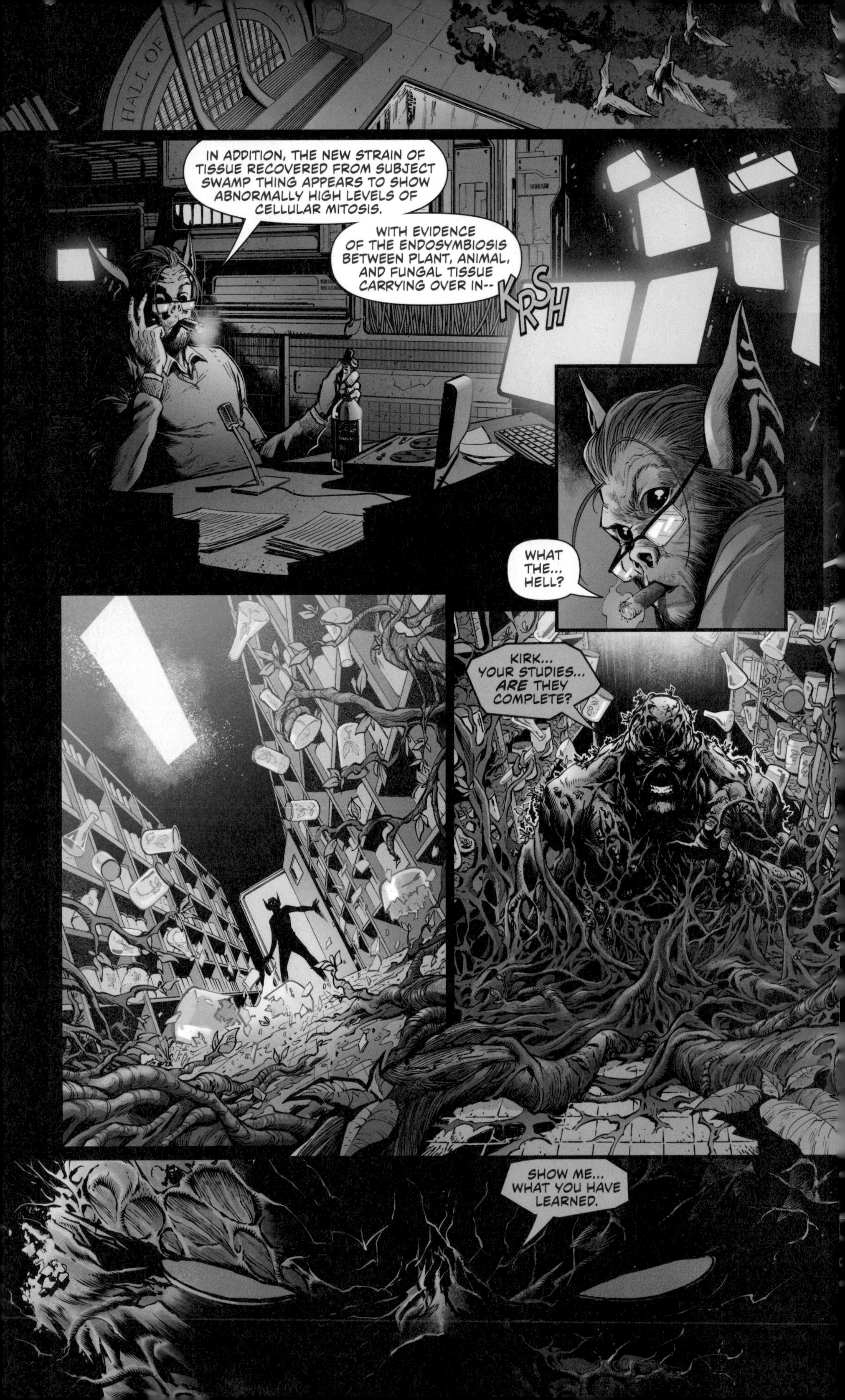
HALL OF
IN ADDITION, THE NEW STRAIN OF TISSUE RECOVERED FROM SUBJECT SWAMP THING APPEARS TO SHOW ABNORMALLY HIGH LEVELS OF CELLULAR MITOSIS.
WITH EVIDENCE OF THE ENDOSYMBIOSIS BETWEEN PLANT, ANIMAL, AND FUNGAL TISSUE CARRYING OVER IN--
KRSH
WHAT THE... HELL?
KIRK... YOUR STUDIES... ARE THEY COMPLETE?
SHOW ME... WHAT YOU HAVE LEARNED.

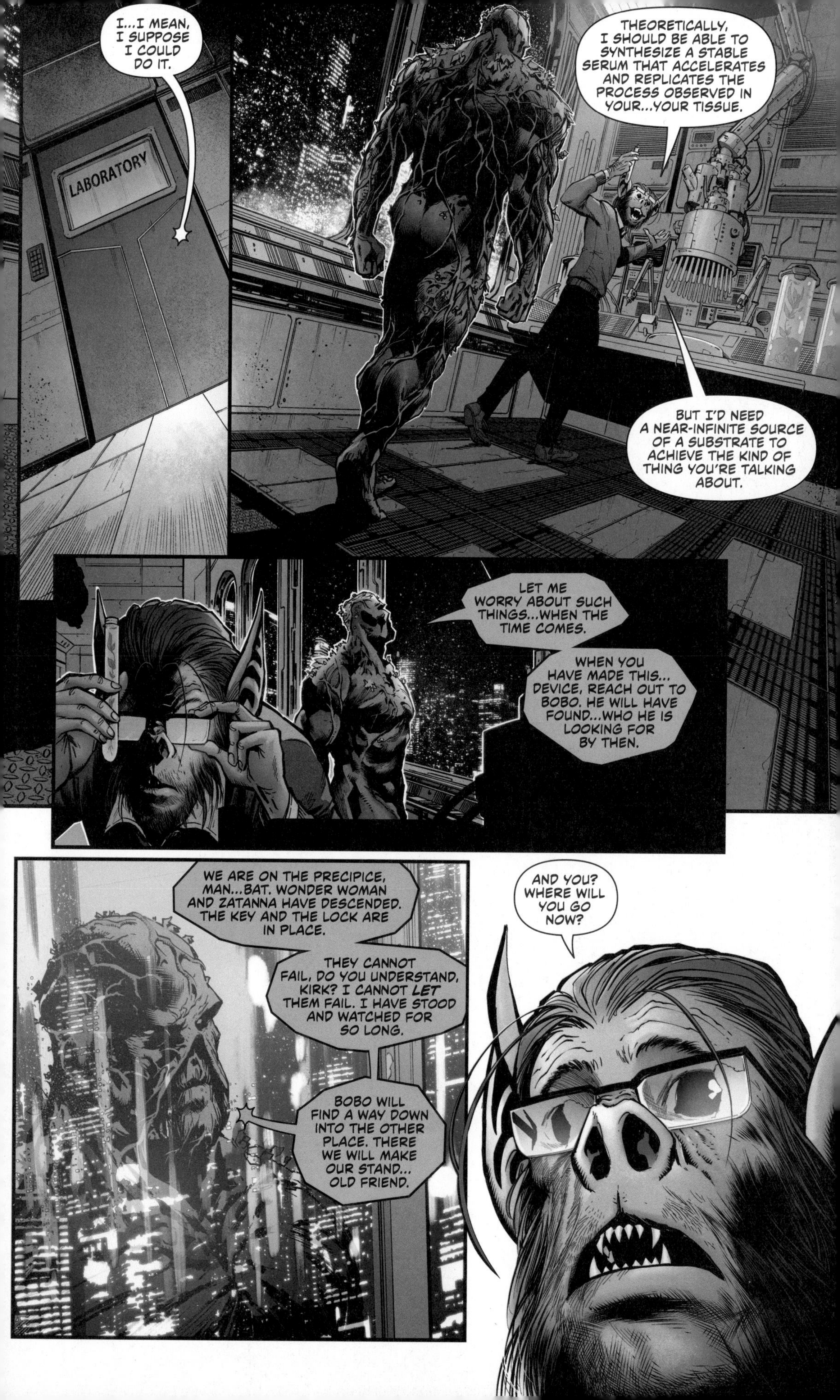
LABORATORY
I...I MEAN, I SUPPOSE I COULD DO IT.
THEORETICALLY, I SHOULD BE ABLE TO SYNTHESIZE A STABLE SERUM THAT ACCELERATES AND REPLICATES THE PROCESS OBSERVED IN YOUR...YOUR TISSUE.
BUT I'D NEED A NEAR-INFINITE SOURCE OF A SUBSTRATE TO ACHIEVE THE KIND OF THING YOU'RE TALKING ABOUT.
LET ME WORRY ABOUT SUCH THINGS...WHEN THE TIME COMES.
WHEN YOU HAVE MADE THIS... DEVICE, REACH OUT TO BOBO. HE WILL HAVE FOUND...WHO HE IS LOOKING FOR BY THEN.
WE ARE ON THE PRECIPICE, MAN...BAT. WONDER WOMAN AND ZATANNA HAVE DESCENDED. THE KEY AND THE LOCK ARE IN PLACE.
THEY CANNOT FAIL, DO YOU UNDERSTAND, KIRK? I CANNOT *LET* THEM FAIL. I HAVE STOOD AND WATCHED FOR SO LONG.
BOBO WILL FIND A WAY DOWN INTO THE OTHER PLACE. THERE WE WILL MAKE OUR STAND... OLD FRIEND.
AND YOU? WHERE WILL YOU GO NOW?

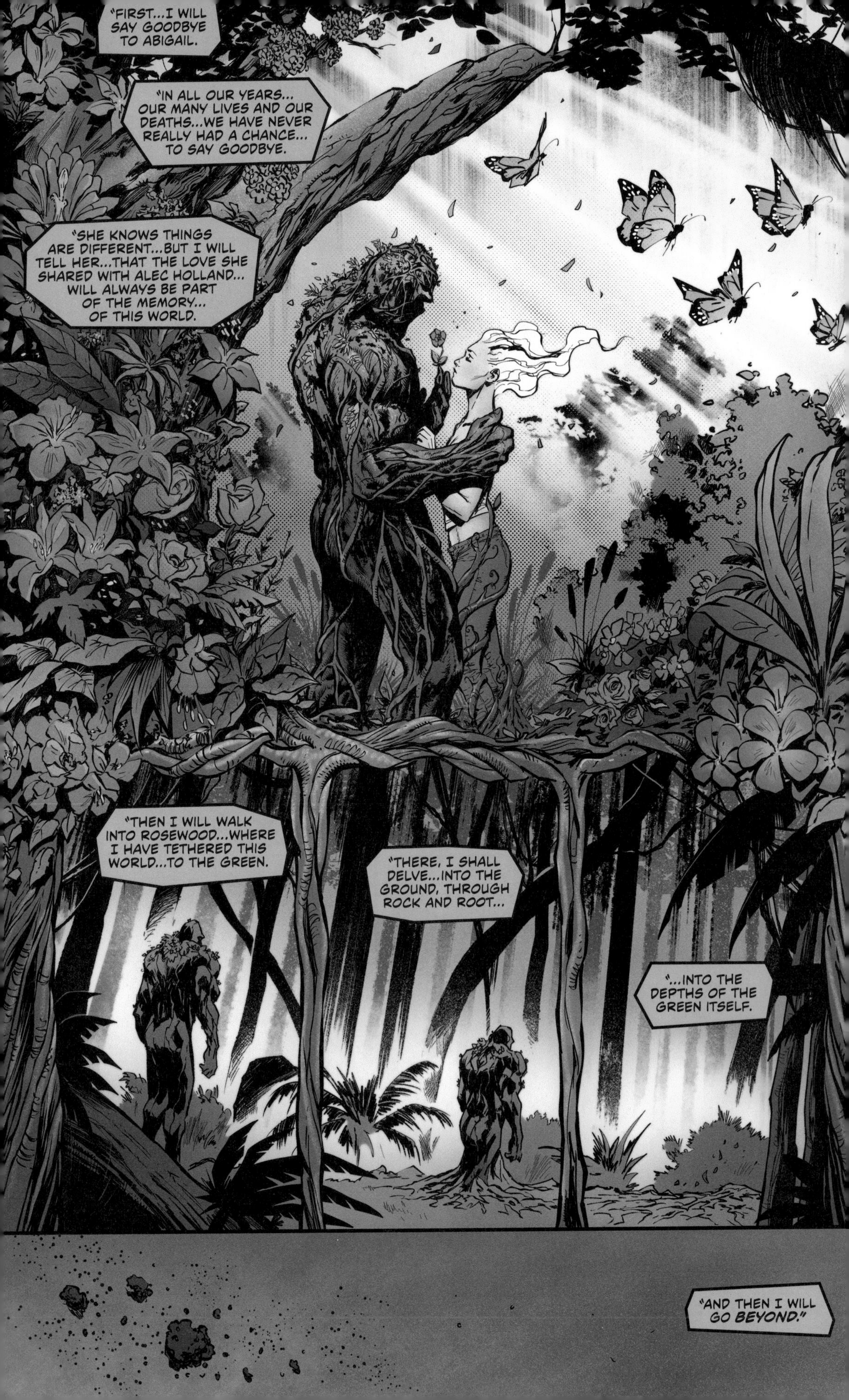
"FIRST...I WILL SAY GOODBYE TO ABIGAIL.
"IN ALL OUR YEARS... OUR MANY LIVES AND OUR DEATHS...WE HAVE NEVER REALLY HAD A CHANCE... TO SAY GOODBYE.
"SHE KNOWS THINGS ARE DIFFERENT...BUT I WILL TELL HER...THAT THE LOVE SHE SHARED WITH ALEC HOLLAND... WILL ALWAYS BE PART OF THE MEMORY... OF THIS WORLD.
"THEN I WILL WALK INTO ROSEWOOD...WHERE I HAVE TETHERED THIS WORLD...TO THE GREEN.
"THERE, I SHALL DELVE...INTO THE GROUND, THROUGH ROCK AND ROOT...
"...INTO THE DEPTHS OF THE GREEN ITSELF.
"AND THEN I WILL GO *BEYOND*."

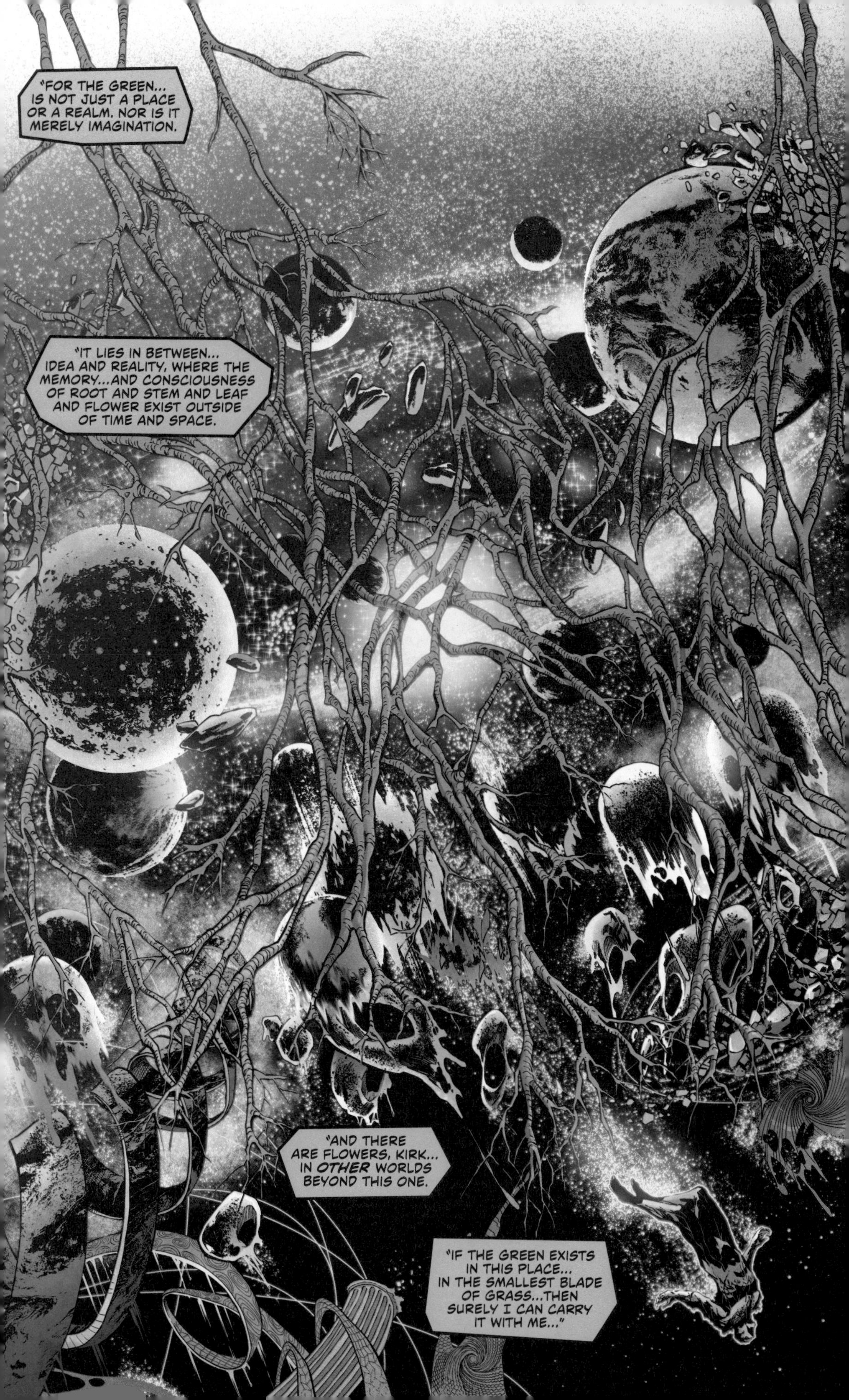
"FOR THE GREEN... IS NOT JUST A PLACE OR A REALM. NOR IS IT MERELY IMAGINATION.
"IT LIES IN BETWEEN... IDEA AND REALITY, WHERE THE MEMORY...AND CONSCIOUSNESS OF ROOT AND STEM AND LEAF AND FLOWER EXIST OUTSIDE OF TIME AND SPACE.
"AND THERE ARE FLOWERS, KIRK... IN *OTHER* WORLDS BEYOND THIS ONE.
"IF THE GREEN EXISTS IN THIS PLACE... IN THE SMALLEST BLADE OF GRASS...THEN SURELY I CAN CARRY IT WITH ME..."

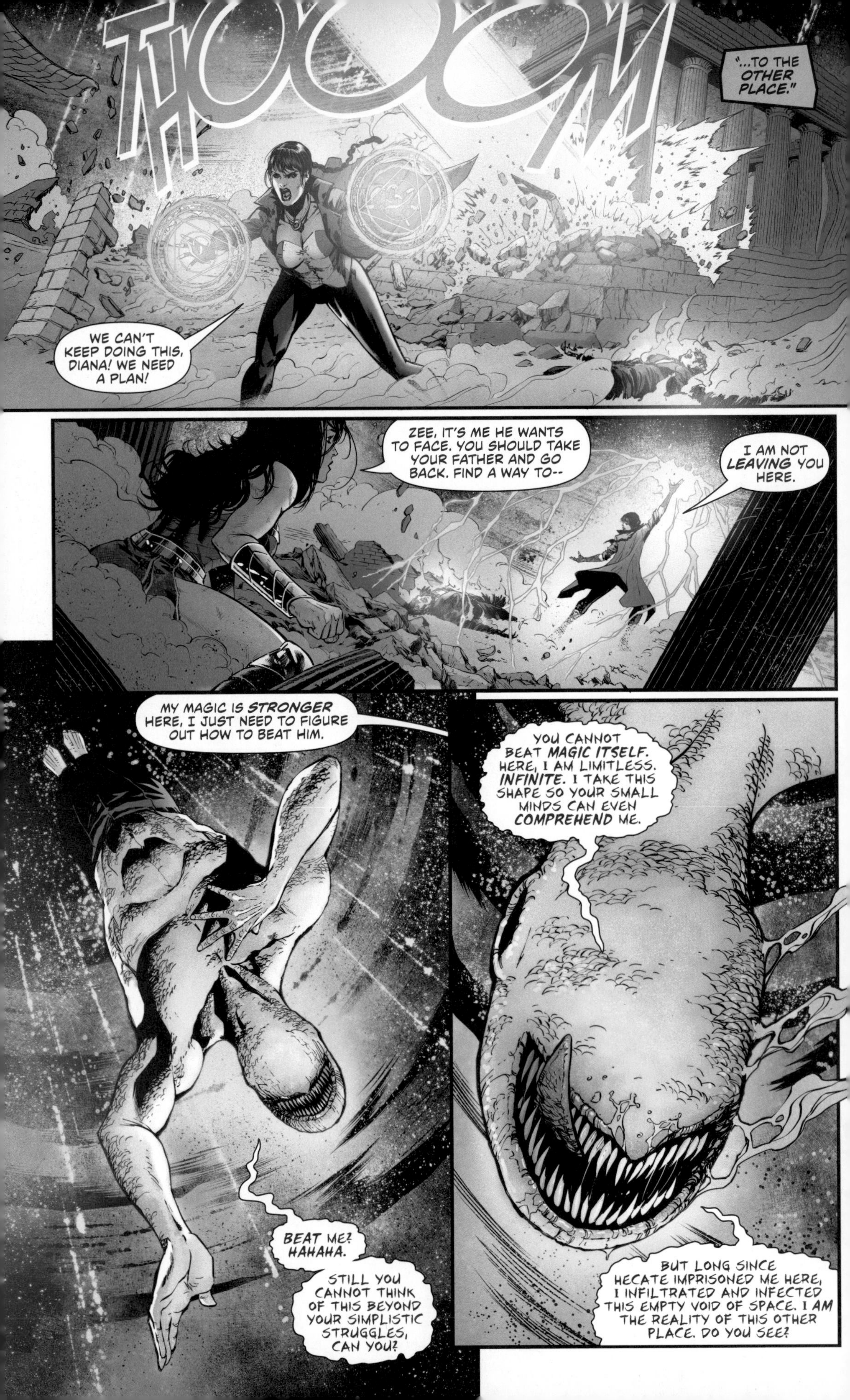
THOOOM
"...TO THE OTHER PLACE."
WE CAN'T KEEP DOING THIS, DIANA! WE NEED A PLAN!
ZEE, IT'S ME HE WANTS TO FACE. YOU SHOULD TAKE YOUR FATHER AND GO BACK. FIND A WAY TO--
I AM NOT LEAVING YOU HERE.
MY MAGIC IS STRONGER HERE, I JUST NEED TO FIGURE OUT HOW TO BEAT HIM.
BEAT ME? HAHAHA.
STILL YOU CANNOT THINK OF THIS BEYOND YOUR SIMPLISTIC STRUGGLES, CAN YOU?
YOU CANNOT BEAT MAGIC ITSELF. HERE, I AM LIMITLESS. INFINITE. I TAKE THIS SHAPE SO YOUR SMALL MINDS CAN EVEN COMPREHEND ME.
BUT LONG SINCE HECATE IMPRISONED ME HERE, I INFILTRATED AND INFECTED THIS EMPTY VOID OF SPACE. I AM THE REALITY OF THIS OTHER PLACE. DO YOU SEE?

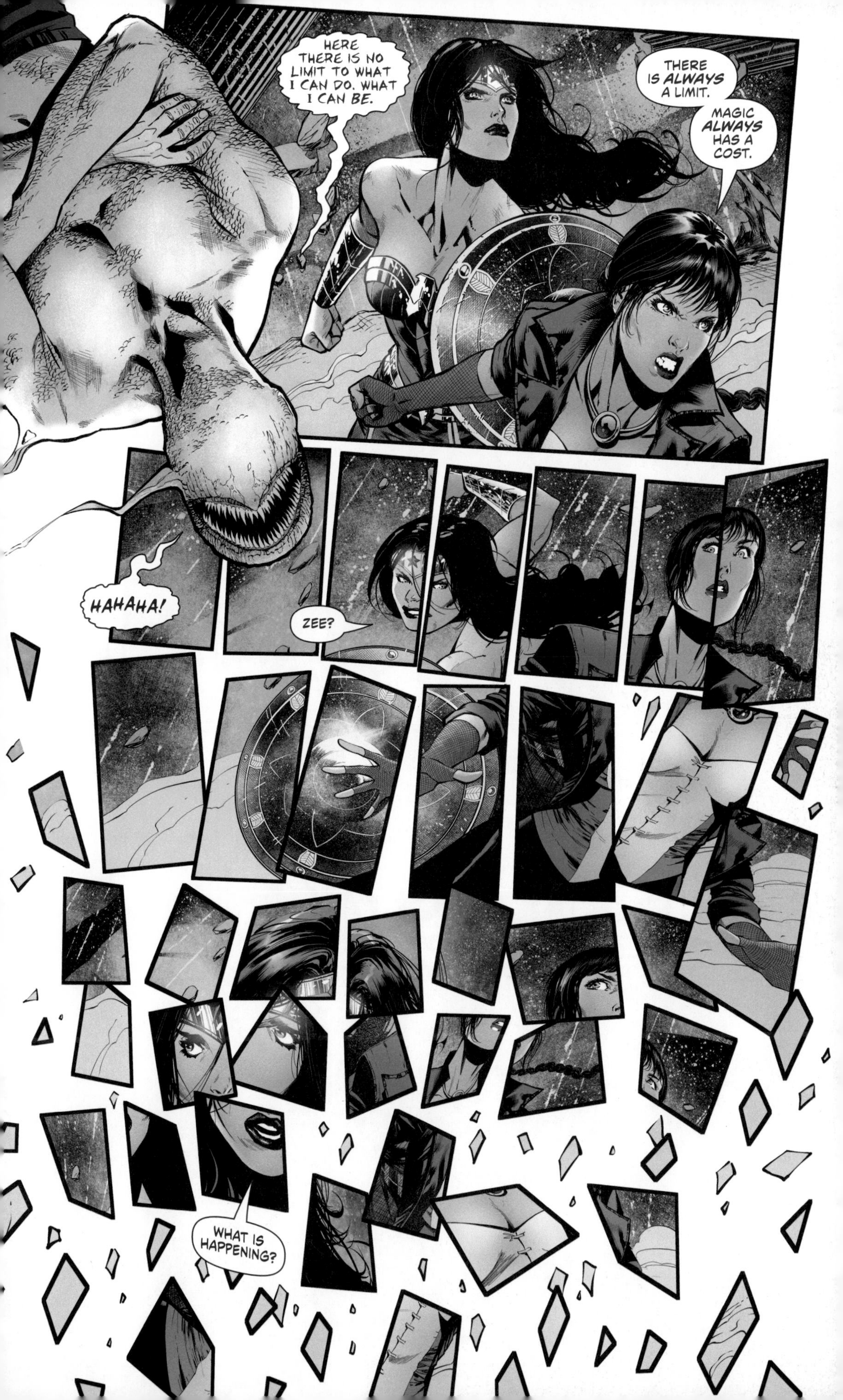
HERE THERE IS NO LIMIT TO WHAT I CAN DO. WHAT I CAN BE.
THERE IS ALWAYS A LIMIT.
MAGIC ALWAYS HAS A COST.
HAHAHA!
ZEE?
WHAT IS HAPPENING?

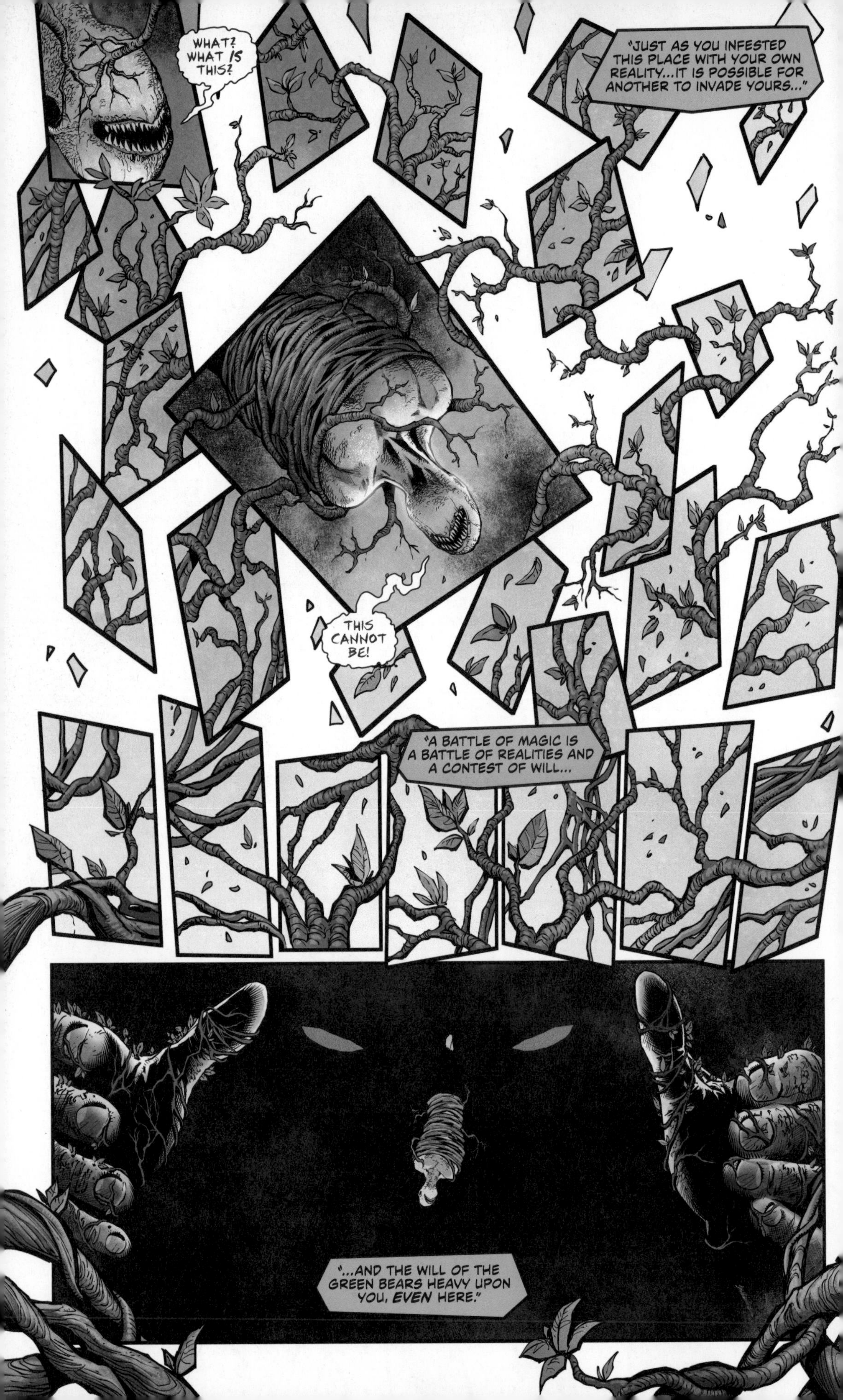
WHAT? WHAT IS THIS?
"JUST AS YOU INFESTED THIS PLACE WITH YOUR OWN REALITY...IT IS POSSIBLE FOR ANOTHER TO INVADE YOURS..."
THIS CANNOT BE!
"A BATTLE OF MAGIC IS A BATTLE OF REALITIES AND A CONTEST OF WILL...
"...AND THE WILL OF THE GREEN BEARS HEAVY UPON YOU, EVEN HERE."

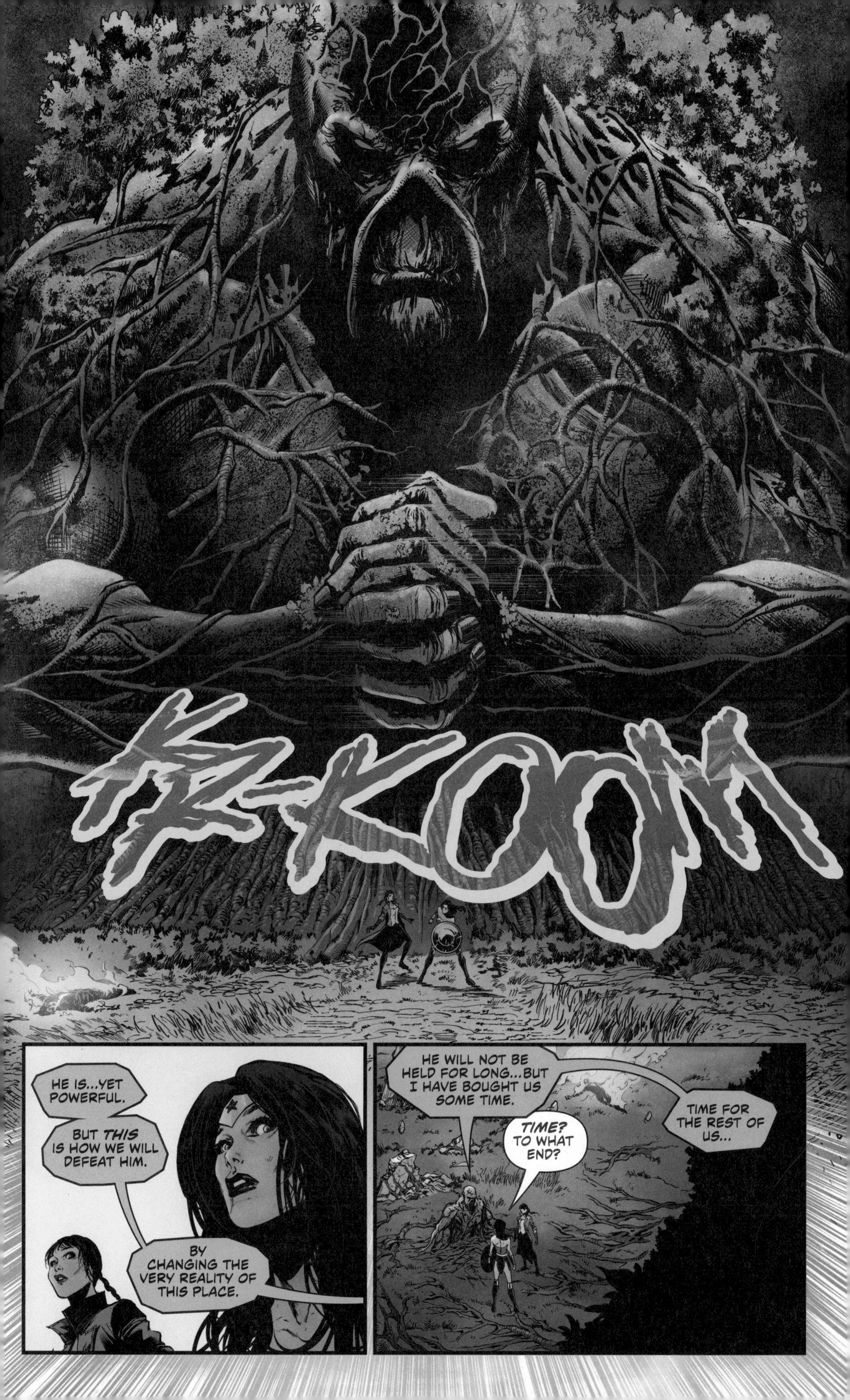
KZ-KOOM
HE IS...YET POWERFUL.
BUT THIS IS HOW WE WILL DEFEAT HIM.
BY CHANGING THE VERY REALITY OF THIS PLACE.
HE WILL NOT BE HELD FOR LONG...BUT I HAVE BOUGHT US SOME TIME.
TIME? TO WHAT END?
TIME FOR THE REST OF US...

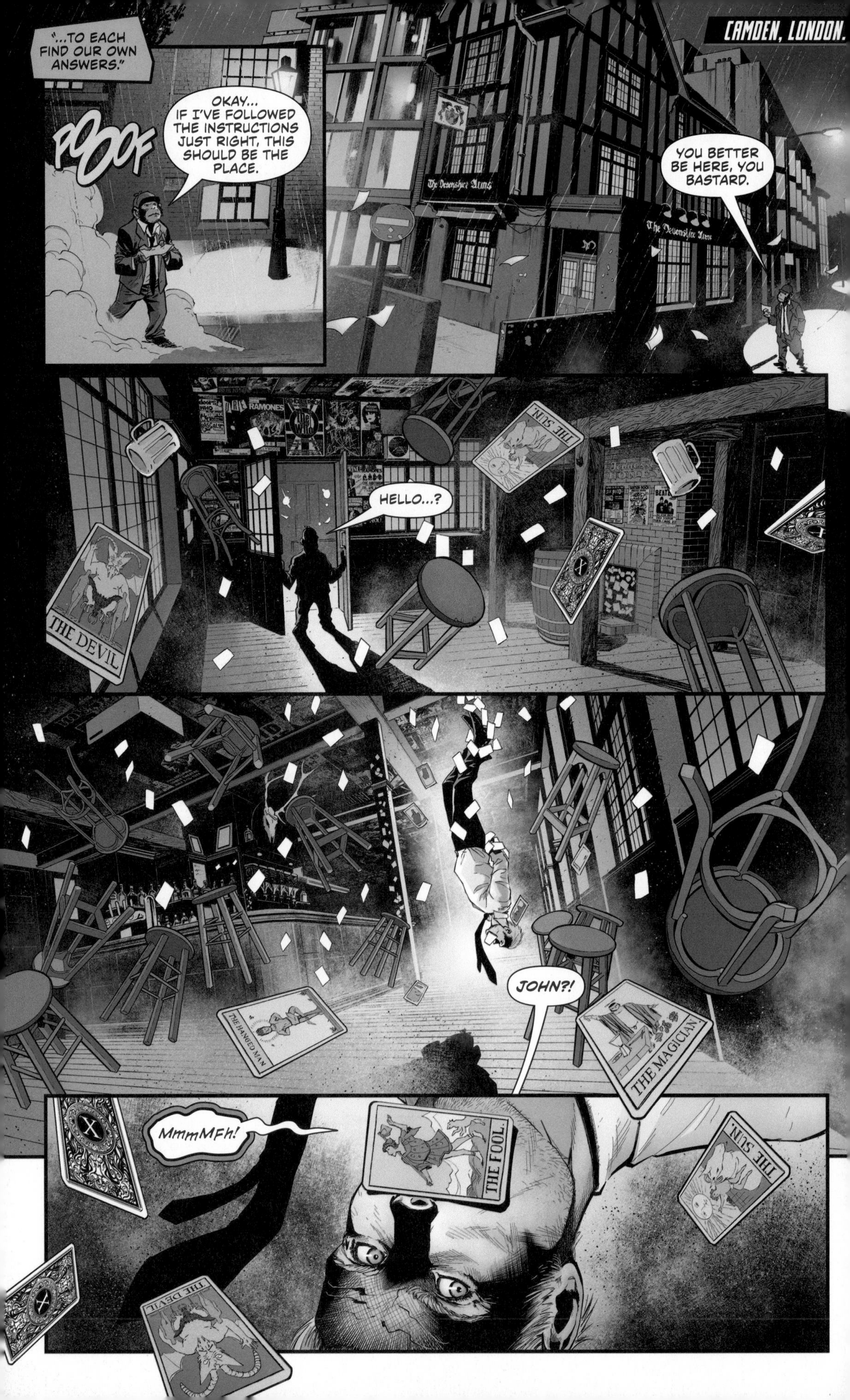
CAMDEN, LONDON.
"...TO EACH FIND OUR OWN ANSWERS."
POOOF
OKAY... IF I'VE FOLLOWED THE INSTRUCTIONS JUST RIGHT, THIS SHOULD BE THE PLACE.
The Devonshire Arms
YOU BETTER BE HERE, YOU BASTARD.
RAMONES
HELLO...?
THE SUN
THE DEVIL
JOHN?!
THE HANGED MAN
THE MAGICIAN
MmmMFh!
THE FOOL.
THE SUN.
THE DEVIL

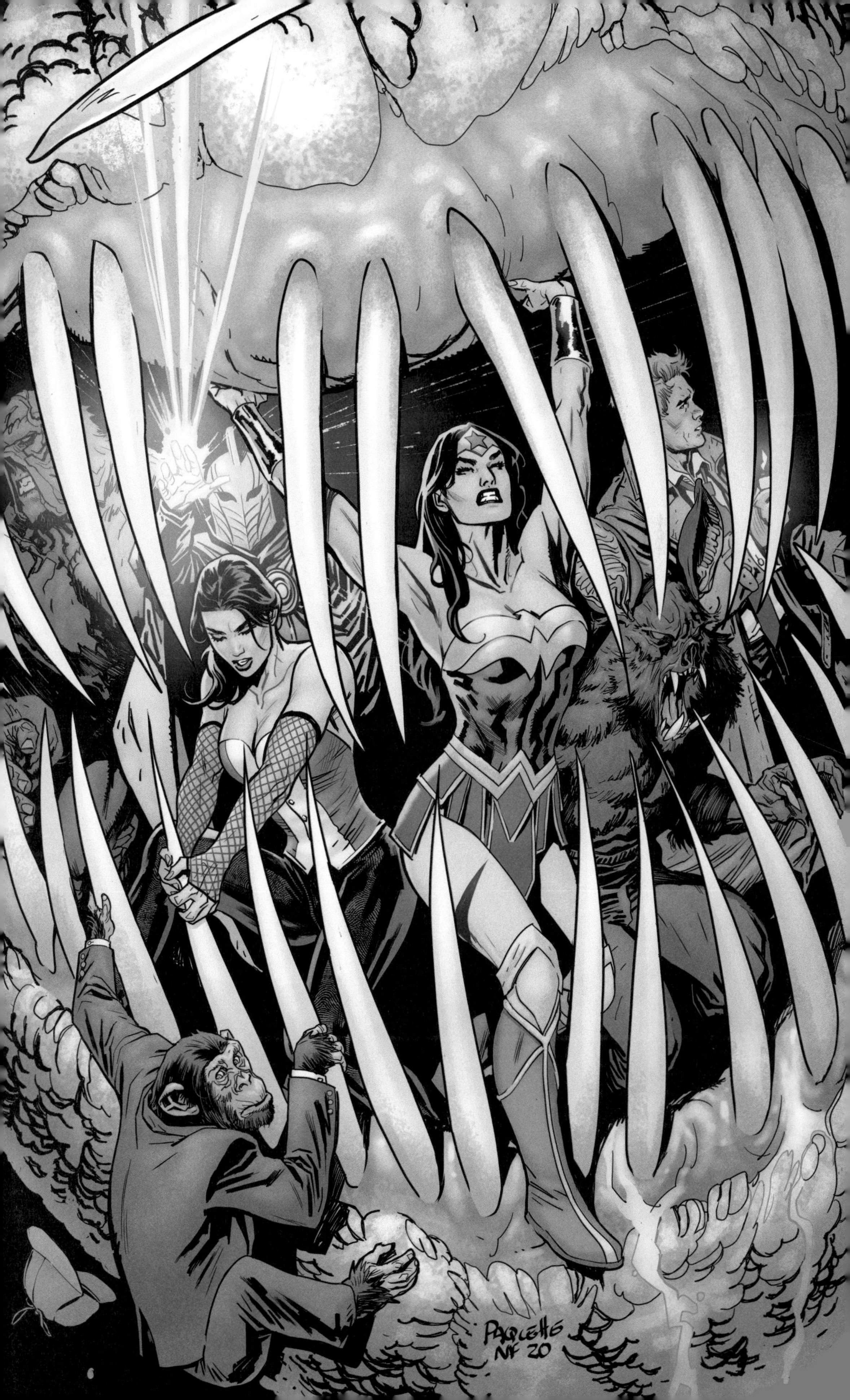

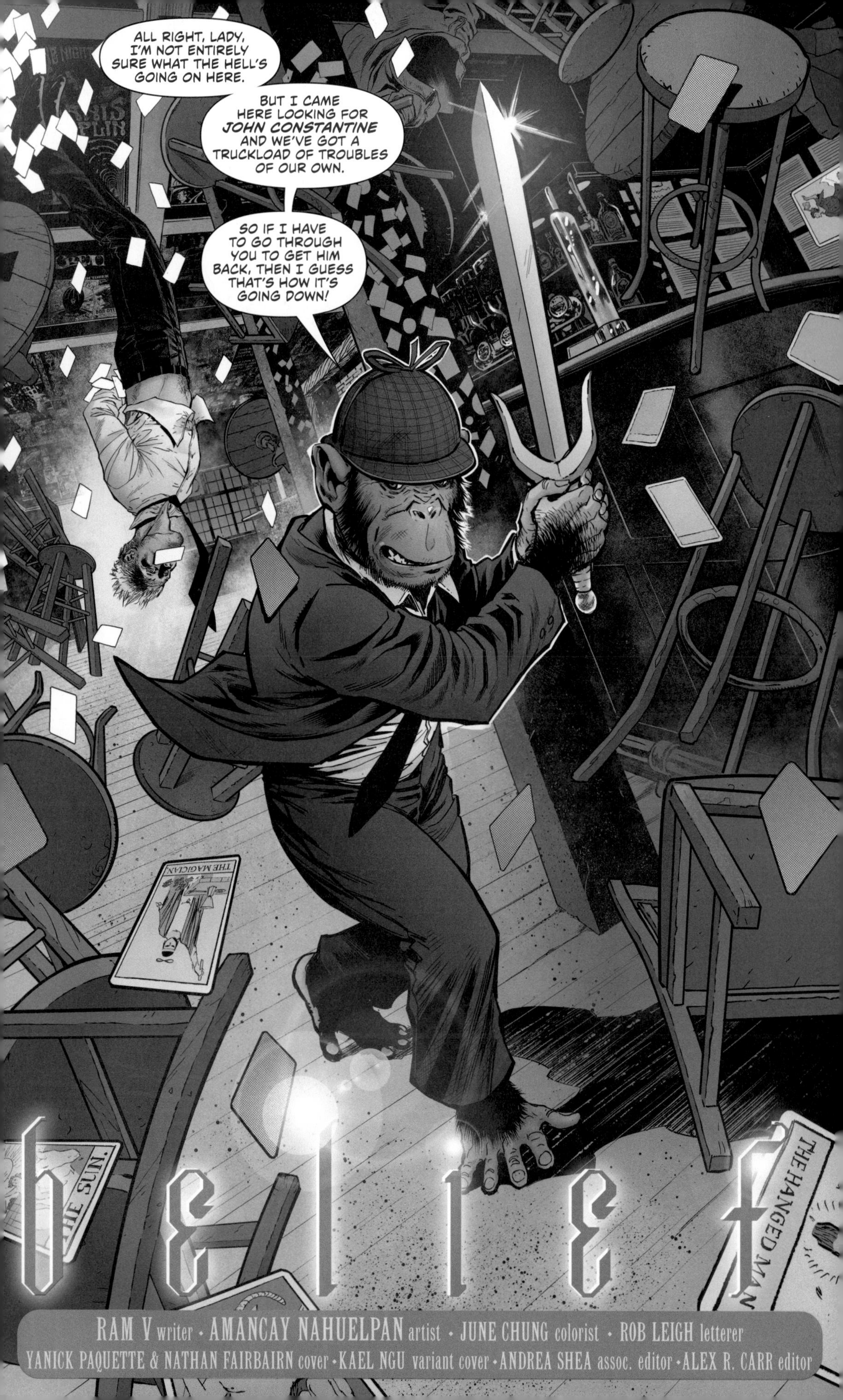
ALL RIGHT, LADY, I'M NOT ENTIRELY SURE WHAT THE HELL'S GOING ON HERE.
BUT I CAME HERE LOOKING FOR JOHN CONSTANTINE AND WE'VE GOT A TRUCKLOAD OF TROUBLES OF OUR OWN.
SO IF I HAVE TO GO THROUGH YOU TO GET HIM BACK, THEN I GUESS THAT'S HOW IT'S GOING DOWN!
THE MAGICIAN.
THE SUN.
THE HANGED MAN
belief
RAM V writer • AMANCAY NAHUELPAN artist • JUNE CHUNG colorist • ROB LEIGH letterer
YANICK PAQUETTE & NATHAN FAIRBAIRN cover • KAEL NGU variant cover • ANDREA SHEA assoc. editor • ALEX R. CARR editor

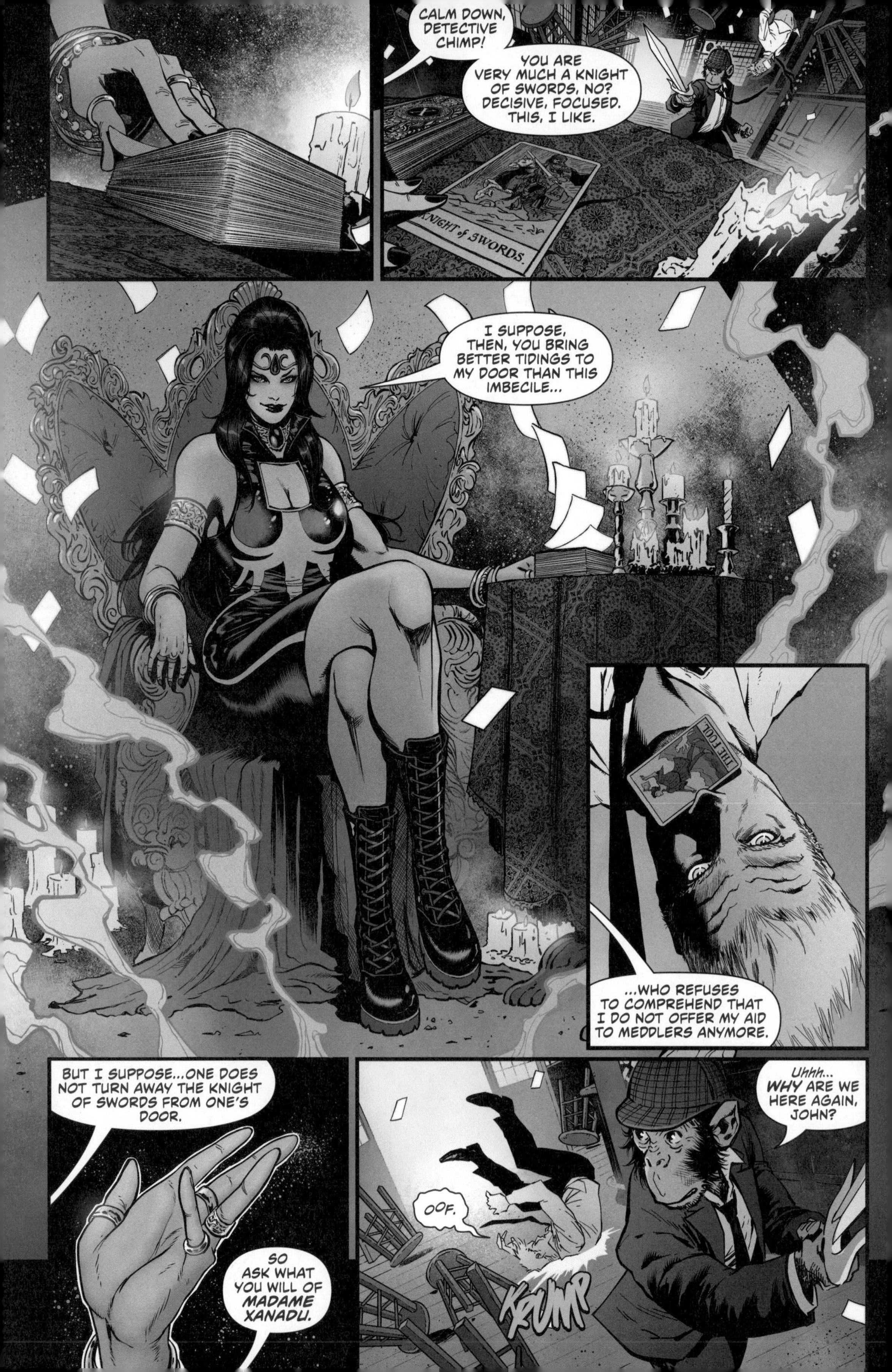
CALM DOWN, DETECTIVE CHIMP!
YOU ARE VERY MUCH A KNIGHT OF SWORDS, NO? DECISIVE, FOCUSED. THIS, I LIKE.
KNIGHT of SWORDS.
I SUPPOSE, THEN, YOU BRING BETTER TIDINGS TO MY DOOR THAN THIS IMBECILE...
THE FOOL
...WHO REFUSES TO COMPREHEND THAT I DO NOT OFFER MY AID TO MEDDLERS ANYMORE.
BUT I SUPPOSE...ONE DOES NOT TURN AWAY THE KNIGHT OF SWORDS FROM ONE'S DOOR.
SO ASK WHAT YOU WILL OF MADAME XANADU.
Uhhh... WHY ARE WE HERE AGAIN, JOHN?
OOF.
KRUMP

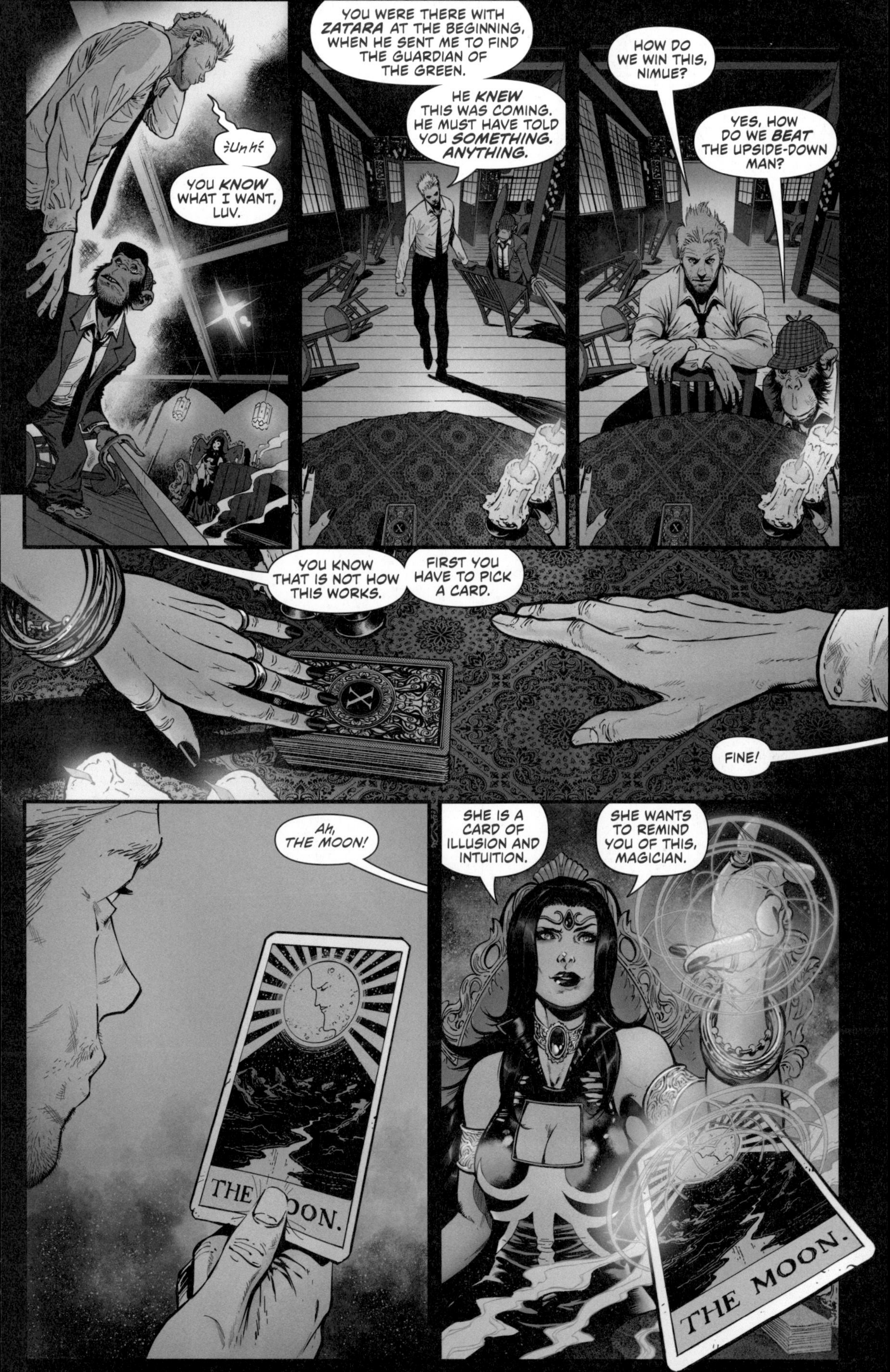

Unh
YOU KNOW WHAT I WANT, LUV.
YOU WERE THERE WITH ZATARA AT THE BEGINNING, WHEN HE SENT ME TO FIND THE GUARDIAN OF THE GREEN.
HE KNEW THIS WAS COMING. HE MUST HAVE TOLD YOU SOMETHING. ANYTHING.
HOW DO WE WIN THIS, NIMUE?
YES, HOW DO WE BEAT THE UPSIDE-DOWN MAN?
YOU KNOW THAT IS NOT HOW THIS WORKS.
FIRST YOU HAVE TO PICK A CARD.
FINE!
Ah, THE MOON!
THE MOON.
SHE IS A CARD OF ILLUSION AND INTUITION.
SHE WANTS TO REMIND YOU OF THIS, MAGICIAN.
THE MOON.

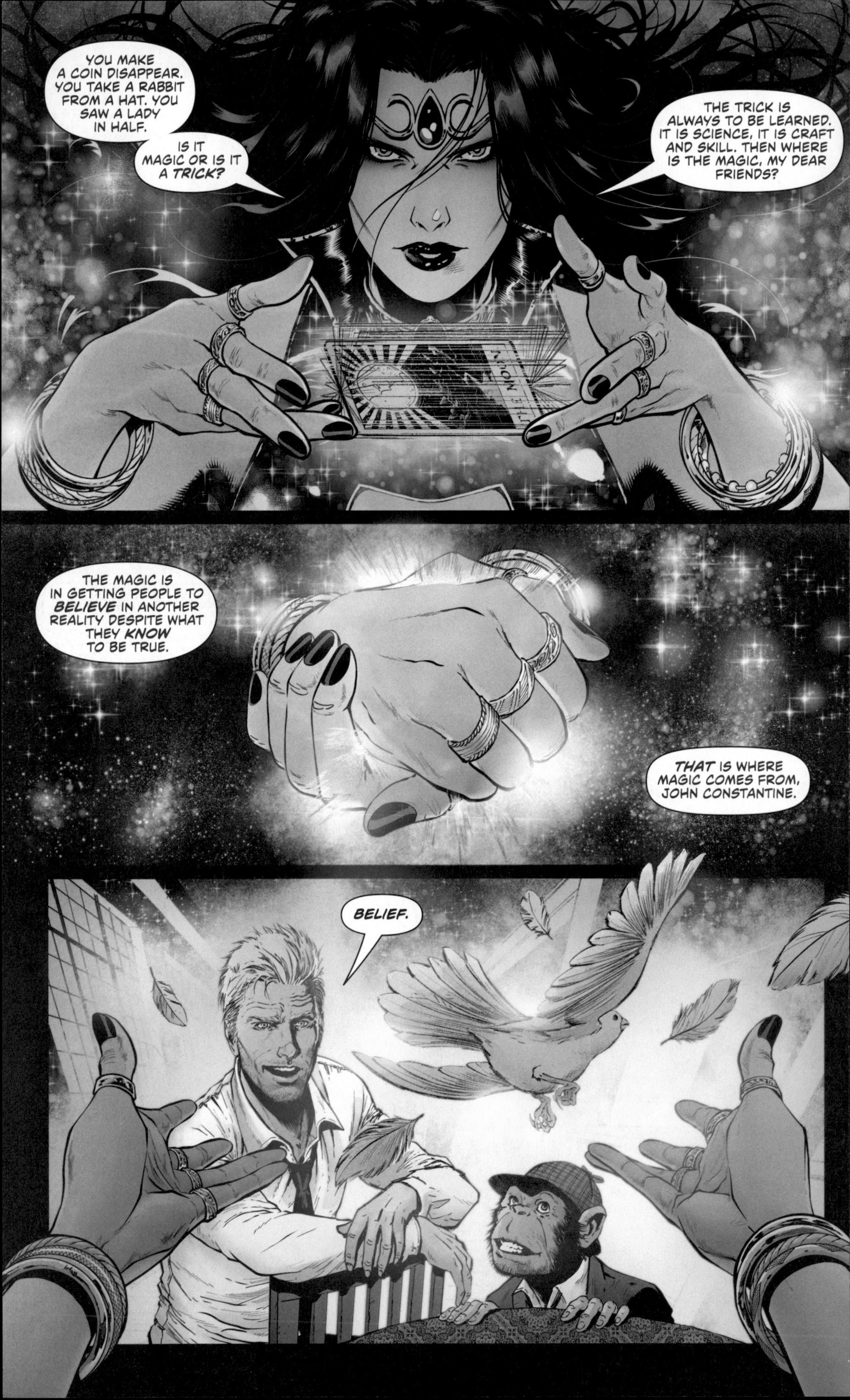
YOU MAKE A COIN DISAPPEAR. YOU TAKE A RABBIT FROM A HAT. YOU SAW A LADY IN HALF.
IS IT MAGIC OR IS IT A *TRICK?*
THE TRICK IS ALWAYS TO BE LEARNED. IT IS SCIENCE, IT IS CRAFT AND SKILL. THEN WHERE IS THE MAGIC, MY DEAR FRIENDS?
THE MAGIC IS IN GETTING PEOPLE TO ***BELIEVE*** IN ANOTHER REALITY DESPITE WHAT THEY ***KNOW*** TO BE TRUE.
THAT IS WHERE MAGIC COMES FROM, JOHN CONSTANTINE.
BELIEF.

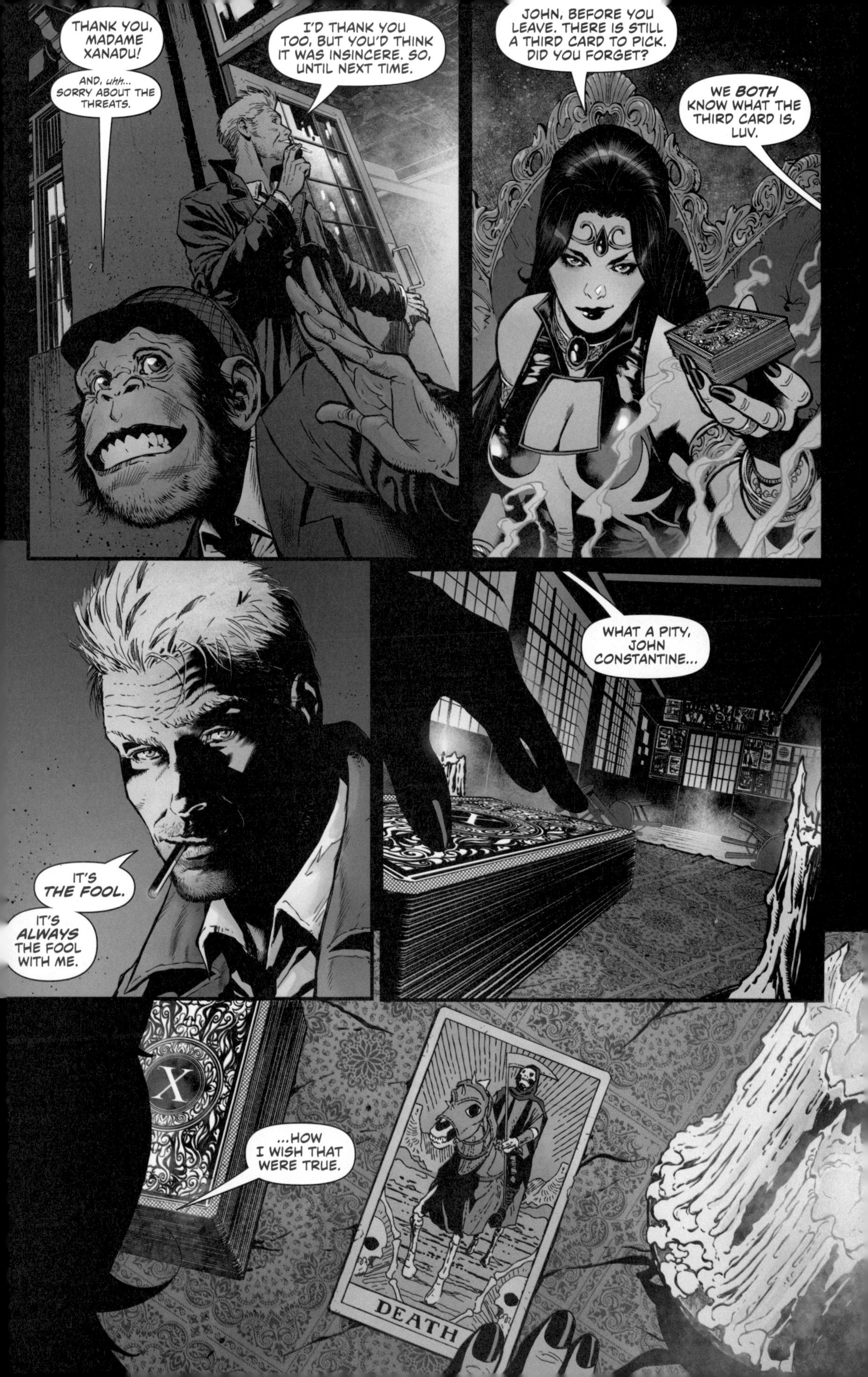
THANK YOU, MADAME XANADU!
AND, *uhh*... SORRY ABOUT THE THREATS.
I'D THANK YOU TOO, BUT YOU'D THINK IT WAS INSINCERE. SO, UNTIL NEXT TIME.
JOHN, BEFORE YOU LEAVE. THERE IS STILL A THIRD CARD TO PICK. DID YOU FORGET?
WE *BOTH* KNOW WHAT THE THIRD CARD IS, LUV.
IT'S *THE FOOL.*
IT'S *ALWAYS* THE FOOL WITH ME.
WHAT A PITY, JOHN CONSTANTINE...
...HOW I WISH THAT WERE TRUE.
X
DEATH

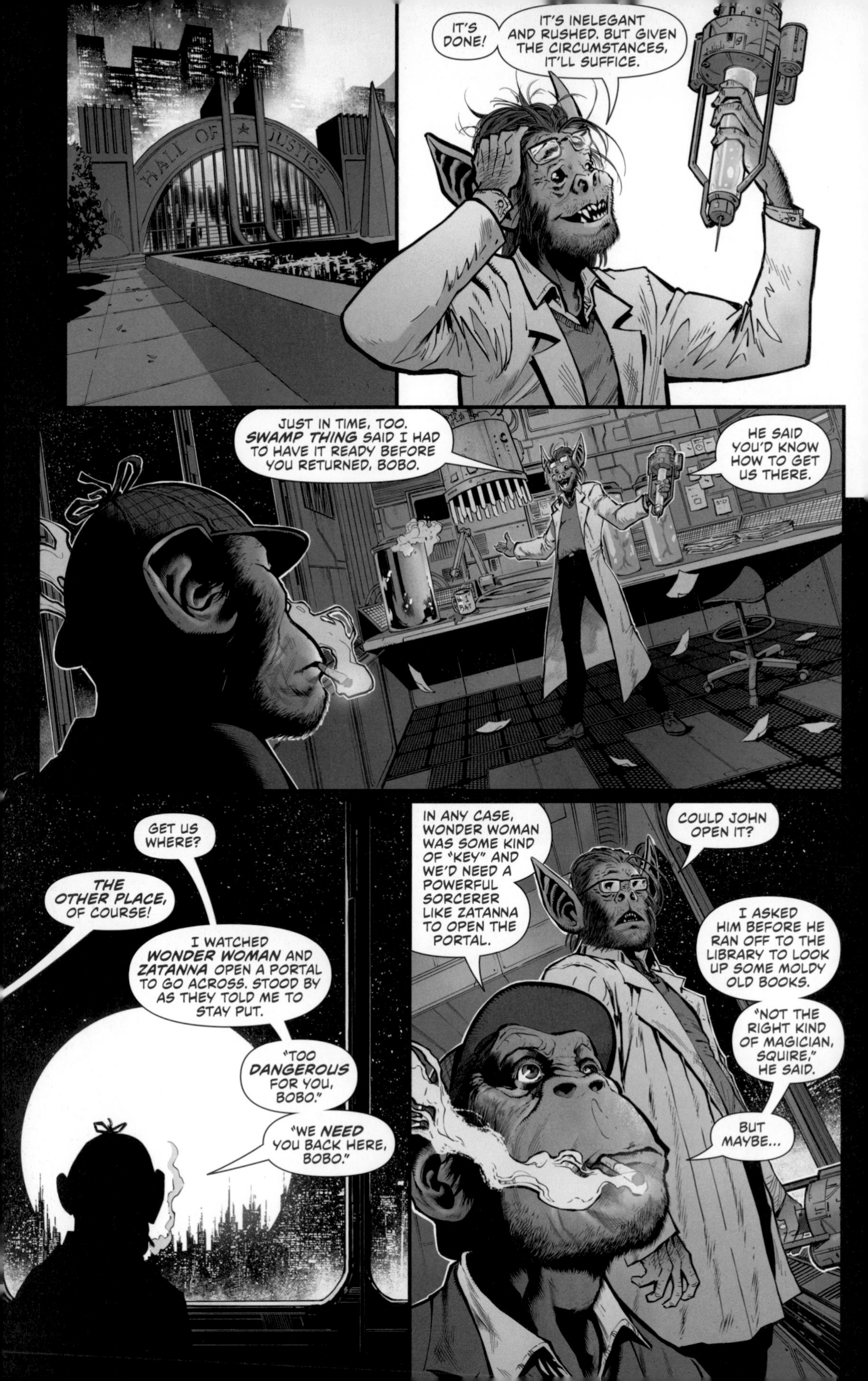
HALL OF JUSTICE
IT'S DONE!
IT'S INELEGANT AND RUSHED. BUT GIVEN THE CIRCUMSTANCES, IT'LL SUFFICE.
JUST IN TIME, TOO. SWAMP THING SAID I HAD TO HAVE IT READY BEFORE YOU RETURNED, BOBO.
HE SAID YOU'D KNOW HOW TO GET US THERE.
GET US WHERE?
THE OTHER PLACE, OF COURSE!
I WATCHED WONDER WOMAN AND ZATANNA OPEN A PORTAL TO GO ACROSS. STOOD BY AS THEY TOLD ME TO STAY PUT.
"TOO DANGEROUS FOR YOU, BOBO."
"WE NEED YOU BACK HERE, BOBO."
IN ANY CASE, WONDER WOMAN WAS SOME KIND OF "KEY" AND WE'D NEED A POWERFUL SORCERER LIKE ZATANNA TO OPEN THE PORTAL.
COULD JOHN OPEN IT?
I ASKED HIM BEFORE HE RAN OFF TO THE LIBRARY TO LOOK UP SOME MOLDY OLD BOOKS.
"NOT THE RIGHT KIND OF MAGICIAN, SQUIRE," HE SAID.
BUT MAYBE...

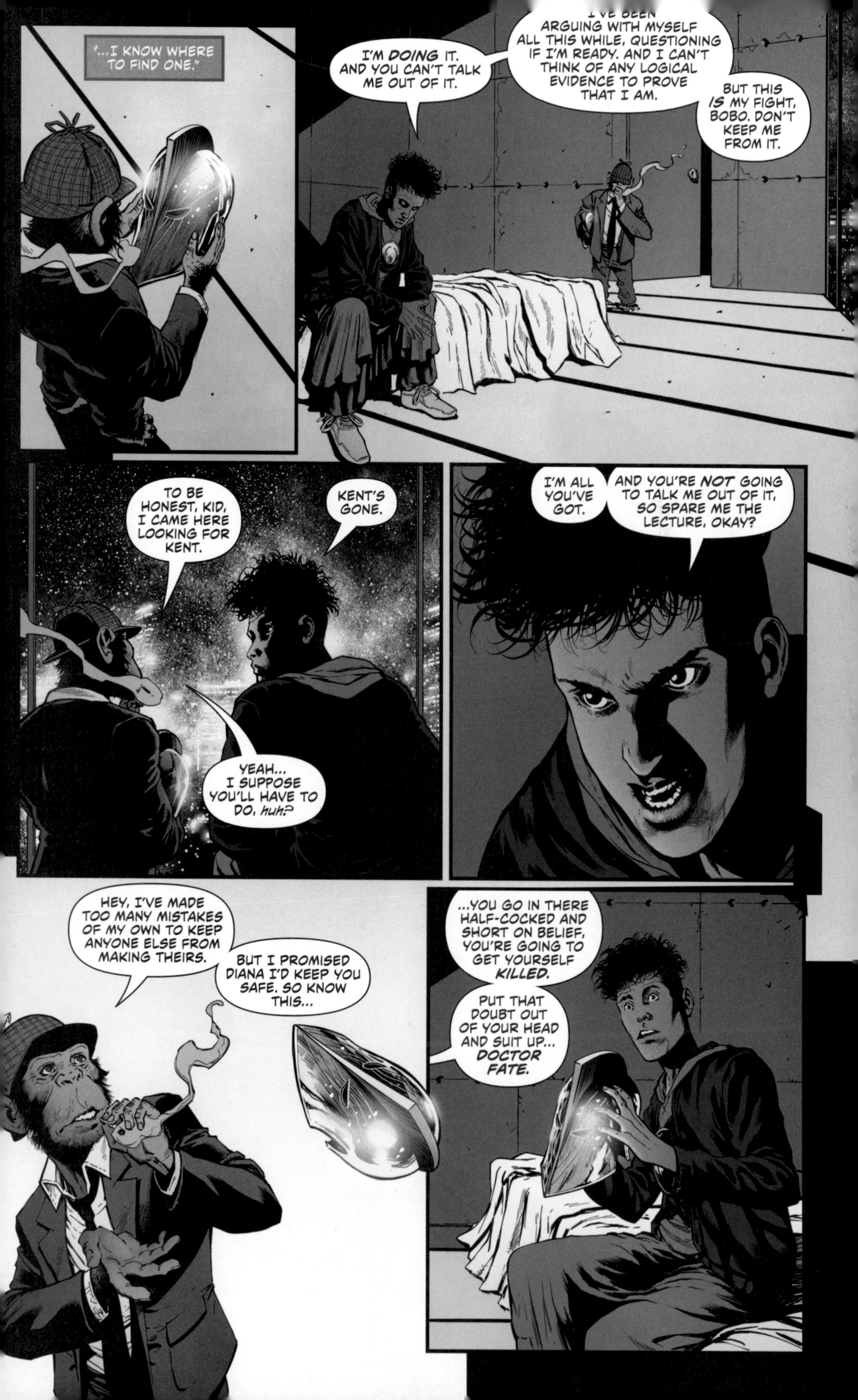
"...I KNOW WHERE TO FIND ONE."
I'M DOING IT. AND YOU CAN'T TALK ME OUT OF IT.
I'VE BEEN ARGUING WITH MYSELF ALL THIS WHILE, QUESTIONING IF I'M READY. AND I CAN'T THINK OF ANY LOGICAL EVIDENCE TO PROVE THAT I AM.
BUT THIS IS MY FIGHT, BOBO. DON'T KEEP ME FROM IT.
TO BE HONEST, KID, I CAME HERE LOOKING FOR KENT.
KENT'S GONE.
YEAH... I SUPPOSE YOU'LL HAVE TO DO, huh?
I'M ALL YOU'VE GOT.
AND YOU'RE NOT GOING TO TALK ME OUT OF IT, SO SPARE ME THE LECTURE, OKAY?
HEY, I'VE MADE TOO MANY MISTAKES OF MY OWN TO KEEP ANYONE ELSE FROM MAKING THEIRS.
BUT I PROMISED DIANA I'D KEEP YOU SAFE. SO KNOW THIS...
...YOU GO IN THERE HALF-COCKED AND SHORT ON BELIEF, YOU'RE GOING TO GET YOURSELF KILLED.
PUT THAT DOUBT OUT OF YOUR HEAD AND SUIT UP... DOCTOR FATE.

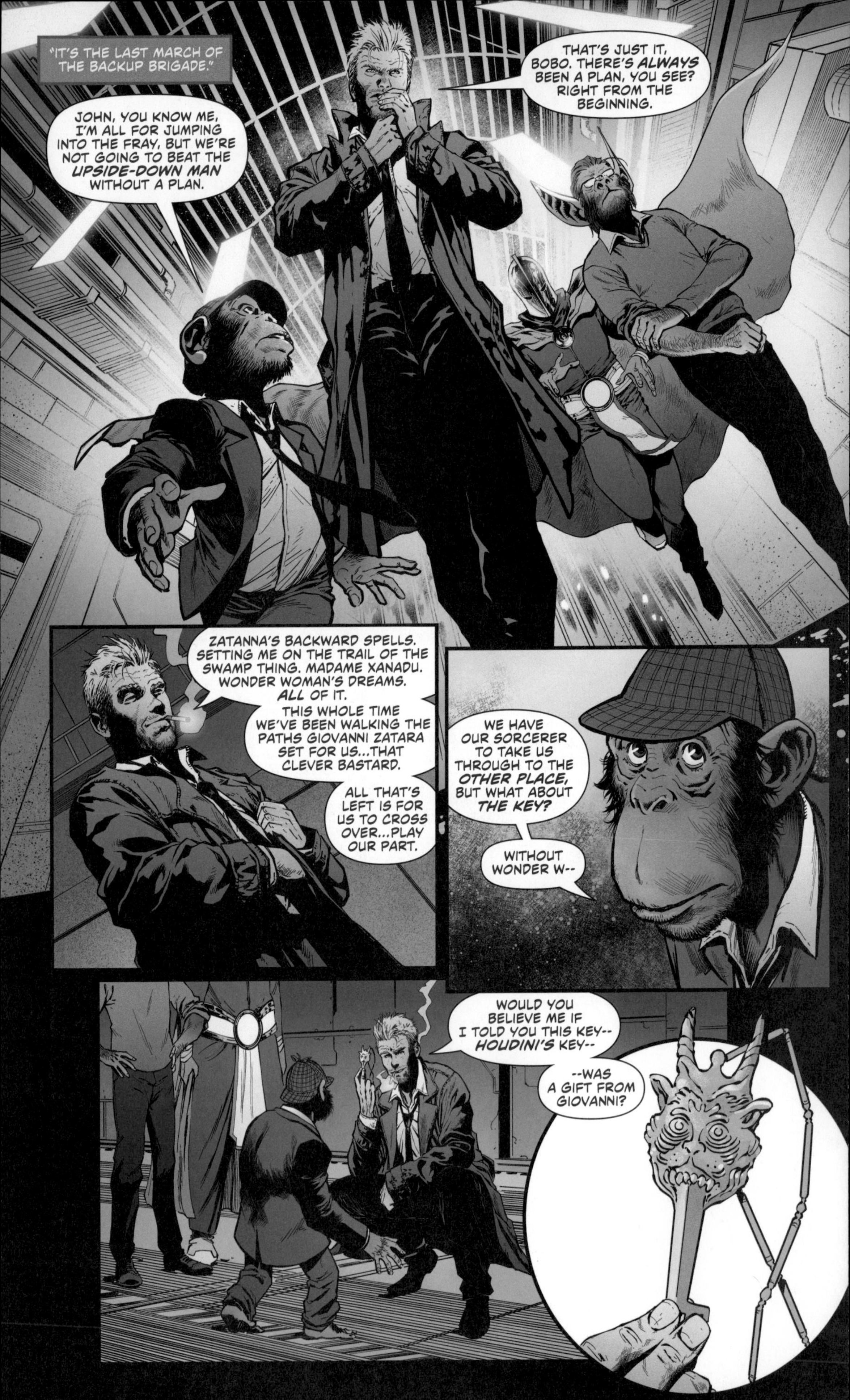
"IT'S THE LAST MARCH OF THE BACKUP BRIGADE."
JOHN, YOU KNOW ME, I'M ALL FOR JUMPING INTO THE FRAY, BUT WE'RE NOT GOING TO BEAT THE UPSIDE-DOWN MAN WITHOUT A PLAN.
THAT'S JUST IT, BOBO. THERE'S ALWAYS BEEN A PLAN, YOU SEE? RIGHT FROM THE BEGINNING.
ZATANNA'S BACKWARD SPELLS. SETTING ME ON THE TRAIL OF THE SWAMP THING. MADAME XANADU. WONDER WOMAN'S DREAMS. ALL OF IT.
THIS WHOLE TIME WE'VE BEEN WALKING THE PATHS GIOVANNI ZATARA SET FOR US...THAT CLEVER BASTARD.
ALL THAT'S LEFT IS FOR US TO CROSS OVER...PLAY OUR PART.
WE HAVE OUR SORCERER TO TAKE US THROUGH TO THE OTHER PLACE, BUT WHAT ABOUT THE KEY?
WITHOUT WONDER W--
WOULD YOU BELIEVE ME IF I TOLD YOU THIS KEY-- HOUDINI'S KEY--
--WAS A GIFT FROM GIOVANNI?

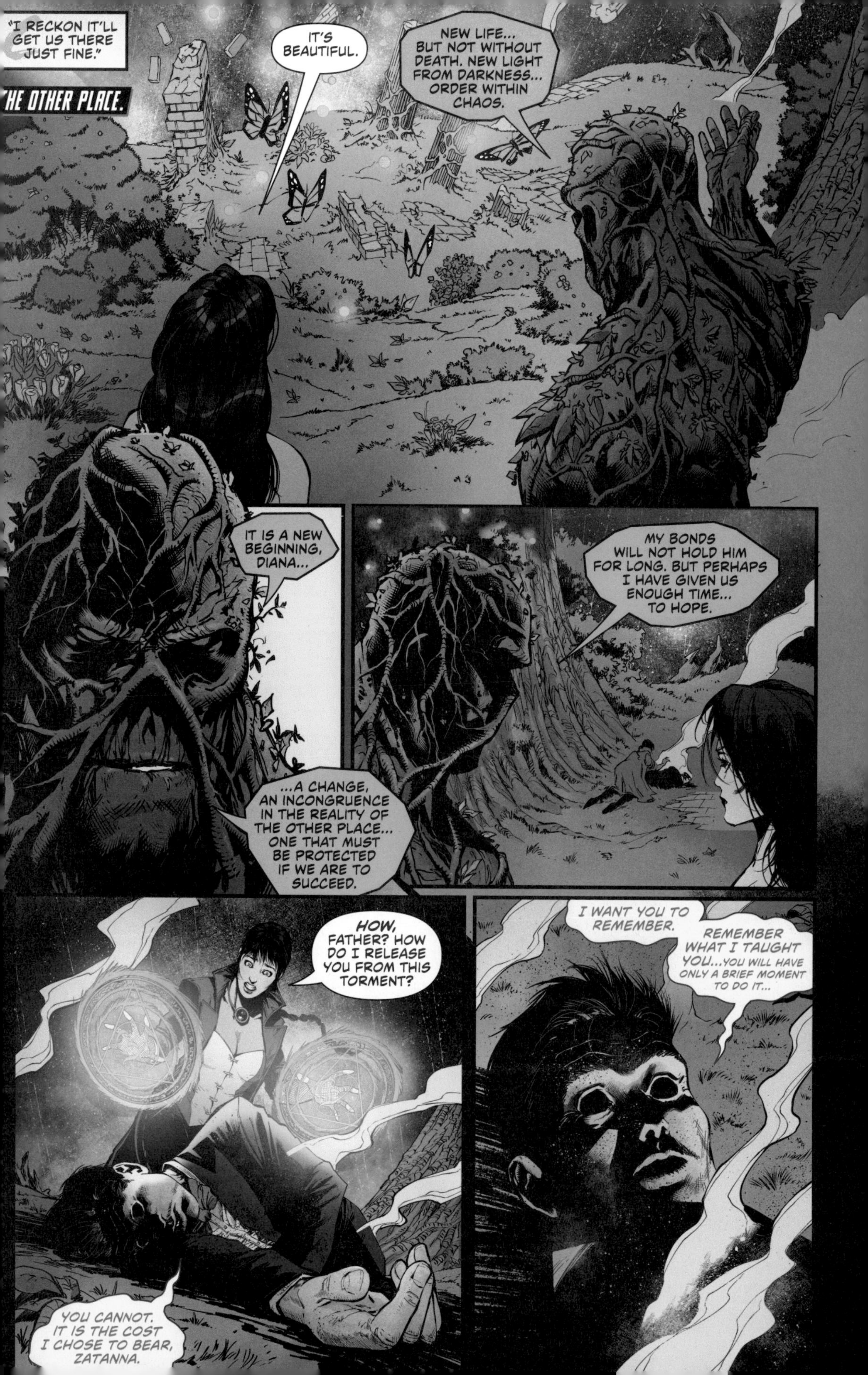
"I RECKON IT'LL GET US THERE JUST FINE."
THE OTHER PLACE.
IT'S BEAUTIFUL.
NEW LIFE... BUT NOT WITHOUT DEATH. NEW LIGHT FROM DARKNESS... ORDER WITHIN CHAOS.
IT IS A NEW BEGINNING, DIANA...
...A CHANGE, AN INCONGRUENCE IN THE REALITY OF THE OTHER PLACE... ONE THAT MUST BE PROTECTED IF WE ARE TO SUCCEED.
MY BONDS WILL NOT HOLD HIM FOR LONG. BUT PERHAPS I HAVE GIVEN US ENOUGH TIME... TO HOPE.
HOW, FATHER? HOW DO I RELEASE YOU FROM THIS TORMENT?
YOU CANNOT. IT IS THE COST I CHOSE TO BEAR, ZATANNA.
I WANT YOU TO REMEMBER.
REMEMBER WHAT I TAUGHT YOU...YOU WILL HAVE ONLY A BRIEF MOMENT TO DO IT...

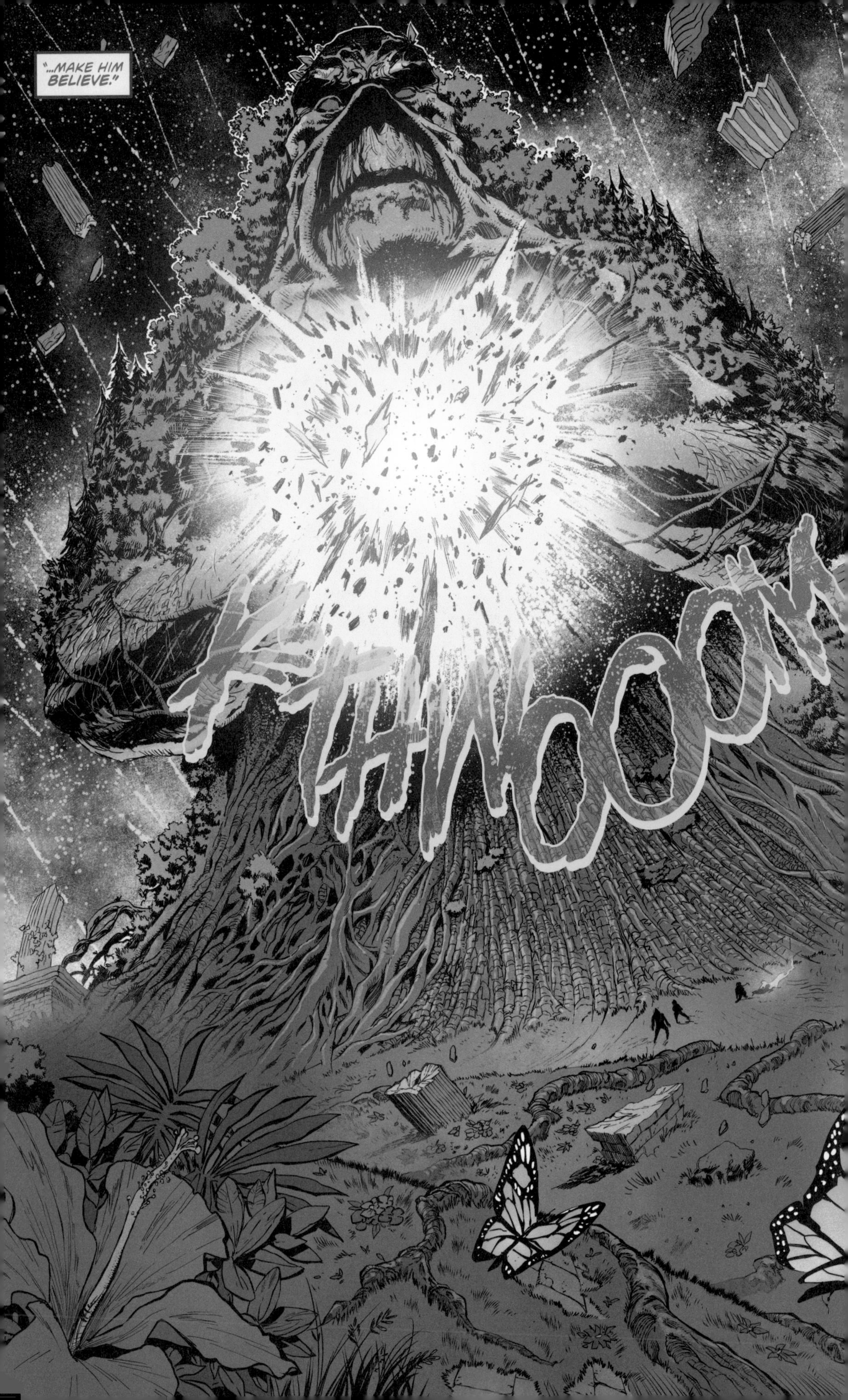
"...MAKE HIM BELIEVE."
KTHWOOOM

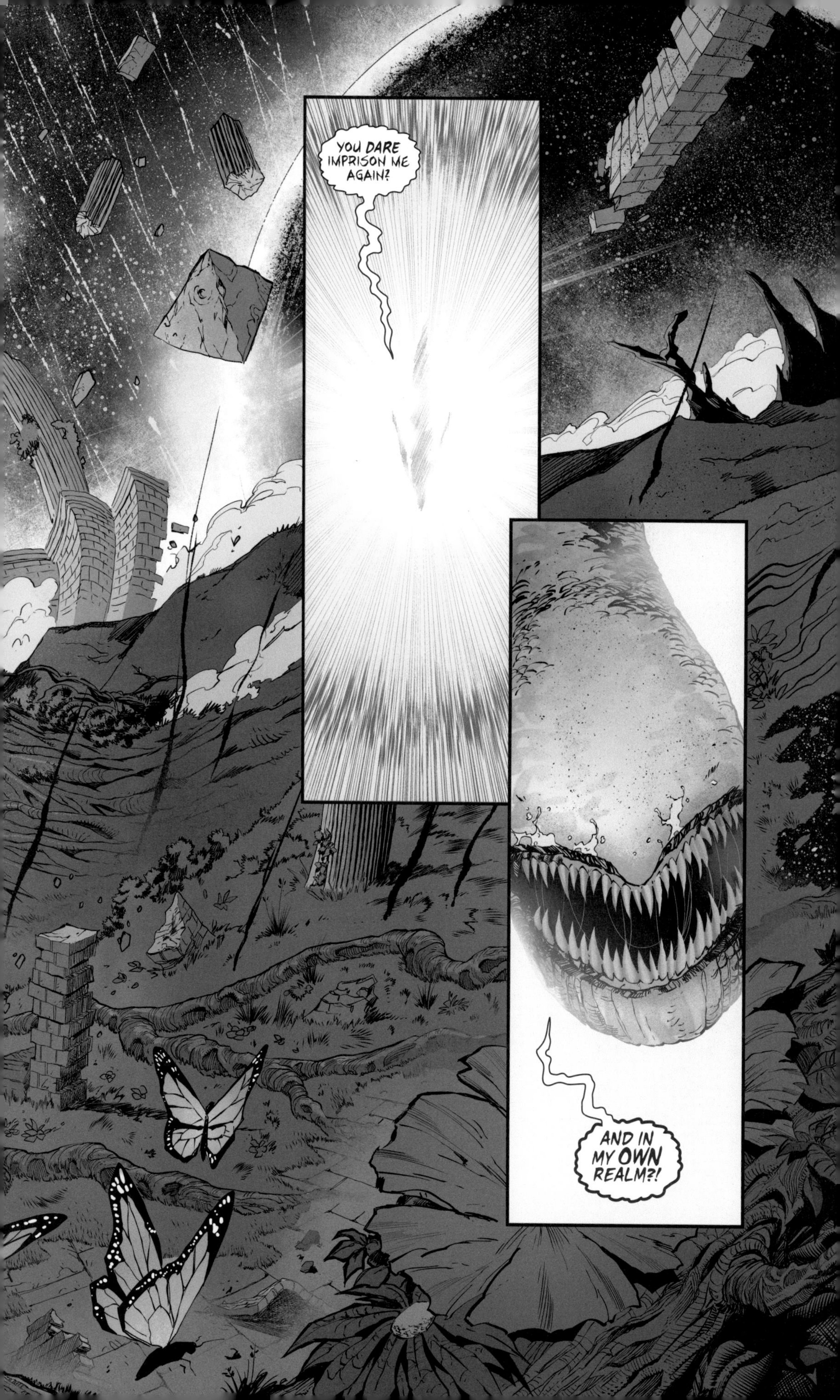
YOU DARE IMPRISON ME AGAIN?
AND IN MY OWN REALM?!

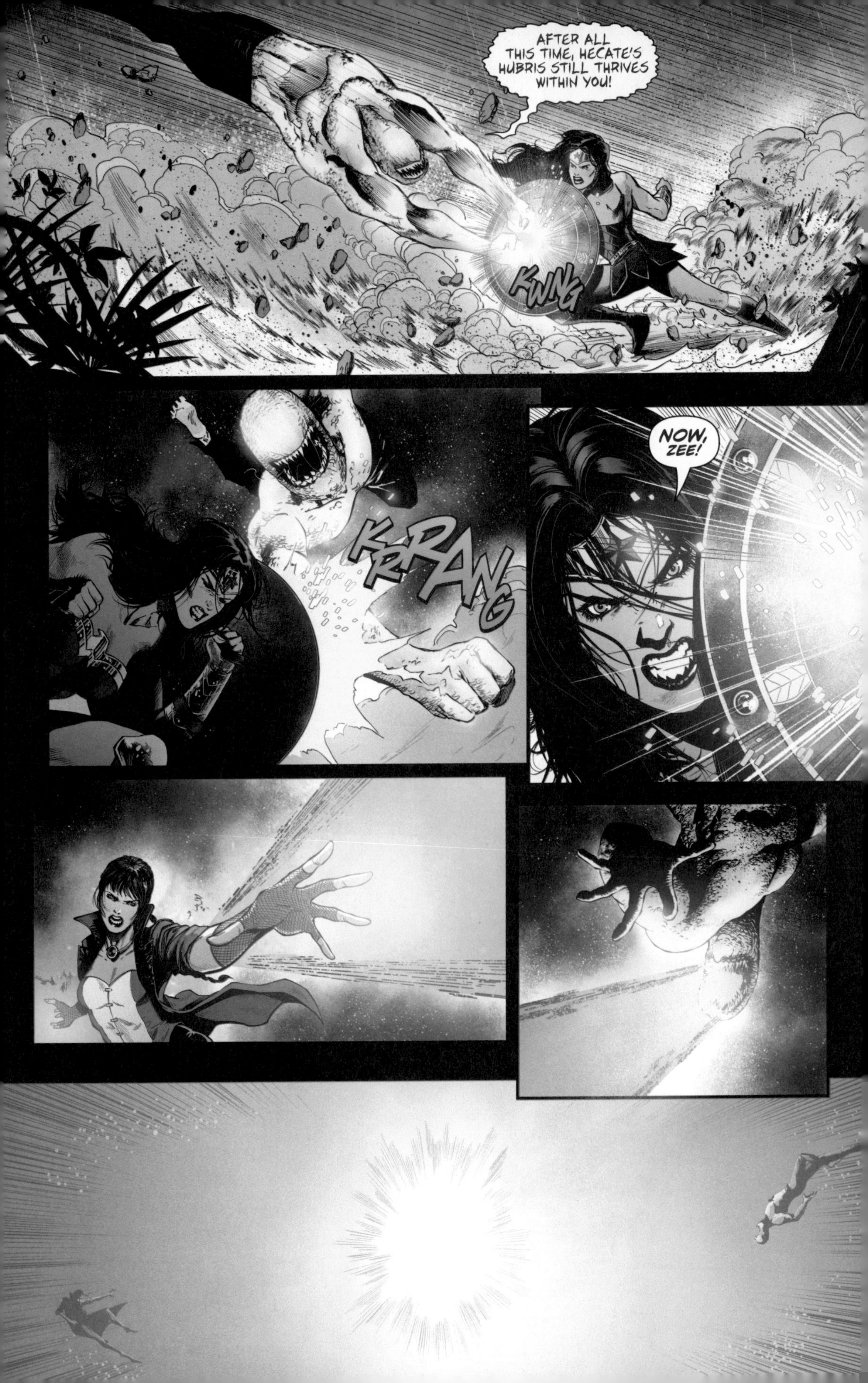
AFTER ALL THIS TIME, HECATE'S HUBRIS STILL THRIVES WITHIN YOU!
KWNG
KRRANG
NOW, ZEE!

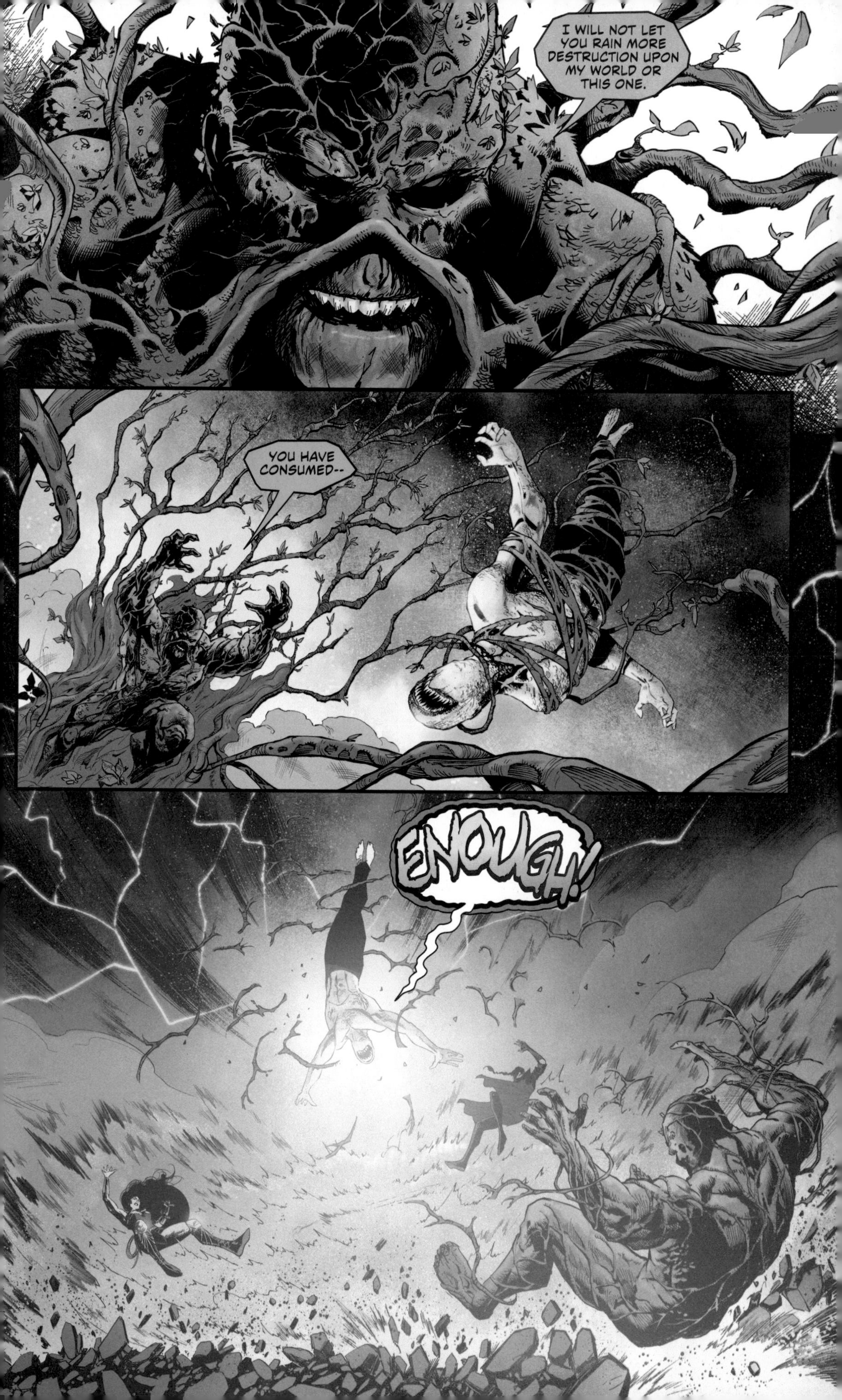
I WILL NOT LET YOU RAIN MORE DESTRUCTION UPON MY WORLD OR THIS ONE.
YOU HAVE CONSUMED--
ENOUGH!

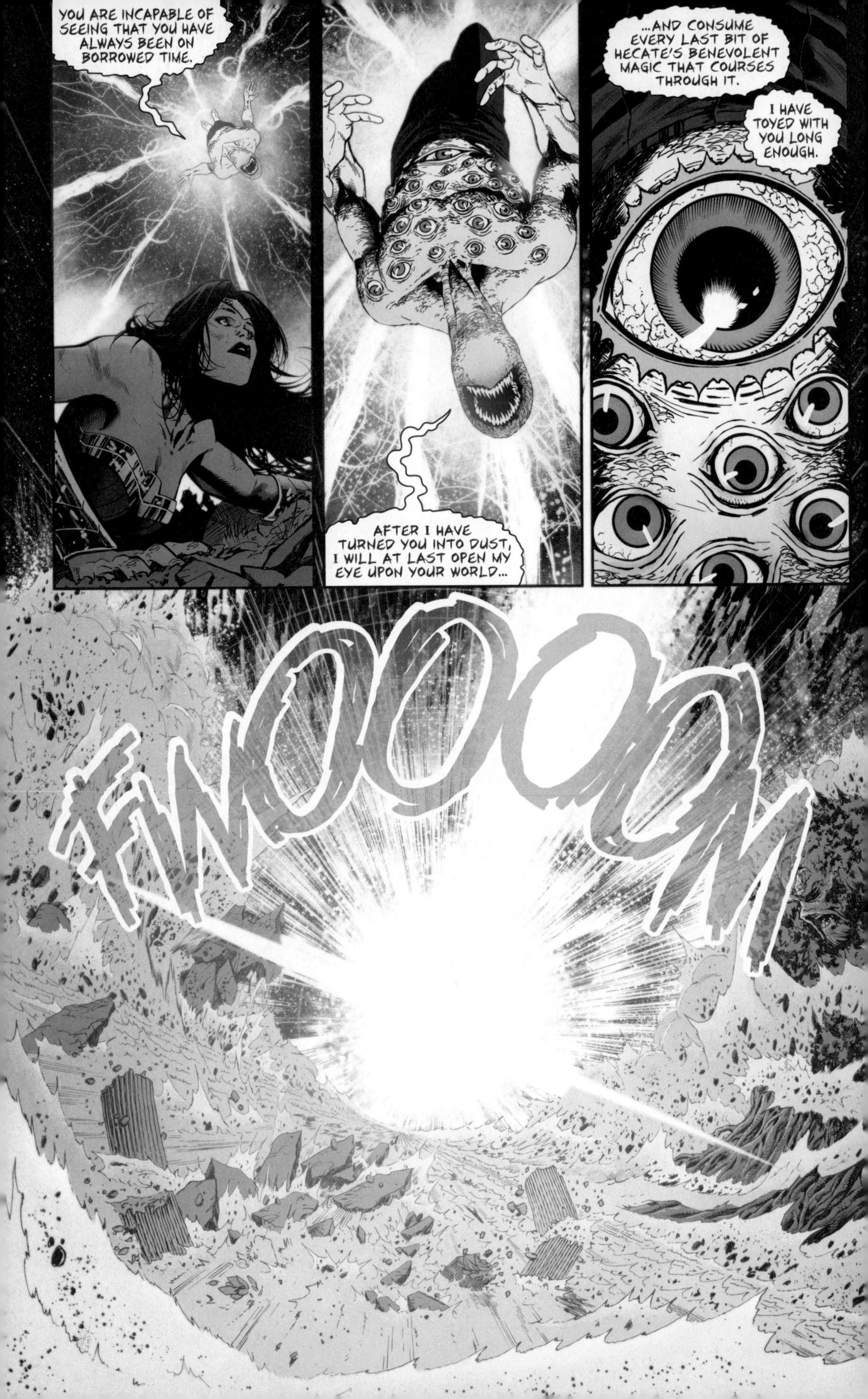
YOU ARE INCAPABLE OF SEEING THAT YOU HAVE ALWAYS BEEN ON BORROWED TIME.
AFTER I HAVE TURNED YOU INTO DUST, I WILL AT LAST OPEN MY EYE UPON YOUR WORLD...
...AND CONSUME EVERY LAST BIT OF HECATE'S BENEVOLENT MAGIC THAT COURSES THROUGH IT.
I HAVE TOYED WITH YOU LONG ENOUGH.
FWOOOOM

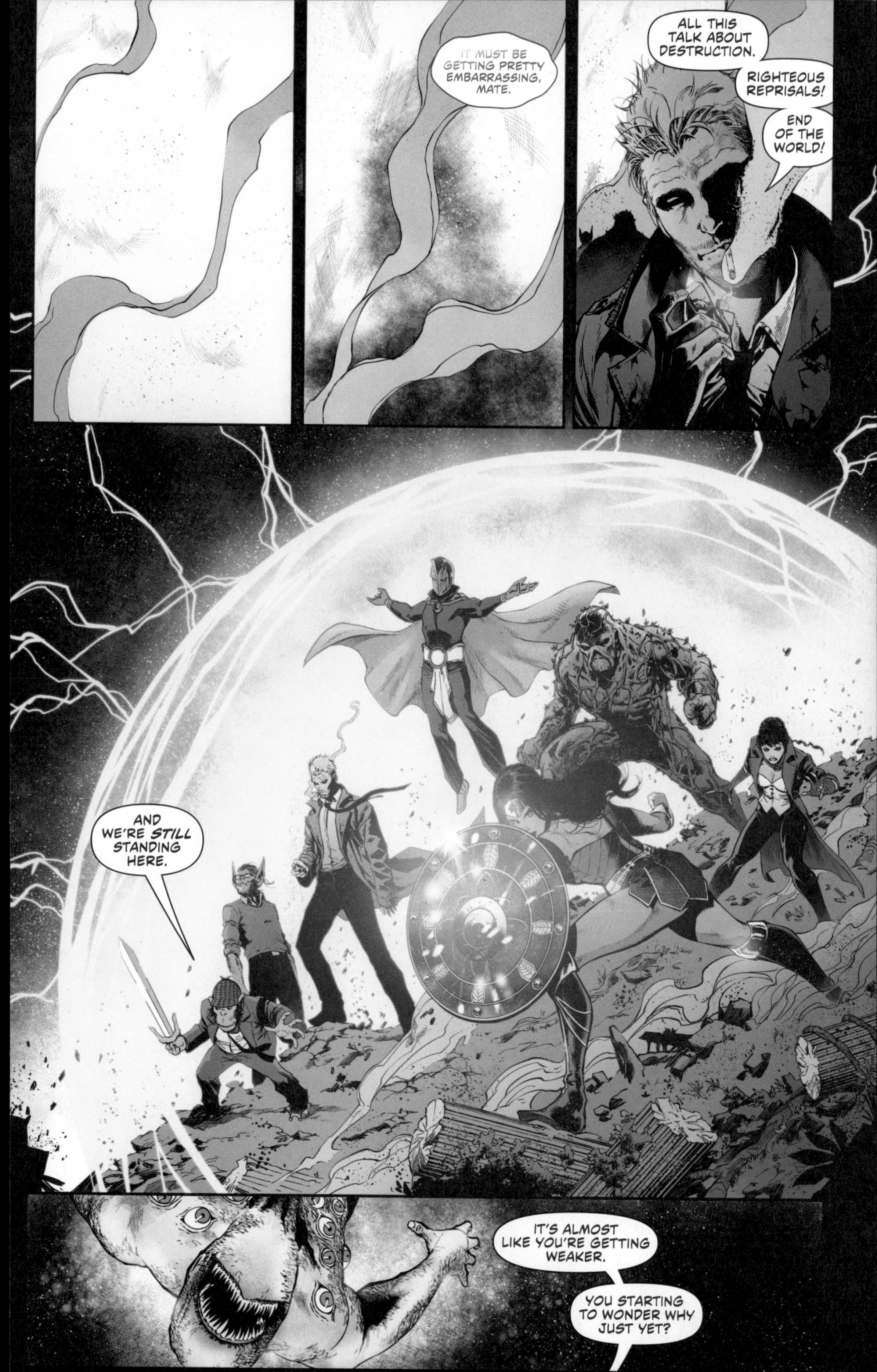
IT MUST BE GETTING PRETTY EMBARRASSING, MATE.
ALL THIS TALK ABOUT DESTRUCTION.
RIGHTEOUS REPRISALS!
END OF THE WORLD!
AND WE'RE *STILL* STANDING HERE.
IT'S ALMOST LIKE YOU'RE GETTING WEAKER.
YOU STARTING TO WONDER WHY JUST YET?

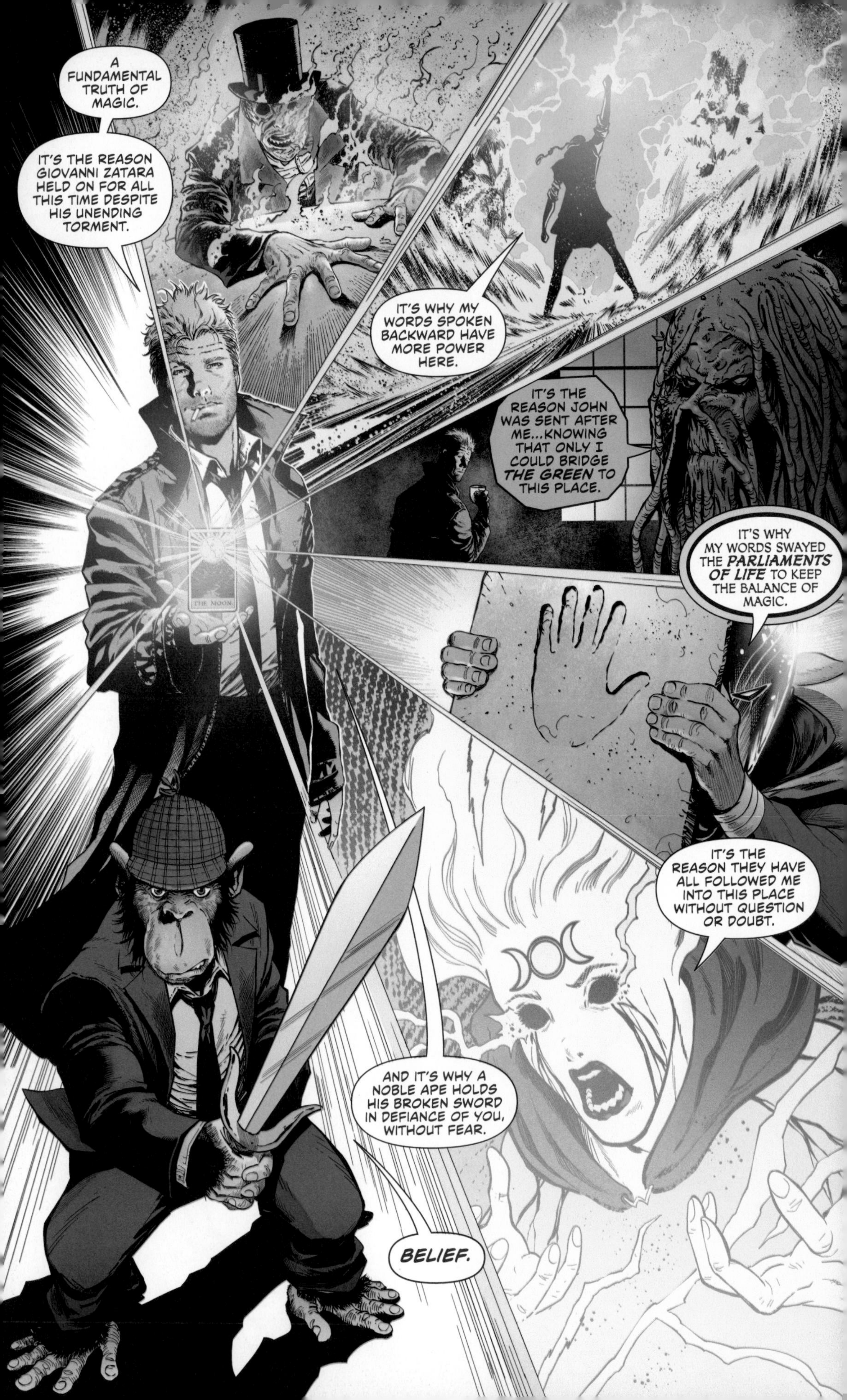
A FUNDAMENTAL TRUTH OF MAGIC.
IT'S THE REASON GIOVANNI ZATARA HELD ON FOR ALL THIS TIME DESPITE HIS UNENDING TORMENT.
IT'S WHY MY WORDS SPOKEN BACKWARD HAVE MORE POWER HERE.
IT'S THE REASON JOHN WAS SENT AFTER ME...KNOWING THAT ONLY I COULD BRIDGE THE GREEN TO THIS PLACE.
THE MOON
IT'S WHY MY WORDS SWAYED THE PARLIAMENTS OF LIFE TO KEEP THE BALANCE OF MAGIC.
IT'S THE REASON THEY HAVE ALL FOLLOWED ME INTO THIS PLACE WITHOUT QUESTION OR DOUBT.
AND IT'S WHY A NOBLE APE HOLDS HIS BROKEN SWORD IN DEFIANCE OF YOU, WITHOUT FEAR.
BELIEF.

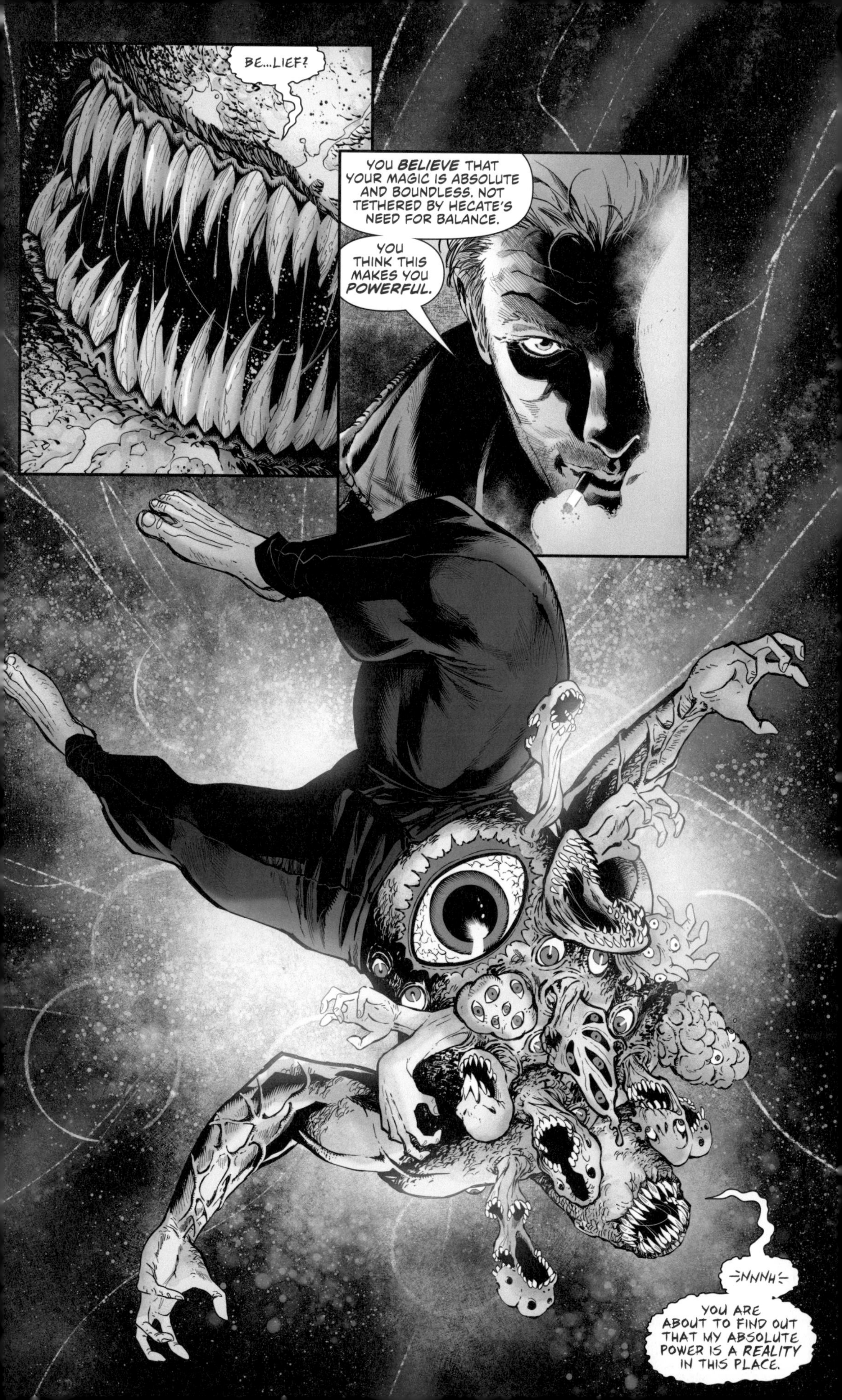

BE...LIEF?
YOU *BELIEVE* THAT YOUR MAGIC IS ABSOLUTE AND BOUNDLESS. NOT TETHERED BY HECATE'S NEED FOR BALANCE.
YOU THINK THIS MAKES YOU *POWERFUL.*
NNNH
YOU ARE ABOUT TO FIND OUT THAT MY ABSOLUTE POWER IS A *REALITY* IN THIS PLACE.

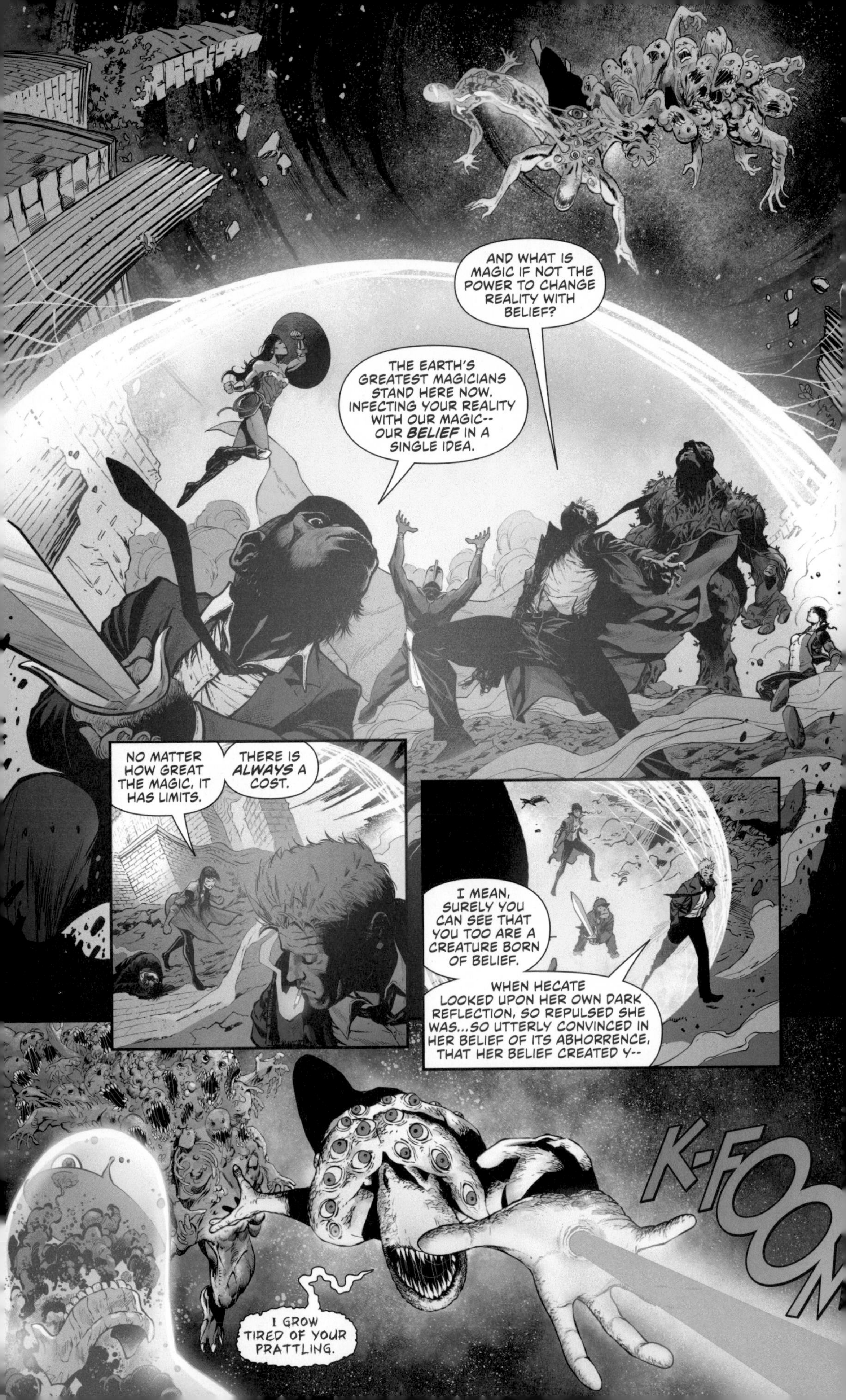
AND WHAT IS MAGIC IF NOT THE POWER TO CHANGE REALITY WITH BELIEF?
THE EARTH'S GREATEST MAGICIANS STAND HERE NOW. INFECTING YOUR REALITY WITH OUR MAGIC-- OUR BELIEF IN A SINGLE IDEA.
NO MATTER HOW GREAT THE MAGIC, IT HAS LIMITS.
THERE IS ALWAYS A COST.
I MEAN, SURELY YOU CAN SEE THAT YOU TOO ARE A CREATURE BORN OF BELIEF.
WHEN HECATE LOOKED UPON HER OWN DARK REFLECTION, SO REPULSED SHE WAS...SO UTTERLY CONVINCED IN HER BELIEF OF ITS ABHORRENCE, THAT HER BELIEF CREATED Y--
K-FOOM
I GROW TIRED OF YOUR PRATTLING.

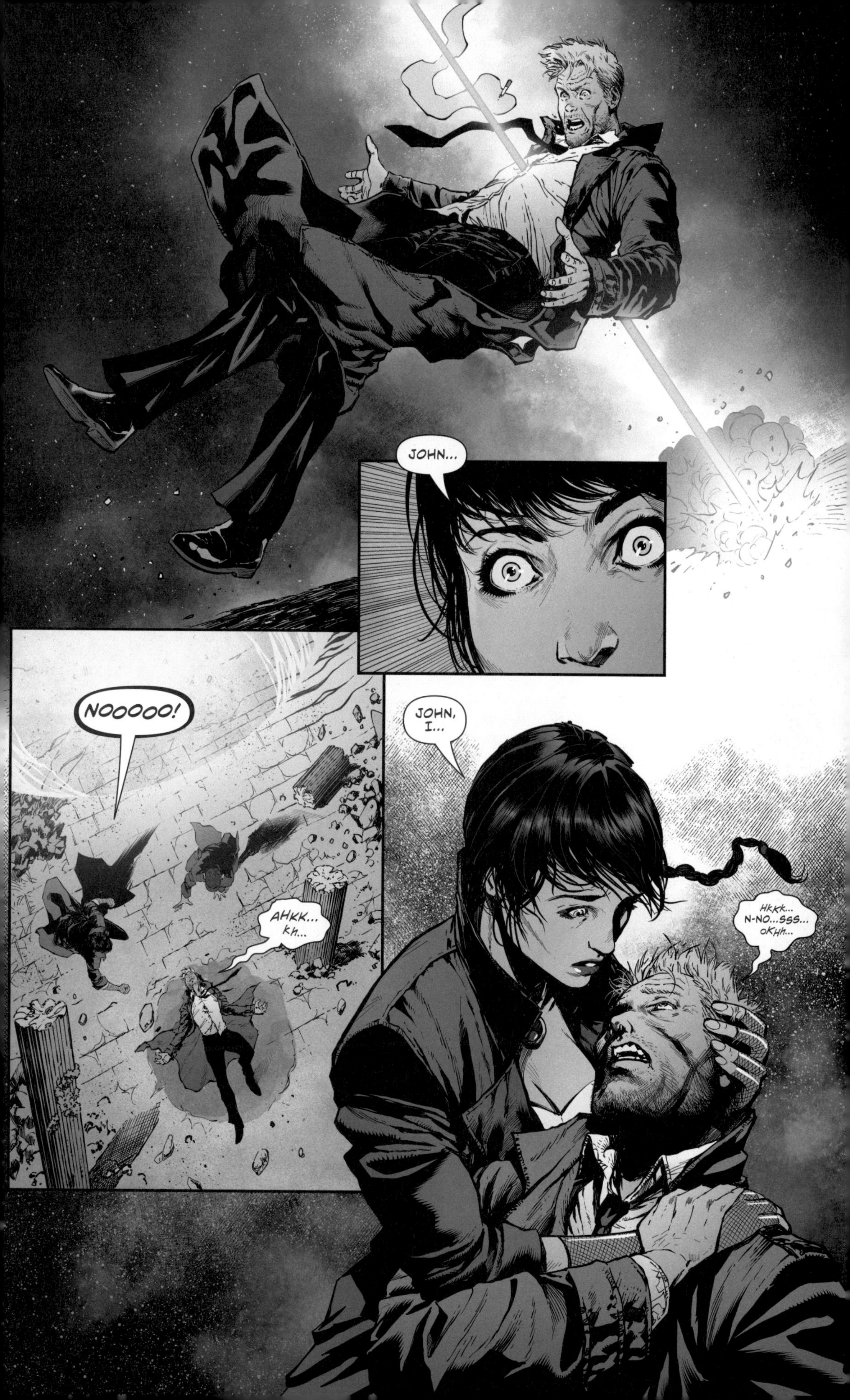
JOHN...
NOOOOO!
AHKK... kh...
JOHN, I...
Hkkk... N-NO...SSS... oKhh...

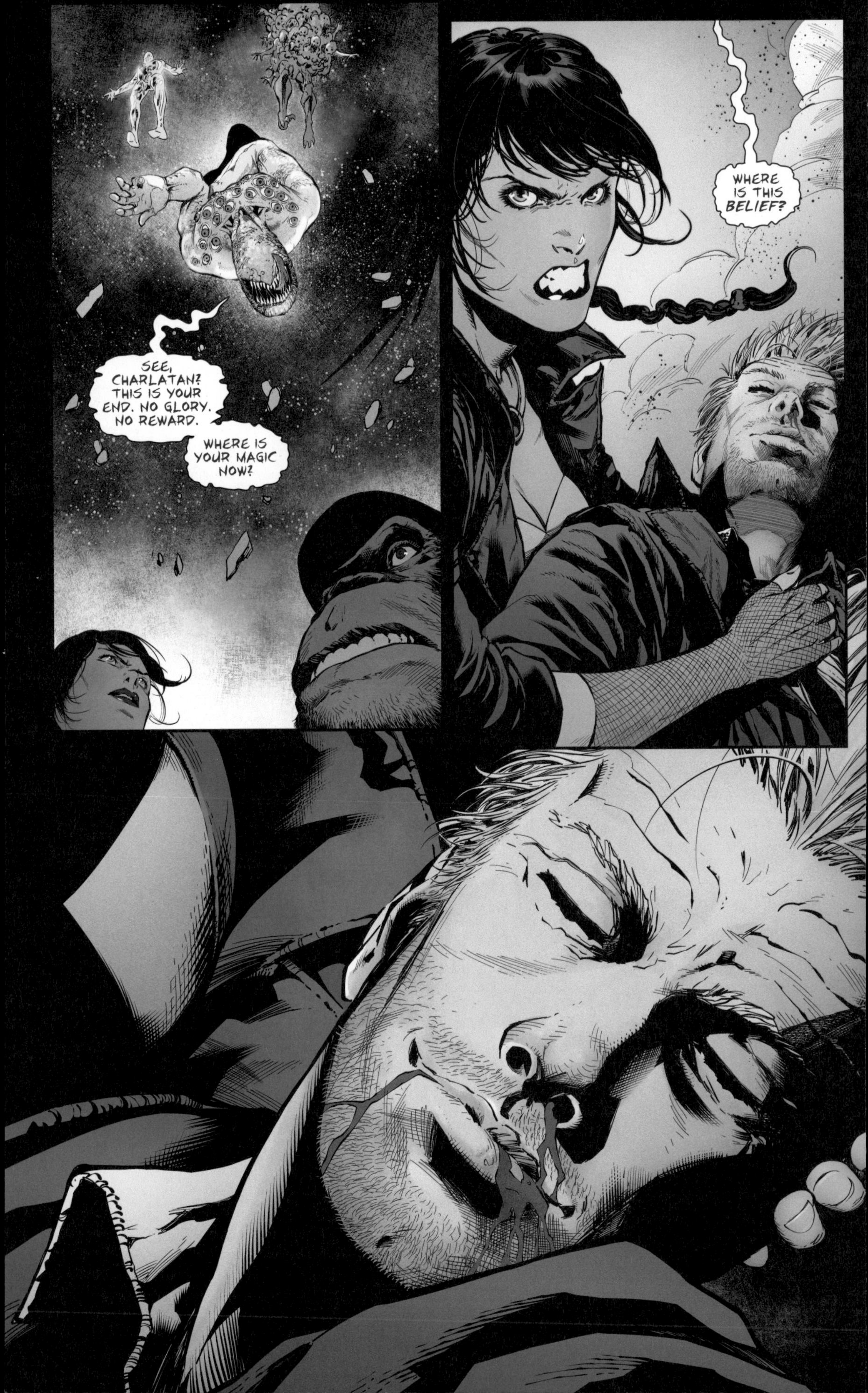

SEE, CHARLATAN? THIS IS YOUR END. NO GLORY. NO REWARD.
WHERE IS YOUR MAGIC NOW?
WHERE IS THIS *BELIEF?*

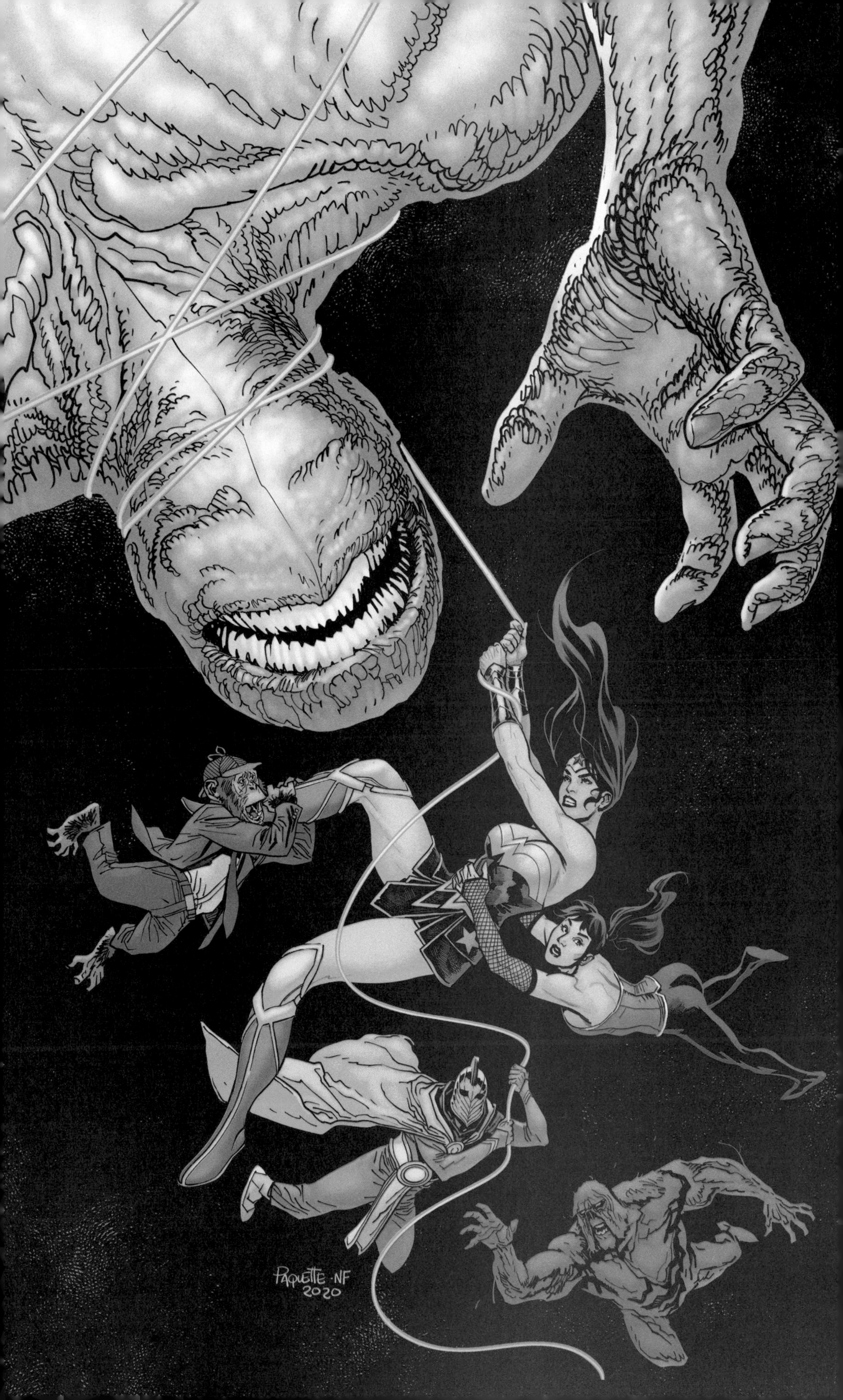
PAQUETTE · NF
2020

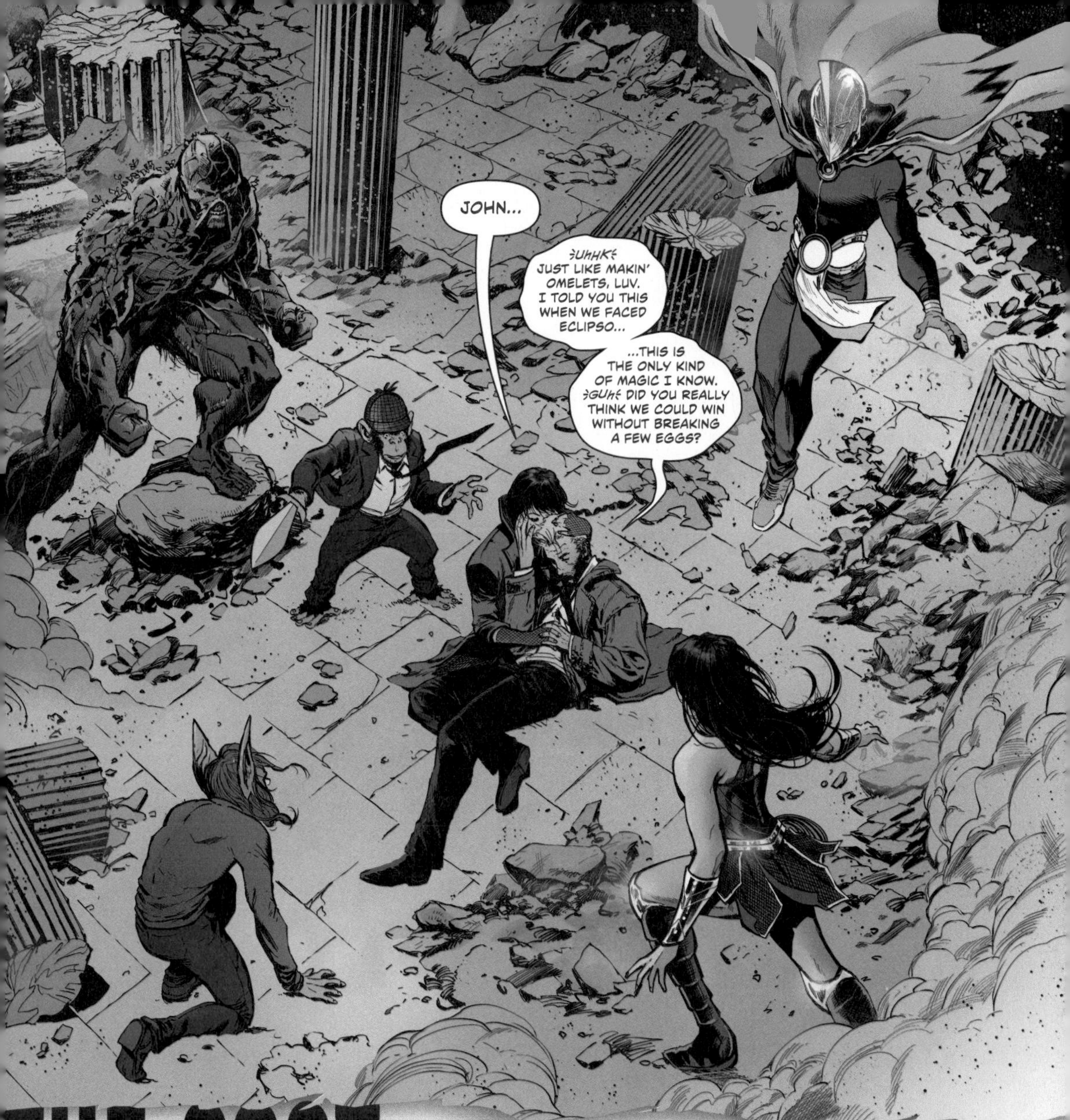
JOHN...
UHHK
JUST LIKE MAKIN' OMELETS, LUV. I TOLD YOU THIS WHEN WE FACED ECLIPSO...
...THIS IS THE ONLY KIND OF MAGIC I KNOW.
GUH
DID YOU REALLY THINK WE COULD WIN WITHOUT BREAKING A FEW EGGS?

THE COST PART 1

RAM V writer AMANCAY NAHUELPAN artist JUNE CHUNG colorist ROB LEIGH letterer
YANICK PAQUETTE & NATHAN FAIRBAIRN cover KAEL NGU variant cover
ANDREA SHEA associate editor ALEX R. CARR editor

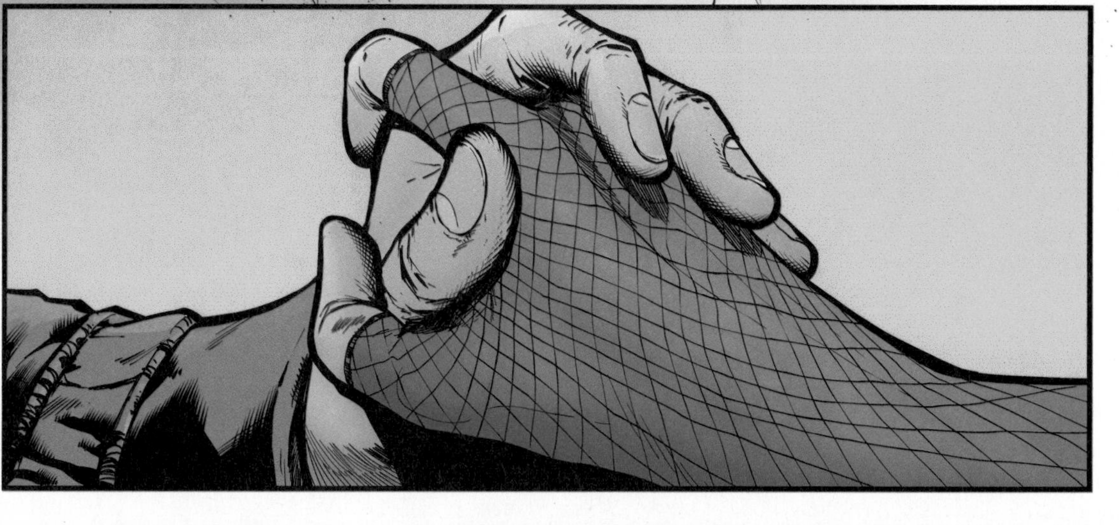

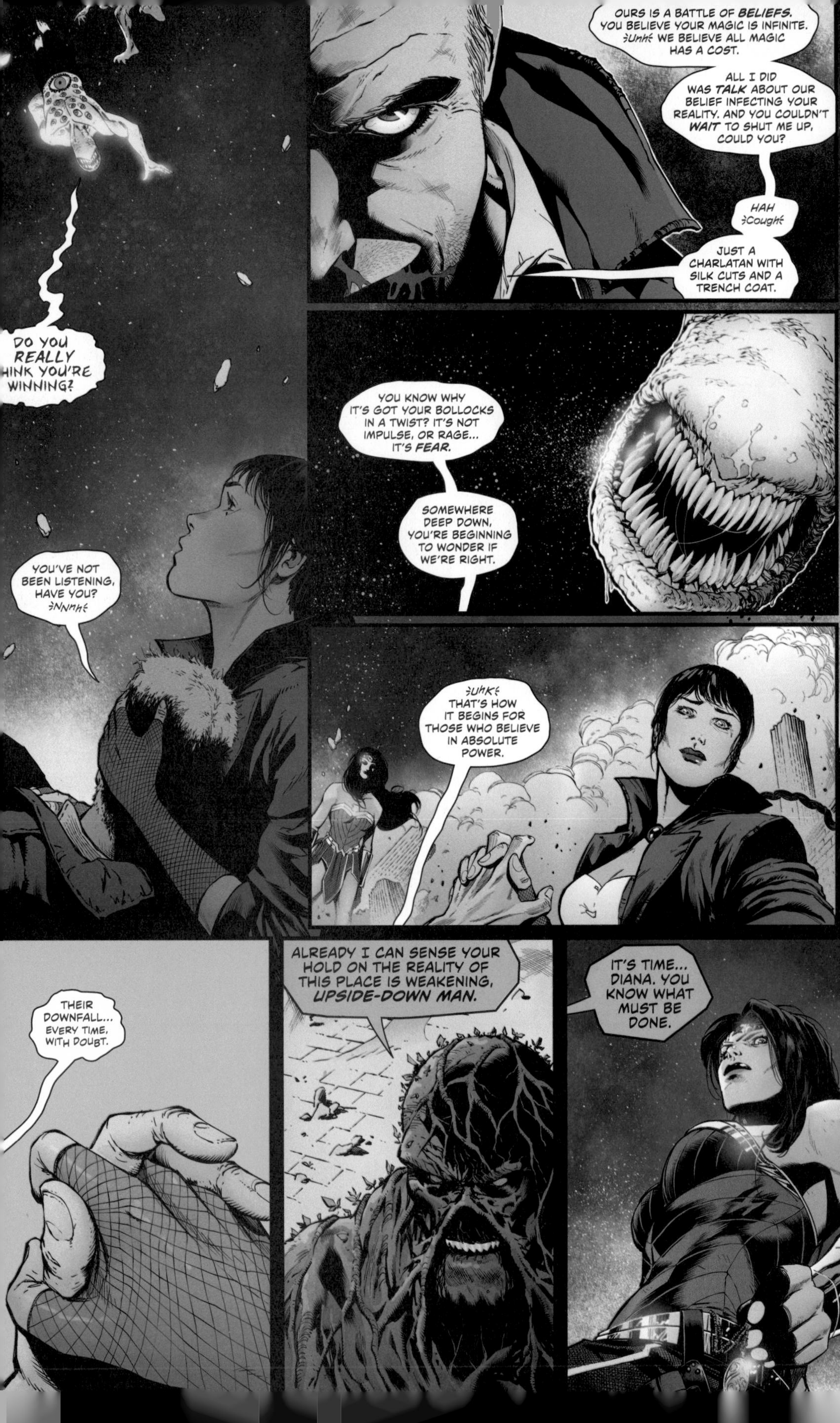
OURS IS A BATTLE OF BELIEFS. YOU BELIEVE YOUR MAGIC IS INFINITE. ≷Unh≶ WE BELIEVE ALL MAGIC HAS A COST.
ALL I DID WAS TALK ABOUT OUR BELIEF INFECTING YOUR REALITY. AND YOU COULDN'T WAIT TO SHUT ME UP, COULD YOU?
HAH ≷Cough≶
JUST A CHARLATAN WITH SILK CUTS AND A TRENCH COAT.
DO YOU REALLY THINK YOU'RE WINNING?
YOU KNOW WHY IT'S GOT YOUR BOLLOCKS IN A TWIST? IT'S NOT IMPULSE, OR RAGE... IT'S FEAR.
SOMEWHERE DEEP DOWN, YOU'RE BEGINNING TO WONDER IF WE'RE RIGHT.
YOU'VE NOT BEEN LISTENING, HAVE YOU? ≷Nnnh≶
≷Uhk≶ THAT'S HOW IT BEGINS FOR THOSE WHO BELIEVE IN ABSOLUTE POWER.
THEIR DOWNFALL... EVERY TIME, WITH DOUBT.
ALREADY I CAN SENSE YOUR HOLD ON THE REALITY OF THIS PLACE IS WEAKENING, UPSIDE-DOWN MAN.
IT'S TIME... DIANA. YOU KNOW WHAT MUST BE DONE.

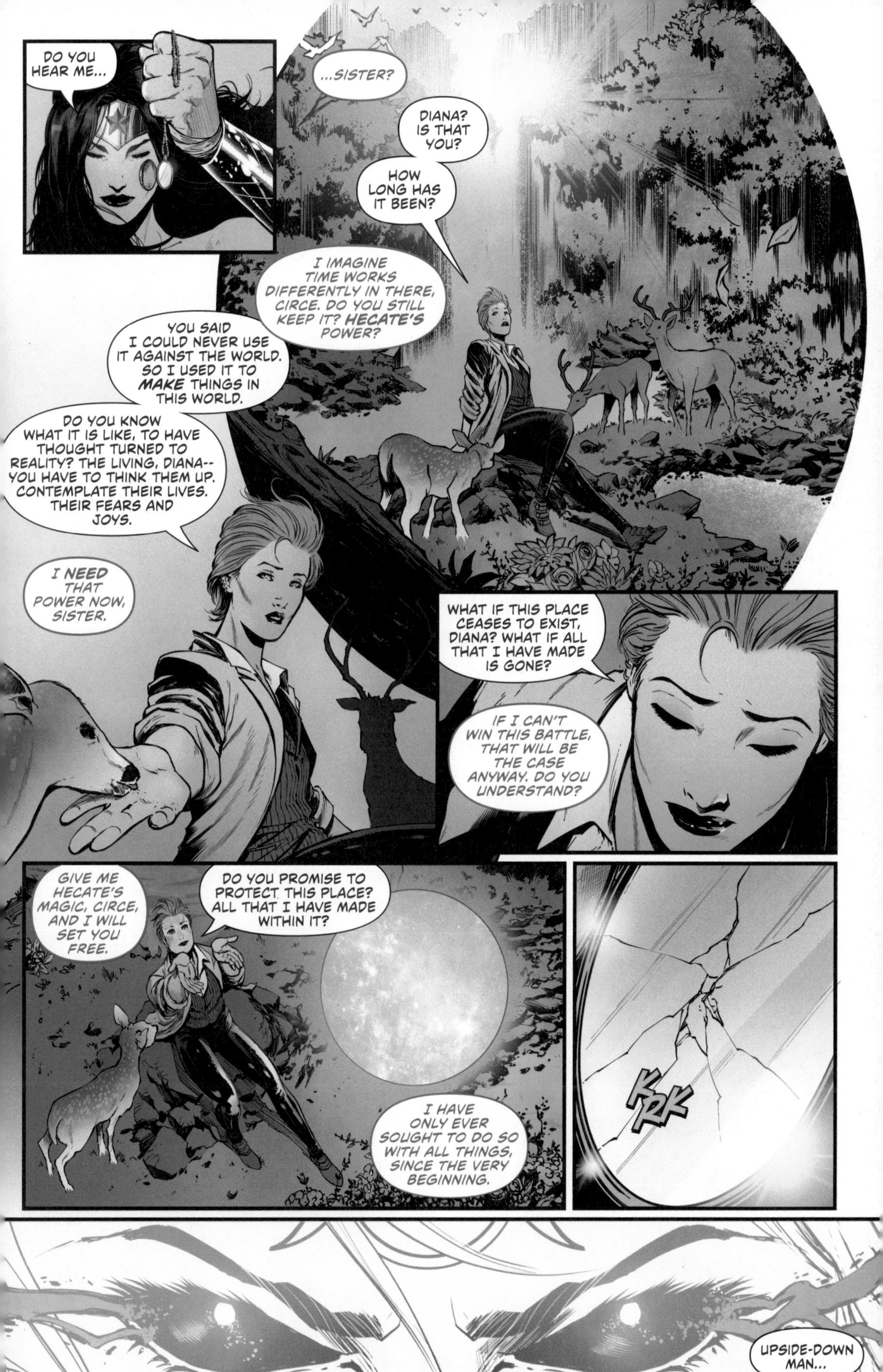
DO YOU HEAR ME...
...SISTER?
DIANA? IS THAT YOU?
HOW LONG HAS IT BEEN?
I IMAGINE TIME WORKS DIFFERENTLY IN THERE, CIRCE. DO YOU STILL KEEP IT? HECATE'S POWER?
YOU SAID I COULD NEVER USE IT AGAINST THE WORLD. SO I USED IT TO MAKE THINGS IN THIS WORLD.
DO YOU KNOW WHAT IT IS LIKE, TO HAVE THOUGHT TURNED TO REALITY? THE LIVING, DIANA-- YOU HAVE TO THINK THEM UP. CONTEMPLATE THEIR LIVES. THEIR FEARS AND JOYS.
I NEED THAT POWER NOW, SISTER.
WHAT IF THIS PLACE CEASES TO EXIST, DIANA? WHAT IF ALL THAT I HAVE MADE IS GONE?
IF I CAN'T WIN THIS BATTLE, THAT WILL BE THE CASE ANYWAY. DO YOU UNDERSTAND?
GIVE ME HECATE'S MAGIC, CIRCE, AND I WILL SET YOU FREE.
DO YOU PROMISE TO PROTECT THIS PLACE? ALL THAT I HAVE MADE WITHIN IT?
I HAVE ONLY EVER SOUGHT TO DO SO WITH ALL THINGS, SINCE THE VERY BEGINNING.
KRK
UPSIDE-DOWN MAN...

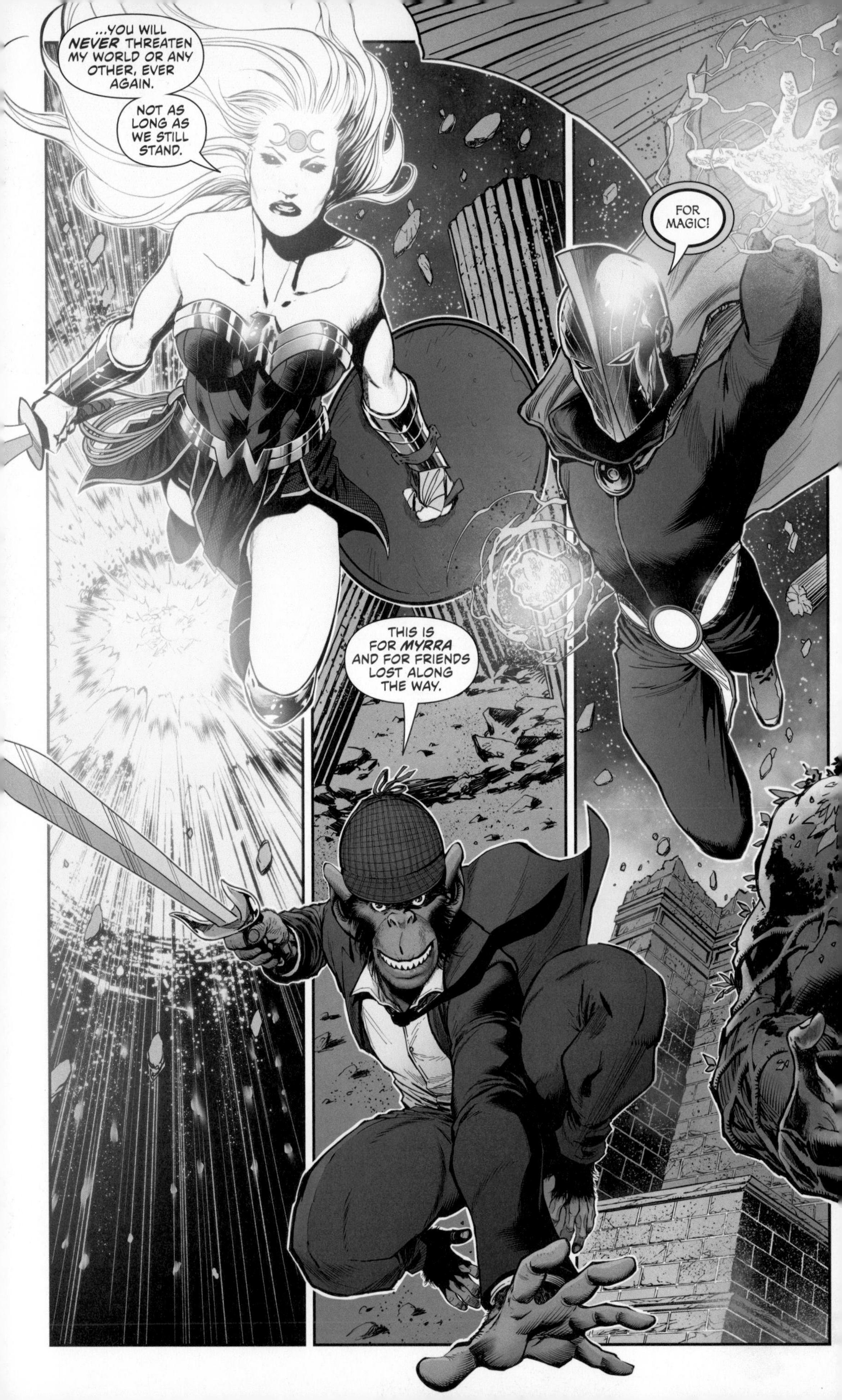
...YOU WILL NEVER THREATEN MY WORLD OR ANY OTHER, EVER AGAIN.
NOT AS LONG AS WE STILL STAND.
FOR MAGIC!
THIS IS FOR MYRRA AND FOR FRIENDS LOST ALONG THE WAY.

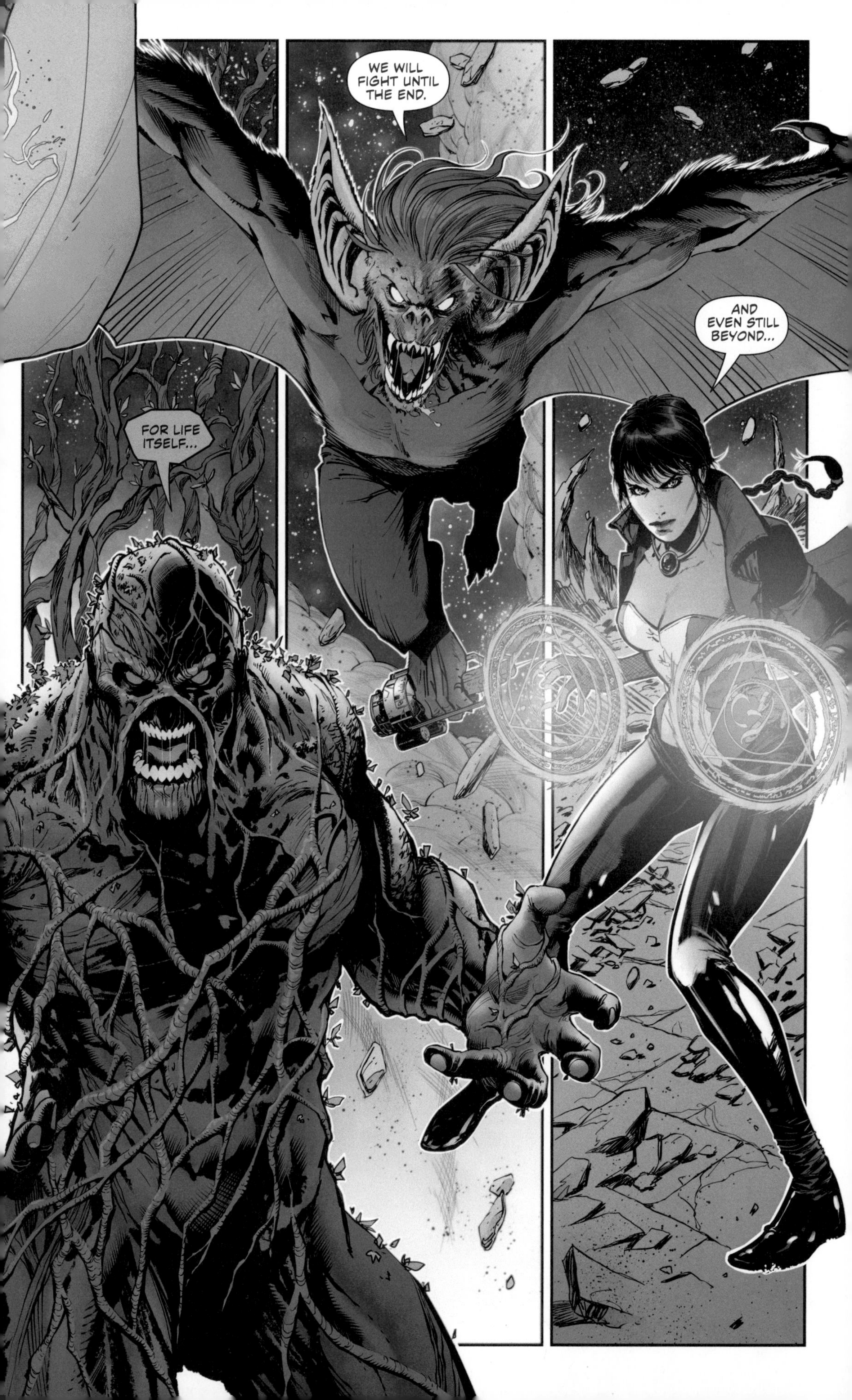
WE WILL FIGHT UNTIL THE END.
AND EVEN STILL BEYOND...
FOR LIFE ITSELF...

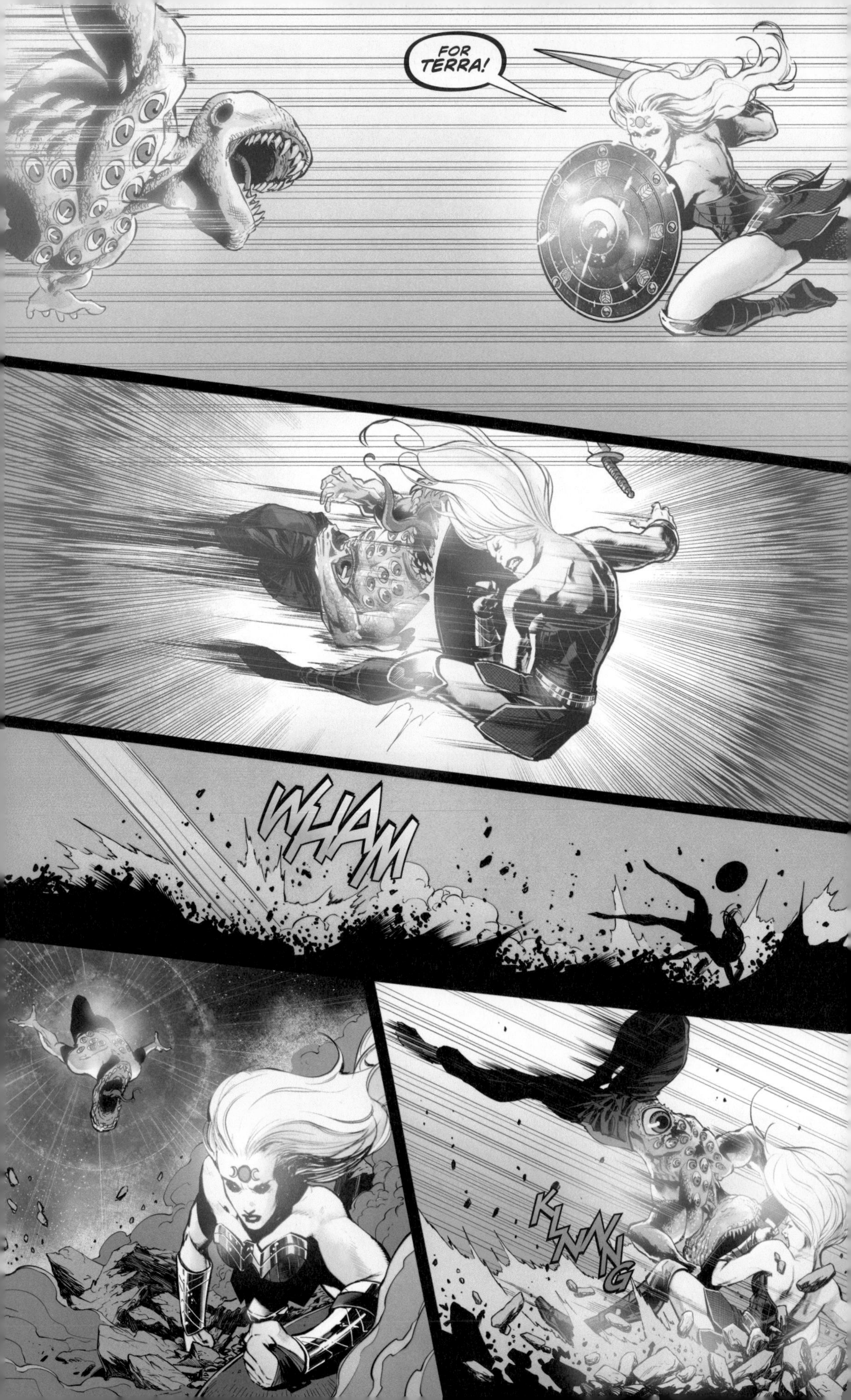
FOR TERRA!
WHAM
KLANG

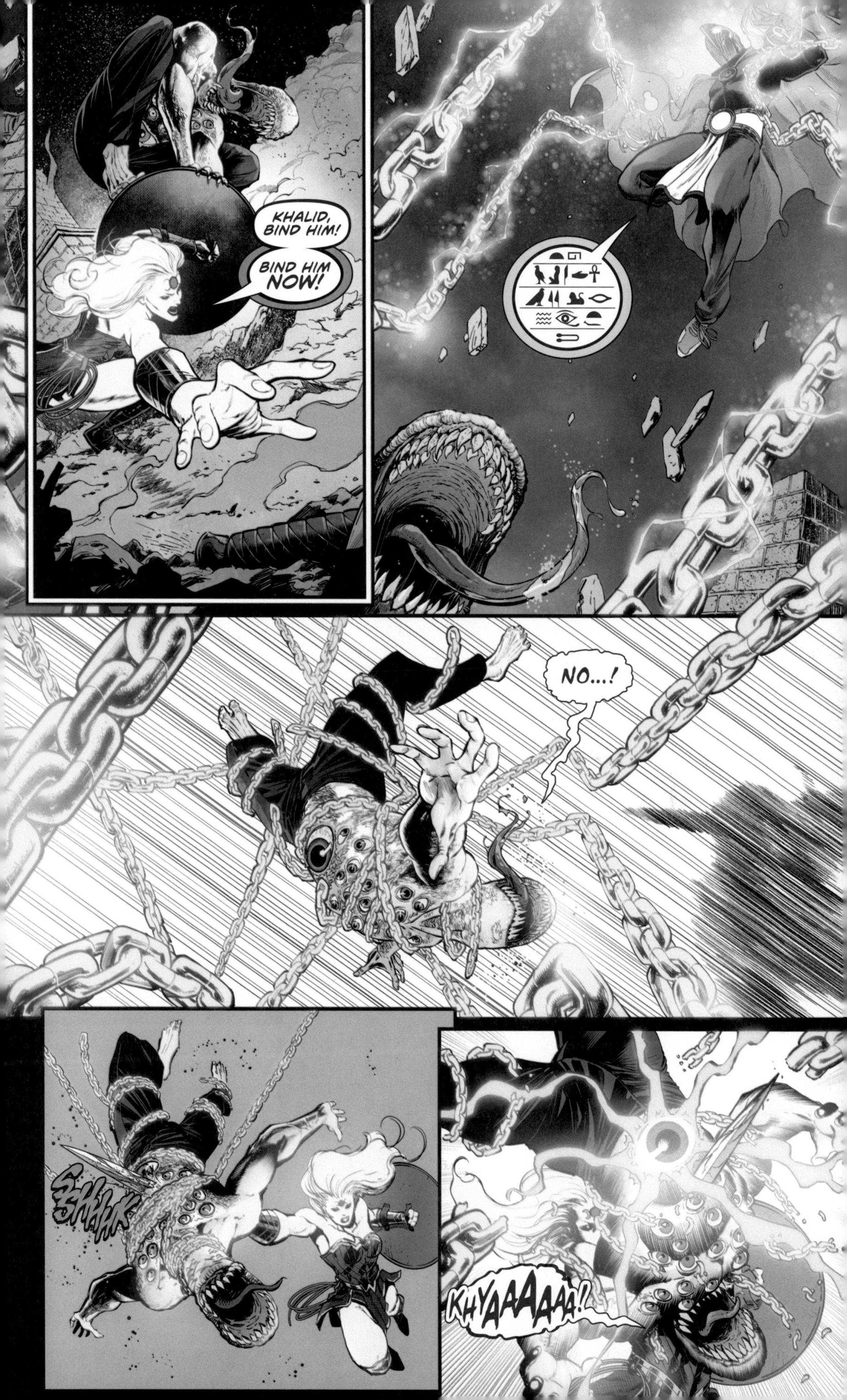
KHALID, BIND HIM!
BIND HIM NOW!
NO...!
SHHHK
KHYAAAAAA!

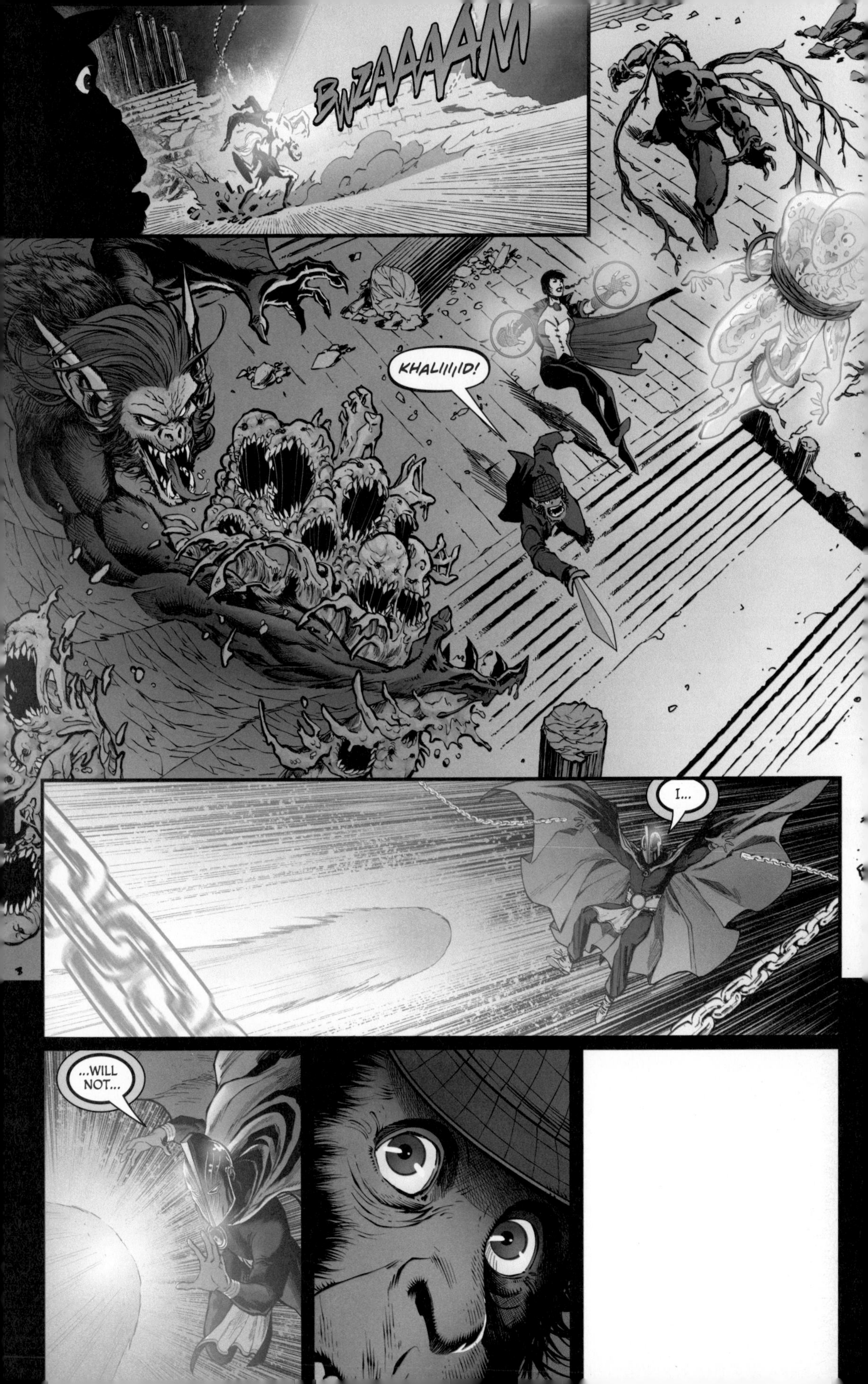
BWZAAAAM
KHALIIIIID!
I...
...WILL NOT...

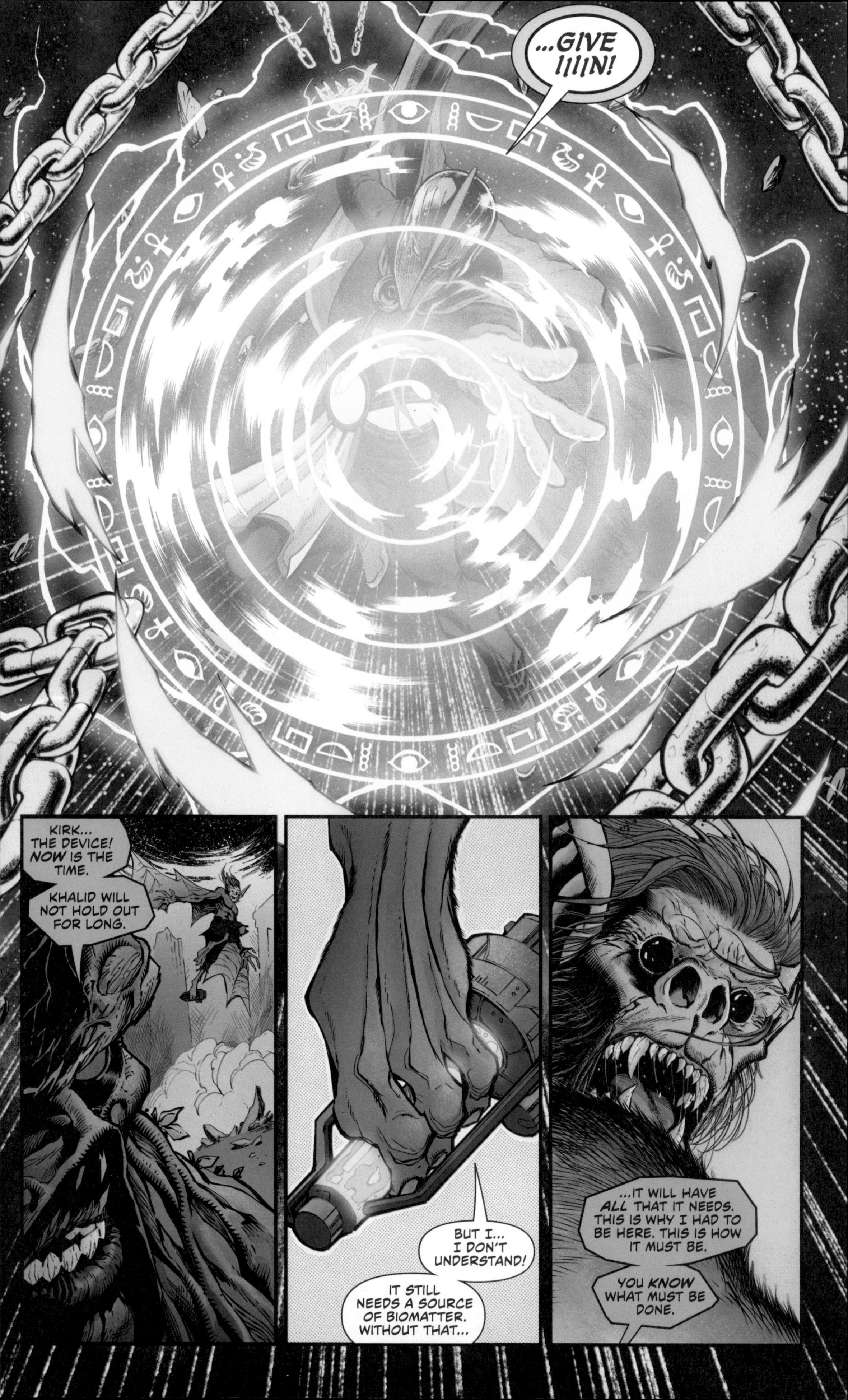
...GIVE IIIIN!
KIRK... THE DEVICE! NOW IS THE TIME.
KHALID WILL NOT HOLD OUT FOR LONG.
BUT I... I DON'T UNDERSTAND!
IT STILL NEEDS A SOURCE OF BIOMATTER. WITHOUT THAT...
...IT WILL HAVE ALL THAT IT NEEDS. THIS IS WHY I HAD TO BE HERE. THIS IS HOW IT MUST BE.
YOU KNOW WHAT MUST BE DONE.

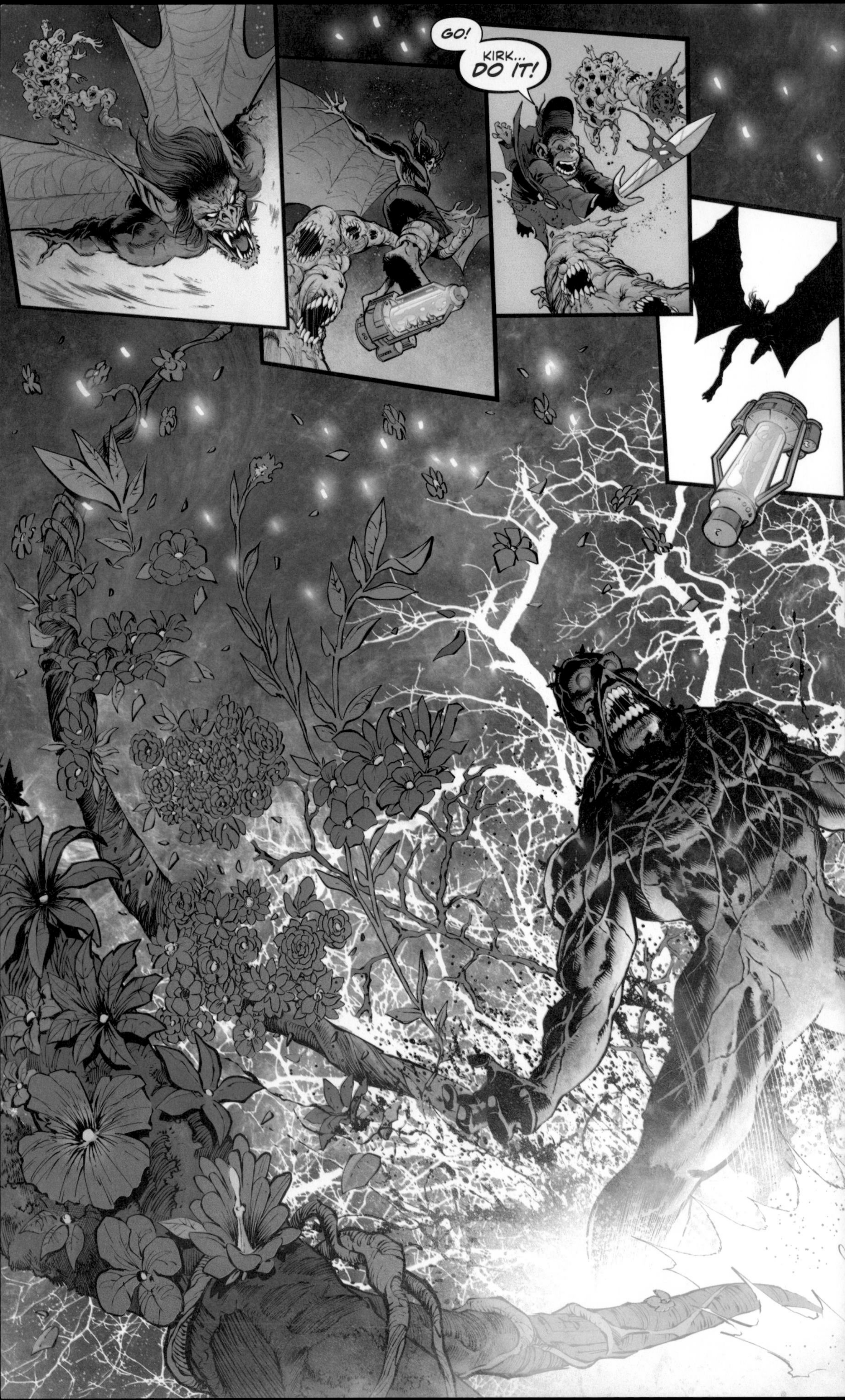
GO!
KIRK... DO IT!

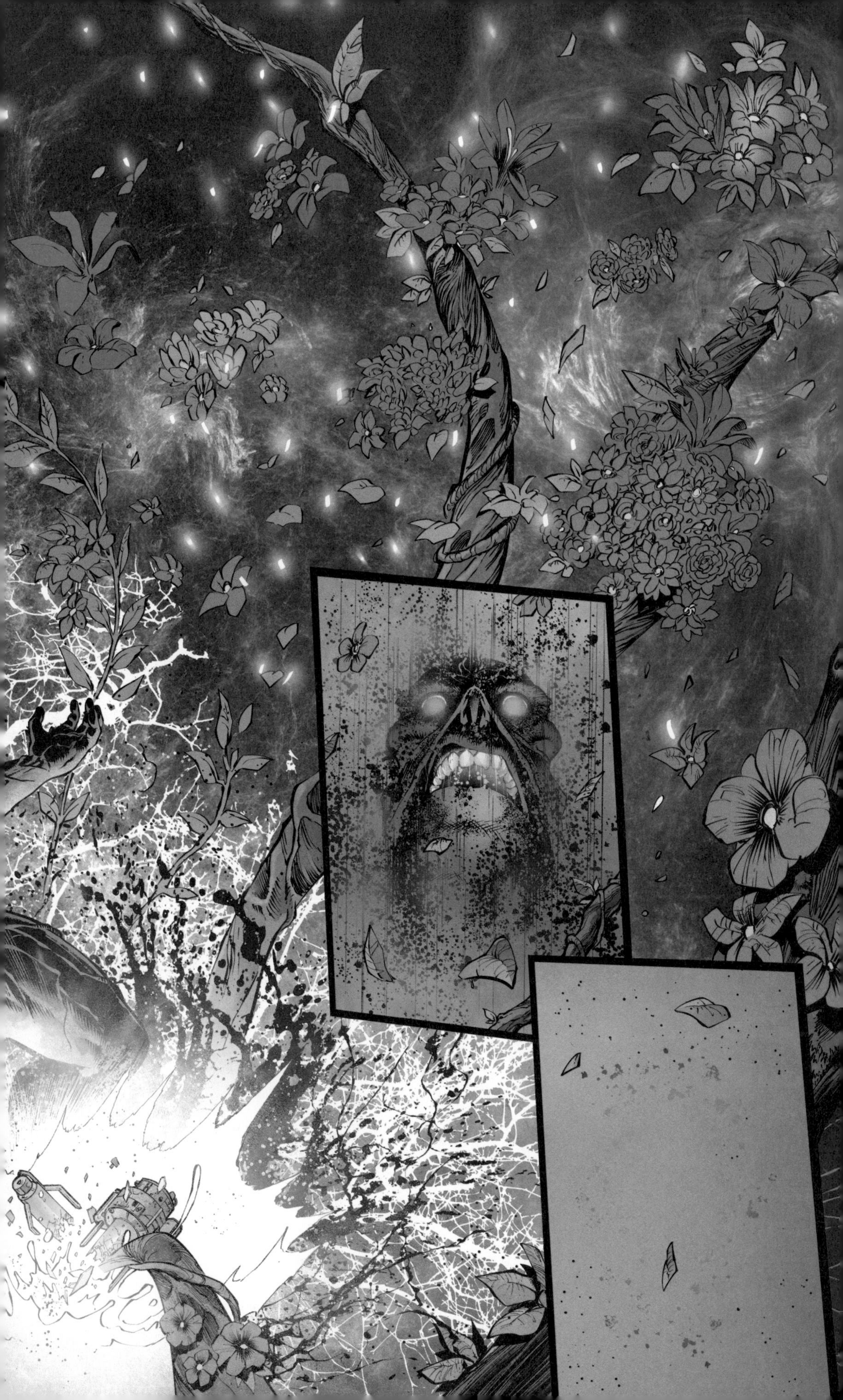

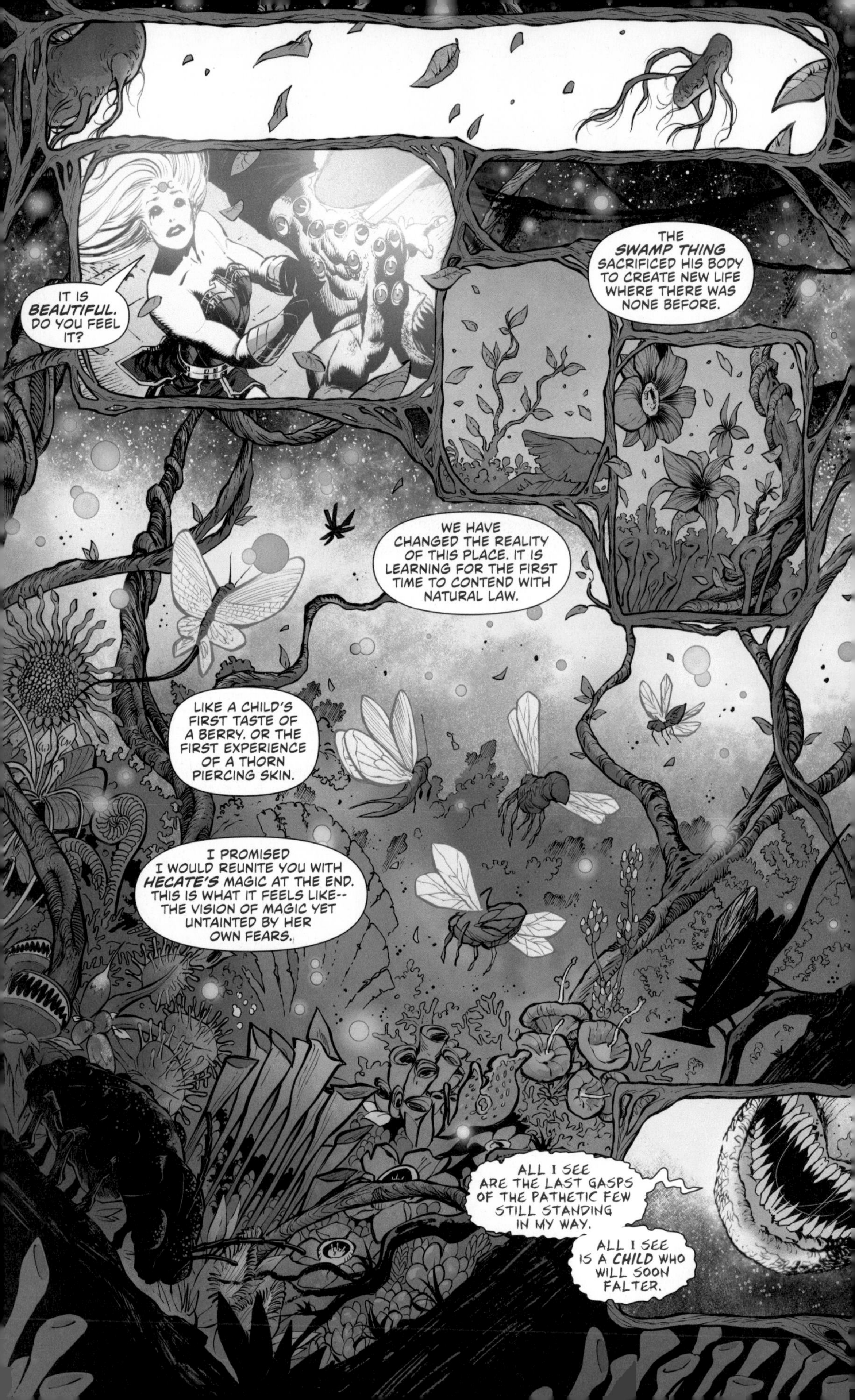

IT IS BEAUTIFUL. DO YOU FEEL IT?
THE SWAMP THING SACRIFICED HIS BODY TO CREATE NEW LIFE WHERE THERE WAS NONE BEFORE.
WE HAVE CHANGED THE REALITY OF THIS PLACE. IT IS LEARNING FOR THE FIRST TIME TO CONTEND WITH NATURAL LAW.
LIKE A CHILD'S FIRST TASTE OF A BERRY. OR THE FIRST EXPERIENCE OF A THORN PIERCING SKIN.
I PROMISED I WOULD REUNITE YOU WITH HECATE'S MAGIC AT THE END. THIS IS WHAT IT FEELS LIKE-- THE VISION OF MAGIC YET UNTAINTED BY HER OWN FEARS.
ALL I SEE ARE THE LAST GASPS OF THE PATHETIC FEW STILL STANDING IN MY WAY.
ALL I SEE IS A CHILD WHO WILL SOON FALTER.

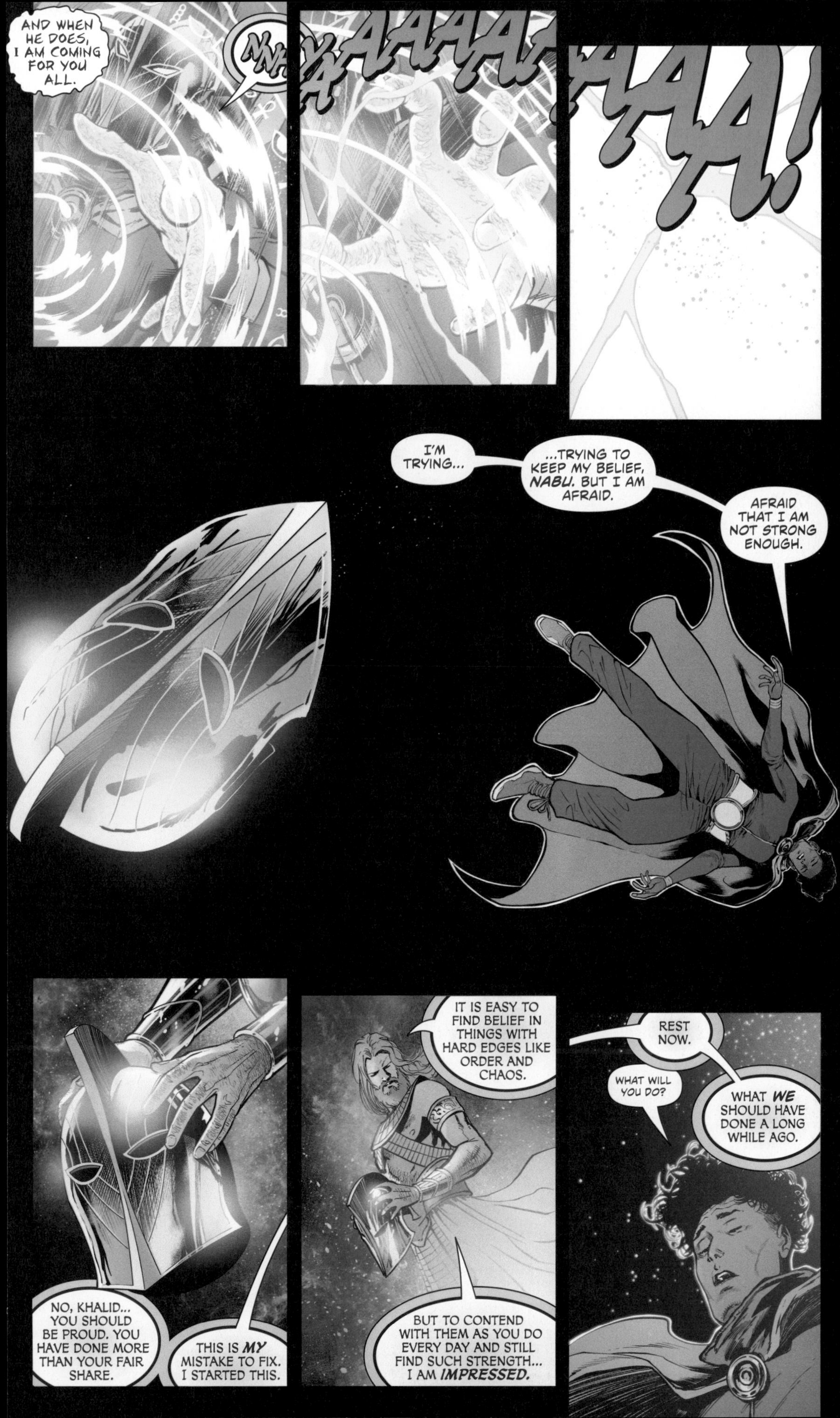
AND WHEN HE DOES, I AM COMING FOR YOU ALL.
NNHYAAAAAAAAAAAAAA!
I'M TRYING...
...TRYING TO KEEP MY BELIEF, NABU. BUT I AM AFRAID.
AFRAID THAT I AM NOT STRONG ENOUGH.
NO, KHALID... YOU SHOULD BE PROUD. YOU HAVE DONE MORE THAN YOUR FAIR SHARE.
THIS IS MY MISTAKE TO FIX. I STARTED THIS.
IT IS EASY TO FIND BELIEF IN THINGS WITH HARD EDGES LIKE ORDER AND CHAOS.
BUT TO CONTEND WITH THEM AS YOU DO EVERY DAY AND STILL FIND SUCH STRENGTH... I AM IMPRESSED.
REST NOW.
WHAT WILL YOU DO?
WHAT WE SHOULD HAVE DONE A LONG WHILE AGO.

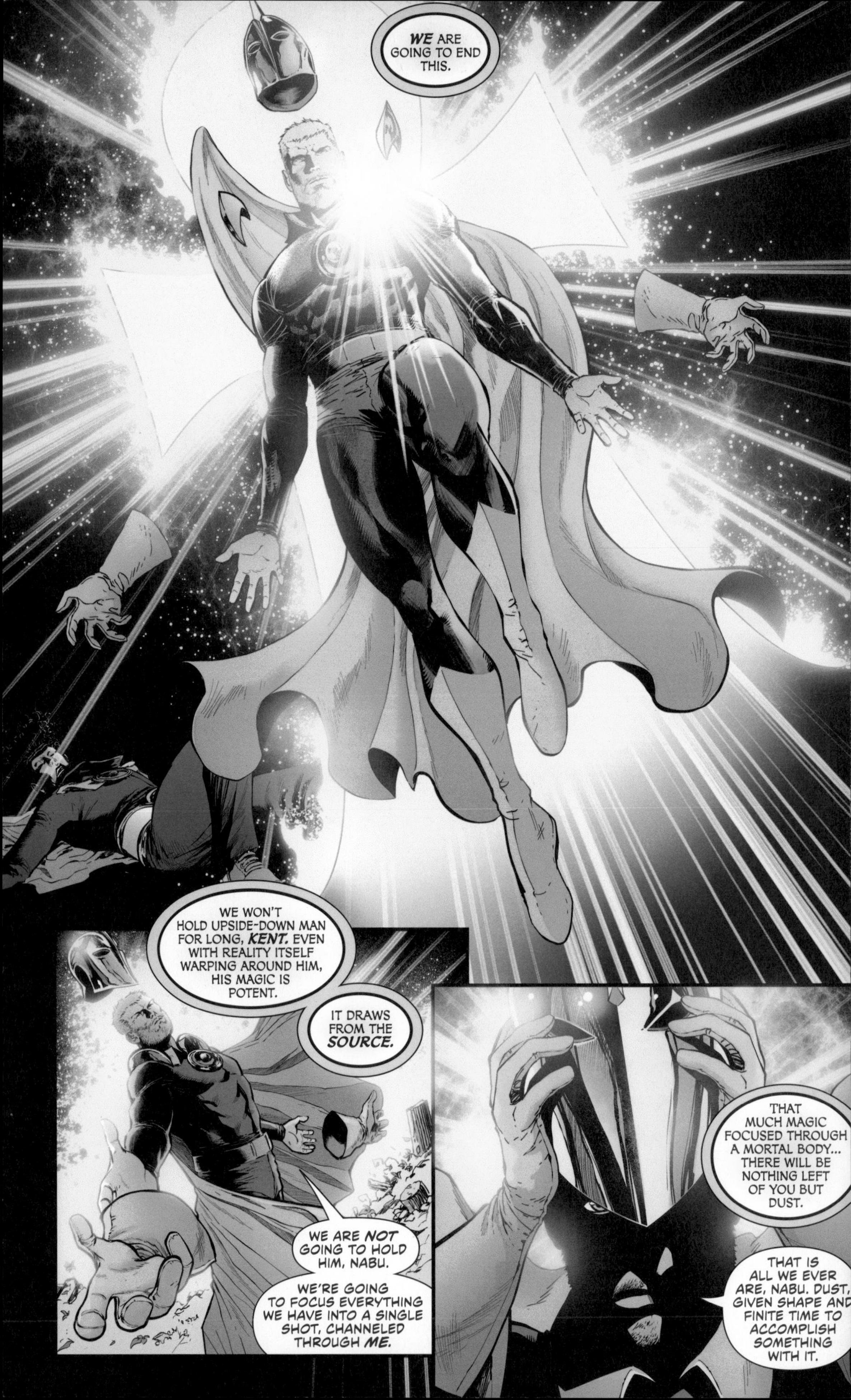

WE ARE GOING TO END THIS.
WE WON'T HOLD UPSIDE-DOWN MAN FOR LONG, KENT. EVEN WITH REALITY ITSELF WARPING AROUND HIM, HIS MAGIC IS POTENT.
IT DRAWS FROM THE SOURCE.
WE ARE NOT GOING TO HOLD HIM, NABU.
WE'RE GOING TO FOCUS EVERYTHING WE HAVE INTO A SINGLE SHOT, CHANNELED THROUGH ME.
THAT MUCH MAGIC FOCUSED THROUGH A MORTAL BODY... THERE WILL BE NOTHING LEFT OF YOU BUT DUST.
THAT IS ALL WE EVER ARE, NABU. DUST, GIVEN SHAPE AND FINITE TIME TO ACCOMPLISH SOMETHING WITH IT.

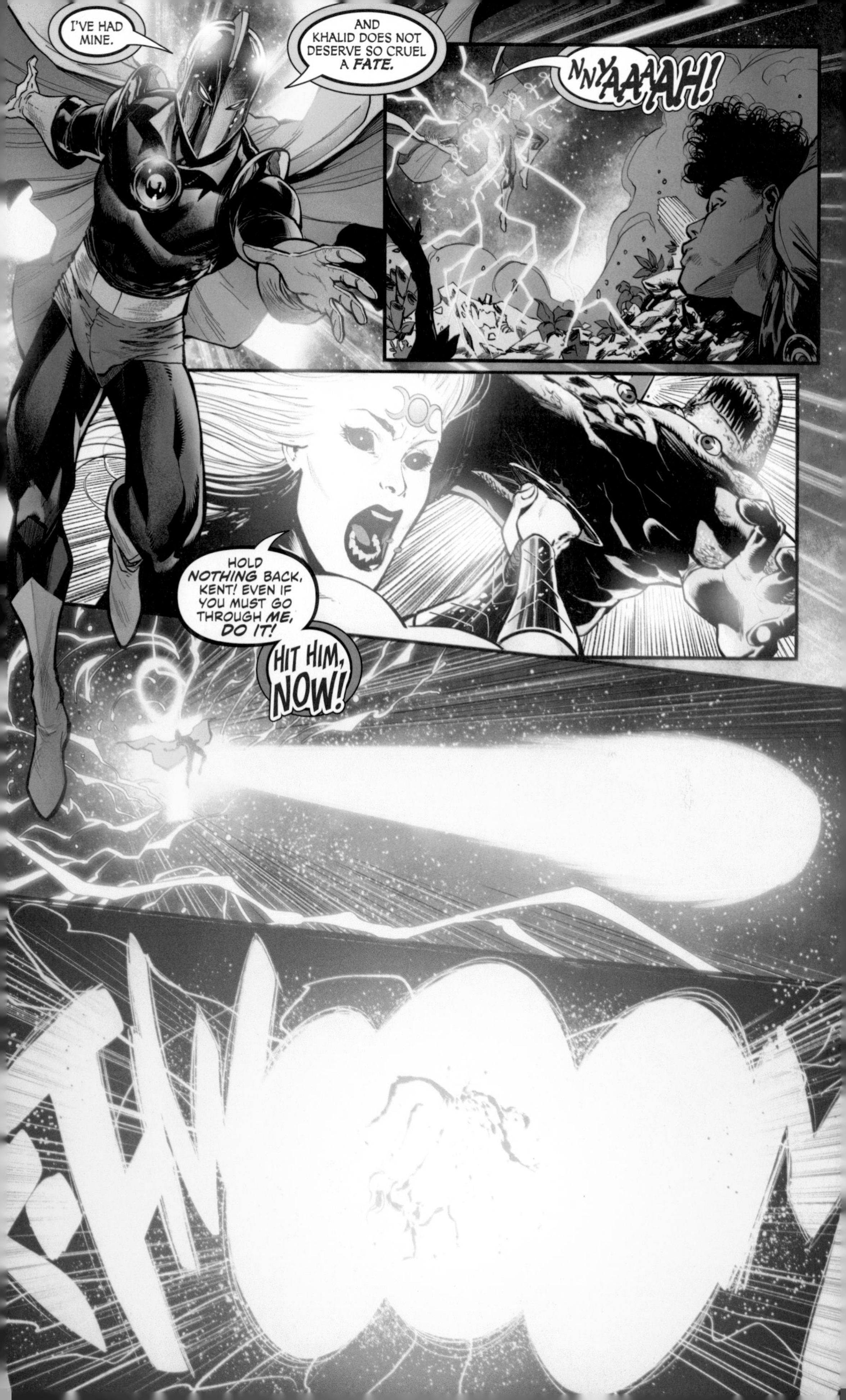
I'VE HAD MINE.
AND KHALID DOES NOT DESERVE SO CRUEL A FATE.
NNYAAAAH!
HOLD NOTHING BACK, KENT! EVEN IF YOU MUST GO THROUGH ME, DO IT!
HIT HIM, NOW!

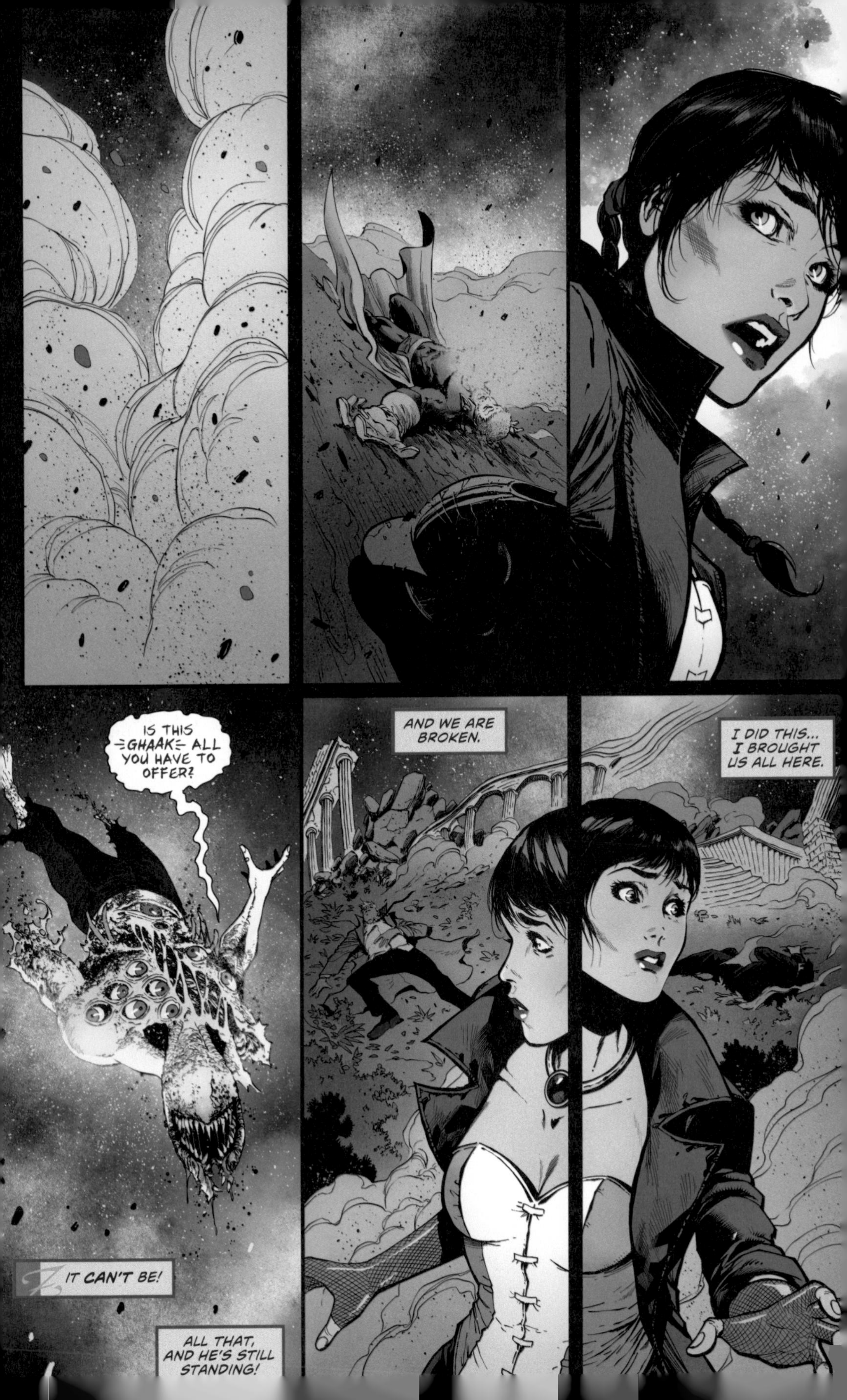
IS THIS =GHAAK= ALL YOU HAVE TO OFFER?
IT CAN'T BE!
ALL THAT, AND HE'S STILL STANDING!
AND WE ARE BROKEN.
I DID THIS... I BROUGHT US ALL HERE.

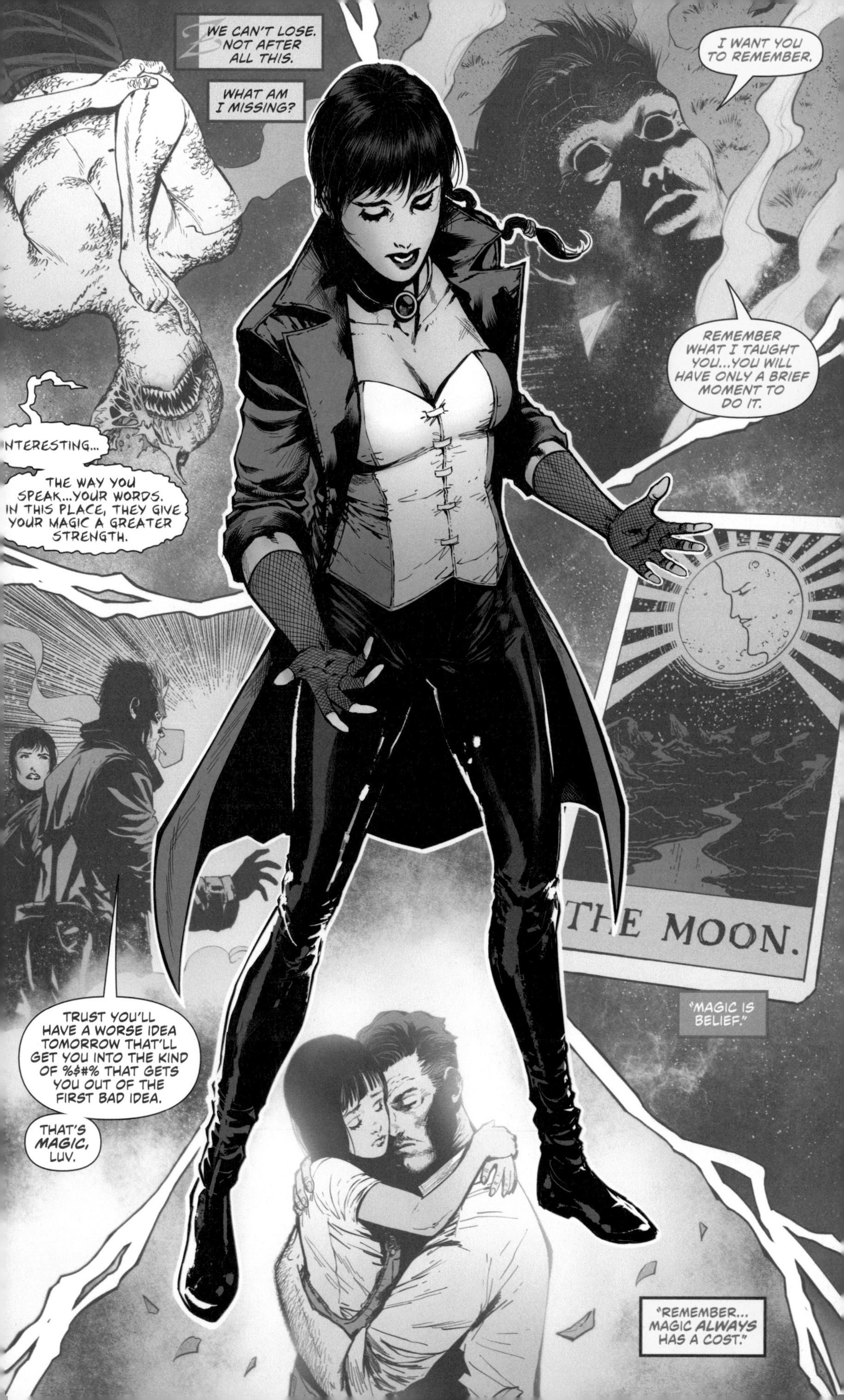
WE CAN'T LOSE. NOT AFTER ALL THIS.
WHAT AM I MISSING?
I WANT YOU TO REMEMBER.
REMEMBER WHAT I TAUGHT YOU...YOU WILL HAVE ONLY A BRIEF MOMENT TO DO IT.
INTERESTING...
THE WAY YOU SPEAK...YOUR WORDS. IN THIS PLACE, THEY GIVE YOUR MAGIC A GREATER STRENGTH.
THE MOON.
"MAGIC IS BELIEF."
TRUST YOU'LL HAVE A WORSE IDEA TOMORROW THAT'LL GET YOU INTO THE KIND OF %$#% THAT GETS YOU OUT OF THE FIRST BAD IDEA.
THAT'S MAGIC, LUV.
"REMEMBER... MAGIC ALWAYS HAS A COST."

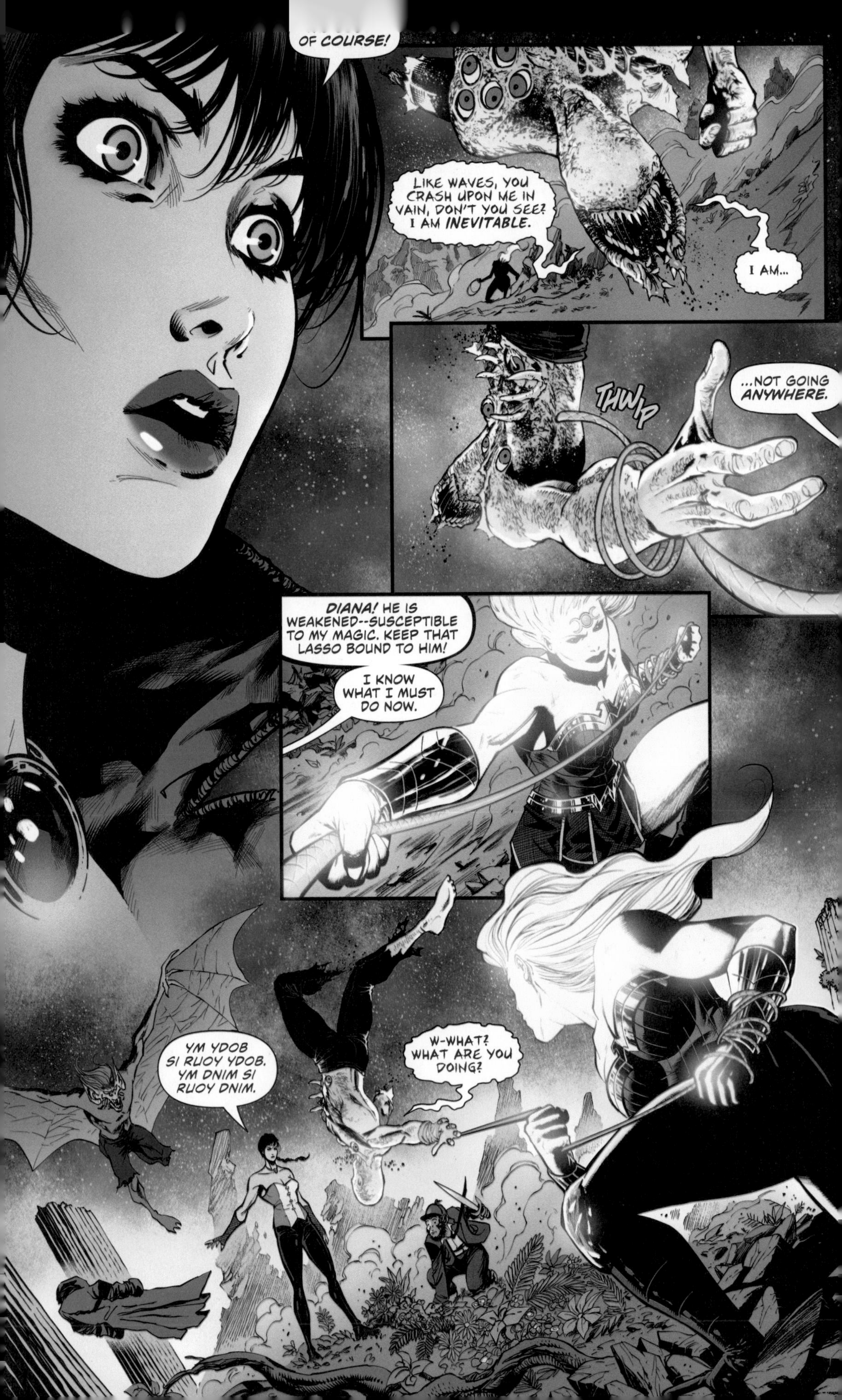

OF COURSE!
LIKE WAVES, YOU CRASH UPON ME IN VAIN, DON'T YOU SEE? I AM INEVITABLE.
I AM...
THWIP
...NOT GOING ANYWHERE.
DIANA! HE IS WEAKENED--SUSCEPTIBLE TO MY MAGIC. KEEP THAT LASSO BOUND TO HIM!
I KNOW WHAT I MUST DO NOW.
YM YDOB SI RUOY YDOB. YM DNIM SI RUOY DNIM.
W-WHAT? WHAT ARE YOU DOING?

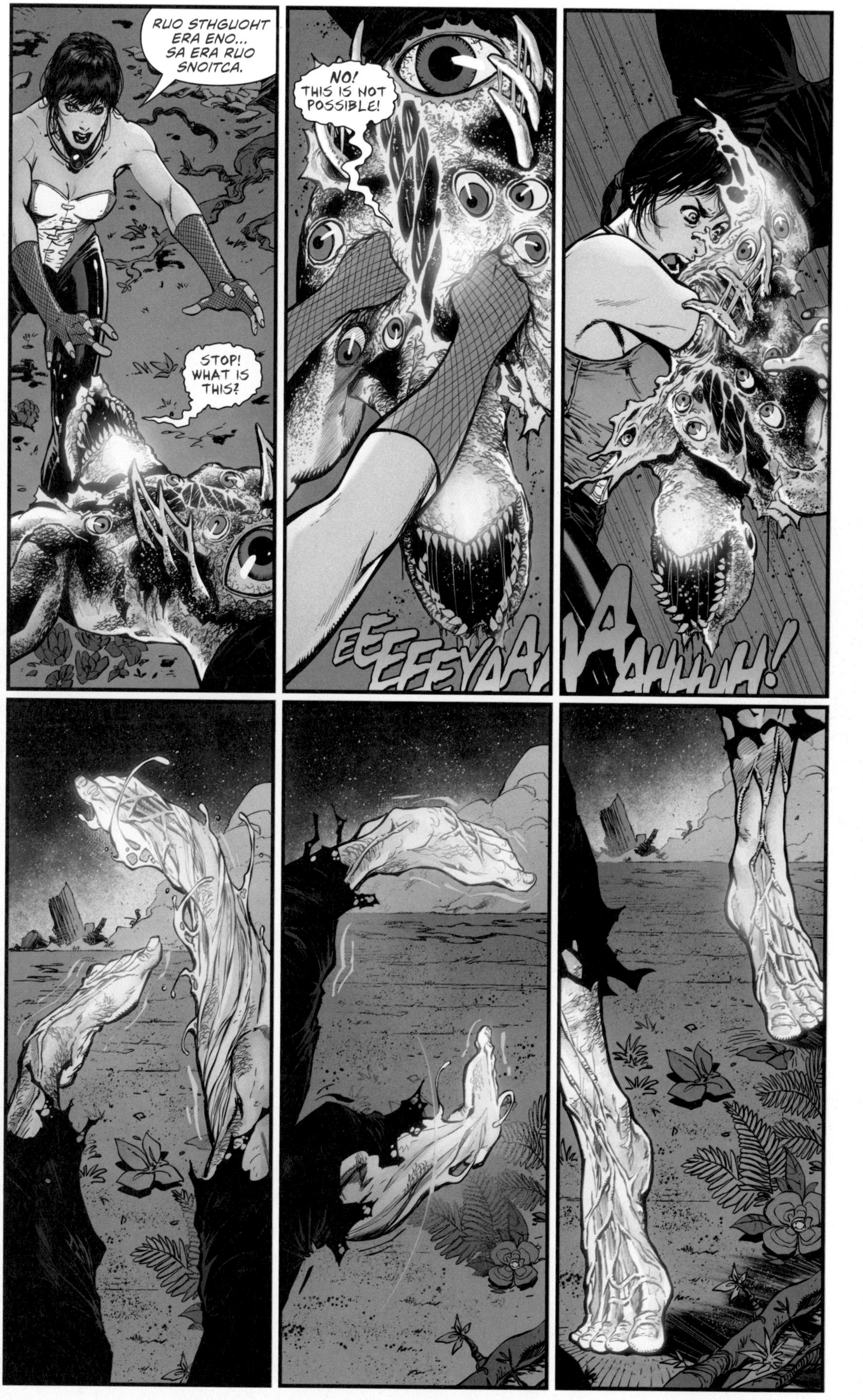

RUO STHGUOHT ERA ENO... SA ERA RUO SNOITCA.
STOP! WHAT IS THIS?
NO! THIS IS NOT POSSIBLE!
EEEEFFEYAAAAAHHHHH!

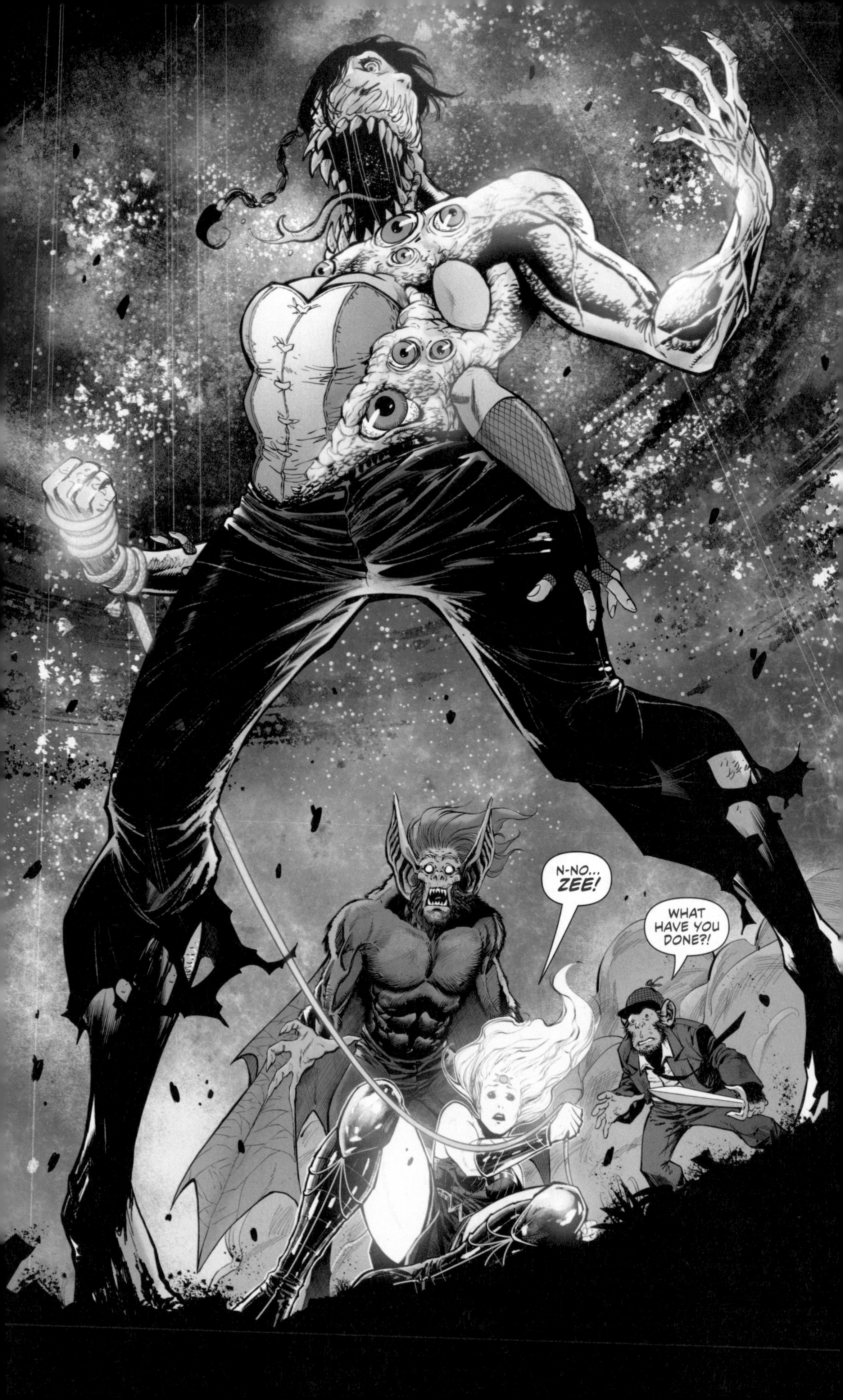
N-NO... ZEE!
WHAT HAVE YOU DONE?!

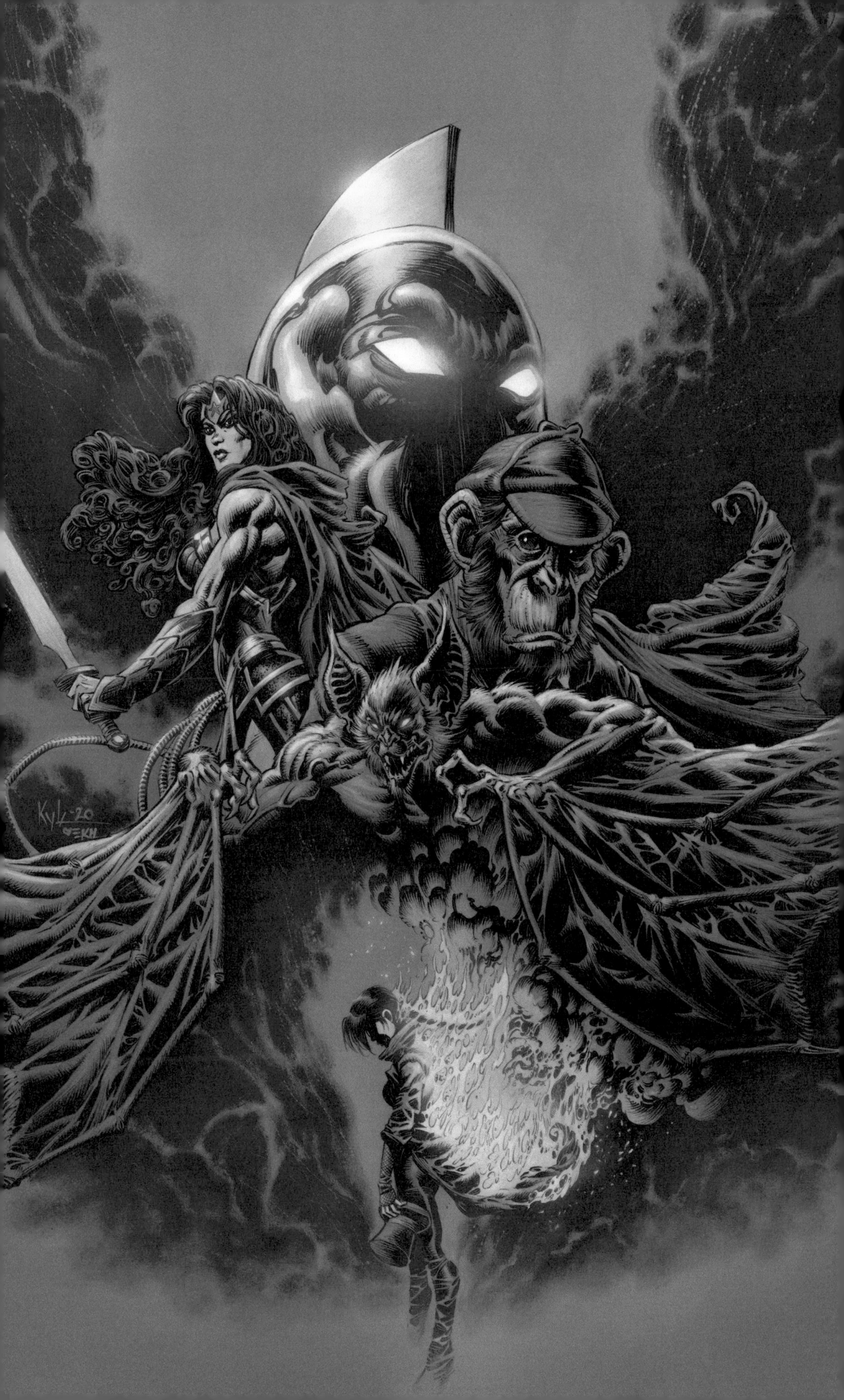

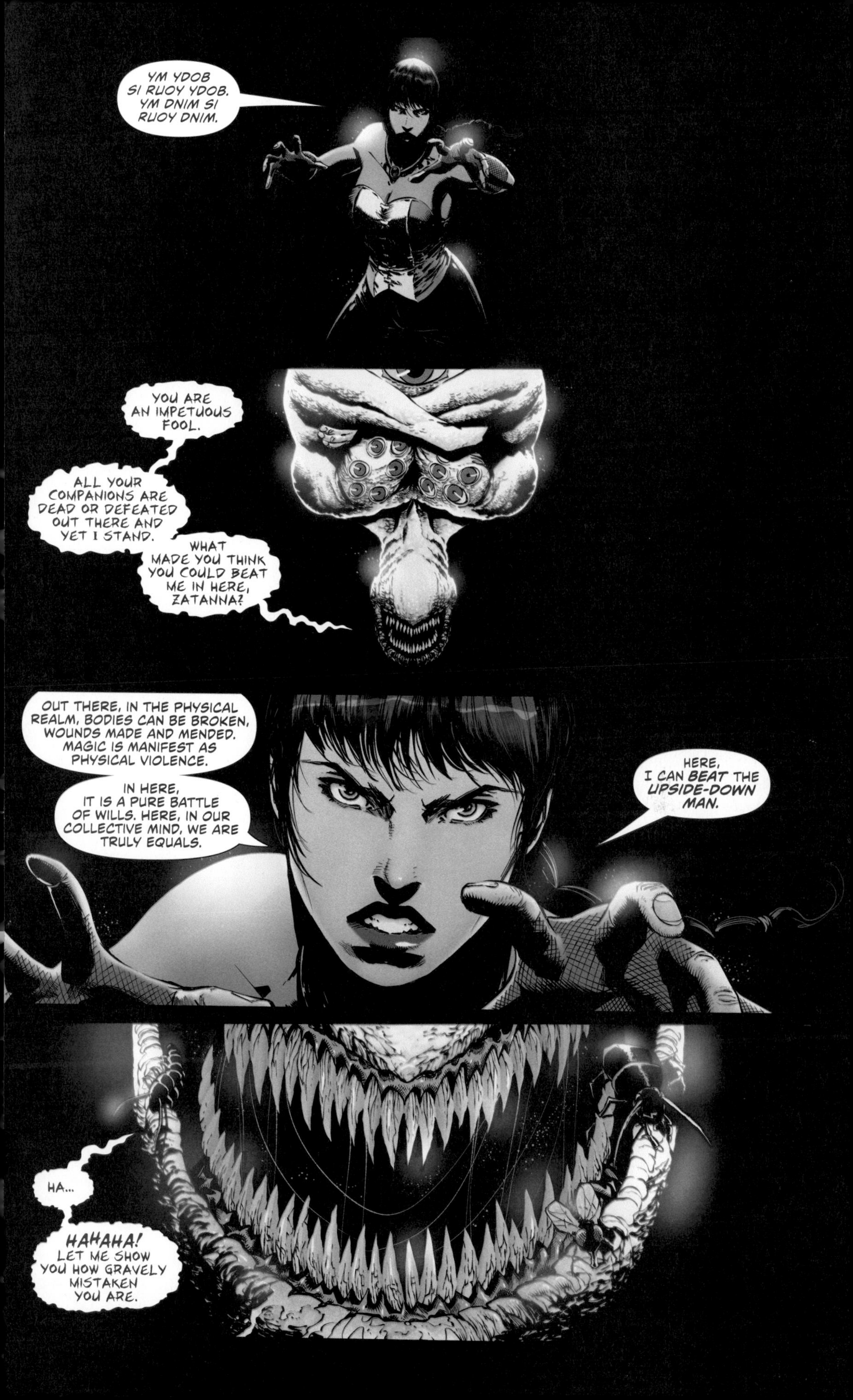
YM YDOB SI RUOY YDOB. YM DNIM SI RUOY DNIM.
YOU ARE AN IMPETUOUS FOOL.
ALL YOUR COMPANIONS ARE DEAD OR DEFEATED OUT THERE AND YET I STAND.
WHAT MADE YOU THINK YOU COULD BEAT ME IN HERE, ZATANNA?
OUT THERE, IN THE PHYSICAL REALM, BODIES CAN BE BROKEN, WOUNDS MADE AND MENDED. MAGIC IS MANIFEST AS PHYSICAL VIOLENCE.
IN HERE, IT IS A PURE BATTLE OF WILLS. HERE, IN OUR COLLECTIVE MIND, WE ARE TRULY EQUALS.
HERE, I CAN *BEAT* THE *UPSIDE-DOWN MAN.*
HA...
HAHAHA! LET ME SHOW YOU HOW GRAVELY MISTAKEN YOU ARE.

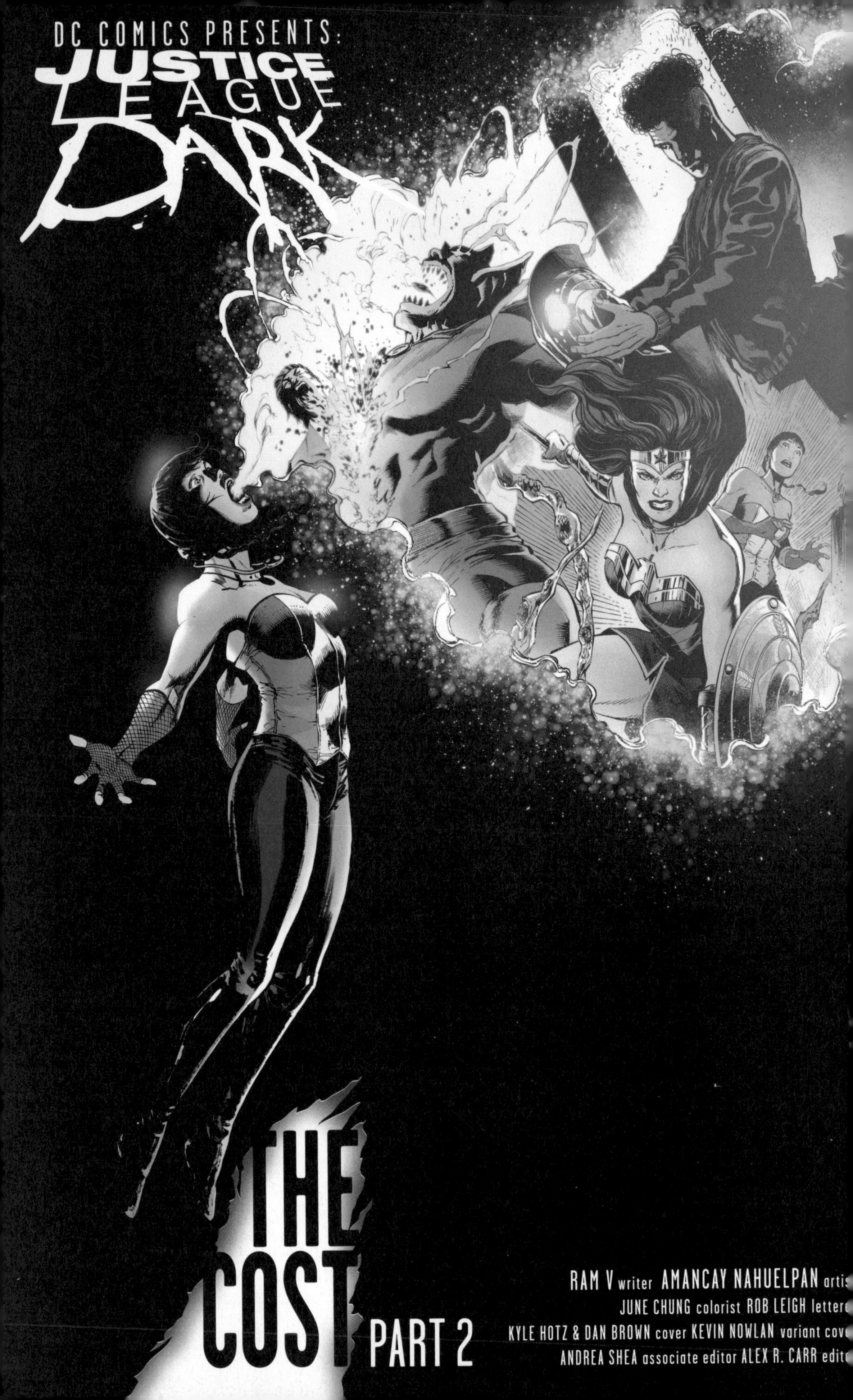
DC COMICS PRESENTS:
JUSTICE LEAGUE DARK
THE COST PART 2
RAM V writer AMANCAY NAHUELPAN artis
JUNE CHUNG colorist ROB LEIGH lettere
KYLE HOTZ & DAN BROWN cover KEVIN NOWLAN variant cove
ANDREA SHEA associate editor ALEX R. CARR edite

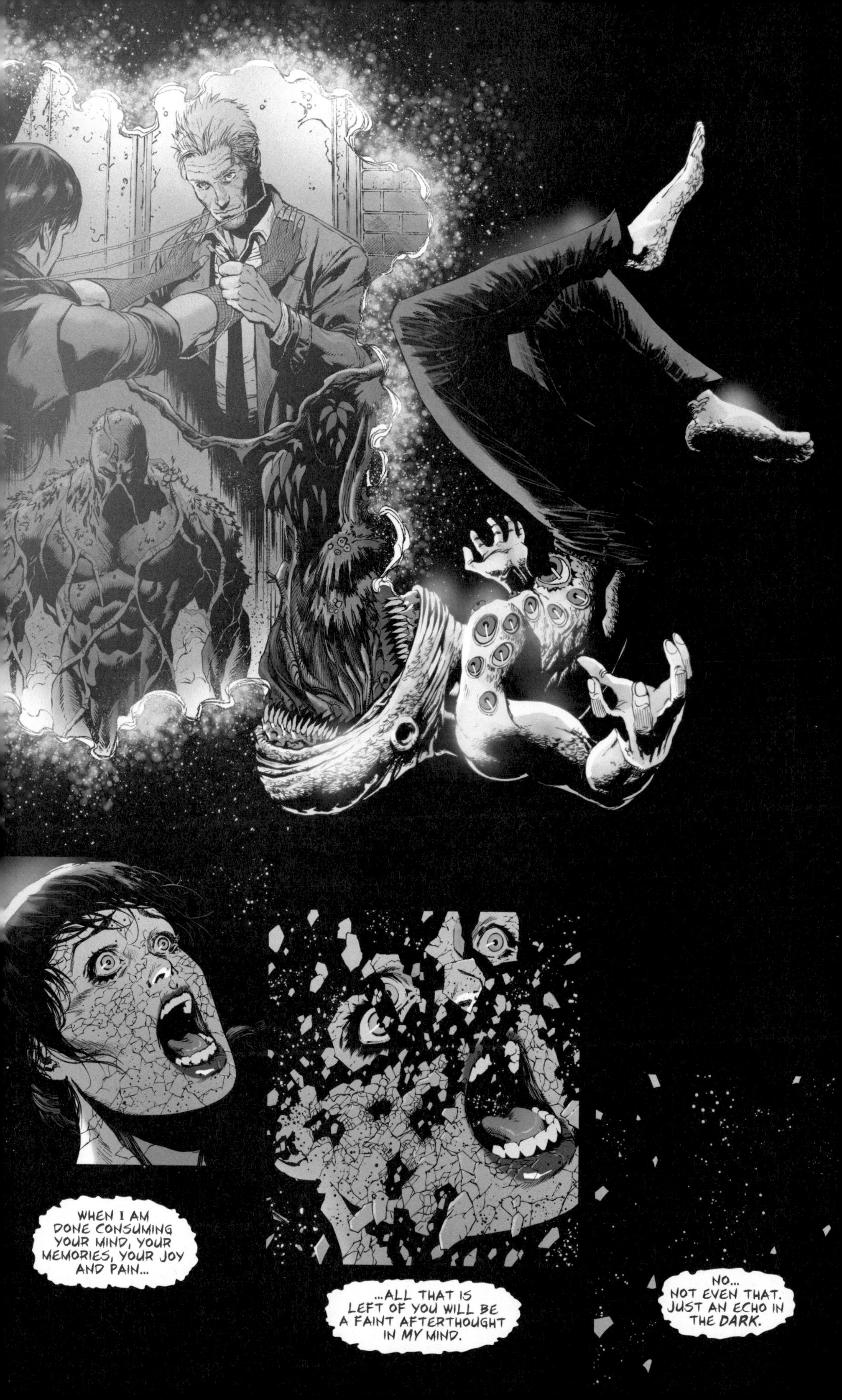
WHEN I AM DONE CONSUMING YOUR MIND, YOUR MEMORIES, YOUR JOY AND PAIN...
...ALL THAT IS LEFT OF YOU WILL BE A FAINT AFTERTHOUGHT IN *MY* MIND.
NO... NOT EVEN THAT. JUST AN ECHO IN THE *DARK*.

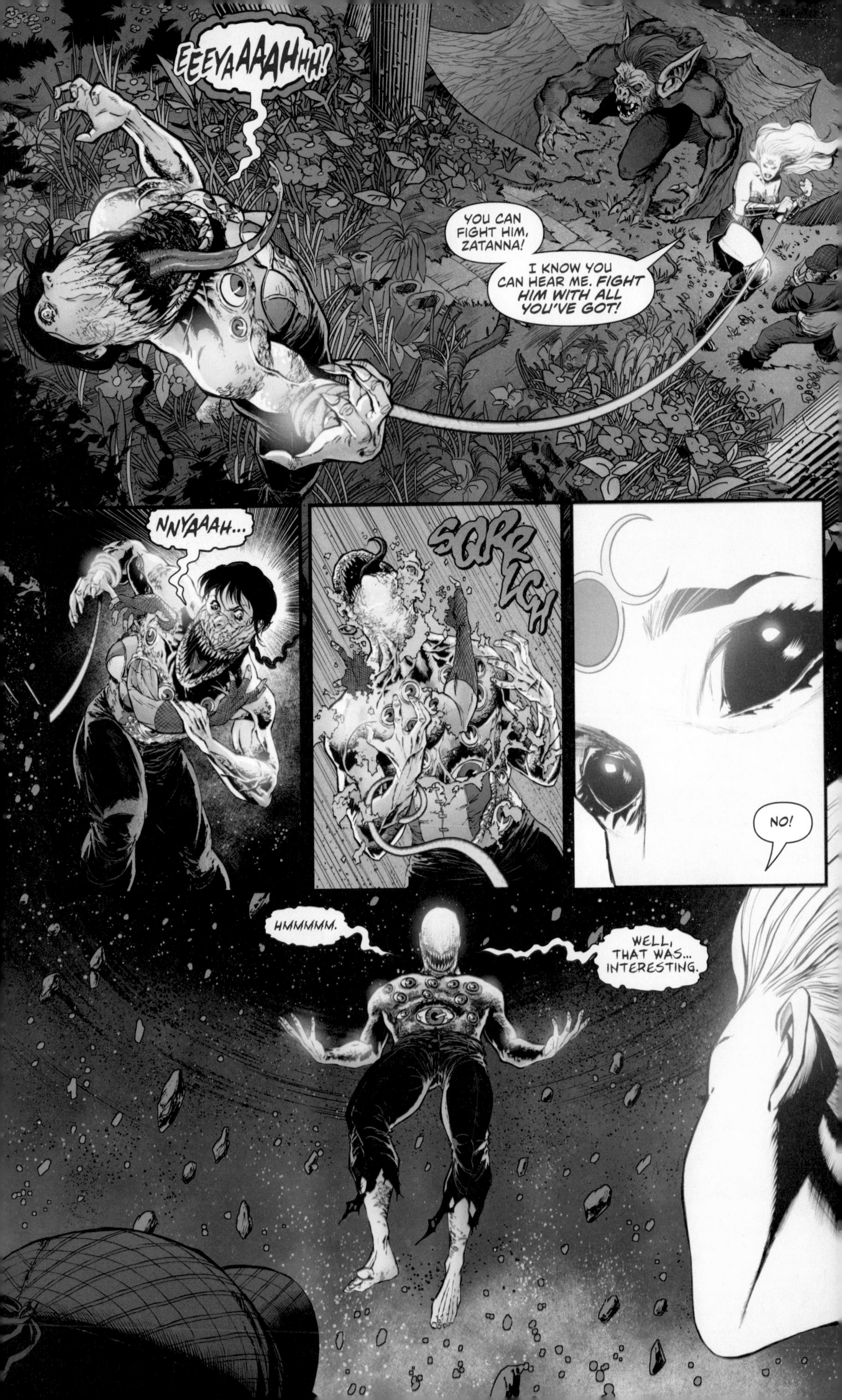
EEEYAAAAHHH!
YOU CAN FIGHT HIM, ZATANNA!
I KNOW YOU CAN HEAR ME. FIGHT HIM WITH ALL YOU'VE GOT!
NNYAAAH...
SQRRLCH
NO!
HMMMMM.
WELL, THAT WAS... INTERESTING.

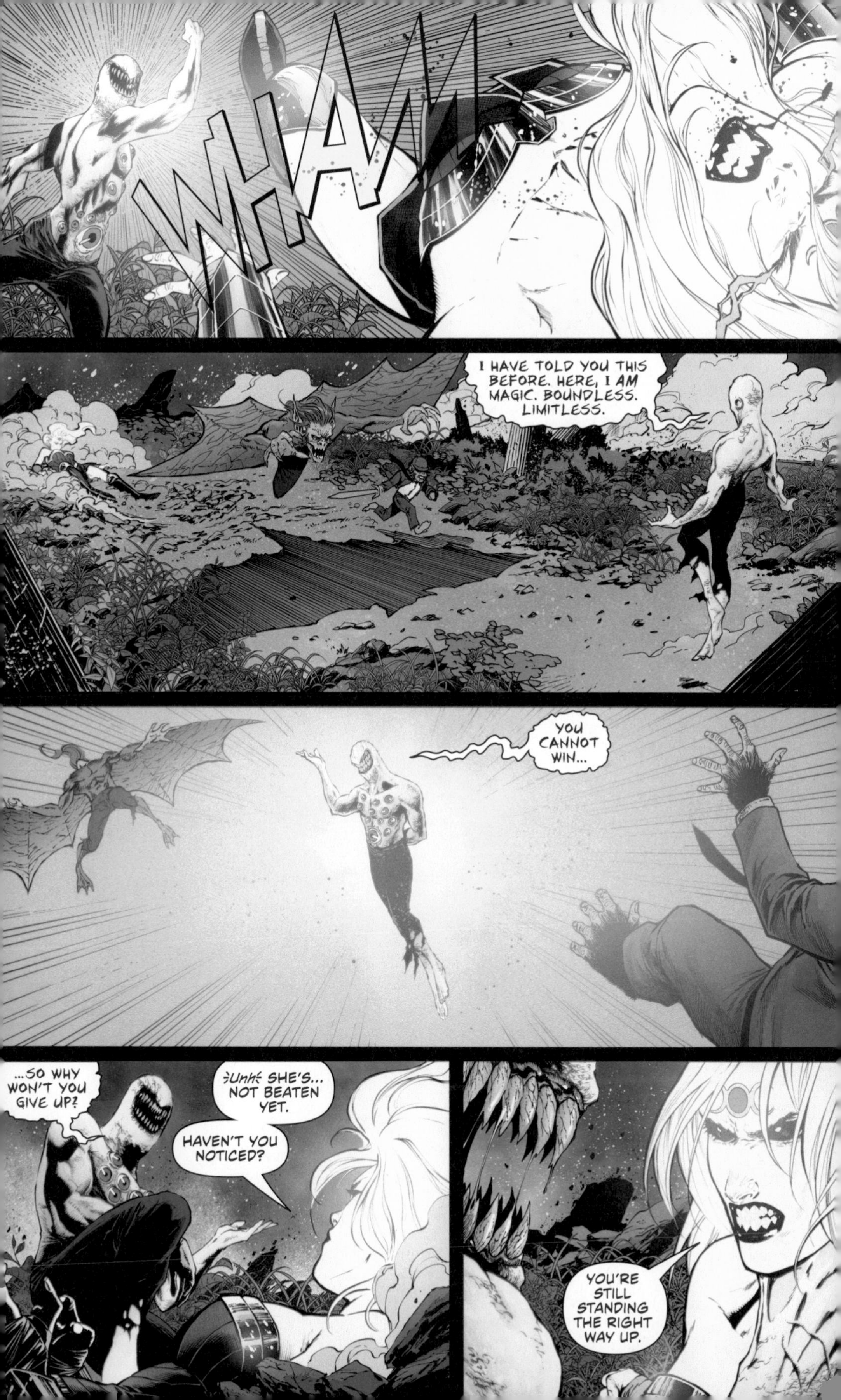
WHAM
I HAVE TOLD YOU THIS BEFORE. HERE, I AM MAGIC. BOUNDLESS. LIMITLESS.
YOU CANNOT WIN...
...SO WHY WON'T YOU GIVE UP?
Unh SHE'S... NOT BEATEN YET.
HAVEN'T YOU NOTICED?
YOU'RE STILL STANDING THE RIGHT WAY UP.

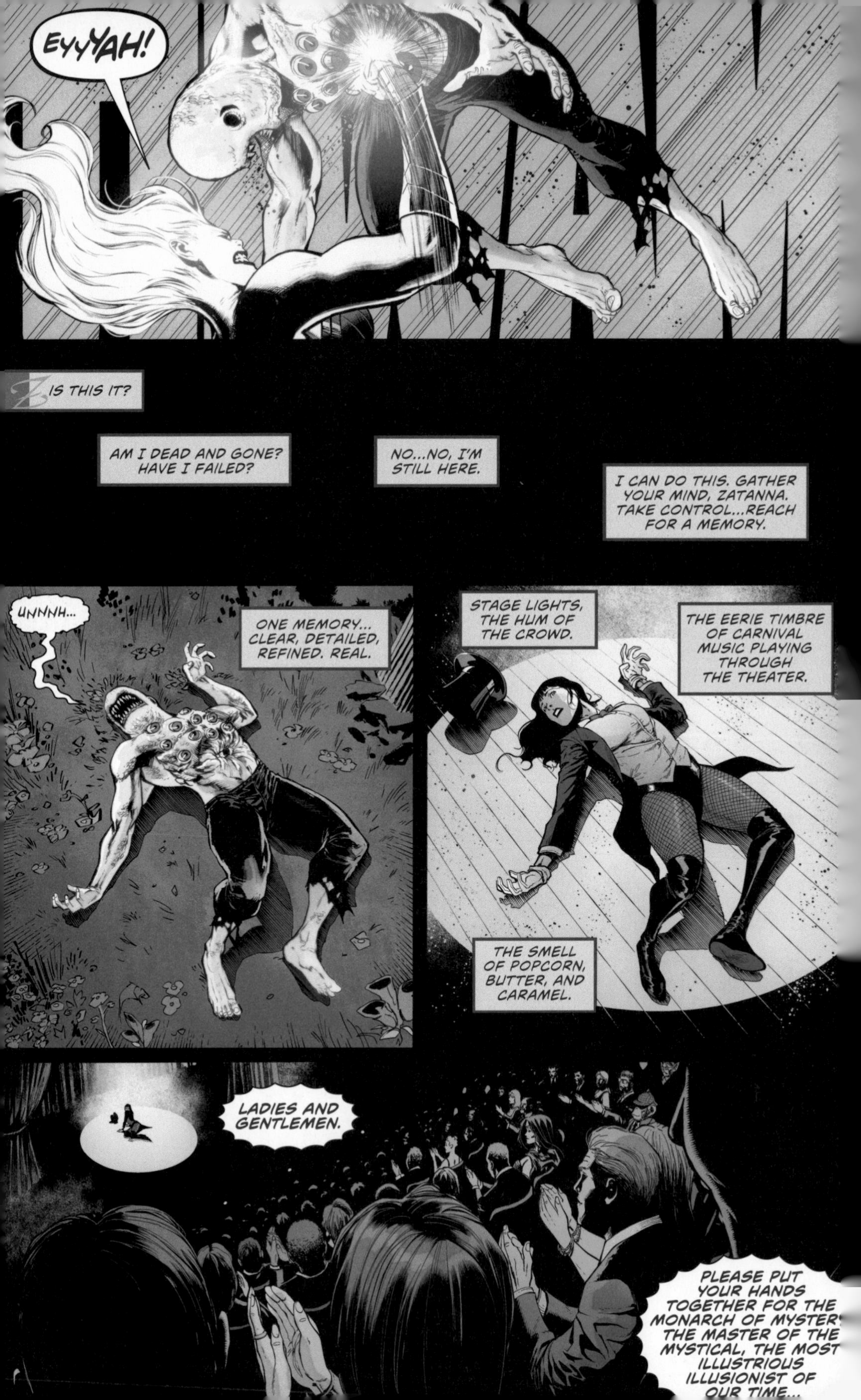
EYYYAH!
IS THIS IT?
AM I DEAD AND GONE? HAVE I FAILED?
NO...NO, I'M STILL HERE.
I CAN DO THIS. GATHER YOUR MIND, ZATANNA. TAKE CONTROL...REACH FOR A MEMORY.
UNNNH...
ONE MEMORY... CLEAR, DETAILED, REFINED. REAL.
STAGE LIGHTS, THE HUM OF THE CROWD.
THE EERIE TIMBRE OF CARNIVAL MUSIC PLAYING THROUGH THE THEATER.
THE SMELL OF POPCORN, BUTTER, AND CARAMEL.
LADIES AND GENTLEMEN.
PLEASE PUT YOUR HANDS TOGETHER FOR THE MONARCH OF MYSTERY THE MASTER OF THE MYSTICAL, THE MOST ILLUSTRIOUS ILLUSIONIST OF OUR TIME...

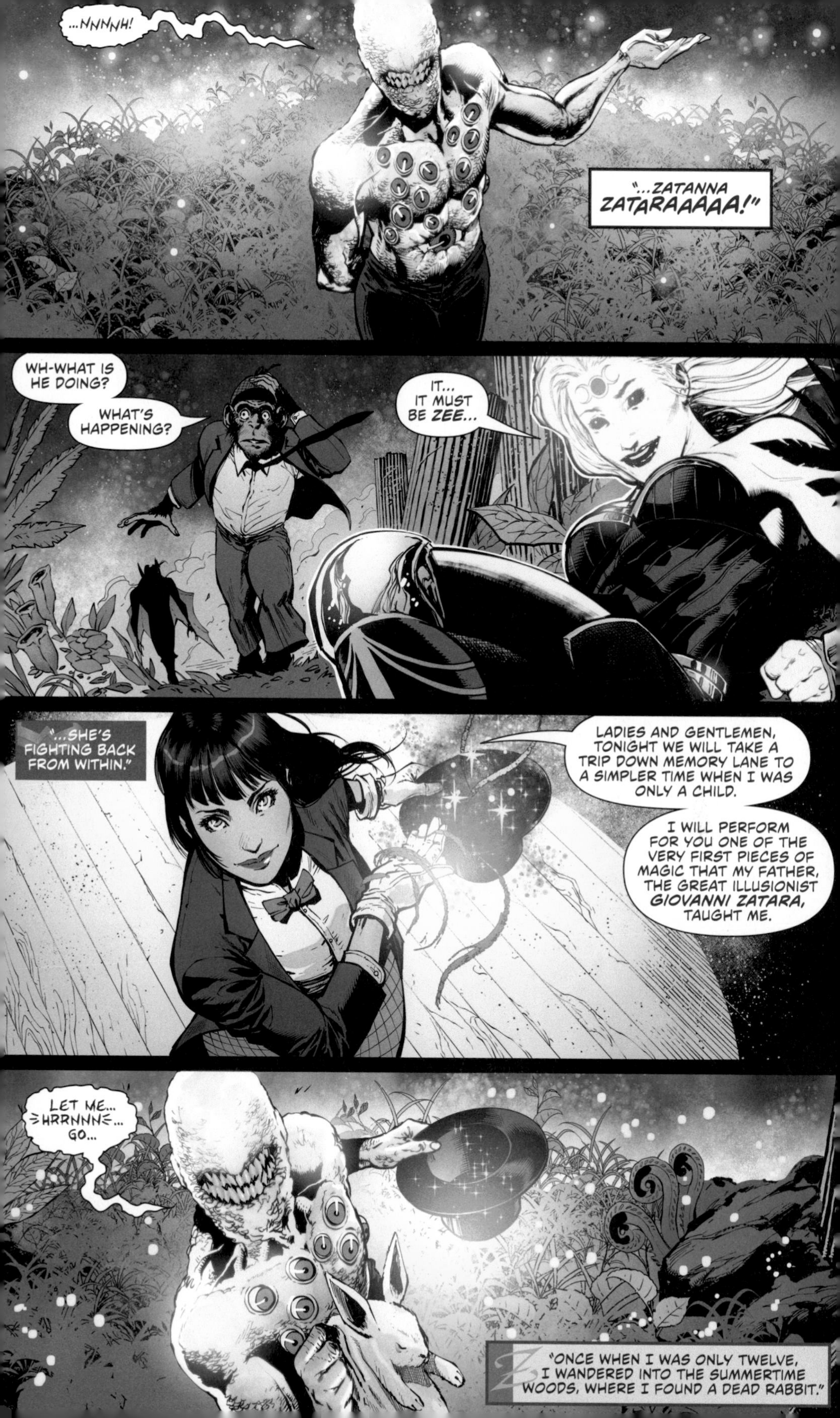
...NNNNH!
"...ZATANNA ZATARAAAAA!"
WH-WHAT IS HE DOING?
WHAT'S HAPPENING?
IT... IT MUST BE ZEE...
"...SHE'S FIGHTING BACK FROM WITHIN."
LADIES AND GENTLEMEN, TONIGHT WE WILL TAKE A TRIP DOWN MEMORY LANE TO A SIMPLER TIME WHEN I WAS ONLY A CHILD.
I WILL PERFORM FOR YOU ONE OF THE VERY FIRST PIECES OF MAGIC THAT MY FATHER, THE GREAT ILLUSIONIST GIOVANNI ZATARA, TAUGHT ME.
LET ME... HRRNNN... GO...
"ONCE WHEN I WAS ONLY TWELVE, I WANDERED INTO THE SUMMERTIME WOODS, WHERE I FOUND A DEAD RABBIT."

I HAD, OF COURSE, SEEN MY FATHER PERFORM THE TRICK BEFORE. THE MAGICIAN PUTS THE DEAD RABBIT INTO HIS HAT.

THE AUDIENCE SITS IN A BEREAVED SILENCE.

A WAVE OF THE WAND. A FEW MAGIC WORDS. ARBADACARBA!

"AND VOILÀ! THE CREATURE NEWLY BROUGHT TO LIFE LEAPS FORTH.

"APPLAUSE.

"JOY.

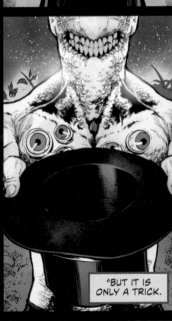

"BUT IT IS ONLY A TRICK.

FALSE BOTTOMS AND HOLES IN TABLES.

RABBITS IN SLEEVES.

"SOMEWHERE UNDERNEATH IT ALL...

"...THERE IS STILL A DEAD RABBIT IN THE DARK."

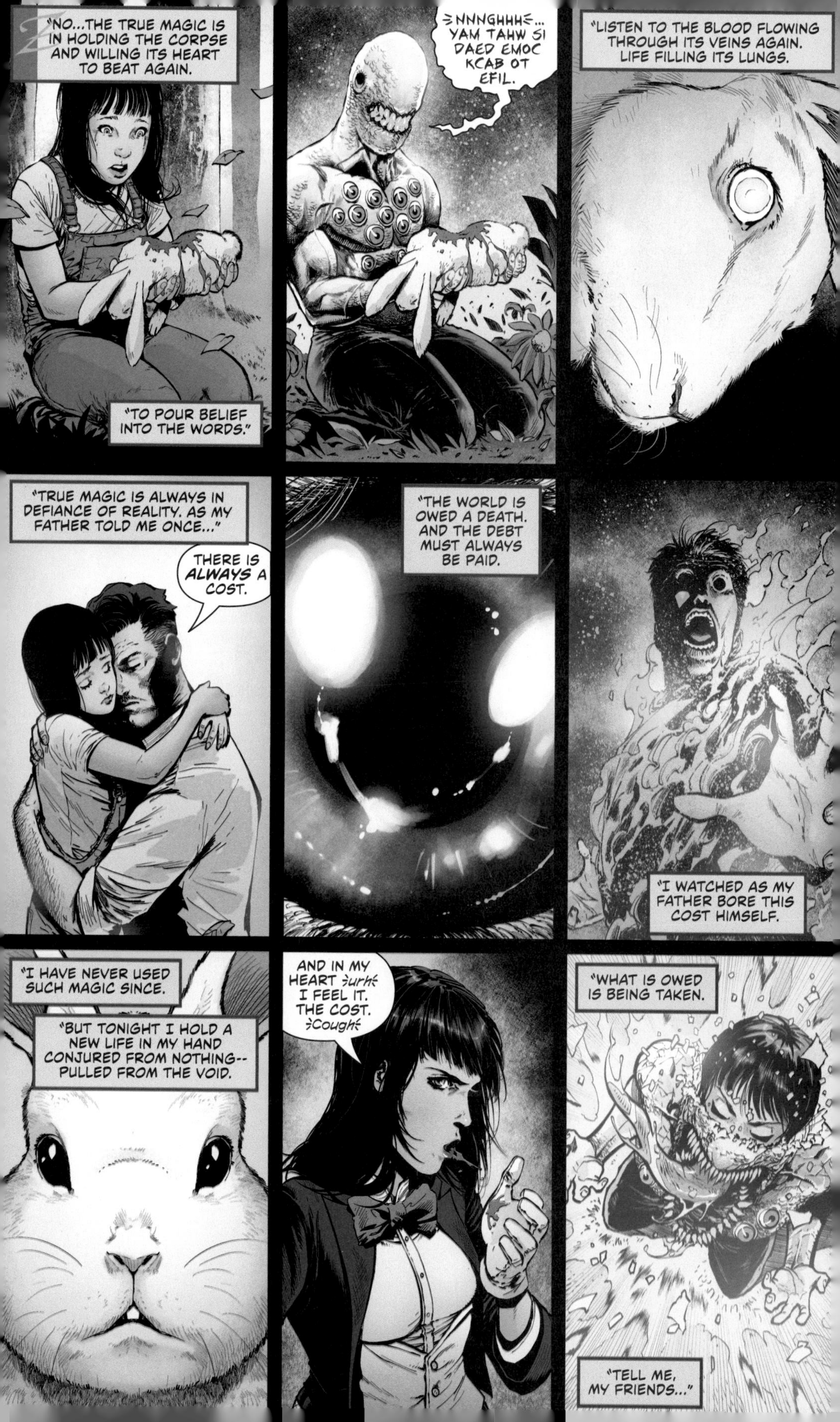
"NO...THE TRUE MAGIC IS IN HOLDING THE CORPSE AND WILLING ITS HEART TO BEAT AGAIN.
"TO POUR BELIEF INTO THE WORDS."
NNNGHHH... YAM TAHW SI DAED EMOC KCAB OT EFIL.
"LISTEN TO THE BLOOD FLOWING THROUGH ITS VEINS AGAIN. LIFE FILLING ITS LUNGS.
"TRUE MAGIC IS ALWAYS IN DEFIANCE OF REALITY. AS MY FATHER TOLD ME ONCE..."
THERE IS ALWAYS A COST.
"THE WORLD IS OWED A DEATH. AND THE DEBT MUST ALWAYS BE PAID.
"I WATCHED AS MY FATHER BORE THIS COST HIMSELF.
"I HAVE NEVER USED SUCH MAGIC SINCE.
"BUT TONIGHT I HOLD A NEW LIFE IN MY HAND CONJURED FROM NOTHING-- PULLED FROM THE VOID.
AND IN MY HEART urh I FEEL IT. THE COST. Cough
"WHAT IS OWED IS BEING TAKEN.
"TELL ME, MY FRIENDS..."

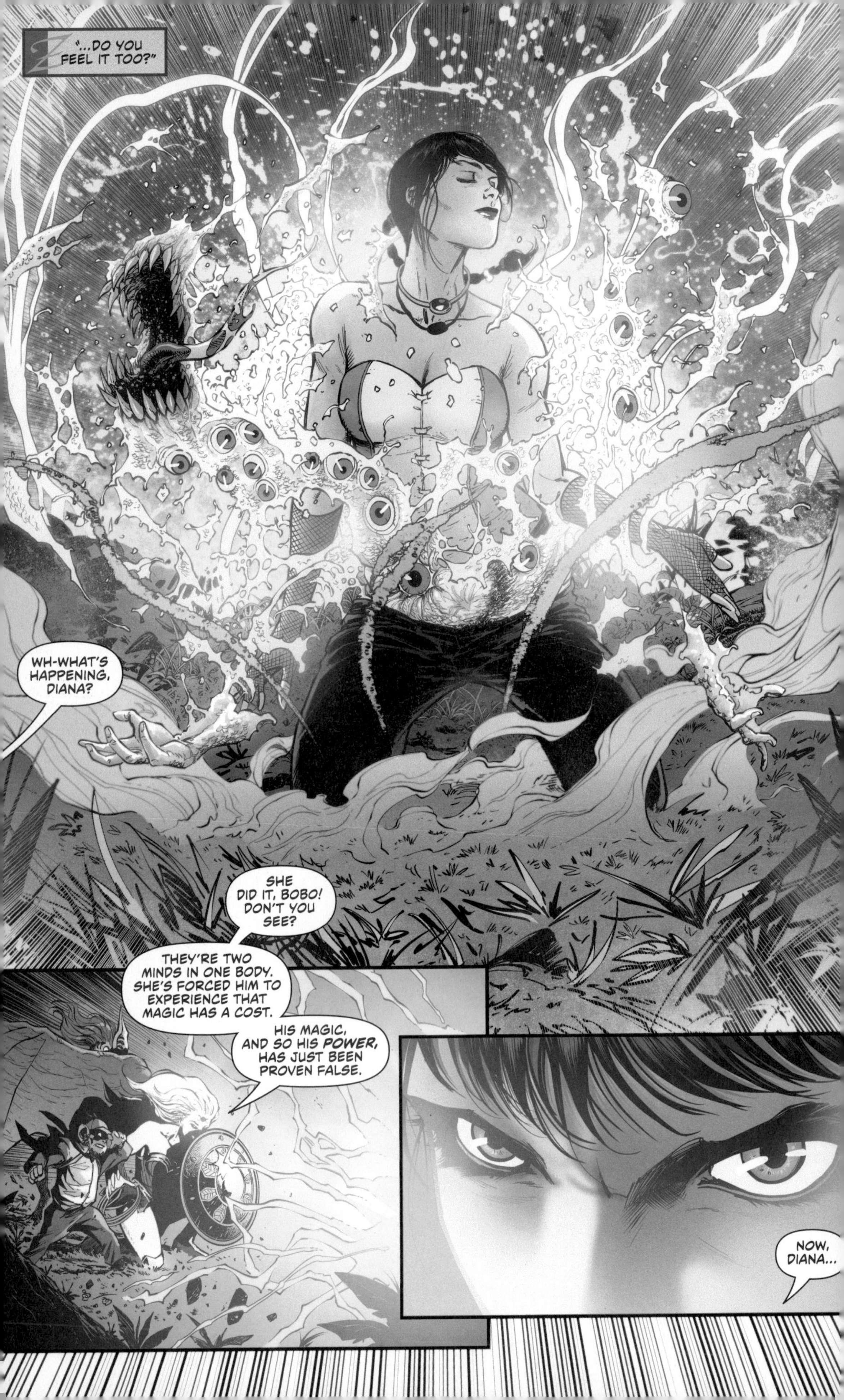
"...DO YOU FEEL IT TOO?"
WH-WHAT'S HAPPENING, DIANA?
SHE DID IT, BOBO! DON'T YOU SEE?
THEY'RE TWO MINDS IN ONE BODY. SHE'S FORCED HIM TO EXPERIENCE THAT MAGIC HAS A COST.
HIS MAGIC, AND SO HIS *POWER*, HAS JUST BEEN PROVEN FALSE.
NOW, DIANA...

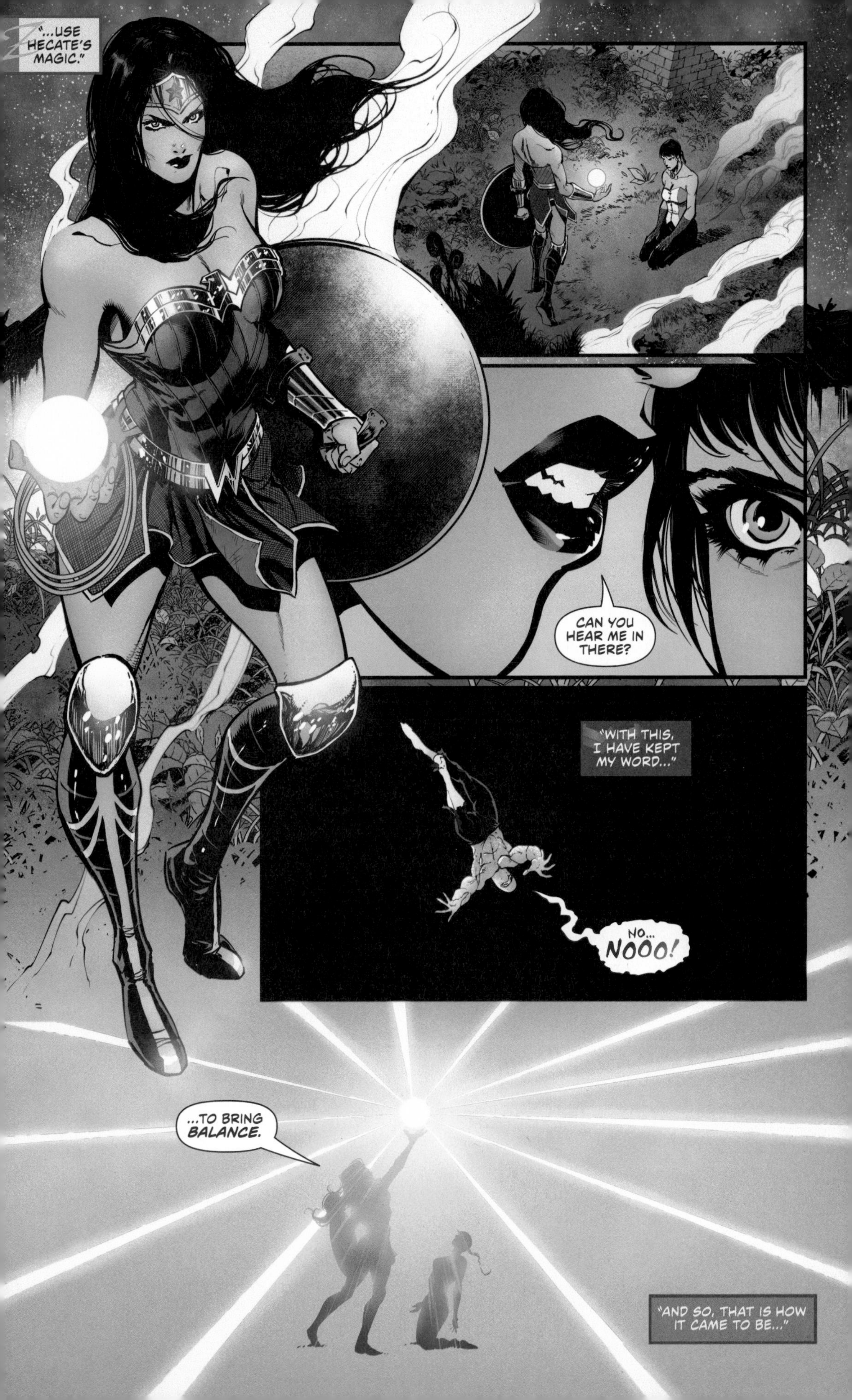
"...USE HECATE'S MAGIC."
CAN YOU HEAR ME IN THERE?
"WITH THIS, I HAVE KEPT MY WORD..."
NO... NOOO!
...TO BRING BALANCE.
"AND SO, THAT IS HOW IT CAME TO BE..."

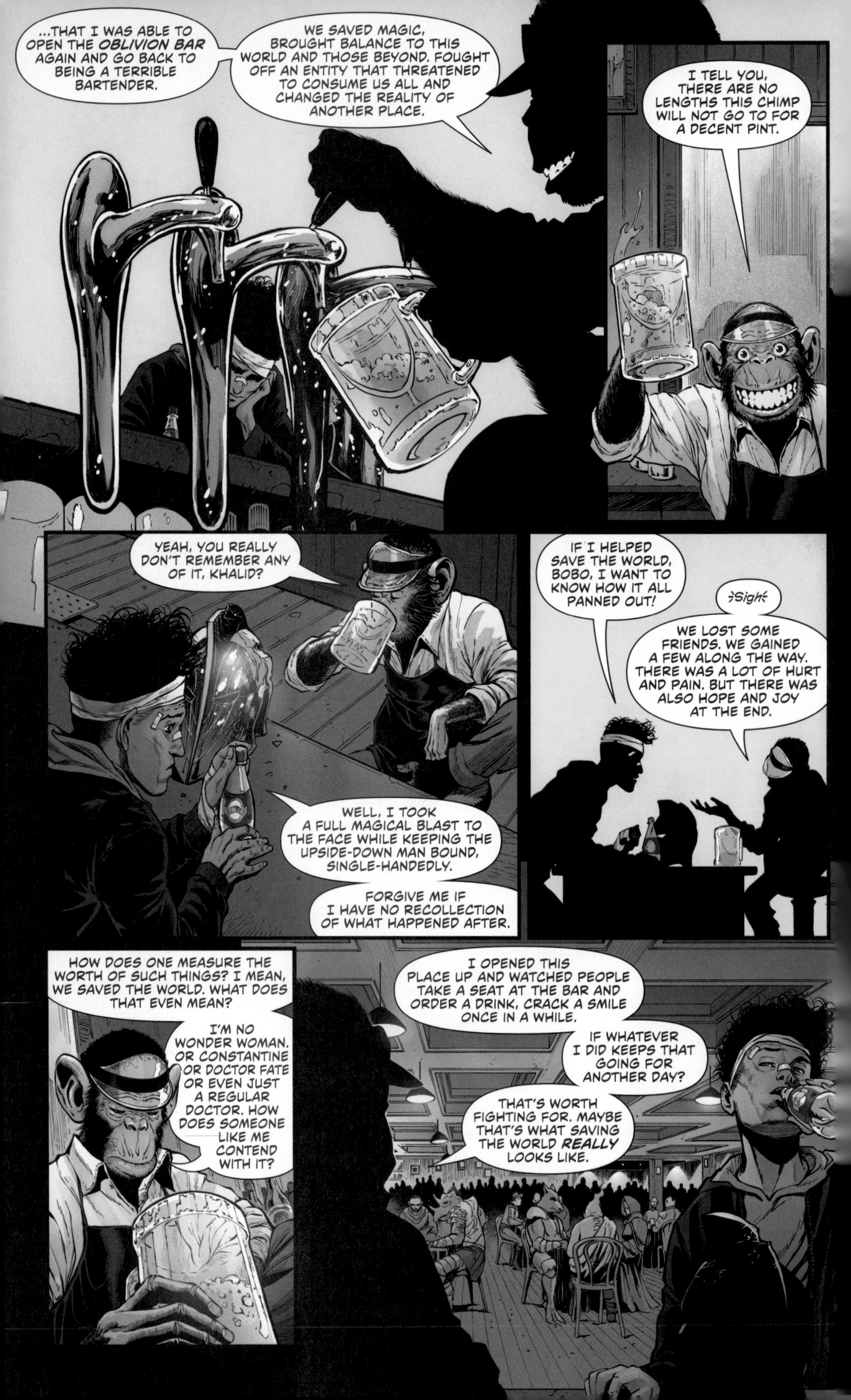
...THAT I WAS ABLE TO OPEN THE *OBLIVION BAR* AGAIN AND GO BACK TO BEING A TERRIBLE BARTENDER.
WE SAVED MAGIC, BROUGHT BALANCE TO THIS WORLD AND THOSE BEYOND. FOUGHT OFF AN ENTITY THAT THREATENED TO CONSUME US ALL AND CHANGED THE REALITY OF ANOTHER PLACE.
I TELL YOU, THERE ARE NO LENGTHS THIS CHIMP WILL NOT GO TO FOR A DECENT PINT.
YEAH, YOU REALLY DON'T REMEMBER ANY OF IT, KHALID?
WELL, I TOOK A FULL MAGICAL BLAST TO THE FACE WHILE KEEPING THE UPSIDE-DOWN MAN BOUND, SINGLE-HANDEDLY.
FORGIVE ME IF I HAVE NO RECOLLECTION OF WHAT HAPPENED AFTER.
IF I HELPED SAVE THE WORLD, BOBO, I WANT TO KNOW HOW IT ALL PANNED OUT!
Sigh
WE LOST SOME FRIENDS. WE GAINED A FEW ALONG THE WAY. THERE WAS A LOT OF HURT AND PAIN. BUT THERE WAS ALSO HOPE AND JOY AT THE END.
HOW DOES ONE MEASURE THE WORTH OF SUCH THINGS? I MEAN, WE SAVED THE WORLD. WHAT DOES THAT EVEN MEAN?
I'M NO WONDER WOMAN. OR CONSTANTINE OR DOCTOR FATE OR EVEN JUST A REGULAR DOCTOR. HOW DOES SOMEONE LIKE ME CONTEND WITH IT?
I OPENED THIS PLACE UP AND WATCHED PEOPLE TAKE A SEAT AT THE BAR AND ORDER A DRINK, CRACK A SMILE ONCE IN A WHILE.
IF WHATEVER I DID KEEPS THAT GOING FOR ANOTHER DAY?
THAT'S WORTH FIGHTING FOR. MAYBE THAT'S WHAT SAVING THE WORLD *REALLY* LOOKS LIKE.

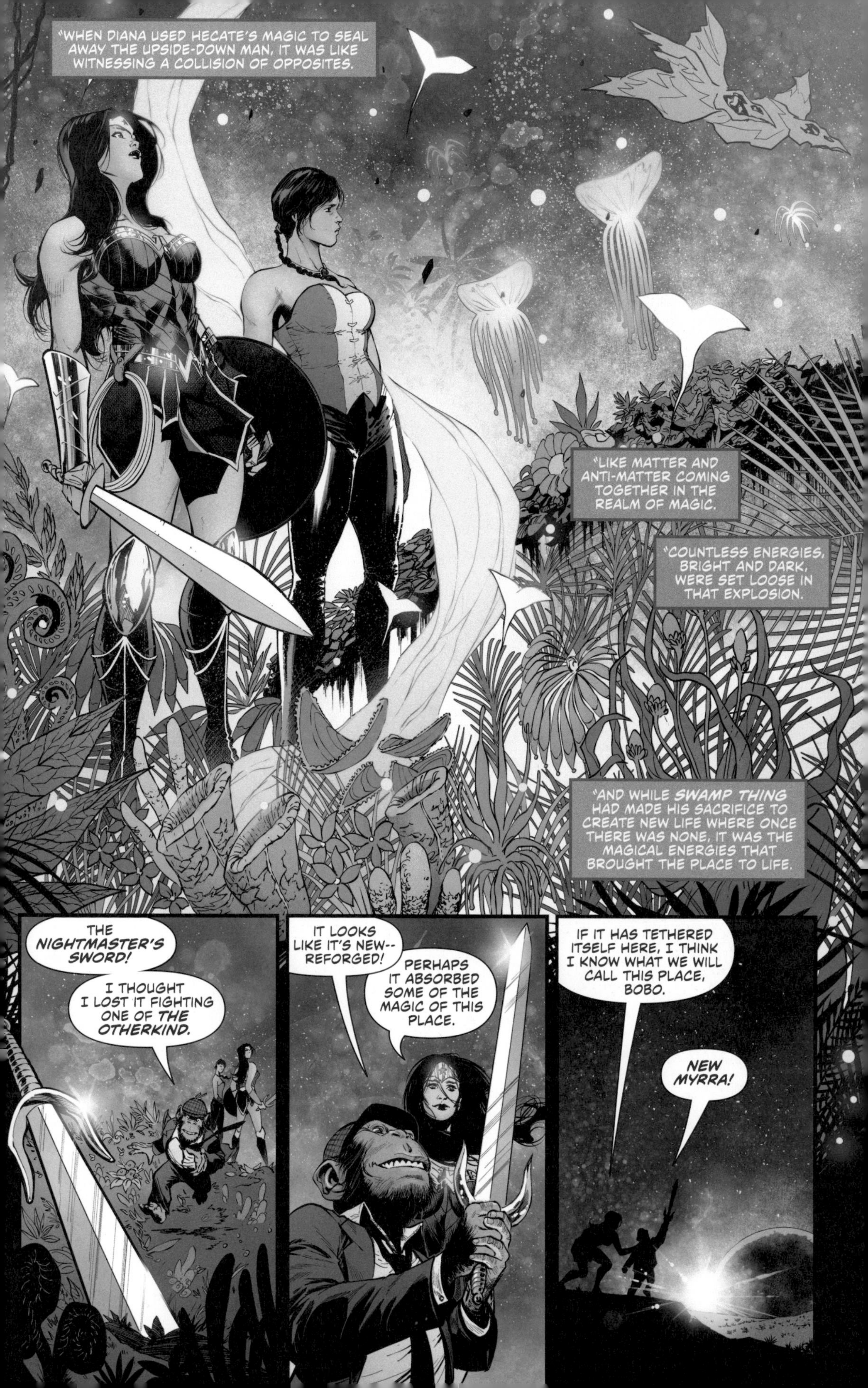
"WHEN DIANA USED HECATE'S MAGIC TO SEAL AWAY THE UPSIDE-DOWN MAN, IT WAS LIKE WITNESSING A COLLISION OF OPPOSITES.
"LIKE MATTER AND ANTI-MATTER COMING TOGETHER IN THE REALM OF MAGIC.
"COUNTLESS ENERGIES, BRIGHT AND DARK, WERE SET LOOSE IN THAT EXPLOSION.
"AND WHILE SWAMP THING HAD MADE HIS SACRIFICE TO CREATE NEW LIFE WHERE ONCE THERE WAS NONE, IT WAS THE MAGICAL ENERGIES THAT BROUGHT THE PLACE TO LIFE.
THE NIGHTMASTER'S SWORD!
I THOUGHT I LOST IT FIGHTING ONE OF THE OTHERKIND.
IT LOOKS LIKE IT'S NEW-- REFORGED!
PERHAPS IT ABSORBED SOME OF THE MAGIC OF THIS PLACE.
IF IT HAS TETHERED ITSELF HERE, I THINK I KNOW WHAT WE WILL CALL THIS PLACE, BOBO.
NEW MYRRA!

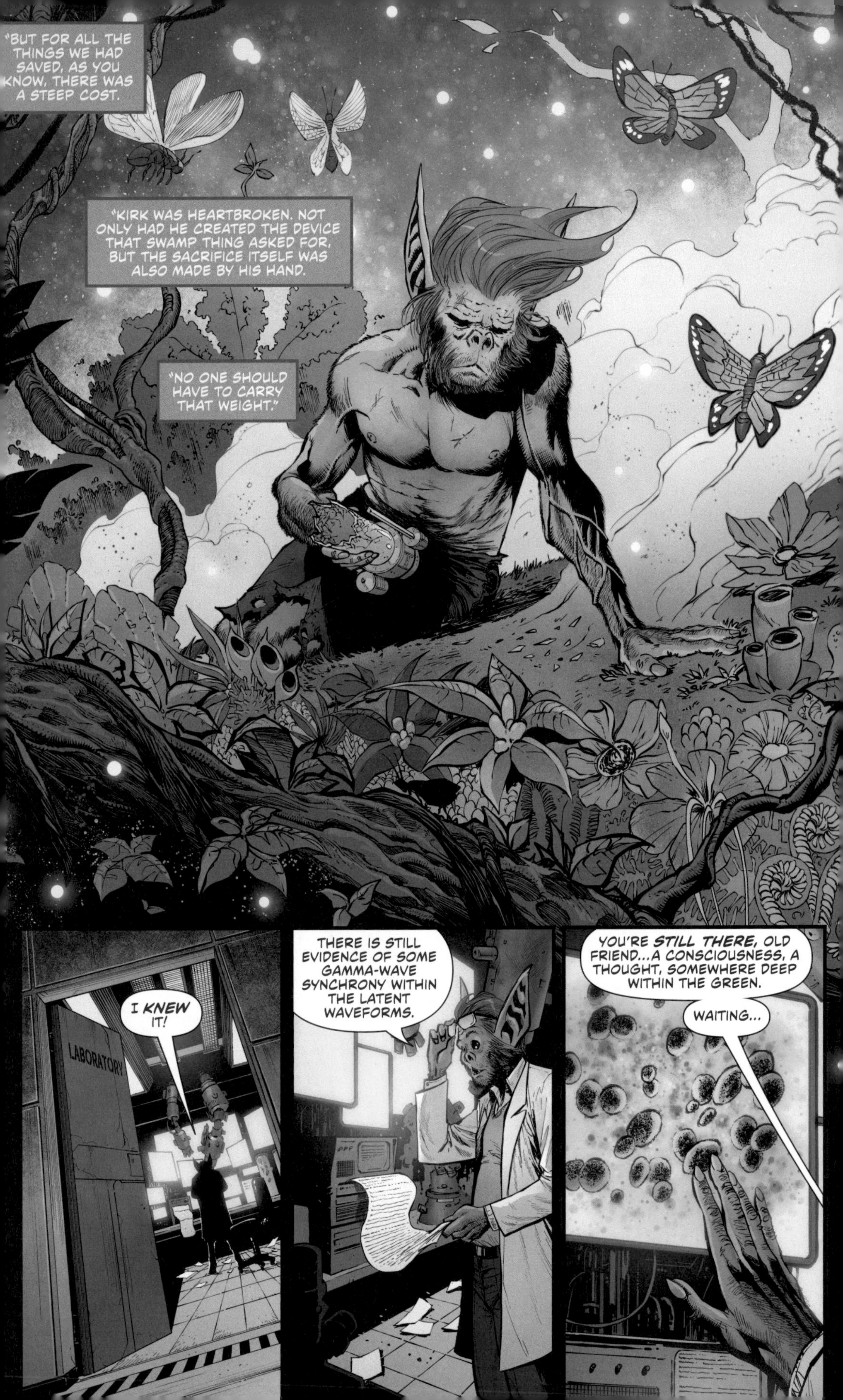
"BUT FOR ALL THE THINGS WE HAD SAVED, AS YOU KNOW, THERE WAS A STEEP COST.
"KIRK WAS HEARTBROKEN. NOT ONLY HAD HE CREATED THE DEVICE THAT SWAMP THING ASKED FOR, BUT THE SACRIFICE ITSELF WAS ALSO MADE BY HIS HAND.
"NO ONE SHOULD HAVE TO CARRY THAT WEIGHT."
LABORATORY
I KNEW IT!
THERE IS STILL EVIDENCE OF SOME GAMMA-WAVE SYNCHRONY WITHIN THE LATENT WAVEFORMS.
YOU'RE STILL THERE, OLD FRIEND...A CONSCIOUSNESS, A THOUGHT, SOMEWHERE DEEP WITHIN THE GREEN.
WAITING...

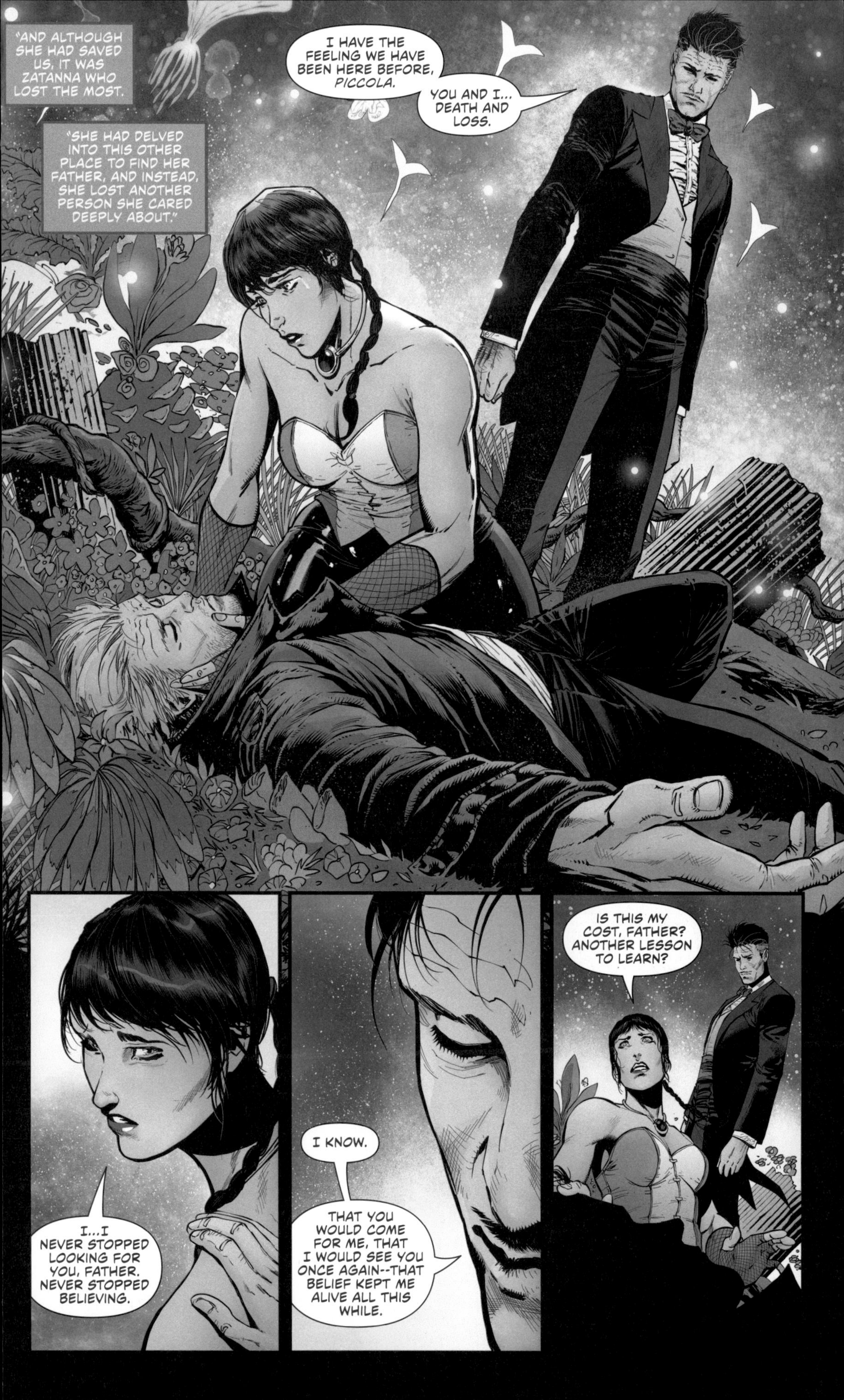
"AND ALTHOUGH SHE HAD SAVED US, IT WAS ZATANNA WHO LOST THE MOST.
"SHE HAD DELVED INTO THIS OTHER PLACE TO FIND HER FATHER, AND INSTEAD, SHE LOST ANOTHER PERSON SHE CARED DEEPLY ABOUT."
I HAVE THE FEELING WE HAVE BEEN HERE BEFORE, *PICCOLA.*
YOU AND I... DEATH AND LOSS.
I...I NEVER STOPPED LOOKING FOR YOU, FATHER. NEVER STOPPED BELIEVING.
I KNOW.
THAT YOU WOULD COME FOR ME, THAT I WOULD SEE YOU ONCE AGAIN--THAT BELIEF KEPT ME ALIVE ALL THIS WHILE.
IS THIS MY COST, FATHER? ANOTHER LESSON TO LEARN?

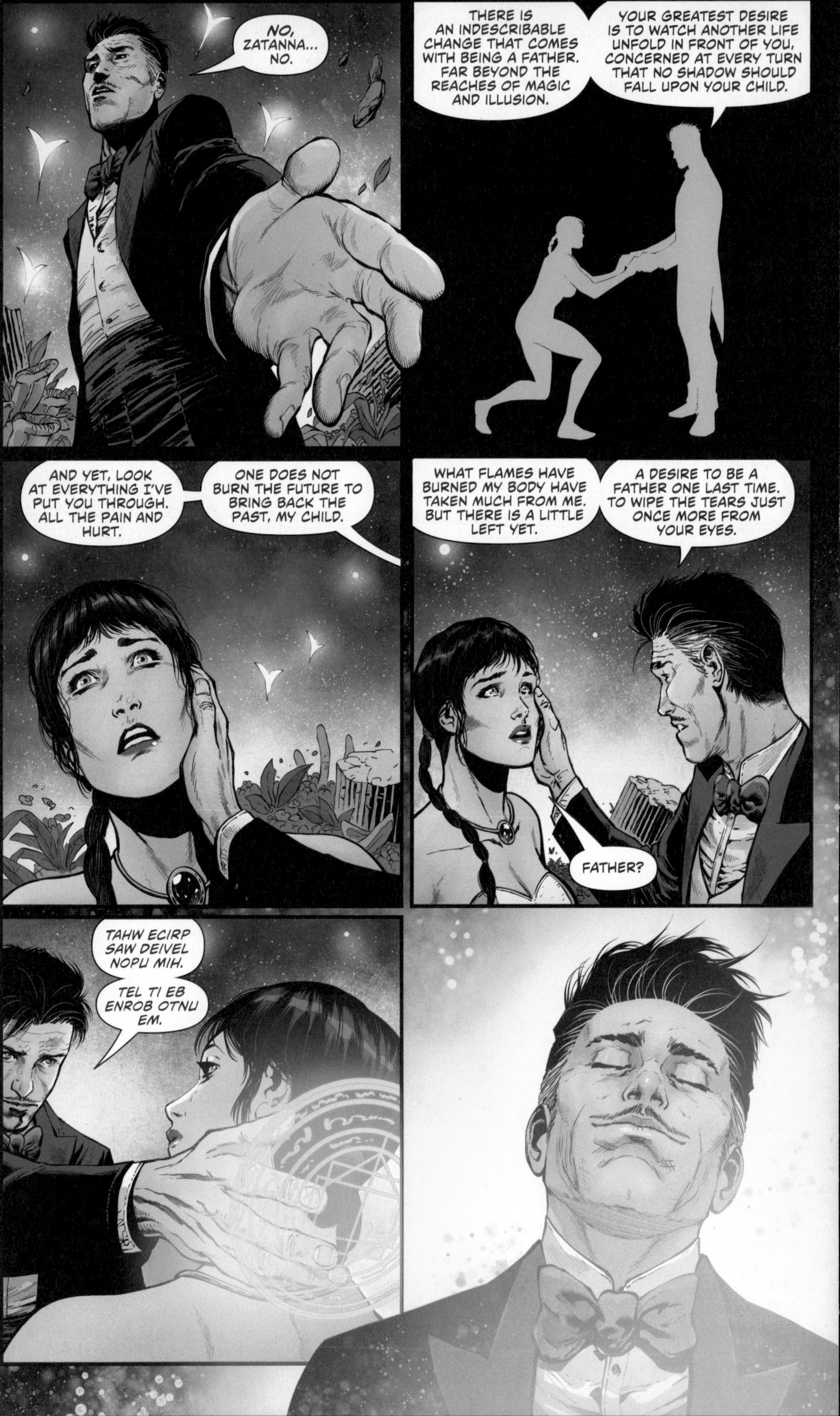
NO, ZATANNA... NO.
THERE IS AN INDESCRIBABLE CHANGE THAT COMES WITH BEING A FATHER. FAR BEYOND THE REACHES OF MAGIC AND ILLUSION.
YOUR GREATEST DESIRE IS TO WATCH ANOTHER LIFE UNFOLD IN FRONT OF YOU, CONCERNED AT EVERY TURN THAT NO SHADOW SHOULD FALL UPON YOUR CHILD.
AND YET, LOOK AT EVERYTHING I'VE PUT YOU THROUGH. ALL THE PAIN AND HURT.
ONE DOES NOT BURN THE FUTURE TO BRING BACK THE PAST, MY CHILD.
WHAT FLAMES HAVE BURNED MY BODY HAVE TAKEN MUCH FROM ME. BUT THERE IS A LITTLE LEFT YET.
A DESIRE TO BE A FATHER ONE LAST TIME. TO WIPE THE TEARS JUST ONCE MORE FROM YOUR EYES.
FATHER?
TAHW ECIRP SAW DEIVEL NOPU MIH.
TEL TI EB ENROB OTNU EM.

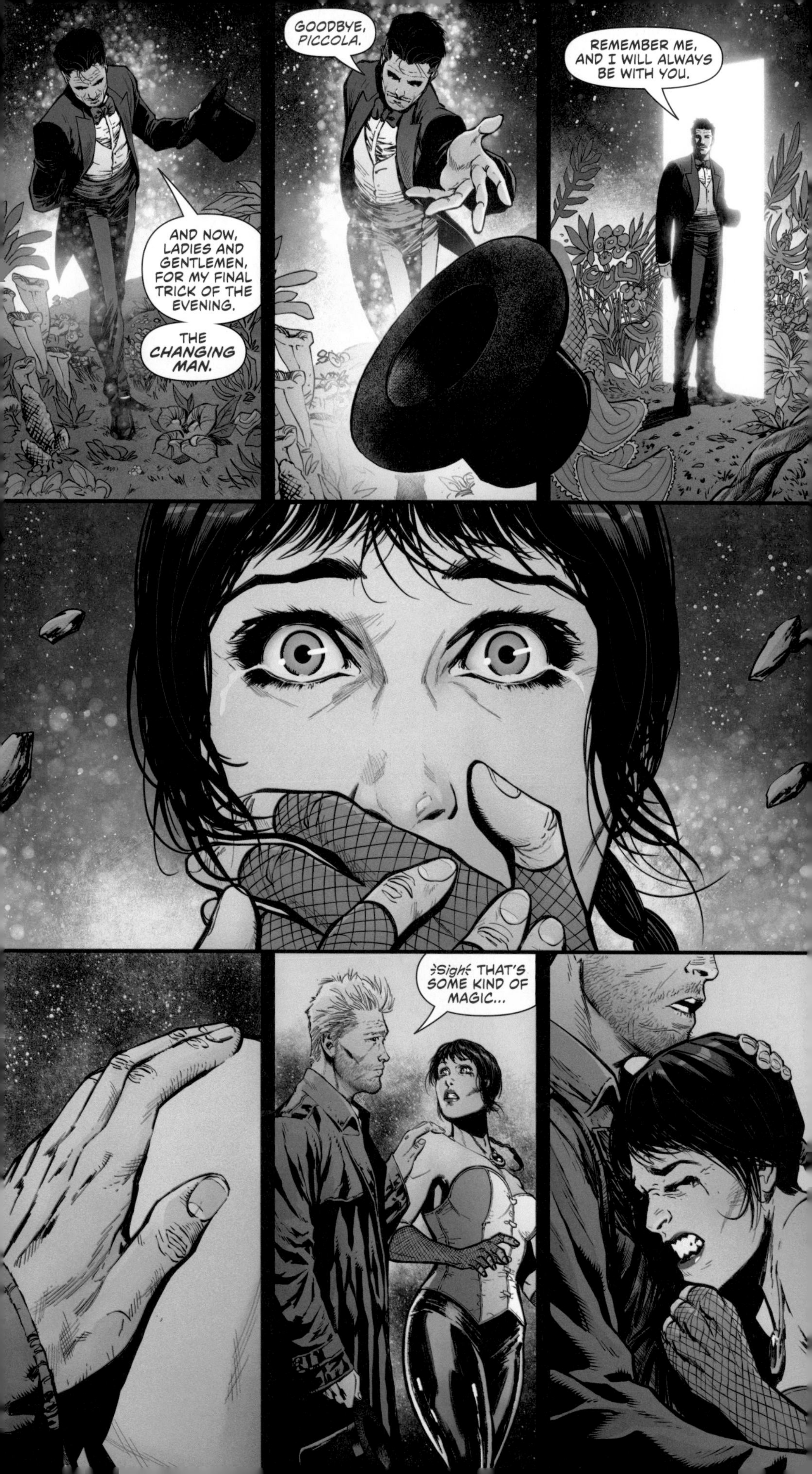
AND NOW, LADIES AND GENTLEMEN, FOR MY FINAL TRICK OF THE EVENING.
THE CHANGING MAN.
GOODBYE, PICCOLA.
REMEMBER ME, AND I WILL ALWAYS BE WITH YOU.
Sigh THAT'S SOME KIND OF MAGIC...

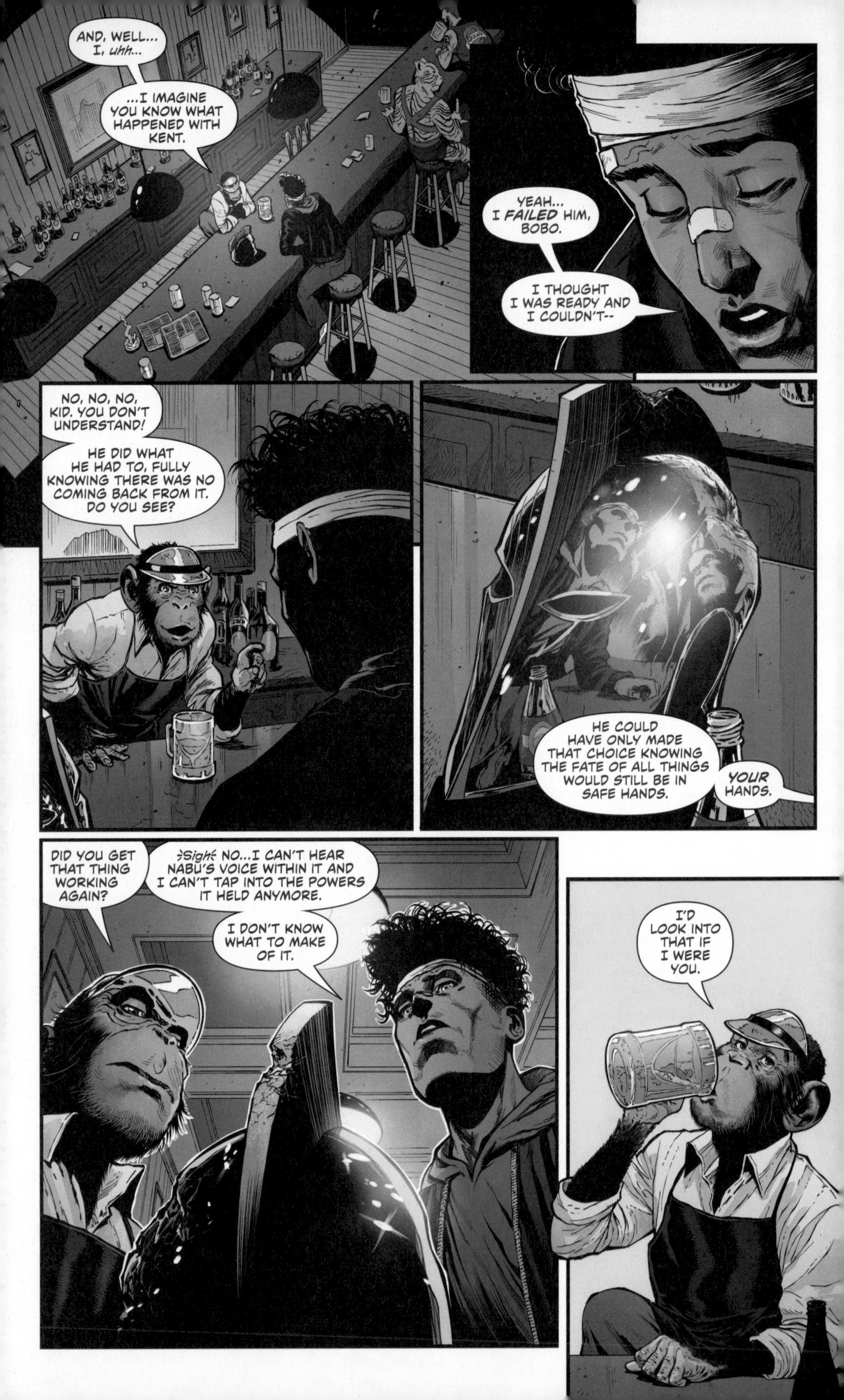
AND, WELL... I, *uhh*...
...I IMAGINE YOU KNOW WHAT HAPPENED WITH KENT.
YEAH... I *FAILED* HIM, BOBO.
I THOUGHT I WAS READY AND I COULDN'T--
NO, NO, NO, KID. YOU DON'T UNDERSTAND!
HE DID WHAT HE HAD TO, FULLY KNOWING THERE WAS NO COMING BACK FROM IT. DO YOU SEE?
HE COULD HAVE ONLY MADE THAT CHOICE KNOWING THE FATE OF ALL THINGS WOULD STILL BE IN SAFE HANDS.
YOUR HANDS.
DID YOU GET THAT THING WORKING AGAIN?
Sigh NO...I CAN'T HEAR NABU'S VOICE WITHIN IT AND I CAN'T TAP INTO THE POWERS IT HELD ANYMORE.
I DON'T KNOW WHAT TO MAKE OF IT.
I'D LOOK INTO THAT IF I WERE YOU.

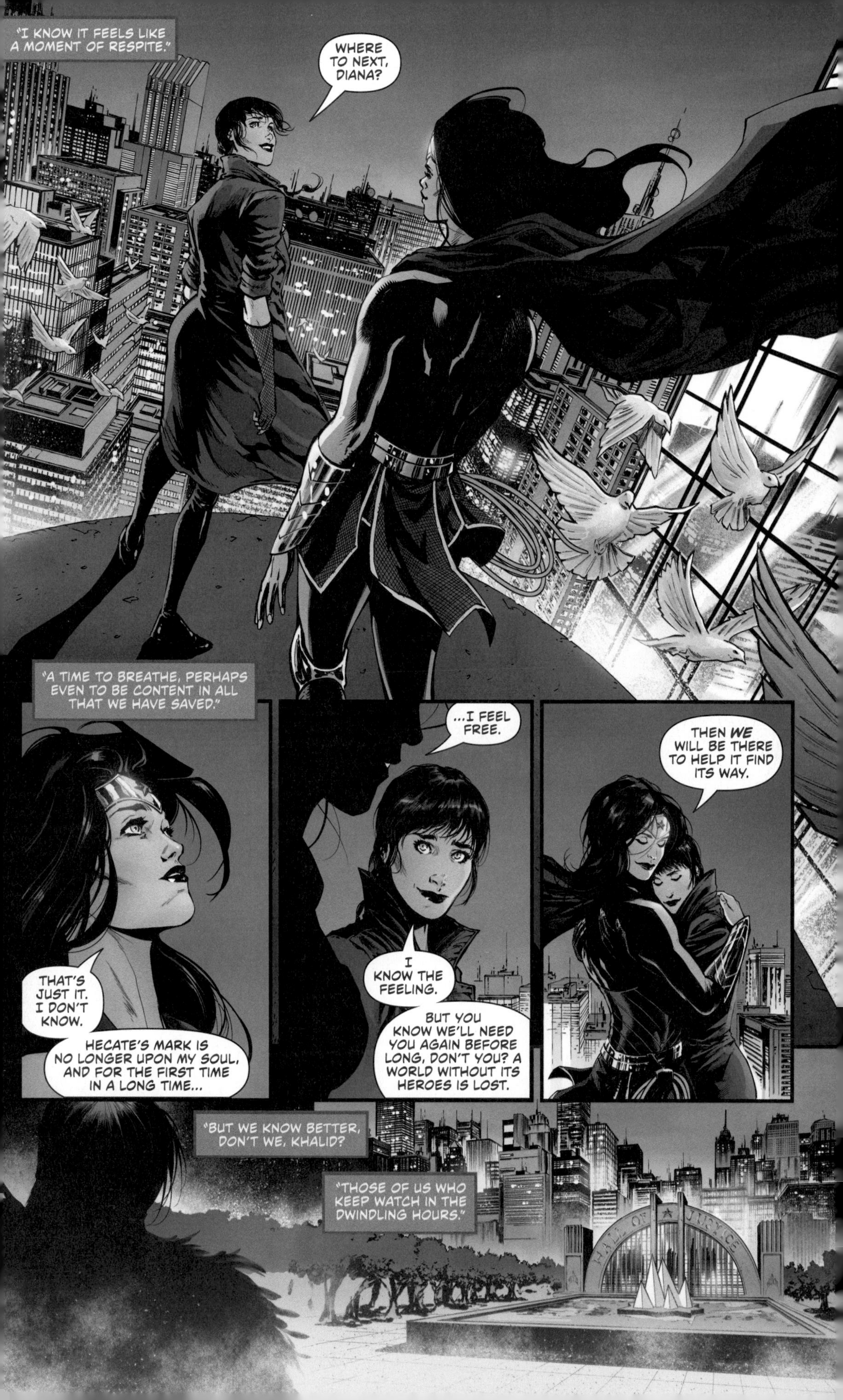
"I KNOW IT FEELS LIKE A MOMENT OF RESPITE."
WHERE TO NEXT, DIANA?
"A TIME TO BREATHE, PERHAPS EVEN TO BE CONTENT IN ALL THAT WE HAVE SAVED."
THAT'S JUST IT. I DON'T KNOW.
HECATE'S MARK IS NO LONGER UPON MY SOUL, AND FOR THE FIRST TIME IN A LONG TIME...
...I FEEL FREE.
I KNOW THE FEELING.
BUT YOU KNOW WE'LL NEED YOU AGAIN BEFORE LONG, DON'T YOU? A WORLD WITHOUT ITS HEROES IS LOST.
THEN WE WILL BE THERE TO HELP IT FIND ITS WAY.
"BUT WE KNOW BETTER, DON'T WE, KHALID?
"THOSE OF US WHO KEEP WATCH IN THE DWINDLING HOURS."
HALL OF JUSTICE

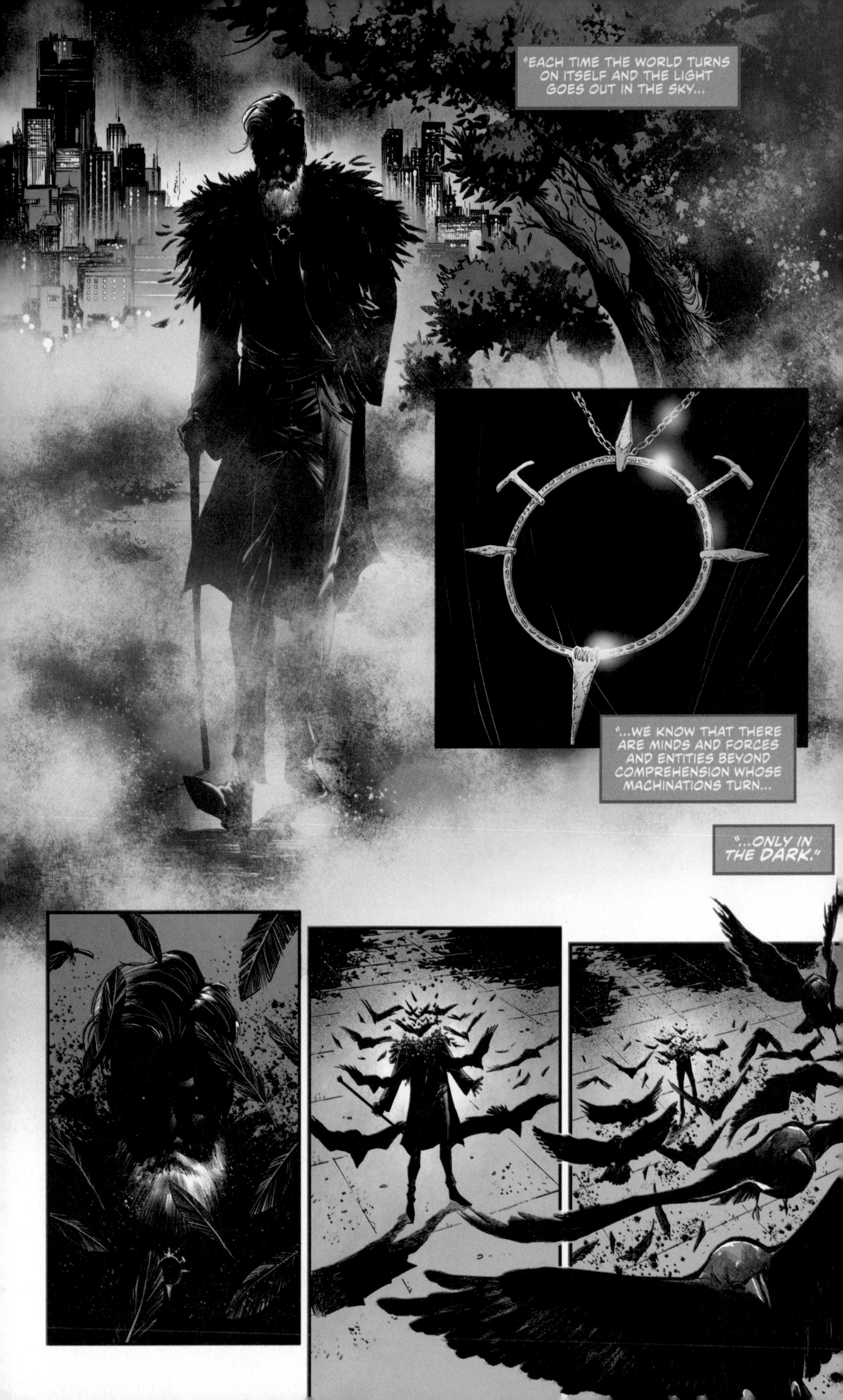
"EACH TIME THE WORLD TURNS ON ITSELF AND THE LIGHT GOES OUT IN THE SKY...
"...WE KNOW THAT THERE ARE MINDS AND FORCES AND ENTITIES BEYOND COMPREHENSION WHOSE MACHINATIONS TURN...
"...ONLY IN THE *DARK*."

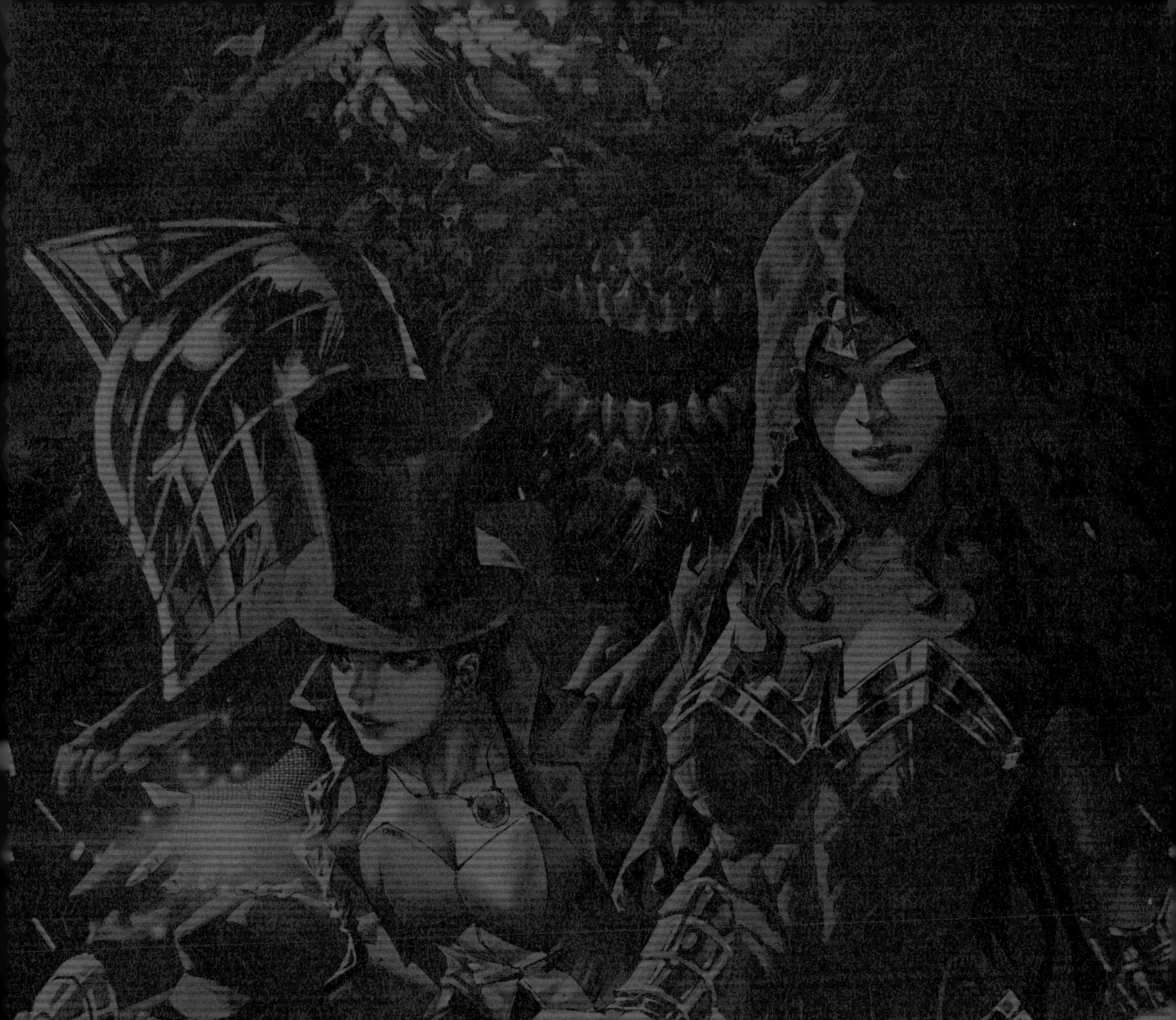

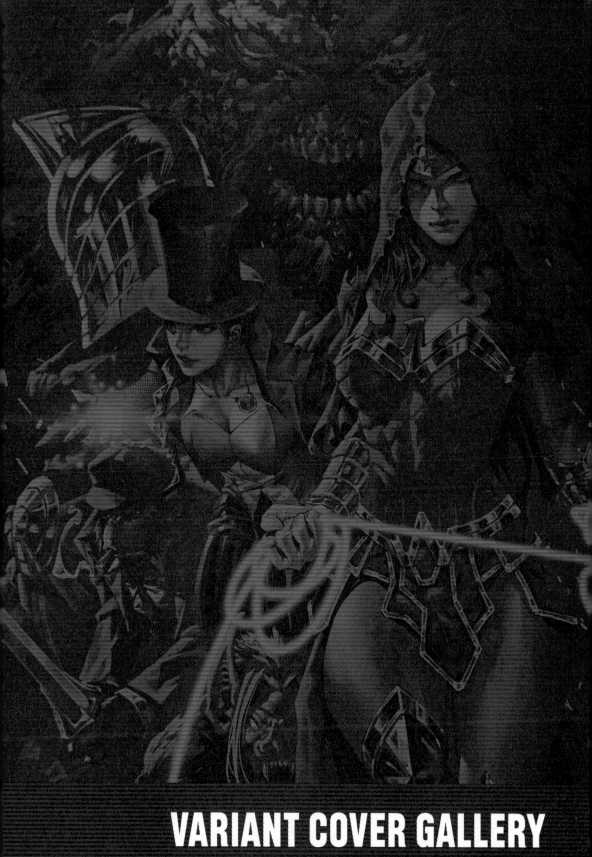

VARIANT COVER GALLERY

Justice League Dark **#20** variant cover
by CLAYTON CRAIN

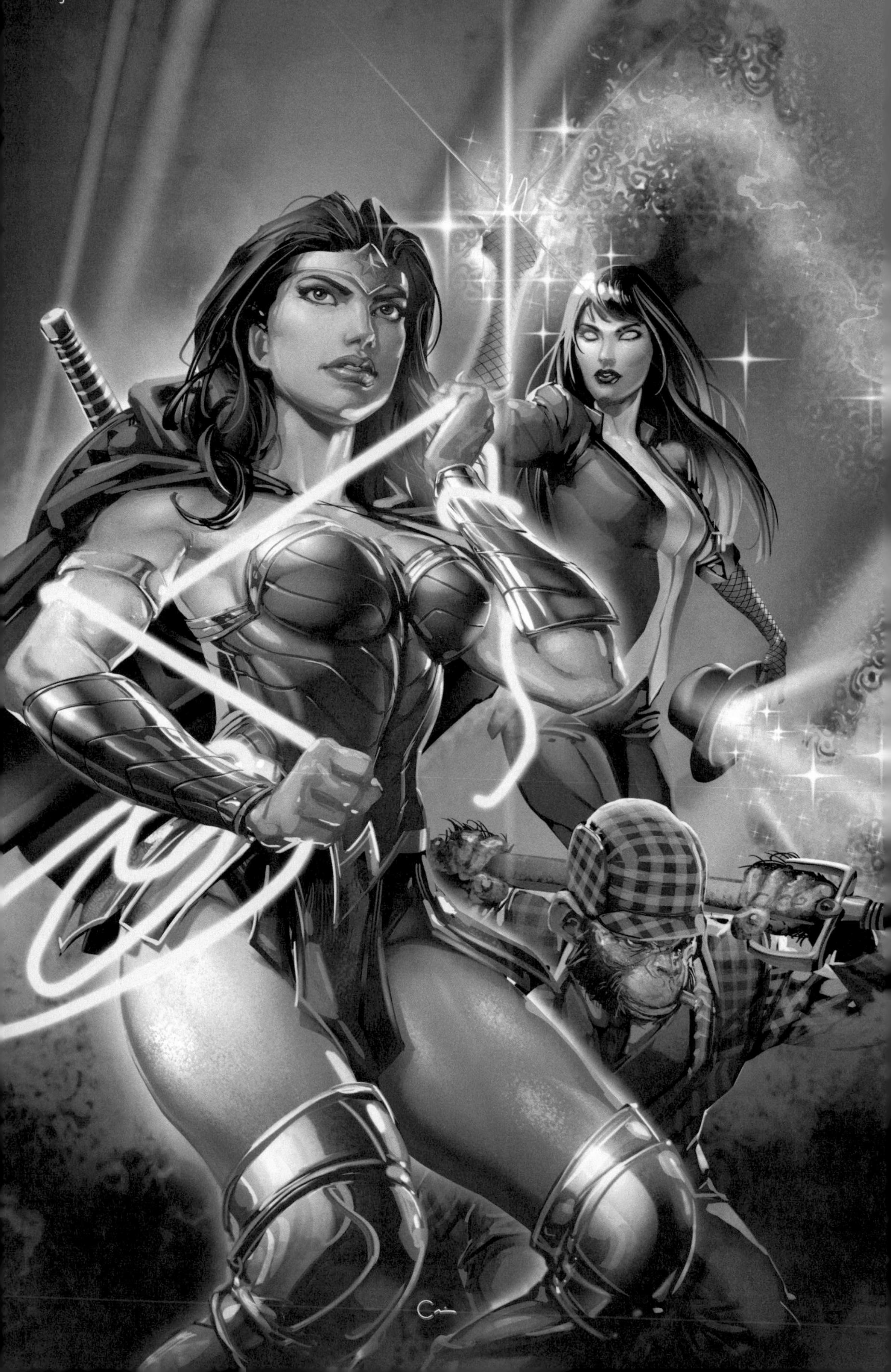

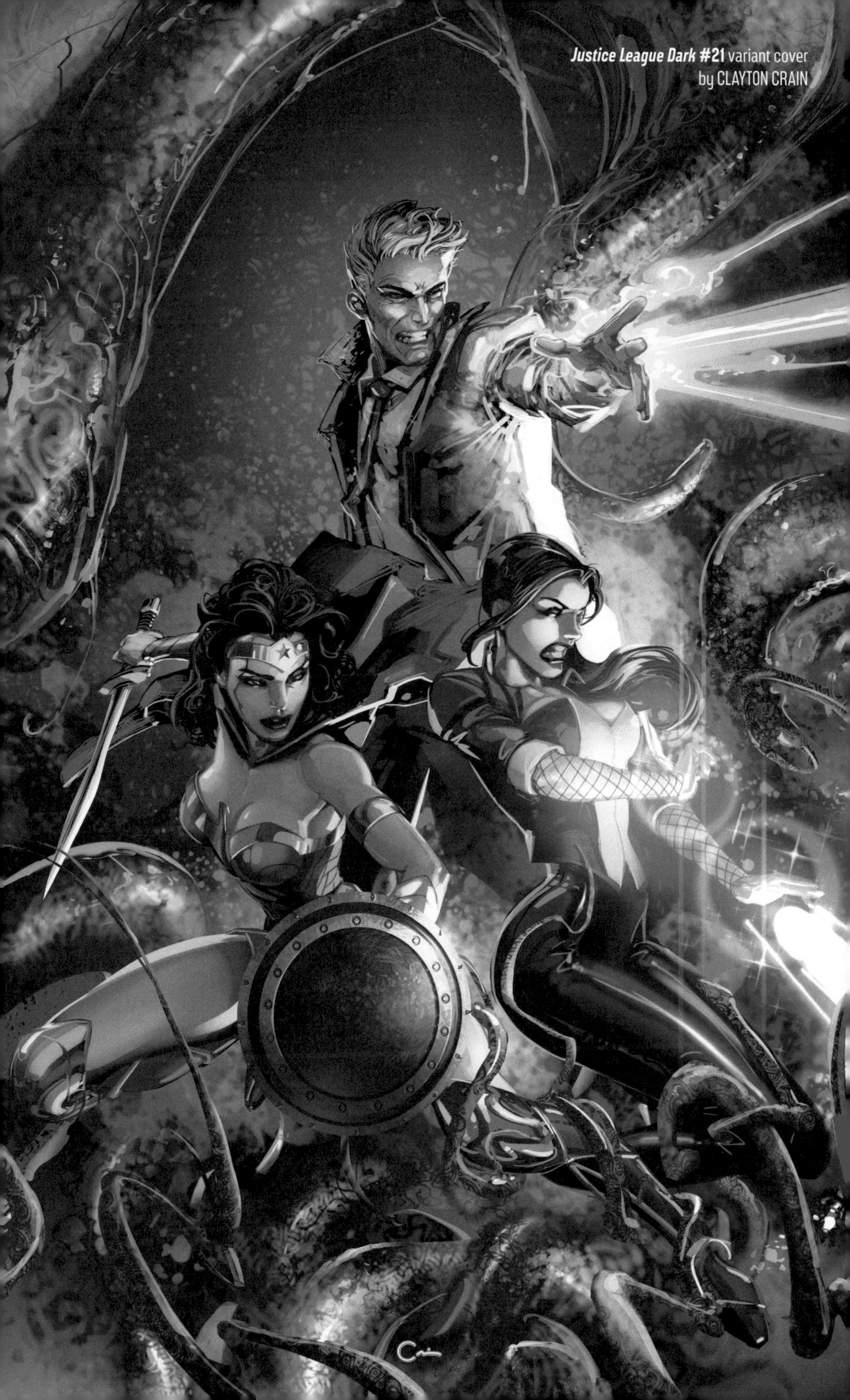

***Justice League Dark* #21** variant cover
by CLAYTON CRAIN

Justice League Dark **#22** variant cover
by CLAYTON CRAIN

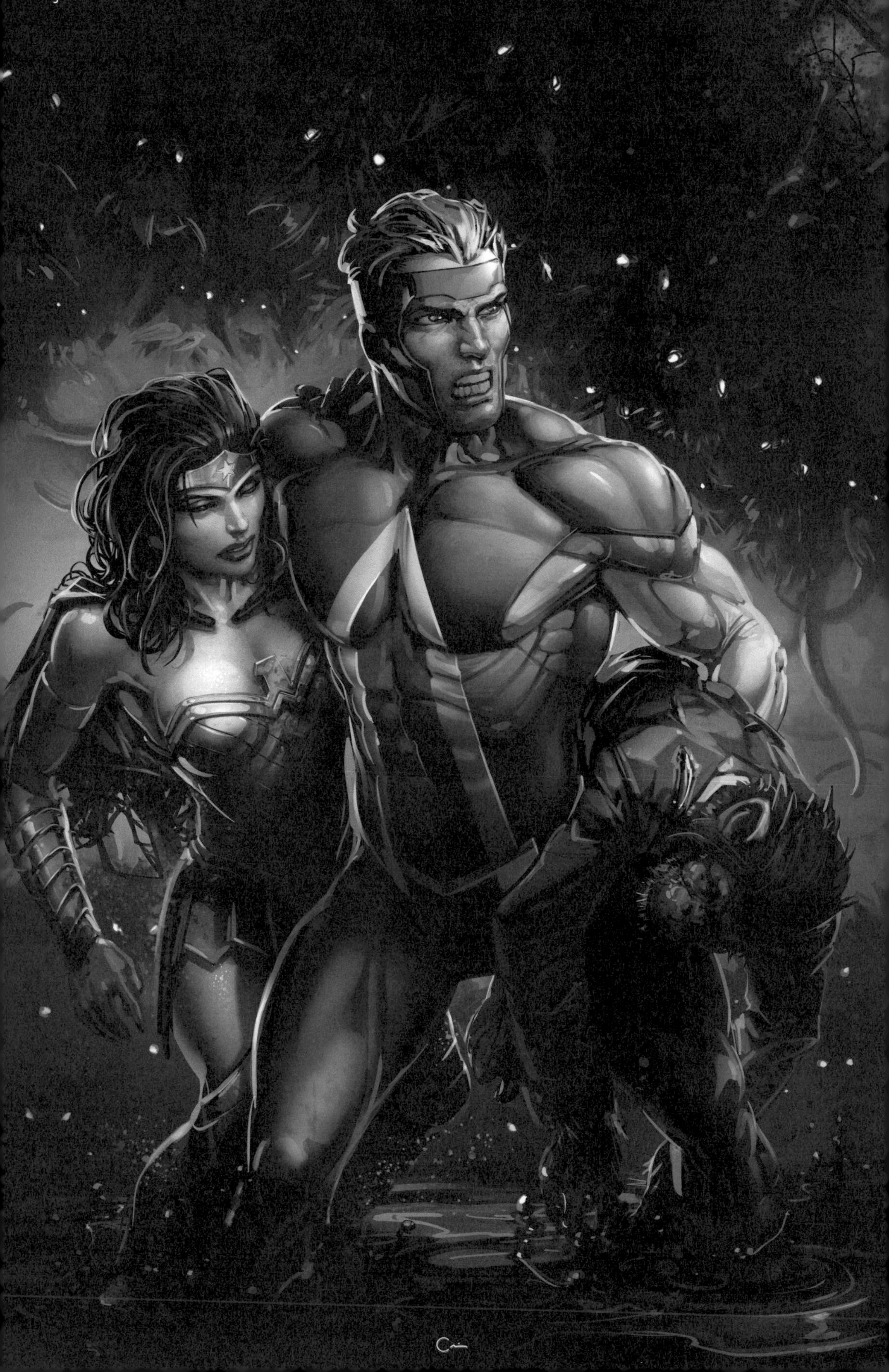

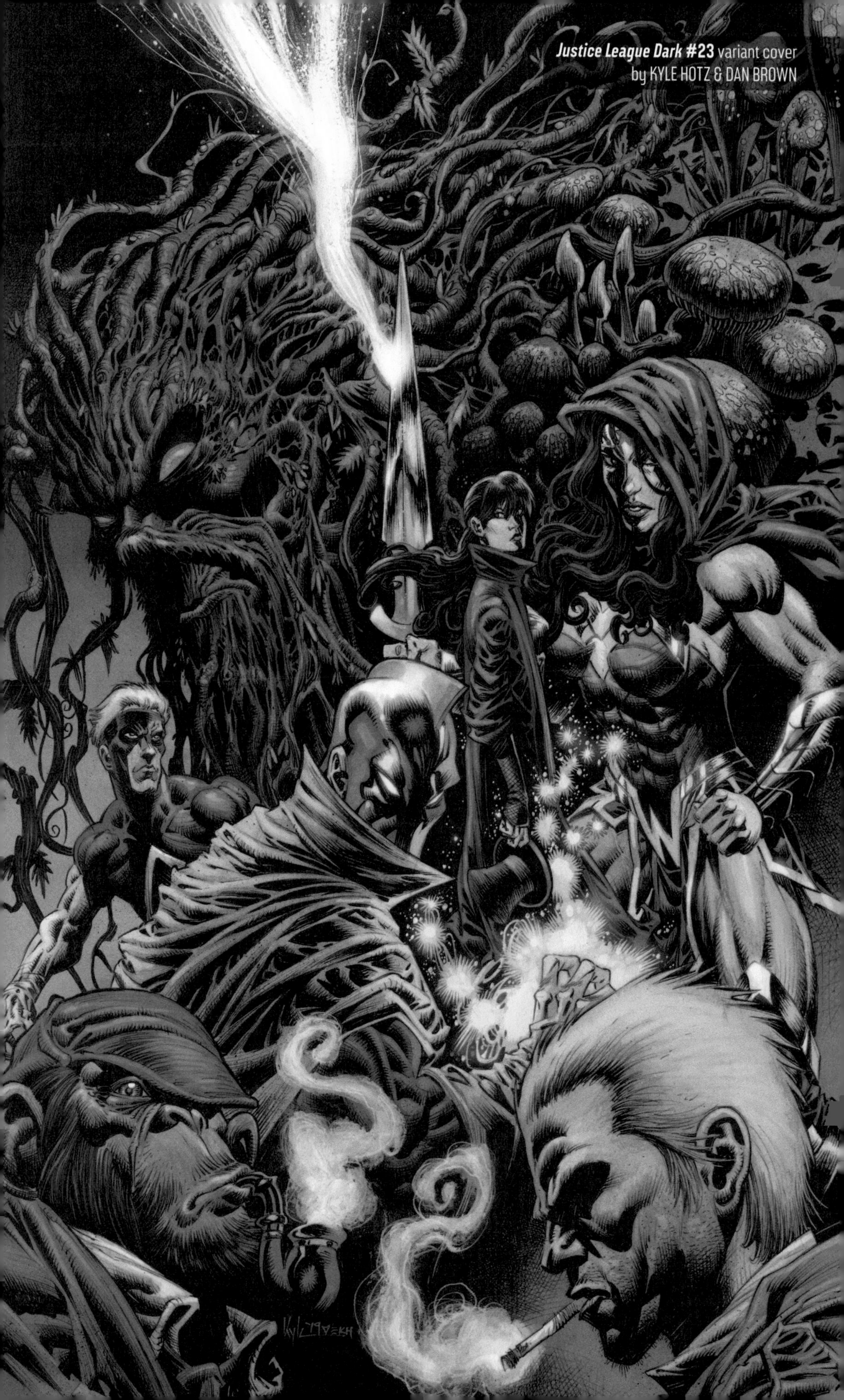

Justice League Dark **#23** variant cover
by KYLE HOTZ & DAN BROWN

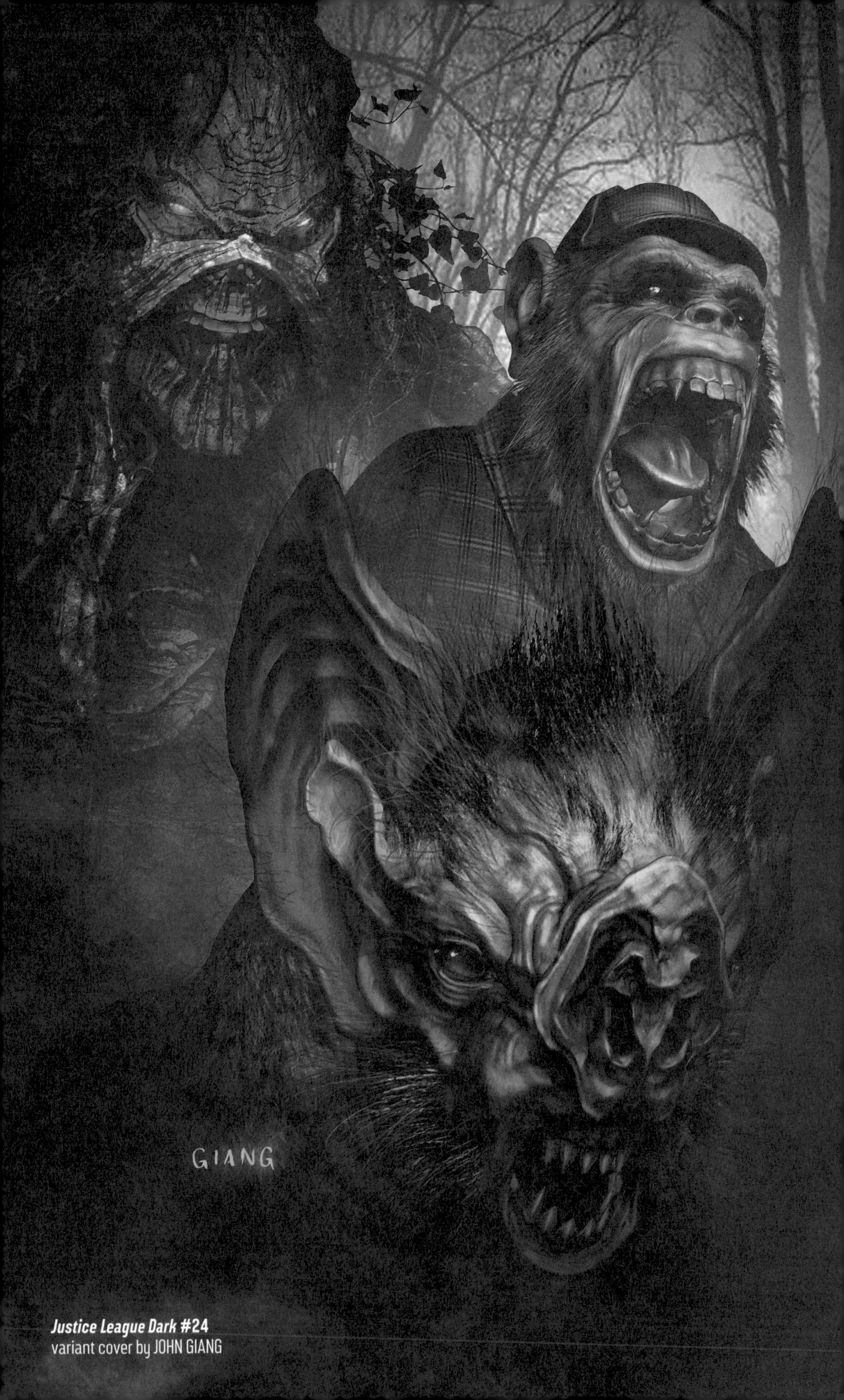
GIANG

***Justice League Dark* #24**
variant cover by JOHN GIANG

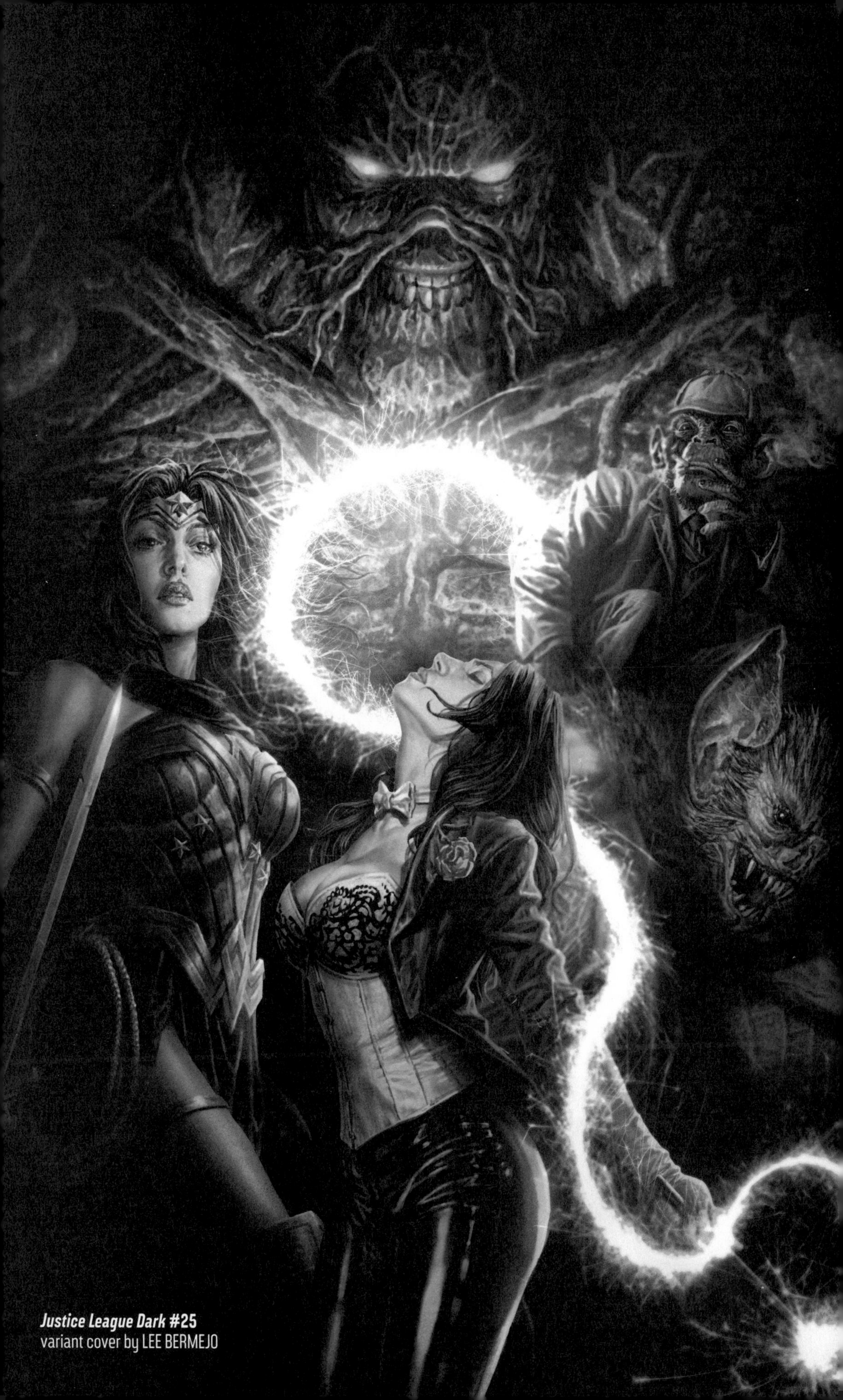

***Justice League Dark* #25**
variant cover by LEE BERMEJO

Justice League Dark #26
variant cover by KAEL NGU

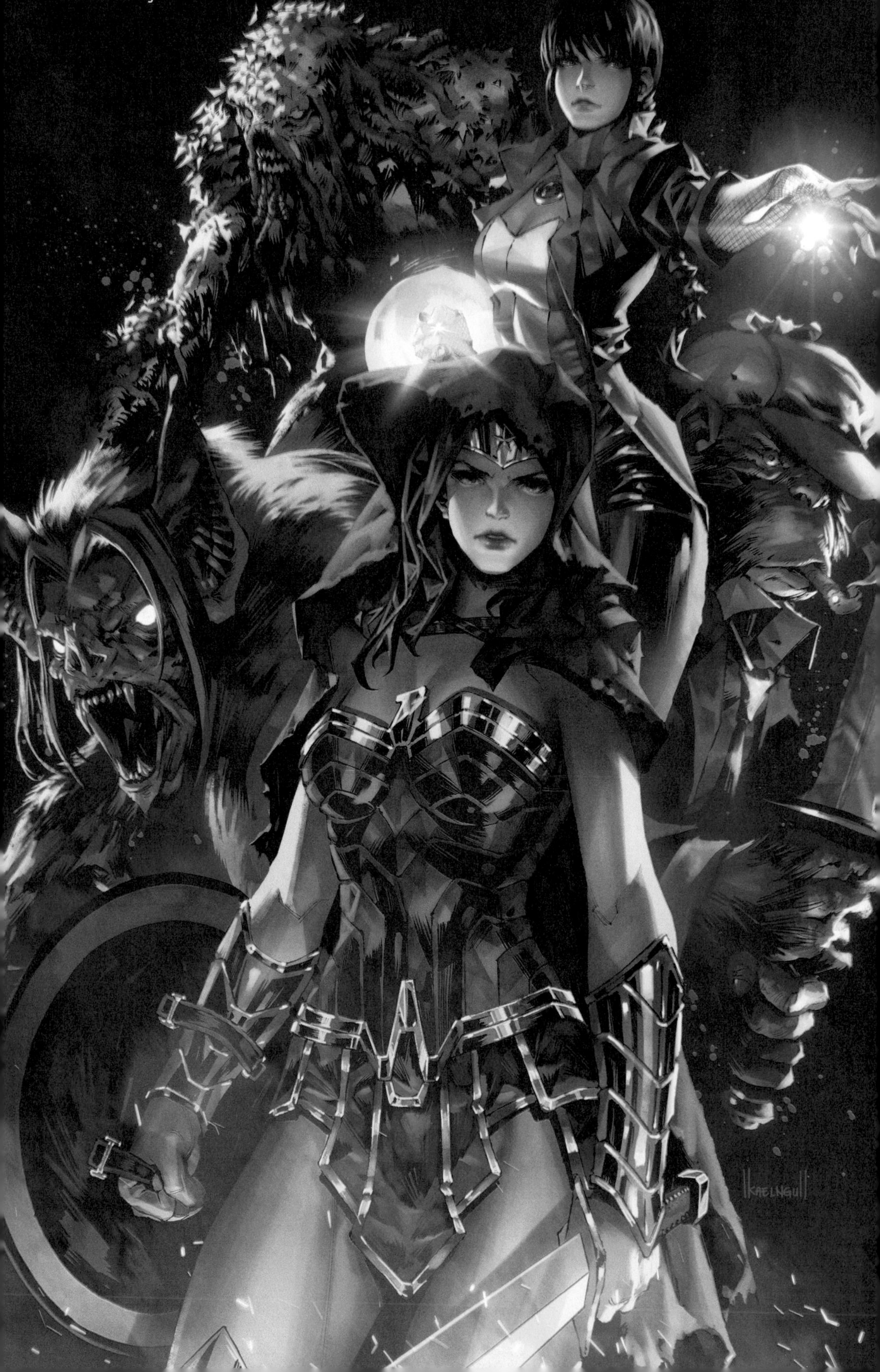

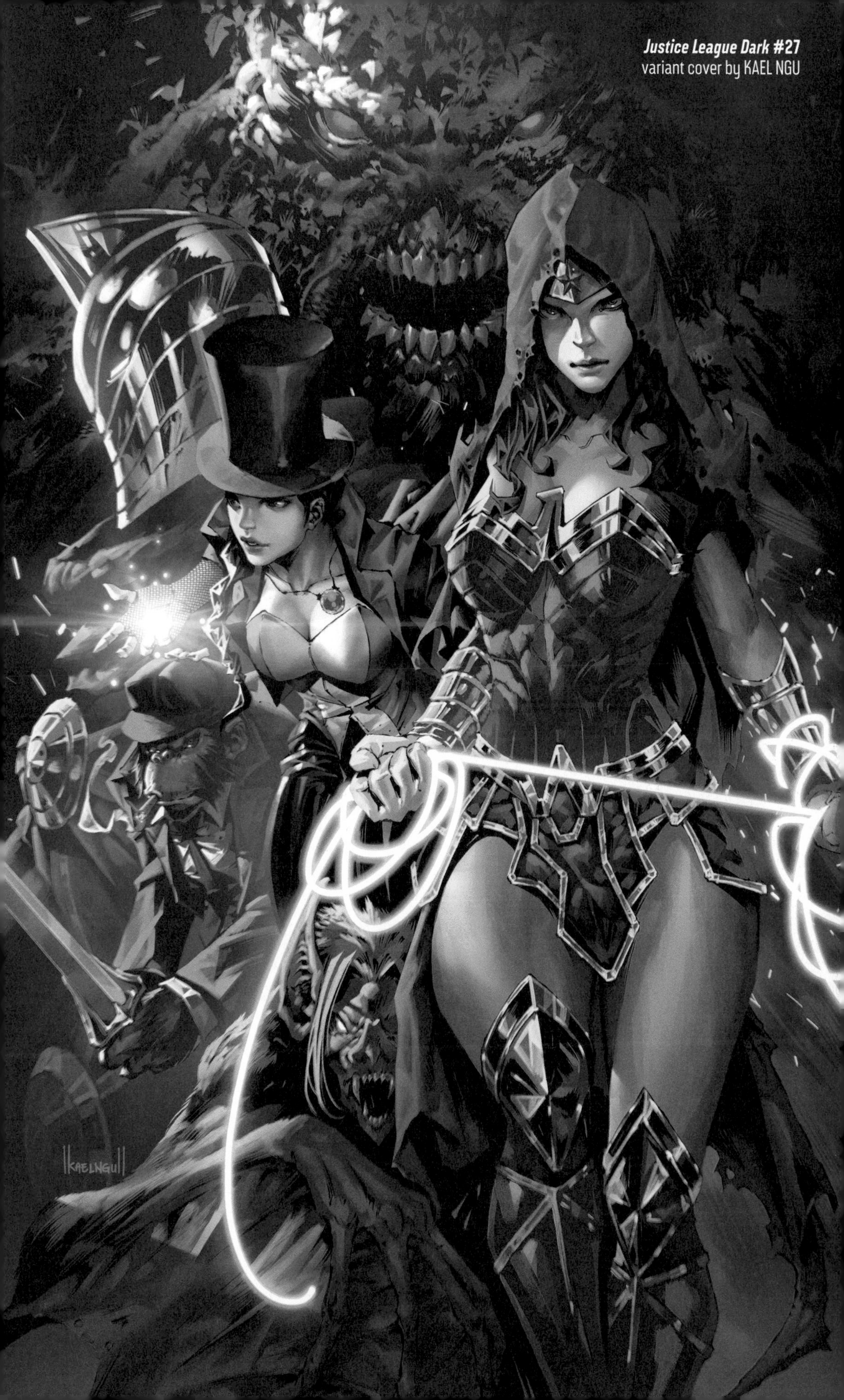
KAELNGU

***Justice League Dark* #27**
variant cover by KAEL NGU

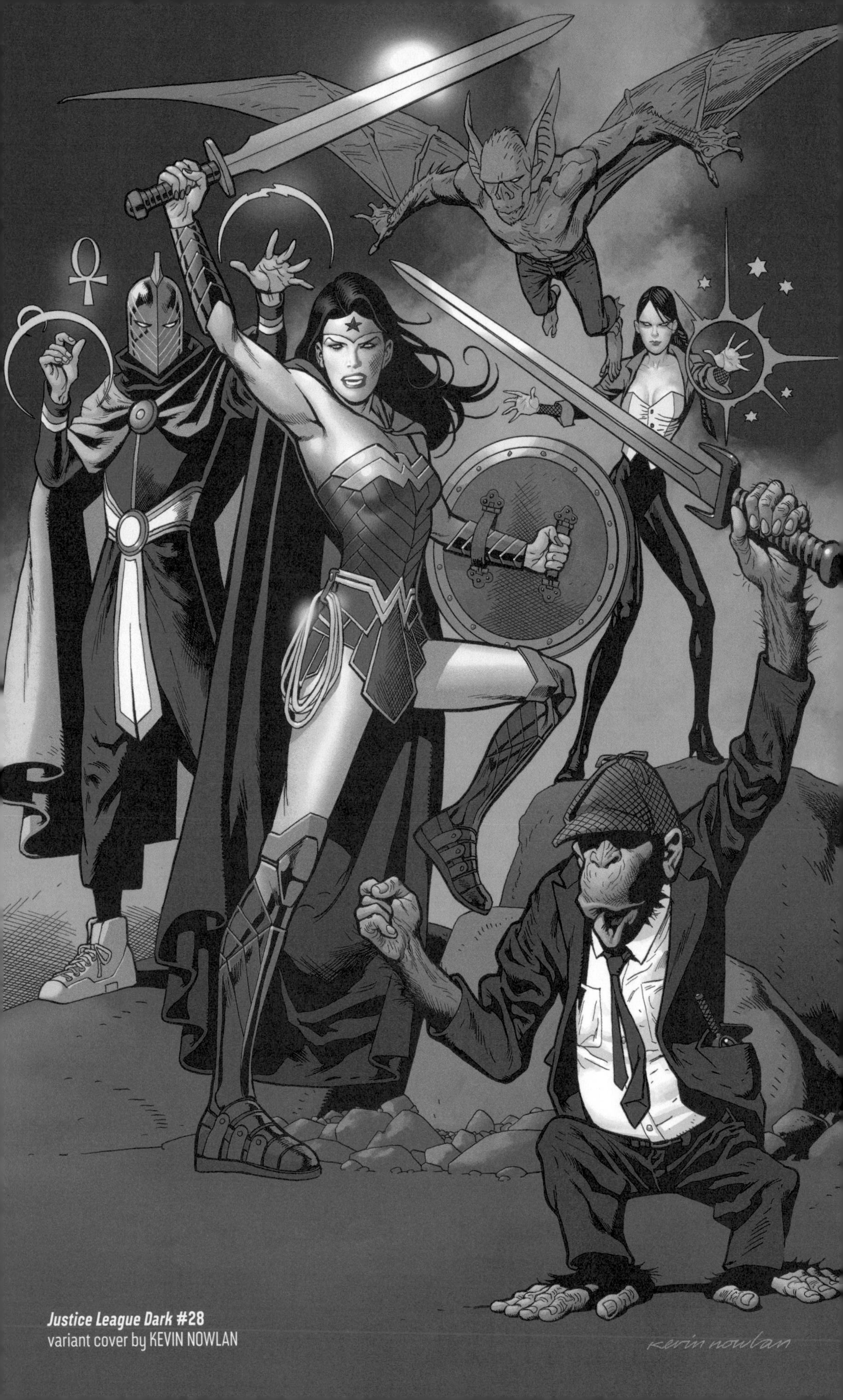
kevin nowlan

***Justice League Dark* #28**
variant cover by KEVIN NOWLAN

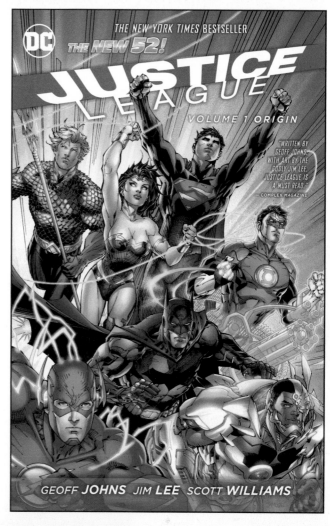

"Welcoming to new fans looking to get into superhero comics for the first time and old fans who gave up on the funny-books long ago."
– SCRIPPS HOWARD NEWS SERVICE

JUSTICE LEAGUE
VOL. 1: ORIGIN
GEOFF JOHNS and JIM LEE

JUSTICE LEAGUE VOL. 2: THE VILLAIN'S JOURNEY

JUSTICE LEAGUE VOL. 3: THRONE OF ATLANTIS

READ THE ENTIRE EPIC!

JUSTICE LEAGUE VOL. 4:
THE GRID

JUSTICE LEAGUE VOL. 5:
FOREVER HEROES

JUSTICE LEAGUE VOL. 6:
INJUSTICE LEAGUE

JUSTICE LEAGUE VOL. 7:
DARKSEID WAR PART 1

JUSTICE LEAGUE VOL. 8:
DARKSEID WAR PART 2

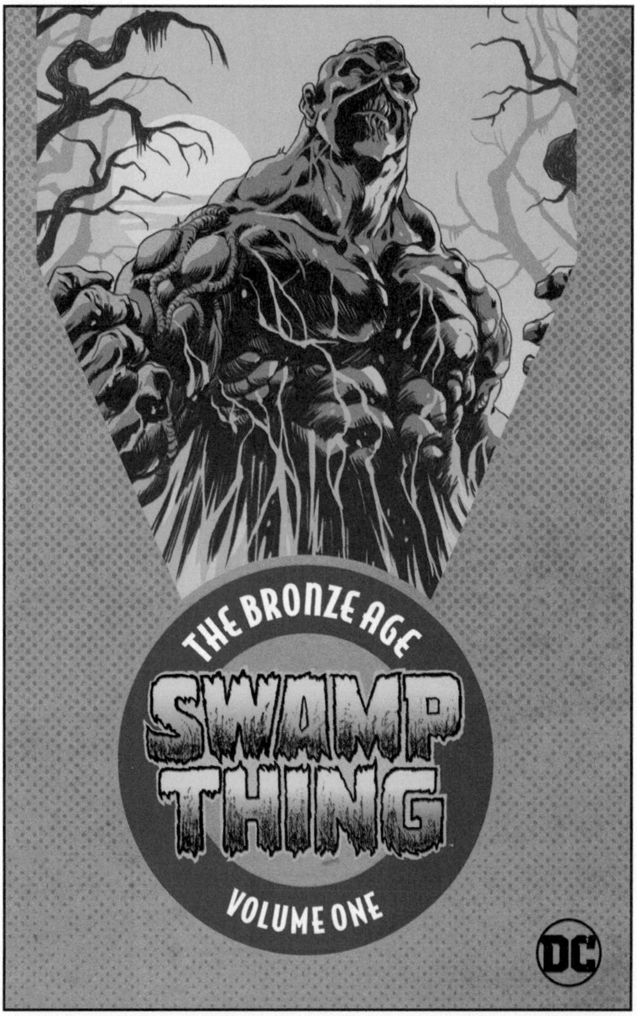
THE BRONZE AGE
SWAMP THING
VOLUME ONE

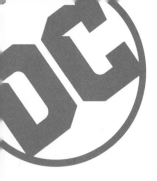

Read the classic early tales of the protector of the Earth!

SWAMP THING

THE BRONZE AGE VOL. 1

By Len Wein and Bernie Wrightson

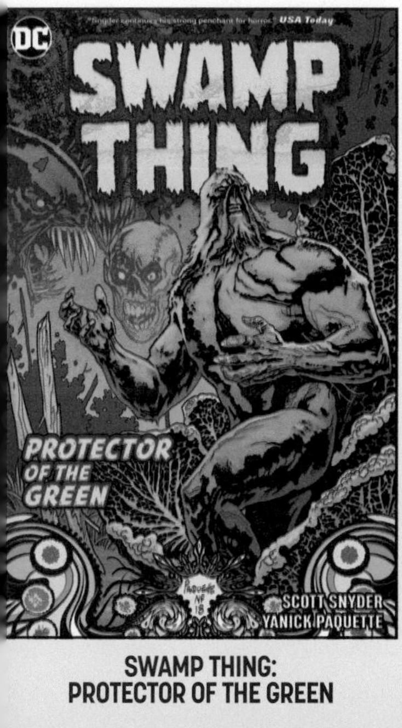
SWAMP THING
PROTECTOR OF THE GREEN
SCOTT SNYDER
YANICK PAQUETTE

SWAMP THING: PROTECTOR OF THE GREEN

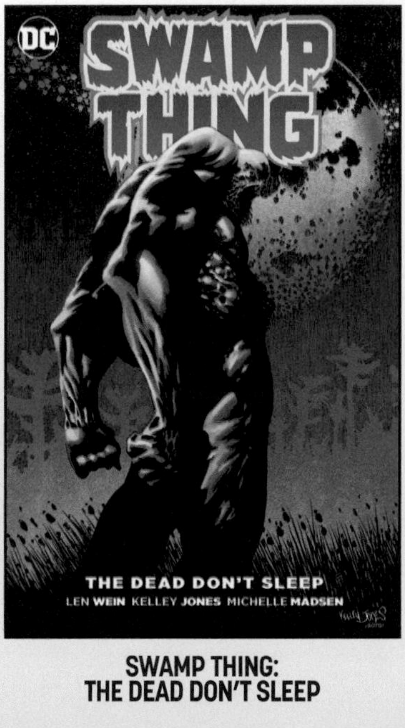
SWAMP THING
THE DEAD DON'T SLEEP
LEN WEIN KELLEY JONES MICHELLE MADSEN

SWAMP THING: THE DEAD DON'T SLEEP

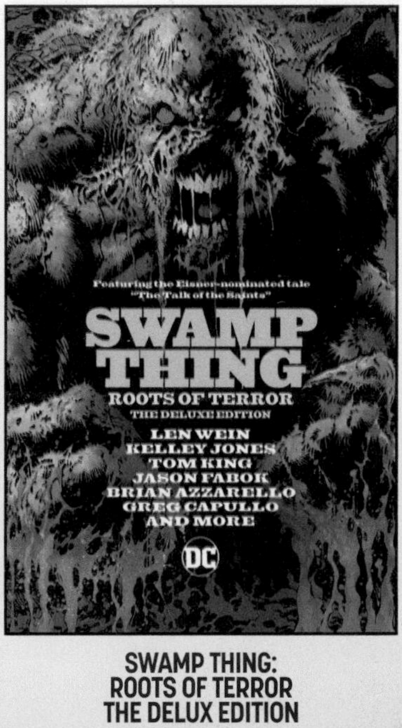
Featuring the Eisner-nominated tale "The Talk of the Saints"
SWAMP THING
ROOTS OF TERROR
THE DELUXE EDITION
LEN WEIN
KELLEY JONES
TOM KING
JASON FABOK
BRIAN AZZARELLO
GREG CAPULLO
AND MORE

SWAMP THING: ROOTS OF TERROR THE DELUX EDITION

Get more DC graphic novels wherever comics and books are sold!

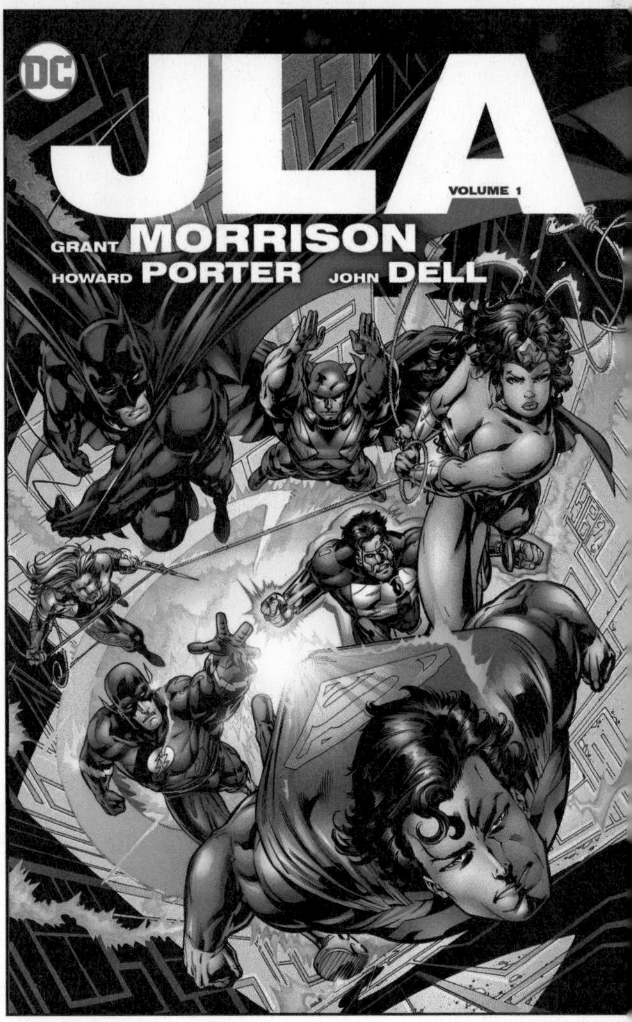
JLA
VOLUME 1
GRANT MORRISON
HOWARD PORTER JOHN DELL

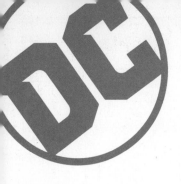

Read more adventures of the World's Greatest Super Heroes in these graphic novels!

JLA VOL. 1

GRANT MORRISON and HOWARD PORTER

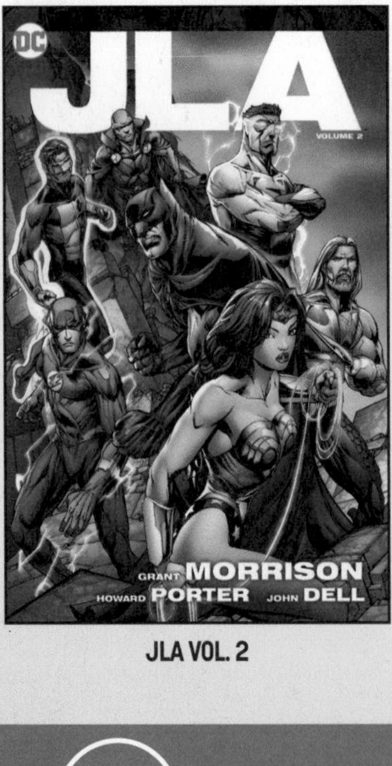
JLA
VOLUME 2
GRANT MORRISON
HOWARD PORTER JOHN DELL

JLA VOL. 2

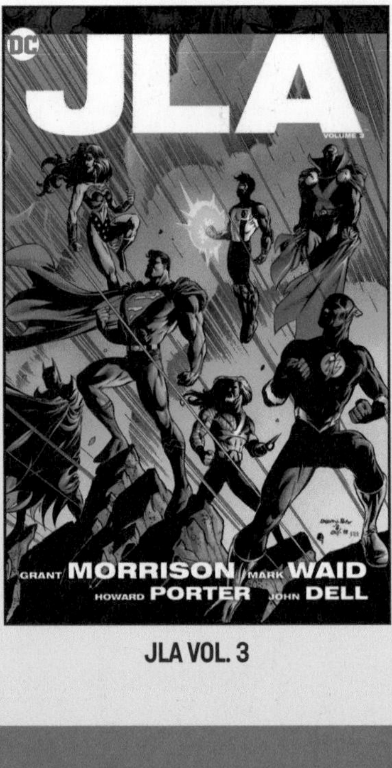
JLA
GRANT MORRISON MARK WAID
HOWARD PORTER JOHN DELL

JLA VOL. 3

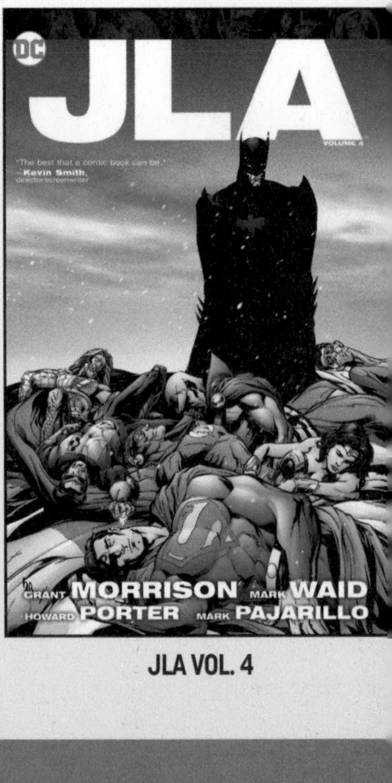
JLA
GRANT MORRISON MARK WAID
HOWARD PORTER MARK PAJARILLO

JLA VOL. 4

Get more DC graphic novels wherever comics and books are sold!